AF541234

MOTIVATIONAL PRACTICES IN ORGANISATIONS

MOTIVATIONAL PRACTICES IN ORGANISATIONS

Edited by

G. BALACHANDAR
Lecturer in Business Administration,
Annamalai University,
Annamalainagar, Tamilnadu.

and

DR. N. PANCHANATHAM
Professor and Head, Department of Business Administration,
Annamalai University,
Annamalainagar, Tamilnadu.

DEEP & DEEP PUBLICATIONS PVT. LTD.
F-159, Rajouri Garden, New Delhi-110027

MOTIVATIONAL PRACTICES IN ORGANISATIONS

ISBN 978-81-8450-328-9

Typeset by S.S. COMPOSERS
3190, Mohindra Park, Shakur Basti, Delhi-110034.

Printed in India at MAYUR ENTERPRISES
WZ Plot No. 3, Gujjar Market, Tihar Village, New Delhi-110018.

Published by DEEP & DEEP PUBLICATIONS PVT. LTD.
F-159, Rajouri Garden, New Delhi-110027.
Phones: 25435369, Telefax: 25440916
E-mail: ddpbooks@yahoo.co.in • ddpubs@gmail.com
Showroom:
2/13, Ansari Road, Daryaganj, New Delhi-110002 • Telefax: 23245122

Contents

E. Thirumudi Pandian
Regional Sales Manager
Tamil Nadu, Pondicherry, Kerala

Foreword

Dear All,

Today the word **"MOTIVATION"** plays a vital role in everybody's life whether it is official or personal. A small pat on the back or offering a small bicycle will motivate your child to excel in his career.

With regard to official life, motivation is required right from MD to Office Boy. A small word of Appreciation to your Assistant will help to bring best out of him. Motivation will vary from individual to individual. For somebody it may be money and for somebody it may be a recognition. If we are able to identify from each individual then that is the KEY OF SUCCESS.

The Author of this book: Dr. N. Panchanatham, Professor and HOD, Business Administration, Annamalai Univeristy and Mr. G. Balachandar, Lecturer, Business Administration, Annamalai University have shown lot of interest and taken much pains to bring out this worthy book Motivational Practices in Organisations. This book will help the readers to understand the impact of motivation and can very well implement in their day-to-day life.

Yours sincerely,

E. Thirumudi Pandian
Areas Sales Manager

Preface

The impact of globalization on organisations, the work environment and workforce have caused a sea change on work motivation related strategies to be followed. The importance of motivational practices in organisations is expected to escalate drastically in the near future. Understanding the different dimensions and dynamics of motivation is the need of the hour. Theories of motivation have existed for years together but it is important to note that, time is an important aspect of motivation to be considered. It is, thus, clear that recent motivational practices in organisations are yet to be explored.

Good motivation is pivotal for a better economy. Although this may not just happen in one day or a month, it is important that we now start doing our part to attain what we really dreamt for. It may take time to achieve the goals for the betterment of our economy, but the seeds sown today will definitely bear the fruits tomorrow. Our objective in bringing out an edited volume on **"Motivational Practices in Organisations"** was to address practical problems in this area, provide suitable solutions to those problems. The contributing authors have addressed motivation related issues from his or her specific area of expertise. The contents of this edited volume span a broad array of topics on concepts and theories of recent motivational practices in organisations, its impact on organisational commitment, employee relations, employee retention and employee empowerment.

The contributions of the authors have opened of new vistas for research in motivational practices in organisations. Their different articles suggest that there are excellent opportunities available for linking motivation in other areas such as human factors, nation's economy, psychology and labour economics.

We thank Deep and Deep Publications Private Ltd., New Delhi for their meticulous professional work. We are grateful to Annamalai University for the encouragement in all our activities. This list is incomplete and we apologize to anyone we omitted. We owe a special note of thanks to all the authors who have contributed to this book and all those who have indirectly helped us to bring out this book. We hope this edited book provokes some strong reactions, positive and negative!

G. BALACHANDAR
DR. N. PANCHANATHAM

List of Contributors

Dr. A. Kalaimathi, Director, School of Distance Education, Mother Teresa Women's University, Kodaikanal.

A.L. Gowri, Higher Grade Assistant, LIC of India, Divisional Office, Tirunelveli.

Ayeesha Zawahir, Research Scholar, University of Madras, Chennai.

B. Poongodi, Lecturer, CMS College of Science and Commerce, Coimbatore.

Dr. B. Revathy, Associate Professor and Head i/c, Department of Commerce, School of Business Studies, Manonmaniam Sundaranar University, Tirunelveli.

Dr. B. Senthil Arasu, Assistant Professor in Management Studies, National Institute of Technology, Trichy.

Prof. Chithra Regis, Lecturer, Loyola College, Chennai.

Cyriac Meppuram, Lecturer in Management Studies, FX Engg. College, Tirunelveli.

D.J. Lini Mol, Lecturer, Dept. of Business Administration, Syed Hameedha Arts and Science College, Kilakarai.

E.V. Rigin, Sr. Lecturer, Department of Management Studies, V.H.N.S.N. College, Virudhunagar.

G. Bhuvaneswari, Lecturer, RVS College of Engineering and Technology, Dindigul.

Dr. G. Vanishree, Professor and HOD of Management Studies, Institute of Aeronautical Engineering, Hyderabad.

G. Sri Devi, Lecturer in Management Studies, AVC College of Engineering, Mayiladuthurai.

H. Muthu Ganesh, Sales Manager, ICICI Bank, Chennai.

J. Dhilipan, Assistant Professor, SRM University, Ramapuram, Chennai.

Jayaprakash Jala, Asst. Training Manager, Academic Staff College, VIT University, Vellore.

Jeyakodeeswari Pratap, Lecturer, Lady Doak College, Madurai.

Dr. K. Chandrasekaran, Faculty in Management Studies, Directorate of Distance Education, Madurai Kamaraj University, Madurai.

Dr. K. Muthuraman, Reader in English, Department of English, Annamalai University, Chidambaram.

K. Sankar Ganesh, Assistant Professor and HOD, Department of Management Studies, Sri Vidya College of Engineering and Technology, Virudhunagar.

Dr. K. Subramanian, Reader in Commerce, Sadakathullah Appa College, Tirunelveli.

Dr. Kalaimathi, Reader, Mother Terasa University, Kodaikanal.

Dr. Kalpana, Sr. Lecturer, Cygmax Institute of Management Studies, Coimbatore.

Kannan, Lecturer, SRM University, Ramapuram, Chennai.

K. Sankar Ganesh, Lecturer, Department of Business Administration, Kalasalingam University, Virudhunagar District, Tamilnadu.

K. Sirajunisa, Department of Business Administration, Annamalai University, Tamilnadu.

M. Balasubramanian, Professor of Management Studies, J.J. College of Engg. and Technology, Ammapettai, Trichy.

M. Jaisun, Lecturer in Management Studies, V.H.N.S.N. College, Virudhunagar.

M. Manikandan, Senior Lecturer, SRM School of Management, SRM University, Chennai.

M. Shunmuga Sundaram, Lecturer, Kalasalingam University, Krishnankoil, Virudhunagar District.

N. Palaniappan, Faculty Member, Mentoris School of Management, Tirunelveli.

Dr. N. Panchanatham, Professor and Head, Department of Business Administration, Annamalai University, Tamilnadu.

Dr. N.R.V. Prabhu, Director, Department of Management Studies, Sri Veerasamy Chettiar College of Engineering and Technology, Puliangudi, Tamil Nadu, Email: drnrvprabhu@yahoo.com

P. Geetha, Lecturer in Commerce, Wavoo Wajeeha Women's College of Arts and Science, Kayalpatanam, Tuticorin District.

Dr. P. Kameswara Rao, Professor and Head, Department of Business Administration, Kalasalingam University, Virudhunagar District, Tamilnadu.

P.N. Kanchana, Assistant Professor, J.J. College of Engineering and Technology, Tiruchirappalli-620 009.

P. Sumathi, Lecturer, Business Administration, Kalasalingam University, Virudhunagar District.

Dr. P. Sundara Pandian, Associate Professor, Commerce Research Centre, VHNSN College, Virudhunagar.

Dr. P.C. Sekar, Prof. and Head in Management Studies, D.D.E., M.K. University, Madurai.

Dr. P.T. Vijaya Rajakumar, Assistant Professor, RVS College of Engineering and Technology, Dindigul.

R. Ayyamperumal, Lecturer in Management Studies, V.H.N.S.N College, Virudhunagar.

R. Banila, Lecturer in Management Studies, Francis Xavier Engg. College, Tirunelveli.

R. Christina Jeya Nithila, Lecturer in Management Studies, FX Engg. College, Tirunelveli.

R. Harini Hingnekar, Lecturer in Vinayaka Mission Business School, Chennai.

R. Rajalakshmi, P.G. Assistant, Guntur Subbiah Pillai T. Nagar Girls Higher Secondary School, Chennai-17.

Rajkumar, Lecturer in Management Studies, Francis Xavier Engg. College, Tirunelveli.

Dr. R. Shobana Devi, UGC Research Fellow, Commerce Research Centre, VHNSN College, Virudhunagar.

R. Thamarai Kannan, Faculty in Management Studies, Directorate of Distance Education, Madurai Kamaraj University, Madurai.

Reena, Lecturer in Management Studies, FX Engineering College, Thirunelveli.

S. Nasar, H.O.D., Dept. of Business Administration, Syed Hameedha Arts and Science College, Kilakarai.

Dr. S. Dhinesh Babu, Professor, Department of Management Studies, J.J. College of Engineering and Technology, Tiruchirapalli.

Dr. S. Kaliyamoorthy, Director, Alagappa Institute of Management, Karaikudi.

S. Lalitha Bhuvaneswari, Lecturer, Department of Management Studies, J.J. College of Engineering and Technology, Tiruchirapalli.

Dr. S. Sakthivel Rani, Assistant Professor, Department of Management Studies, Kalasalingam University, Krishnan Koil, Virudhunagar Dt.

S. Sekar Subramanian, Associate Professor, Department of Business Administration, V.H.N.S.N. College, Virudhunagar.

Dr. S. Varadaraj, Associate Professor of Management Studies, Gobi College of Arts and Science (Autonoums), Gobichettipalayam.

S. Venkatesan, Faculty, Department of Management Studies, DDE, M.K. University, Madurai.

S.C. Sivasundaram Anushan, Assistant Professor, Department of Management Studies, V.H.N.S.N. College, Virudhnagar

S.M. Asyed Mohamed Khaja, Lecturer in Commerce (Computer Applications), Sadakathullah Appa College, Tirunelveli.

Sheeba, E., Ph.D. Scholar, Department of Commerce, School of Business Studies, Manonmaniam Sundaranar University, Tirunelveli.

T. Lalitha Devi, Lecturer, Department of Commerce, Avinashilingam University for Women, Coimbatore.

Dr. T. Ramachandran, Professor, SRM School of Management, SRM University, Chennai.

T.S. Uma Rani, Lecturer in Management Studies, J.J. College of Engg. and Technology, Trichy.

Dr. U. Jerinabi, Reader, Department of Commerce, Avinashilingam University for Women, Coimbatore.

Dr. V. Bharathi Ramani, Reader in Commerce, Ambai Arts College, Ambasamudram, Tirunelveli District.

Dr. V. Parthiban, Dept of Management Studies, Gobi Arts and Science College (Autonoums), Gobichettipalayam, Tamilnadu.

CHAPTER

1

Motivational Practices: A Tool for Sustaining Competitiveness in Organisations

S.C. Sivasundaram Anushan

INTRODUCTION

In this age, any company that wants to get ahead needs to have motivated workers. Traditional incentive programs have been based upon extrinsic motivators such as salary and benefits. Intrinsic motivation, however, is needed in order to arouse a person's passion or commitment to the job. Shared vision, leadership, teamwork, training, increased capability, and goal accomplishment are powerful motivators which can be encouraged, embedded, or "designed in" to create a high performance culture.

A 1993 public relations brochure on the Opel production system makes a surprising statement: "Employee motivation represents one of our largest productivity reserves and is therefore a key element for increasing the international competitiveness of German automobile manufacturers." Continuous improvement at Open Essence is part of the team concept. People on the job understand their immediate work environment and are expected to optimize the process, to change details of the assembly, or to develop new procedures. There are two more lessons to consider. One is the surprising level of work motivation created by giving people full control over their jobs and letting them organize their workplace to reach the highest possible degree of overall efficiency. This changes the role of management to becoming a resource of advice and support, based on close partnership and open communications. The other is the importance of learning, or continuous skill acquisition. Learning with the team and across the team structure at Opel Eisenach provides the people with a good understanding of the conceptual framework of the facility and everyone's role within it.

EXAMPLES: MOTIVATIONAL PRACTICES

1. *Mars, Inc.*: Every employee, including the president, gets a weekly 10% bonus by coming to work on time each day that week.
2. *Japanese Companies*: Employees meet regularly to hear inspirational speeches, sing company songs, and chant the corporate litany.
3. *Tupperware and Mary Kay Cosmetics*: Hold inspirational get-togethers for sales force organisations.
4. *Procter and Gamble*: Encourages competition among brand managers; system breeds people who love to compete and excel.

CONTEMPORARY ISSUES IN MOTIVATION

Understanding and predicting employee motivation continues to be one of the most popular areas in management research. Several significant workplace issues are important to look at in understanding motivation.

A. To maximize motivation among today's diversified work force, managers need to think in terms of being flexible. Many of the so-called family-friendly programmes and flexible working schedules that organisations have developed are a response to the varied needs of a diverse workforce.
   1. A compressed workweek is a workweek comprised of four 10-hour days.
   2. Flexible work hours (also known as flextime) describes a scheduling system in which employees are required to work a number of hours a week, but are free, within limits, to vary the hours of work.
   3. Job sharing is the practice of having two or more people split a forty-hour-a-week job.
   4. Telecommuting allows employees to do their work at home through the linking by computer and modem of the employee and the office.
   5. Cultural differences also play a role in motivating a diverse workforce. Managers need to be aware of cultural differences in developing appropriate motivation programmes.

B. Pay-for-performance programs are compensation plans that pay employees on the basis of some performance measure.

C. Employee stock ownership plans (ESOPs) is a compensation program in which employees become part owners of the organisation by receiving stock as a performance incentive.

D. Motivating minimum-wage employees is one of the toughest motivation challenges a manager faces. Since money typically can't be used as a reward, managers look for other types of rewards such as employee recognition programs. But managers can also look to job design and expectancy theories of motivation to find some help in motivating these workers.

FROM THEORY TO PRACTICE: SUGGESTIONS FOR MOTIVATING EMPLOYEES

Several suggestions for motivating employees are given and are based upon what is currently known about motivation.

A. Recognise individual differences in terms of needs, attitudes, personality, and other important individual factors.

B. Match people to jobs by identifying what needs are important to individuals and trying to provide jobs that allow them to fulfil those needs.

C. Use goals since the literature on goal setting suggests that managers should ensure that employees have hard, specific goals and feedback on how well they are doing in pursuit of those goals.

D. Ensure that goals are perceived as attainable. Employees who see goals as unattainable will reduce their level of effort.

E. Individualize rewards. Because employees have different needs, what is a reward and reinforcer to one may not work for another.

F. Link rewards to performance by making rewards contingent on desired levels of performance.

G. Check the system for equity. Employees should perceive that the rewards or outcomes are equal to the inputs given.

H. Don't ignore money. The allocation of performance-based wage increases, piecework bonuses, and other pay incentives are important in determining employee motivation.

MOTIVATION'S THREE CRITICAL PRE-REQUISITES

Motivation = Productivity
Communication = Execution of Strategy
Motivation + Communication = Sustained Productivity

This is the mantra of success for any organisation. Motivation is directly proportional to productivity. A proper motivated workforce is known to have achieved amazing target when certain hygiene factors are not present. The essence of Motivation management is: confidence, trust and satisfaction. The cost of neglecting motivation can lead to declined performance of the employee which in turn leads to reduced productivity. Performance deteriorates or the propensity to leave increases, when the motivational level drops. When poor-performing employees are not motivated to improve, they drag results down, reduce productivity among their team members and, worse, seldom leave because they have no place to go.

The crux of motivation management is to understand that employees are motivated by what they believe is going to happen, not by what managers' promise will happen. Managers can motivate employees by setting in motion the three conditions required for motivation-confidence, trust and satisfaction and by creating an environment that reinforces those conditions.

1. Confidence

Most importantly, managers can improve motivation by assigning work to employees that they naturally do well and that they enjoy. When employees can do the job well naturally, they know they can perform and there will be no confidence problems.

2. Trust

Employees face a major motivational roadblock when they believe, "Outcomes are not tied to my performance. I will not get what my performance deserves." This is a trust problem. Trust problems tend to be easier for managers to spot because employees usually are vocal about them. There are two difficulties, however, that managers face. Trust problems cannot be corrected quickly. It takes time to build trust and courage for managers to give employees what their performance deserves. It may be easy to reward the high performers, but it is sometimes uncomfortable to withhold rewards when people perform poorly. It is particularly difficult when the poor-performing employee is either an outspoken troublemaker or a loyal, dedicated and hard-working employee. But giving employees what their performance deserves is important. To do otherwise might send a crippling message to the under performing employee and his team-mates. It is like a parent who tells two children they can have ice cream if they clean their rooms, and then lets both have the reward when only one completes the chore. This teaches both children that they do not have to perform to get what they want.

3. Satisfaction

It is difficult for employees to put out the effort necessary to get their work done when they realize, "The outcomes offered to me are not satisfying. I'm not getting what I want from my job." People may believe they can do the job (confidence) and that outcomes will be tied to performance (trust), but they will not be motivated if they believe the outcomes will be dissatisfying. It does not make sense for anyone to work hard for something he doesn't want. Many managers fail to take the time to find out what is satisfying and dissatisfying to each employee. When motivating employees, many managers make the mistake of believing and acting as though everyone is motivated in the same way. This simply is not true. What motivates one person may even de-motivate another. Challenging work, for example, is motivating to some employees, intimidating to others; some employees prefer the certainty of a fixed routine, while others thrive on task variety.

CONCLUSION

Managers also cannot assume that each employee will be satisfied if the three "big outcomes"—money, advancement and job security—are fulfiled. Another outcome, such as praise, recognition, openness or honesty, may be more of a motivating factor to some employees. Another interesting point is that when the work itself is satisfying, employees tend to be very forgiving when there is a shortfall in rewards. This is because employees are getting something that is highly prized by most people in today's work environment—enjoyment from their work. Motivation is related to the above three factors. If any one of them is not up to the mark, performance suffers; thus, there is a loss of productivity to the organisation.

Motivate to Inspire

AYEESHA ZAWAHIR

The word "motivation" comes from the Latin word "movere"—"to move." And managers often view motivation in exactly those terms—"I need to get my people moving!" Hence, work motivation is looked upon as a process that initiates and maintains goal-oriented performance. Consequently, the managers use the trigger that will spark employees' best efforts, whether it is money, power or responsibility, bigger challenges or interesting works, which form the basis of motivation equation.

Employees are the lifeblood of any organisation. Building a positive work environment is an important strategy in attracting, retaining and motivating employees. But lasting passion and commitment to a job comes from an inner sense of being inspired. Perhaps that's the reason why February second is celebrated as "Inspire your employees to excellence day" world over.

"Inspiration to me is the stimulus that generates enthusiasm and energy within and results in a higher level of demonstrated behaviour or action. Motivation stirs you while inspiration fills you," says Lipika Mohanty, Head of HR, Authbridge. Inspiration is more enduring and lasting. Inspiration was traditionally believed to be the privilege of artistic people but no longer so. Today, a career means much more than just a source of livelihood for every individual. The workplace is the primary and sometimes the sole source of social interaction, appreciation and fulfilmentf or many individuals, which makes it all the more imperative for them to be inspired about their jobs. "Every job has a purpose and reason for existence. It may not be easy for each individual to identify with each and every job; but they can if they want, be inspired by it. All that it requires is to understand and appreciate the significance of the job in the whole, the challenges, the achievements and the rewards associated with the job," says Mohanty.

Performance disparity exists whenever individuals evade starting something afresh, persist in continuing old methods, resist change, don't prioritize, or refuse to "work smart" and get stranded with inadequate solutions to solve a problem. Motivation plays a crucial role in avoiding such disparities. It energizes the thought process, fuels the enthusiasm, steers the mental force and converts abilities into performance. If this motivation could move the inner self, then there will be no stopping of the performance. In simple words, it makes the employee work at his best continually.

Motivation in most companies is considered as a tool to channelize human energy towards goal achievement. As a result, managers focus too much on what might get their employees moving like hefty bonus or a coveted promotion rather than thinking about how to keep them moving in the right direction once they've started. They treat motivation like a bulb which, when switched on, gives light. But most experts see motivation as an ongoing process--one in which managers need to continually focus on how to successfully channel or support employees once they "get moving."

Jon Katzenbach, CEO of Katzenbach Partners and author of "The Discipline of Teams and the Wisdom of Teams," writes, "The key to encouraging people has more to do with figuring out how to connect them emotionally to their work than throwing money or promotions at them." Developments in many areas of life, which occurred at an astonishing pace in the last decade, have produced a turbulent business environment for which the causes are global, technical, economical, and social. With intense competition in industry today, simply meeting or beating past performance will not result in the level of improvement necessary to remain competitive. The employees need to be kept alive, active and aware if the company is to sustain or improve. Inspiration, unlike motivation, is sourced in the heart, draws on an inner sense of meaning and gives rise to creativity. Accordingly if the managers don't motivate to inspire the company may expire in due course of time.

Motivation is a result of external stimulus. Inspiration is the result of an internal trust. By providing a meaning and purpose in the work, the employees can be inspired. Employees need to have a reason for their organisation's existence that extends beyond the stock price, next month's sales, and year-end profits. "Companies must have a product, a mission, or simply a vision of the industry that employees find exciting and energizing. These employees may not be with you for the long-term but, while they are part of your workforce, they want to accomplish something worthwhile," say Joseph H. Boyett and Jimmie T. Boyett, co-authors of "Beyond Workplace 2000". They quote in an empirical study, (a project designed to identify the best ideas shared by top management thinkers about workplace best practices to deal with a changing environment) "Merck is a good example of a company that provides such a purpose. This pharmaceutical manufacturer promotes a company that puts people before profits and backs up that commitment with action such as putting a below-market price on its anti-AIDS drug and giving away medicine to developing countries. Maybe that's why in a recent survey, 97 percent of Merck's employees said they were proud to work for the company and 86 percent said they thought their work had special meaning. Merck demonstrates a higher purpose than profits."

Stephen R. Covey declares, "An empowered organisation is one in which individuals have the knowledge, skill, desire, and opportunity to personally succeed in a way that leads to collective organisational success." Today, organisations deal with amalgamations, new technologies, economic policies, stockless or just-in-time distribution, captivated contracts, preferred suppliers, total quality management, continuous improvement, business reengineering, and so forth. To move into the next decade, organisations need to re-think their structures, products, processes, and markets. They must reestablish themselves to be quicker to market, customer focused, innovative, nimble, flexible, and be able to handle rapid change. This can only be achieved by continuously empowering the human resources who are the achievers. Employees who lack critical skills are unlikely to be star performers, no matter how "motivated" they are. Empowerment is not simply another way to "get something" it's a condition that supports you in living life fully. Empowerment is an inner-to-outer dynamic. Actions aligned with inner knowingness and strength is necessary for true empowerment. Motivating to inspire the inner self of the employees to align with the vision of the company is critical if the company is to tread on the success path.

Inspiring employees brings in long-term effects while motivating employees only fills the short-term goals and has to be revived every term. America's most respected scholar on organisational leadership today, Warren Bennis in his book "On Becoming a Leader" stresses the difference between a leader and a manager: "The leader innovates; the manager administrates. The leader focuses on people; the manager focuses on systems and structure. The leader inspires; the manager controls. The leader is his own person; the manager is a good soldier. The leader sees the long-term; the manager sees the short-term." A leader has to inspire rather than motivate his employees if the vision of the company is to be accomplished successfully.

To inspire the employees, their outdated beliefs, repressed fears and resentments must be released. To get inspired output, the employees must be made to start from where they are right now without making them feel wrong or believing that they need to be "fixed". The word "inspire" literally means "to breathe in." Motivating the employees to look in will awaken them to their abilities. It will stimulate them to do what is necessary leading to what is possible and one day you will find them doing the impossible.

People are inspired by the trust they have on their own self and on the people in the workplace. When they are centered, they will not get tipped off by any challenge that comes on the way. Motivation at the workplace should enable to build this trust in the employee. It should be prioritized. "If you want a man to be for you, never let him feel he is dependent on you. Make him feel you are in some way dependent on him".—General George C. Marshall. Without making the human resource powerful company goals cannot be achieved at the right time. Once inspired, the employees will rise up to their highest level of functioning. Then prosperity easily submits to the inspired soul.

Such an inspiration can be instilled in employees by motivating them through innovative training, establishing work values, creating trust, and by compensation, rewards, recognition, communication, and favouring participatory management. As Thomas Jefferson observes, "In matters of style, swim with the current; in matters of principle, stand like a rock." The companies need to adopt the best practices of motivation and at the same get their values engraved in employees' hearts.

In the new economy, the days of sticking to a single job and moral binding are in jeopardy. Employers readily announce layoffs. Employees just as readily leave for better offers. Effective management of human resources has become all the more critical. At this juncture motivating people to higher and higher levels of performance and retaining them is possible only by inspiring them.

Inspiration is value-based. Motivation is benefit-based. Inspiration works out of love while motivation works out of ego. Hence inspiration leads while motivation drives. An inspired person enjoys what he does while a motivated person is pressurized. Motivation makes people work hard while inspiration makes people work smart. Inspiration boosts the employee's morale to result in creative and effective productivity. Motivation just propels productivity. Inspiration longs for inherent satisfaction rather than for some separable consequence. Inspiration makes one genuinely incline to take interest in novelty, to actively assimilate and to creatively apply one's skills that affects performance, persistence and well-being. Companies need to favour conditions that elicit, sustain and enhance such an inspiration if their human resources are to be utilized to the maximum level in performance.

"Don't tell people how to do things, tell them what to do and let them surprise you with their results," argues George S. Patton. Companies must guide the employees to motivate themselves. That is the key. People will motivate themselves in their own way if you gently guide them. If the motivation comes from inside that is inspiration. The companies should be the cause and activate. They should be the producers of the cause which will make things happen. Then they will enable the employees to play far beyond their own self-concepts.

Inspiration makes one perform out of interest and to satisfy the innate psychological needs for competence and autonomy. It is the prototype of self-determined behaviour. It is intrinsic. In order to make employees invincible external or extrinsic motivation is the means. It should be instrumental in internalizing and integrating self-determination. The company should earn the respect of the employees. When this respect runs deep enough, the employee ends up in loving the company. Then that love will inspire the employee to be at his/her best automatically. It can be achieved if the motivating activities of the company aim at constructing an affirmative atmosphere. Where every human thrives cherishing the role he plays.

A good way to inspire is by motivating employees to gain confidence in their self and in the company by eliminating context obstacles that might prevent employees from doing an outstanding job. In other words, company needs to do what it can to ensure that it or the company isn't somehow getting in employees' way. This will make them put their mind, body and spirit in the work they do with dedication. This devotion when rewarded will inspire them to perseverance. It is a matter of simple exchange, the employee's inspired loyalty and commitment in return for peace and happiness at the work atmosphere.

Companies must motivate to inspire the employees. Such a motivation will lead employees to invest more or less cognitive effort to enhance both the quality and quantity of their work performance. Today, value lies in love, knowledge and skill, which are applied to create, innovate, produce, service, entertain, and excite, and the employees need to be inspired to unleash their full potential and not just motivated.

References

Joseph, H. Boyett and Henry P. Conn., 'Maximum Performance Management', Joseph H. Boyett and Henry P. Conn. Glenbridge Publishing Ltd., 1988.

Steve, Chandler and Scott Richardson, '100 ways to Motivate Others—How great leaders can produce insane results without driving people crazy', The Career Press, Inc., 3 Tice Road, PO Box 687, Franklin Lakes, NJ 07417, 2008

Peter, Vaill, 'Managing as a Performing Art—New Ideas for a World of Chaotic Change', Jossey-Bass Inc. Publishers, 350, Sansome Street, California-94104, 1989.

Richard, E. Clark, 'Fostering the Work Motivation of Individuals and Teams', Rossier School of Education, University of Southern California, 2003.

Clark, R.E. and Estes, F., 'Turning Research into Results: A guide to selecting the right performance solutions', CEP Press, Atlanta, GA, 2002

Bandura, A., 'Self-efficacy: The exercise of control', W.H. Freeman, New York, NY, 1997.

Druckman, D., and Bjork, R. (Eds.), 'Learning, remembering, and believing: Enhancing human performance', National Academy Press, Washington, D.C., 1994.

Spitzer, D., 'Super Motivation', AMACOM Books, New York, NY, 1995.

An Empirical Study on Sales Force Motivation and its Application

M. BALASUBRAMANIAN

ABSTRACT

With the growing diversity of today's sales force, it is becoming more and more important to find ways to motivate leaders and followers to engage in trusting and give-and-take relationships. Trust has been found to lead to many positive organisational outcomes (Dirks, 2002). The proposed article attempts to examine the role of motivation by discussing (a) the concept of motivation, (b) the steps in motivation, (c) the different types of motivation, (d) theories of Motivation and application to sales force, (e) cultural differences and motivation, (f) Sales Force Motivation Mix, (g) creating sales force motivation, and (h) guidelines for motivating sales employees and the managers.

INTRODUCTION

"Motivation means a process of stimulating people to action to accomplish desired goals". According to Berelson and Steiner, "A motive is an inner state that energizes, activates, or moves and directs or channels behaviour toward goals". Tolma observes, "More specifically, the term motivation has been called an intervening variable." Intervening variables are internal and psychological process which are not directly observable and which, in turn, account for behaviour.

Characteristics of Motivation

1. Motivation is an internal feeling

2. Person in totality, not in part, is motivated
3. Motivation is the product of anticipated values from an action and the perceived probability that these values will be achieved by the action.

Importance of Motivation

1. High Performance level
2. Low employee turnover and absenteeism
3. Acceptance of organisational changes

MOTIVATION, SATISFACTION, INSPIRATION AND MANIPULATION

Motivation refers to the drive and efforts to satisfy a want or goal, whereas satisfaction refers to the contentment experienced when a want is satisfied. In contrast, inspiration brings about a change in the thinking pattern. On the other hand manipulation gets things done from others in a predetermined manner.

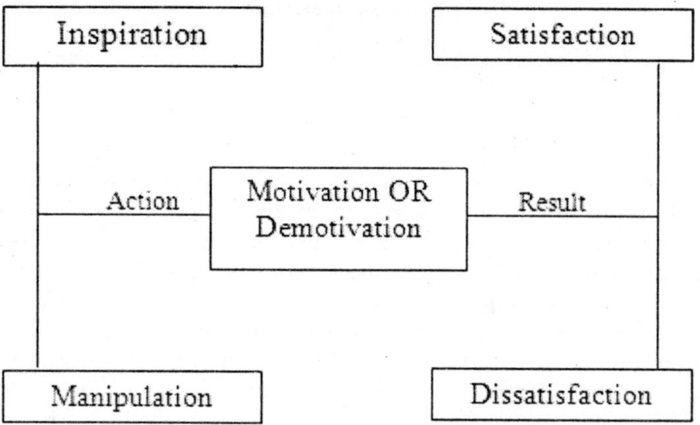

Hence, manipulation or external stimulus as well as inspiration or internal stimulus acts as carriers of either demotivation or motivation which in turn either results into dissatisfaction or satisfaction depending upon.

Steps in Motivation

According to Jucius, the following steps are adopted in motivation:

- *Sizing up*: This involves ascertaining motivational needs. All employees need motivation, but of varying kinds degrees. For example, one may need proper facilities for the education of one's children; others may want higher education for them. One may take pride in producing quality work; another may be interested only in quality. Stress at size-up stage must, therefore, be laid up as individual differences.

- *Preparing a set of motivation tool*: This requires' a selection of specific tools of motivation. An executive, from personal experience or from the experiences of others, and with the help of the personnel department, may draw up a list of the devices that may motivate different types of people under different circumstances.
- *Selecting and applying motivators*: The executive should decide about the words, the tone of voice, the gestures, etc. to be used and make a necessary rehearsal for their proper use. Besides, it has also to be considered where and when motivation is to be applied. The place and timing for this purpose are important.
- *Feedback*: This involves the finding out of whether an individual has been motivated. If not, some other device may be applied. He further suggests that while establishing the steps of motivation, an executive should be guided by certain rules such as:
- *Variability*: The methods of motivation should not be the same but should change according to the circumstances, and also because no one set of motivators will be effective for everybody or for the same person over a period of time.
- *Self-interest and Motivation*: People are, by nature, selfish. When a person realizes that his own interests are best served by the attainment of an organisation's goals, he is likely to be motivated.
- *Attainability*: It is necessary to establish goals which are reasonable and attainable. When such goals are attained, employee satisfaction is achieved. Unattainable goals often frustrate people.
- *Participation*: The desirability of the participation of those to be motivated ensures that their co-operation is enlisted. This reduces suspicion of a management's motivational aims.
- *Proportioning Rewards*: Motivation should be in proportion to the efforts made.
- *The Human Element*: Motivation appeals to the emotions. The executive who is most successful as a motivator can trace his success invariably to his skill in dealing with other people's feelings.
- *Individual Group Relationship*: Motivation must be based on group as well as individual stimuli.
- *Situational*: Motivation must be based on a sound managerial theory.

EXECUTIVE MOTIVATION

Managers are persons responsible for achieving organisational goals through people. They are held accountable for their own performance as well as the performance. They have the responsibility to see that the behaviour of their subordinates is supportive of the organisation rather than detrimental to it.

The very nature of the manager's role brings inherent pressures. Scott has said that "Every manager lives with pressures to produce successfully, to adapt to the demands of change, to live with great uncertainties in a hostile environment, to conform to the demand of others, to perform conflicting roles, and sometimes to survive in a socially ostracized position."

The heavy demands under which many managers work shape their actions and expectations. Since they are human beings, they need to give attention, to the typical human needs. But their needs do differ in urgency. As McClelland puts, "the manager tend to exhibit a greater degree of the need for achievement than do those who are non-managers."

According to Castle, managers are induced to work when they feel that (i) they are doing something that they call their own; (ii) they do tasks they have set for themselves; (iii) they can see what they have done; (iv) they feel that their job is important; (v) they are secure; and (vi) they are doing something useful.

Seven Rules of Motivation

- Set a major goal, but follow a path.
- Finish what you start.
- Socialize with others of similar interest.
- Learn how to learn.
- Harmonize natural talent with interest that motivates.
- Increase knowledge of subjects that inspires.
- Take risk.

MOTIVATION IS BUILT ON THREE BASIC ELEMENTS

1. Motivation starts with need, vision, dream or desire to achieve the seemingly impossible. Creativity is associated with ideas, projects and goals, which can be considered a path to freedom. President Abraham Lincoln never went to school; he became President because he had a vision that motivated him. In addition, his vision was so powerful that it motivated everyone around him and that energy motivated the country.
2. Develop a love-to-learn, become involved with risky ventures and continually seek new opportunities. Success is based on learning what works and does not work.
3. Develop the ability to overcome barriers and to bounce back from discouragement or failure. Achievers learn to tolerate the agony of failure. In any endeavor, barriers and failure will be there. Bouncing back requires creative thinking as it is a learning process. In addition, bouncing back requires starting again at square one.

TYPES OF MOTIVATION

There are various types of motivation that influence human beings. These different motivation types have different short and long-term effects on people. We can use the most suitable motivation type to fit the particular situation or individual we are dealing with. There are two main broad categories of motivation: intrinsic motivation and extrinsic motivation.

Intrinsic motivation comes from within. It comes from the personal enjoyment and educational achievement that we derive from doing that particular thing. For example, for people who love music, their motivation to practice the instrument, attend classes, etc. is intrinsic motivation.

Extrinsic motivation comes from things or factors that are outside the individual. For example, one is motivated to work hard at the office because one is looking for a promotion .Social recognition, money, fame, competition or material achievements are all examples of extrinsic motivation.

ACHIEVEMENT

This is the motivation of a person to attain goals. The longing for achievement is inherent in every man, but not all persons look to achievement as their motivation. They are motivated by a goal. In order to attain that goal, they are willing to go as far as possible. The complexity of the goal is determined by a person's perception. It is similar to 'Kaizen' approach to Japanese Management.

Socialization: Some people consider socialization to be their main motivation for actions. This is especially evident in the situation of peer pressure. Some people are willing to do anything to be treated as an equal within a group structure. The idea of being accepted among a group of people is their motivation for doing certain things.

Incentive Motivation

This motivation involves rewards. People who believe that they will receive rewards for doing something are motivated to do everything they can to reach a certain goal. While achievement motivation is focused on the goal itself, incentive motivation is driven by the fact that the goal will give people benefits. Incentive motivation is used in companies through bonuses and other types of compensation for additional work.

By offering incentives, companies hope to raise productivity and motivate their employees to work harder.

Fear Motivation

When incentives do not work, people often turn to fear and punishment as the next tools. Fear motivation involves pointing out various consequences if someone does not follow a set of prescribed behaviour. This is often seen in companies as working hand-in-hand with incentive motivation. Workers are often faced with a reward and punishment system, wherein they are given incentives if they accomplish a certain goal, but they are given punishments when they disobey certain policies.

Change Motivation

Sometimes people do things just to bring about changes within their immediate environment. Change motivation is often the cause of true progress. People just become tired of how things are and thus, think of ways to improve it.

Affiliation Motivation

It is a drive to relate to people on a social basis. Persons with affiliation motivation perform work better when they are complimented for their favourable attitudes and co-operation.

Competence Motivation

It is the drive to be good at something, allowing the individual to perform high quality work. Competence motivates people seek job mastery, take pride in developing and using their problem-solving skills and strive to be creative when confronted with obstacles. They learn from their experience.

Power Motivation

It is the drive to influence people and change situations. Power motivates people to create an impact on their organisation.

Attitude Motivation

Attitude motivation is how people think and feel. It is their self-confidence, their belief in themselves, and their attitude to life. It is how they feel about the future and how they react to the past.

MOTIVATING DIFFERENT PEOPLE IN DIFFERENT WAYS

Motivation is not only in a single direction, i.e. downwards. In the present scenario, where the workforce is more informed, more educated and more goal-oriented, the role of motivation has left the boundaries of the hierarchy of management. Apart from superior motivating a subordinate, encouragement and support to colleagues as well as helpful suggestions on the right time, even to the superior, brings about a rapport at various work levels. Besides, where workforce is self-motivated, just the acknowledgement of the same makes people feel important and wanted.

How to Understand Sales Force Motivation?

Motivation can be understood at two levels:

(a) What motivates salespeople?
(b) How do salespeople choose their action?

The first one attempts to identify the reason behind the intensity and persistence of physical and mental efforts expended; the second one tells about the directions or decisions to engage in specific actions in specific situation.

THEORIES OF MOTIVATION AND APPLICATION TO SALESFORCE

Need Hierarchy Theory

As people progress up the pyramid, needs become increasingly psychological and social. Soon, the need for love, friendship and intimacy become important. Further up the pyramid, the need for personal esteem and feelings of accomplishment become important. Like Carl Rogers, Maslow emphasizes the importance of self-actualization, which is a process of growing and developing as a person to achieve individual potential.

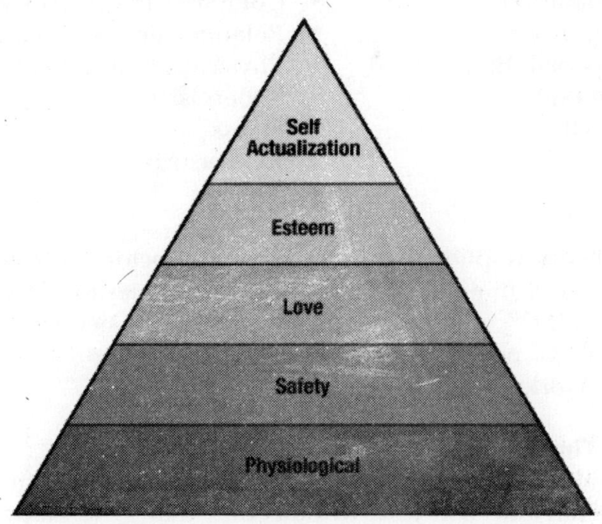

Physiological needs (e.g., basic salary)
Security needs (e.g., pension plan)
Belongingness needs (e.g., friends in work group)
Esteem needs (e.g., job title)
Self-actualisation needs (e.g., challenging job)

Salespeople are Motivated by Different Needs

- o *Need for status* (e.g., need for recognition and promotion)
- o *Need for control* (e.g., need to be in control and influence others)
- o *Need for respect* (e.g., need to be seen as experts who can give advice)
- o *Need for routine* (e.g., need to follow a routine that must not be interrupted)

- o Need for accomplishment (e.g., need more money and challenges)
- o Need for stimulation (e.g., need to seek outside stimulation and challenges)
- o Need for honesty (e.g., need to believe in the rightness of their practices)

Two Factor Theory

Two factor theory of Frederick Herzberg talks about two things: Motivator Factors and Hygiene Factors.

Motivator Factors	*Hygiene Factors*
• Achievement	• Pay and Benefits
• Recognition	• Company Policy and Administration
• Work Itself	• Relationships with co-workers
• Responsibility	• Physical Environment
• Promotion	• Supervision
• Growth	• Status
	• Job Security
	• Salary

The theory implies that the motivation factors or motivators are the primary causes of motivation, and address the question "why work harder to improve sales?" and the Hygiene factors are necessary conditions to achieve a state of neutrality and address the question "why prefer to work in the same workplace?"

Expectancy Theory

Motivation is a function of a salesperson's anticipation that a particular behaviour will lead to outcomes that s/he values.

Motivation = Function of (Expectancy × Instrumentality × Valence)

Expectancy is the salesperson's perception that a certain amount of effort will lead to successful performance (e.g., Can I do it?).

Instrumentality refers to salesperson's perception of the probability that performance will lead to certain outcomes or rewards. (e.g., What do I get for doing it?).

Valence is the perceived attractiveness or unattractiveness of an outcome or reward (e.g., How much do I value the reward?).

Goal Setting Theory

Motivated behaviour is the result of conscious goals and intentions. The theory starts from the point that a salesperson has determined to engage in an activity and argues that a person's inclination to act in a particular way is influenced by the:

- o Anticipated result (*goal*)
- o Intention (*will*), which implies
- o Effort (*will-act*); and
- o Strategy to reach the goal (*object-oriented content*).

Goal difficulty and goal specificity are two important aspects that shape performance.

Cultural differences and motivation

Cultures differ on at least six bipolar dimensions:

Universalism (e.g., *rules, laws*)
Particularism (e.g., *exceptions, unique relations*)
Individualism (e.g., *competitiveness*)
Communitarianism (e.g., *cooperation*)
Specificity (e.g., *atomistic*)
Diffusion (e.g., *holistic*)
Achieved status (e.g., *what you have done*)
Ascribed status (e.g., *who you are*)
Inner direction (e.g., *conscience is located inside*)
Outer directed (e.g., *examples are located outside*)
Sequential time (e.g., *time is a race*)
Synchronous time (e.g., *time is a dance*)

Using examples, explain how differences in values as above might complicate the task of motivating a global sales force.

Motivation is a large concept; it is a product of all that a sales manager or the organisation does in relation to the sales persons. That is why practically all discussions on sales management always center on motivation of sales force. The compensation plan discussed earlier and aspects like building morale, training and development, sales supervisor; sales coordination and achieving effective communication with salesmen are all closely related to motivation. In fact, even sales administration tasks, such as setting personal selling objectives, assigning tasks to individual salesmen and designing their territories have a strong bearing on motivation.

Motivation is the sum total of all that a sales manager does to his salesmen. While a compensation policy no doubt has an impact on motivation, there are many other aspects that make up motivation. Morale building, training and development, sales supervision and coordination and effective communication are all parts of motivation. Sensible management in itself is a motivational element. For example, when the sales task is clearly set out and handed down to the salesmen, their motivation becomes positive; when the sales task is set out in vague and ambiguous terms and the salesmen are left in doubt as to what is expected of them, their motivation sags.

Motivating the sales force is the crux of sales force management. The mettle of sales managers always gets tested on the touchstone of their motivational skill—how well they are able to motivate the salesmen under them.

Sales Force Motivation Mix

1. *Compensation plan*:
   Financial compensation
   Non-financial compensation
2. *Recognition*:
   Awards such as pins, trophies, certificates, etc.
   Praise and encouragement
   Job enrichment
3. *Promotion*
4. *Proper performance evaluation*
5. *Good sales coaching*
6. *Good supervision (in person, by mail, by telephone)*
7. *Sales meetings and conventions*
8. *Sales contests*
9. *Training programmes (induction and continuation)*
10. *Sales planning elements:*
    Good forecasting
    Good budgeting
    Fair quotas
    Fair territories
11. *General management elements :*
    Organisational structure and Climate
    Management's leadership style
12. *Sensible management*

CREATIVE SALES FORCE MOTIVATION OF SUCCESSFUL COMPANIES

Successful companies have found creative ways to harness the competitive, incentive driven nature of good sales people, with a minimum of negative backfires. For Mary Brown, Director of Western Region Sales Operations for *Right Now Technologies*, this includes ingenious approaches that reward individual performance while building camaraderie and teamwork.

For example, the company will sometimes sponsor raffles for trips or special merchandise. The more a sales person achieves, the more "chances" they get in the raffle; yet everyone who produces has a shot at winning. Often, Mary provides non-monetary incentives that are fun for employees and their families: A video camera, a mountain bike or a week-end at *Big*

Sky (a local resort). Or she may provide extra days off if sales quotas are met—to be used at the employees' discretion. The point is, great companies like *Right Now* use innovation and creativity to stay ahead of the employee motivation curve. By developing incentive programs that are exciting and unifying, the company and the employees both win.

The century-old *Owen House* Hardware (an institution in downtown *Bozeman, Montana*), takes a different creative approach. As manager Larry Bowman explains, the key to retailing is to serve with excellence, every customer who walks through the door, whether they are buying a riding lawn mower or a package of thumb tacks. Commissions and bonuses based on individual sales numbers tend to counteract the *Owen House* philosophy, and prompt sales personnel to "push" large ticket items and compete over customers.

Larry has tried a number of things over the years, but is convinced that for his type of business, incentives should be provided to all personnel (both full and part time), based on store-wide performance parameters. Currently, the company is giving to each employee, credit toward in-store purchases based on monthly improvement in average ticket sales. The credit is computed daily, and entered on a calendar where everyone can see their collective progress. As with most incentive programs, it is difficult to measure its success objectively. Larry isn't sure how many employees are knowingly motivated to boost average sales, but at the very least, the program focuses everyone's attention on the worthy goal.

GUIDELINES FOR MOTIVATING SALES EMPLOYEES AND THE MANAGERS

- The management should let his people know that he considers them valuable, capable individuals, i.e. should treat the people with respect and honesty.
- He should make sure that subordinates have the tools to get the job done for achieving the goals.
- The person should be fitted on the job where he can set his own standard, get concrete feedback and deal with moderate risks.
- He should avoid building "dissatisfies" into the job, i.e., he should make sure that salary and working conditions are adequate.
- He should set fair, achievable goals and communicate them to the employees, for understanding what they are shooting for helps them adequate accomplishment of the goals.
- The people should be made known, through feed-back, how they are doing.
- All such techniques as reinforcement incentives, MBO, job enrichment and maintenance of high morale should be utilized.
- Job analysis, selection and training should be used to ensure that the hired people could do the jobs with the required skills and abilities.

CONCLUSION

Motivation is an inner force that drives and directs behaviour. Motivation theories answer questions pertaining to what motivates salespeople and how salespeople choose their actions. The three groupings of motivational theories discussed in this article are content, process and reinforcement. Culture influences motivation through its influence on salespeople's values, attitudes and norms. Sales managers have a range of motivational tools at their disposal. Cultural differences among salespeople should be taken into consideration when designing a motivational program. Motivation, job satisfaction and performance are inextricably related.

Obviously, employee incentive programs do not fit all propositions. As these successful companies demonstrate, different approaches work best in differing situations. But one conclusion I've come to is that "motivating sales people" is a contradiction in terms. Sales people—if they are sales people—are already motivated. The challenge the employers face is channeling that motivation, and maintaining it at peak levels, week in and week out.

Creative, well-conceived commission programs and bonus plans can certainly help in this regard. But ultimately, the most important factor lies within the heart and soul of your business itself. If a salesperson identifies with the culture and mission of your company, and feels a sense of ownership in your company's future, then you will most likely have a loyal, motivated employee whose consistent performance levels will help you reach for the top.

Spice of Life

Dr. V. Bharathi Ramani

Any one to have interest in his life, it must be spicy. The spice which is referred to here is "MOTIVATION".

Motivation is the key to a successful life. It is motivation that helps us in our day to day existence. Only through motivation we get through the most difficult times in our lives and in our careers. Motivation to work, motivation to live healthy and motivation to have a happy family are required by all. Yet sometimes we find ourselves down and unmotivated. When we lose our motivation, we feel frustrated.

MOTIVATION IN THE WORK PLACE

Many business managers today are not aware of the effect of motivation on their business, and it is therefore important that they must learn and understand the factors that determine positive motivation in the work place. The size of the business is irrelevant. Everyone needs some form of motivation. Motivation is something that is approached differently by different businesses. The responsibility of its integration lies with the supervisors or managers. However, it is the business owner who must initiate motivation as a strategy to attain corporate goals.

The key factors that determine the rate of motivation among the employees must be identified. These factors are linked directly to their individual needs, behaviour and attitudes.

WHAT IS MOTIVATION?

Motivation is the force that makes us do things. This is the result of our individual needs being satisfied or met so that we have inspiration to complete the task. These needs vary from person to person as everybody has his individual needs to motivate himself. Depending on how motivated we are, it may further determine the effort we put into our work and therefore increase the standard of the output. Motivation does not always mean high salary. Some employees are motivated by money but not all. Human motivation is personal in nature. Even good music can motivate a person.

THE IMPORTANCE OF MOTIVATION

Motivation can have an effect on the output of the business, and is concerned with both quantity and quality. The employees are the greatest asset and no matter how efficient the technology and equipment of the organisation may be, it is no match for the effectiveness and efficiency of the staff.

With the right employee motivation techniques, the potentials of the employees are unlocked. The tenure is increased. Performance of the employees is improved. Success can be reinforced and it builds behaviour in the entire organisation. The above mentioned are possible through effectively learning the ways to motivate employees by creating opportunities for employees to succeed and earn rewards that are personally meaningful and professionally motivating.

NATURE OF MOTIVATION

Motivation is the inner force that drives employee behaviour. The intensity of one's inner force to do a task or accomplish a goal describes the level of motivation. Most employees prefer to be motivated. Motivating jobs and work environments win praise from employees. Of course what one person finds motivating may be boring, frustrating and debilitating to another person.

Motivating is complex process. No simple set of guidelines guarantees motivated employees. Motivation provides a never ending struggle for both employees and employers.

There are different types of motivation. But the important thing to remember is that the right plan will comfortably align with that particular organisation, its culture and its employees. Inspiring reward options, which are fit to the employees, must be found out.

EMPLOYEE MOTIVATION PROGRAMME

To have a positive impact on an organisation, the following motivation factors must be considered:

- Positive reinforcement along with high expectations and necessary training must be provided to the employees.
- Employees must be treated fairly with respect and honour.
- Employers must understand the employee needs.
- The employees must be taught to set work-related goals.

- The jobs and job descriptions must be restructured whenever necessary.
- There must be a reward system based on job performance.

EMPLOYEE MOTIVATION TECHNIQUES

Employee motivation techniques vary from expert to expert. However, they all have the same goal: getting employees to do their job better and more efficiently.

Motivation is the key to performance improvement. Here some techniques of motivation are discussed which can be included in a simple motivational programme through which the workers in an organisation can be motivated.

Team Development

Team development arises where the team starts to work together as a single unit. When there is a team surely there will be some conflicts and disagreements. Still this keeps the relationships alive and motivates people to think of new ideas and develop solutions for any problem. What is more important is to remain DYNAMIC and not to fall into complacency.

But development of teams is of course very difficult. Every one needs to be matured about things in team development. Arguments and disputes are normal in the early stages of team development, but the team learns to work more smoothly with one another in course of time.

Listen Before Speaking

Good listening is one of the most important skills of an employee in a service organisation. It is needed to solve complex problems quickly and stay competitive in the market. Much can be gained from improving listening skills. A good leader listens more than he speaks letting facts get through before he makes assumptions and decisions. The superiors must be impartial in disputes among co-workers and keep an open mind. The best managers listen and take their employees' concerns seriously enough to make them feel important not only as individual but as part of the team. A good listener is interested in what the speaker is saying. The speaker must be respected. If the conversation involves criticisms from either party or contains personal information, the discussions must be held in private.

Feel You Can Do More

In today's recession, banking is a job that is filled with stress. Many employees fall victims to the recession. Companies are trimming their workforce to save on costs. At that time how can one think that one can do more? It must be made known to the management that the employees are interested in promotions and they are interested in providing better service in a higher capacity. Drive is what more people lack and what they need to get them on the road to promotion. Movies provide a rich source of instant motivation and inspiration for audience. It is not costly. Some movies take the people out of misery.

Hypnotherapy for Motivation

It is connected to the concept of motivation. It will help the employees to push on and bring out the best in them. For this, the real goal must be identified by the employees. Motivation is about realizing one's true potentials. Sometimes these potentials meet certain barriers like unhappy and uneventful experiences in life. Hypnotherapy works toward connecting with their conscious. It is based on sub-conscious suggestions and it works in deeper level.

How to Motivate Unmotivated People?

Motivation comes from inspiration. If the employees are offered inspirational goals, they will take on the job of motivating themselves.

Creating a motivating environment is very essential. Working environment has a greater impact on the productivity than we think. Every business has a culture. The impact of every move made on the culture and the productivity must be watched.

The employees must be involved in decision-making. Employers do not just want a job. They want to be part something more. S. let them play a meaningful role in the organisation.

CONCLUSION

Motivation is the willingness of a person to perform a task when it comes down to him. We all do either what we want to do or what someone or something motivates us to do. Ability and motivation are the core part of any good employee motivation programme. Ability is a person's aptitude to perform a task. Either he has the skills to perform a given task or he does not. Ability can be improved with training and education. This can be a time consuming process, but it needs to be included in the total programme.

Again we have to consider two more important factors in any type of motivational programme. One is pleasure and the other is pain. If we find something pleasurable, we will continue to seek it out. If we find something painful, we usually avoid it. These two factors play an important role in any motivation programme. It is very simple that our focus needs to be on the positive. Gone are the days when effective management meant a tyrant boss running an organisation through intimidation. In the long run, that policy does not work. Well-planned and suitable motivational programme, focusing on ability and motivation, will surely make the life of the employees spicy.

References

www.EnterpriseLeaders.com/
www.inspiration and motivation.com/
www.geocities.com/

Motivational Factors of Organisational Environment in Nationalized Banks—Madurai District

Dr. K. Chandrasekaran and Mr. R. Thamarai Kannan

INTRODUCTION

"There are many forms and degrees of cooperation between the worker and the management", wrote James F. Lincoln. "The worker's attitude can vary all the way from passivity to highly imaginative contributions to efficiency and progress", he marked (Peter F. Drucker, 1986). Motivation depends on having clear objectives. Since motivation is personal, aim to align staff's individual drives with the company's purpose in general and individual units in particular is important. Motivational is reflected on three fields, it induces particular human behaviour, it directs and canalizes that behaviour and it explains how certain forms of behaviours can be maintained or preserved. Motivation in its broader sense includes both positive and negative aspects of human behaviour. In that sense, a term demotivation is introduced meaning lack of motivation, negative motivation or being motivated not to act in a certain way.

AIM OF THE STUDY

The Present study aims at identifying the motivating and demotivating elements and ranking the factors of the focus group in organisational environment.

Objectives

(i) To study the motivational pattern, of the focus group along the lines of identified motivational dimensions.
(ii) To study the ranked importance assigned by the focus group for identified motivational dimensions.

Research Design

Study area constitutes the group of study employed, the middle level officers working in nationalized banks in Madurai District the study group for the motivation study total numbering, 105.Survey method was employed to collect the data from the Population. The period refers to November 2009. Primary data were collected employing the questionnaire method.

The employee motivation Questionnaire indicates the motivation profile in twenty dimensions - Recognition, management, Progression, Business mode, Remuneration, Ethics Interest, Achievement, Growth, Power, Flexibility, Job security, Activity, Status, Autonomy, Customers, Teamwork, Pressure, Competition, Fear of Failure.

The collected data were made to be tabulated, cross-checked and worked out to get analytical information. These produce inferences about the particular dimensions and the dimensional factors concerned with identified motivation/demotivation. Simple percentage analysis, rank analysis as well as comparative analysis was carried out besides hypotheses testing with appropriate statistical tools.

Hypotheses Testing

Hypotheses were formulated and tested using the appropriate statistical testing method. Kendall's coefficient of concordance was identified to be an important testing tool in this regard.

RANK ANALYSIS

Rank analysis exclusively deals with the ranked importance extended to the twenty dimensional factors of the motivational study. Rank analysis is done through two modes. Simple Rank Analysis—using quantifiable data. Projective Rank Analysis—expressing through multi-dimensional factors. Rank analysis studies the mode of importance given by the focus groups in details. To quantitative data scale values and scores are used.

Calculation of scale score: The scale range can vary from greatly reduces my work motivation to greatly increases my work motivation in five modes. This qualitative feature is quantified by assuming values as. Greatly reduces my motivation –2(GR), Tends to reduce my motivation –1(TR), Has no effect on my motivation –0, Tends to increase my motivation +1(TI), Greatly increases my motivation +2(GI)

Recognition which has the highest scale score ranked as first by the focus group falls to the higher level in the motivation scale. All the other

Twenty Dimensions

(n=105)

Factor Dimension Scale Factor	Rank	Scale Score	Motivational Level
Recognition	1	1.2207	GI
Management	2	0.7947	TI
Progression	3	0.7810	TI
Business mode	4	0.7714	TI
Remuneration	5	0.7657	TI
Ethics	6	0.7619	TI
Interest	7	0.7222	TI
Achievement	8	0.6857	TI
Growth	9	0.6524	TI
Power	10	0.6445	TI
Flexibility	11	0.6329	TI
Job security	12	0.6305	TI
Activity	13	0.5746	TI
Status	14	0.4980	TI
Autonomy	15	0.4780	TI
Customers	16	0.3565	TI
Teamwork	17	0.2810	TI
Pressure	18	0.0762	TR
Competition	19	0.1048	TR
Fear of Failure.	20	0.2705	TR

scale values are positive except that to pressure, competition, and fear of failure. It can be inferred these factors are demotivating and the rest belongs to motivating scenario by this ranked importance.

I. Hypotheses Testing

Ho : There is no significant agreement among various job position (designations) to the perceived motivational factors.

Ha : There is significant agreement among various positions (designations) to the perceived motivational factors.

In the case of ranked importance, the significance of agreement among various job positions can be tested. Kendall's co-efficient of concordance, represented b the symbol W, is an important non-parametric of relationship which can be used for determining the degree of association among several (k) sets of ranking of the objects or individuals. This descriptive measure of the agreement has special applications in providing a standard method of ordering object according to consensus when we do not have an objective order of the object and dimensions.

Calculation of Kendell's (refer the following table)

As N is larger than 7, X^2 value is used for determining W's significance as under.

X^2 = k (N–1) w with or N–1 degree of freedom.

Therefore X^2 = s (20–1) (0.6152)

or X^2 = (195) (0.6152) = 58.444.

Table value of X^2 at 1% significance level for N – 1 degrees of freedom is 20-1 = 19 d.f. is 36.191, but the calculated value of X^2 is 58.444 and this is slightly higher than the table value. This does not support the null hypothesis of independence and as such we can infer that W is significant at 1% level. Alternative hypothesis is accepted and the null hypothesis is rejected.

Calculation of Kendell's Co-Efficient (W)
For Job Positions (GI, GII, GIII, GIV, GV)

Factor Dimension	*Rank 105*	*GI*	*GII*	*GIII*	*GIV*	*GV*	R_j	*Kendell's Rank*	$(R_j–R)^2$
Recognition	1	3	2	2	1	1	9	1	1931.60
Management	2	11	8	4	6	4	33	2	398.00
Progression	3	12	11	15	2	2	42	9	119.90
Business mode	4	6	7	7	7	11	38	6	223.50
Remuneration	5	5	6	10	12	3	36	3.5	287.30
Ethics	6	8	1	1	14	13	47	11	35.40
Interest	7	7	15	3	5	8	38	6	223.50
Achievement	8	2	5	6	15	10	38	6	223.50
Growth	9	18	13	8	3	12	54	13	1.10
Power	10	1	4	16	9	6	36	3.5	287.30
Flexibility	11	4	10	9	4	14	41	8	142.80
Job security	12	10	9	5	12	7	43	10	99.00
Activity	13	9	12	13	8	9	51	12	3.80
Status	14	13.5	3	14	10	16	56.5	14	12.60
Autonomy	15	15	14	11	12	5	57	15	16.40
Customers	16	19	17	12	16	15	79	16	678.60
Teamwork	17	17	16	17	17	17	84	17	964.10
Pressure	18	13.5	19	18	19.5	19	89.5	18	1335.90
Competition	19	20	20	19	18	18	96	20	1853.30
Fear of Failure.	20	15	18	18	19.5	20	91	19	1447.80
							ΣR_j 1059		$\Sigma (R_j–R)^2$ 10285.40

$\bar{R}$ = (1059/20) = 52.95. s = S $(R_j–R)^2$ 10285.40. W = s/[1/12k^2(N^3–N)]. Replacing values we get 0.61518

II. Hypotheses Testing

Ho: There is no significant agreement among various age levels to the perceived motivational factors.

Ha: There is significant agreement among various age levels to the perceived motivational factors.

In the case of ranked importance, the significance of agreement among various age levels can be tested. Kendall's co-efficient of concordance, represented b the symbol W, is an important non-parametric of relationship which can be used for determining the degree of association among several (k) sets of ranking of the objects or individuals. This descriptive measure of the agreement has special applications in providing a standard method of ordering object according to consensus when we do not have an objective order of the object and dimensions.

Calculation of Kendell's (Refer the following table)

As N is larger than 7, X^2 value is used for determining W's significance as under.

$X^2 = k\ (N-1)\ w$

$X^2 = 4\ (20-1)\ (0.7373)$

or $X^2 = 4(20-1)\ (0.7373) = 56.03$

Calculation of Kendell's Co-efficient (W). For Age Analysis

Factor Dimension	*Rank 105*	*Age 25-32*	*Age 33-41*	*Age 42-50*	*Age 51-58*	R_j	*Kendell's Rank*	*(Rj-R)²*
Recognition	1	1	1	1	1	4	1	1444
Management	2	11	3	2	12	28	6	196
Progression	3	10	6	7	11	34	7.5	64
Business mode	4	14	2	17	16	49	15	49
Remuneration	5	4	4	8	6	22	3	400
Ethics	6	12	5	4	3	24	5	324
Interest	7	6	7	3	2	18	2	574
Achievement	8	5	9	5	4	23	4	361
Growth	9	8	10	11	5	34	7.5	64
Power	10	15	8	6	17	46	14	16
Flexibility	11	13	12	9.5	7	41.5	11	0.25
Job security	12	7	11	9.5	10	37.5	9.5	2.25
Activity	13	9	13	14	8.5	44	12	6.25
Status	14	3	14	12	8.5	37.5	9.5	20.25
Autonomy	15	16	15	15	14.5	60.5	16	342.25
Customers	16	2	16	13	14.5	45.5	13	12.25
Teamwork	17	17	17	16	13	63	17	441
Pressure	18	18	18	18	18	72	18	900
Competition	19	19	19	19	19	76	19	1156
Fear of Failure.	20	20	20	20	20	80	20	1444
					Σ Rj 840			Σ (Rj-R)² = 7836.50

R = 840/20 or 42. s=S $(Rj-R)^2$ or 7836.50. W = $s/[1/12k^2(N^3-N)]$. Replacing values we get 0.7373.

Table value of X^2 at 1% significance level for N–1 degrees of freedom is 20–1 = 19 d.f. is 36.191, but the calculated value of X^2 is 56.03 and this is slightly higher than the table value. This does not support the null hypothesis of independence and as such we can infer that W is significant at 1% level. Null hypothesis is rejected and the alternative hypothesis is accepted.

CONCLUSION

As far as the employee motivation is concerned in the long run, it is optimal to move employees towards an internal/growth orientation, where they are self-motivated to earn new tasks. But where are they in the short run? To manage them right now, need to recognize what their current preferred work motivates are. The middle level officers working in nationalized banks in Madurai District are self-motivated to perform routine tasks. They would prefer to extend the things from the past than to change the dynamics. Their current motives reflect past habits of management and work.

Thank God it's Monday!!!

PROF. CHITHRA REGIS

INTRODUCTION

Within the present economic climate, the need to positively motivate both the employer and fellow professionals has rarely been more relevant. For a business to perform well, even within adverse trading conditions, it requires employees to be prepared to go the extra mile, and for all the right reasons. A collective sense of purpose is essential to establish if you want people to get behind it. But how does one develop career motivation, self-belief and even progression within an economic context?

Motivation is Infectious

In business, as with other aspects of life, every participant has the opportunity to affect the performance and mood of others in both positive and negative ways. Just as a depressed mood within the office can start to get under the skin of even the most hardened optimist, a refreshed and motivated individual can spread an upbeat philosophy equally as well. Start trying to focus on the positive things and the employee may well see momentum carried across to fellow colleagues, who in turn may inspire further.

Visualise and Actualise

Whether an employer tries to motivate him or another individual or even a whole team, the key initial step is to develop a vision within his mind of the preferred outcomes and the actions required in order to achieve them. Once your objectives and methodology have been fully developed, you can hope to inspire and motivate both yourself and others to get behind the strategy. The more clearly you can communicate this vision, the more actively your colleagues can successfully implement it.

Stay Focused

Motivational workshops or other initiatives, both internally and externally run, are often a good idea to refocus a team and the individuals that populate it. It is worth bearing in mind, however, that the individual will need to initiate processes that serve to motivate the employer and his employees' day in, day out, rather than experiencing around the workshops themselves. With consistent application, motivational practices can weave the way into the cultural fabric of any company.

Staying Motivated in a Changing World

The concept of motivation is, by definition, a relative one. Everybody has times when they feel more or less motivated than they have done in the past, and this can be as the result of both internal and external pressures. Being motivated is a positive state however, and it involves being able to see the opportunities, rather than the pitfalls, in everything you put your mind to. It's an easy habit to create, infinitely preferable to being de-motivated, and could open up avenues within your current and future career that you haven't thought previously possible.

Celebrate Achievements

A huge part of successful motivation and confidence building is the reward received when an objective is reached. Whether this is a financial bonus, taking the team out to lunch, or just a general feeling of individual and collective achievement, it needs to be celebrated. If the employer tries to build motivation, he must make sure that some of the initial goals are fairly easily reached, providing a "quick win" scenario whereby everybody involved feels the satisfaction of achievement early on. This will in turn build motivation to more complex objectives, backed by the knowledge and experience of meeting objectives in the past.

Staying Motivated in a Changing World

The concept of motivation is, by definition, a relative one. Everybody has times when they feel more or less motivated than they have done in the past, and this can be as the result of both internal and external pressures. Being motivated is a positive state however, and it involves being able to see the opportunities, rather than the pitfalls, in everything you put your mind to. It's an easy habit to create, infinitely preferable to being de-motivated, and could open up avenues within your current and future career that you hadn't thought previously possible.

CASE STUDY

A store manager of a large departmental shop in Sydney, Australia, implemented an embarrassing (and happily short-lived) safety incentive: Employees caught violating safety procedures were immediately given a two-foot rubber chicken on a string to wear around their necks in front of customers. To get rid of the chicken, an employee needed to catch another employee behaving "unsafely."

The practice quickly descended into a game of hot potato, with employees chasing one another around the store in search of the slightest violation to rid themselves of the safety chicken.

Many people don't feel motivated at work, and there's a very simple explanation for this: The motivational techniques used by most managers don't work. While few companies use rubber chickens (fortunately), most of the standard motivational tools like promotions, bonuses, employee of the month awards, pep-talks and free-pizza-nights are downright harmful to the drive, energy and commitment of employees. It only leaves them feeling manipulated, cynical and de-motivated.

The result: According to one Gallup study, 60-80% of workers are not engaged at work. They feel little or no loyalty, passion or motivation on the job. They're putting in the hours, but they're not doing a great job and they're certainly not happy at work! Millions of employees especially in India have to drag themselves out of bed 6-7 days a week and report to work although on weekends hardly ever anything happens.

Based on the illustration above, there are four different kinds of motivation. Only one of them works and unfortunately, many managers focus exclusively on the other three. There are actually four:

First, motivation can be intrinsic or extrinsic. Intrinsic motivation is when you want to do something. Extrinsic motivation is when somebody else tries to make you do something.

Secondly, there is positive and negative motivation. Positive motivation is when you want to get something—motivation towards some goal. Negative motivation is away from something you want to avoid. Combining these two dimensions, we get four kinds of motivation.

Extrinsic Motivation doesn't Work

In the laboratory, rats get Rice Krispies. In the classroom the top students get A's, and in the factory or office the best workers get raises. It's an article of faith for most of us that rewards promote better performance.

But a growing body of research suggests that this law is not nearly as ironclad as was once thought... If a reward—money, awards, praise, or winning a contest—comes to be seen as the reason one is engaging in an activity, that activity will be viewed as less enjoyable in its own right.

There are still serious drawbacks in the extrinsic motivation:

1. *Its not sustainable*—As soon as you withdraw the punishment or reward, the motivation disappears.
2. *You get diminishing returns*—If the punishment or rewards stay at the same levels, motivation slowly drops off. To get the same motivation next time requires a bigger reward.
3. *It hurts intrinsic motivation*—Punishing or rewarding people for doing something removes their own innate desire to do it on their own. From now on you must punish/reward every time to get them to do it.

Negative Motivation doesn't Work

Heart patients who've had double or quadruple bypass operations face a very simple choice: They must stop eating unhealthy food, smoking, drinking and working too much or they die. That has got to be the ultimate negative motivation and it carries the ultimate price for not doing it. But how many of them actually manage to change their lifestyle sustainably? Two years after the operation, how many of heart patients have managed to stick to their new habits? Come on, take a guess. 10% faced with the ultimate negative motivation, 9 out of 10 are still not able to make simple lifestyle changes. These pave way for many patients coming in for their second or third heart operations. And it is also a strong evidence that negative motivation does not work.

One doctor created a program where heart patients were instead taught to appreciate life (rather than fear death). They practiced yoga, meditated, got anti-stress counseling and got a healthy diet; all aimed at making them enjoy life more. The result: 2 years later, 70% of the patients maintained their new lifestyles.

When even the threat of death can't make people change their lifestyle sustainably, it becomes clear that motivation based on avoiding something is simply not as effective as motivation based on achieving something.

If people are not inherently motivated, they go to work each day and wait for someone else to light their fire. This belief is common among managers and employees alike...

It is right and human for managers to care about the motivation and morale of their people, it is just that they are not the cause of it. So with extrinsic motivation out and negative motivation out, we're left with only one quadrant: Intrinsic positive. This completely changes the role of the manager as motivator. Rather than being the source of motivation (kind of a ludicrous idea in itself), the manager must help employees to find their own intrinsic motivation.

The main factors that enhance intrinsic motivation are:

- *Challenge*—Being able to challenge yourself (employee/employer) and accomplish new tasks.
- *Control*—Having choice over what you do.
- *Cooperation*—Being able to work with and help others.
- *Recognition*—Getting meaningful, positive recognition for the work.

To Summarise

- *Happiness at work*—People who like their job and their workplace are much more likely to find intrinsic motivation.
- *Trust*—When you trust the people you work with, intrinsic motivation is much easier.

So rather than trying to bribe people to want things using pizzas and promotions, managers should help their people to discover meaning and develop skills at work. What some managers don't realize is that people want to do good work. Create a happy, positive work environment and people are naturally motivated. Even better: They motivate themselves and each other.

And that surely beats the punishments and rewards.

Tips to Welcome Your Monday's

Most of the employees wait for their authorities to motivate. But here are some tips that would help the employee motivate his boss

1. *Take the Initiative*: Don't wait for your boss to "give" you work. Find out what needs to be done and suggest to your boss that you do it.
2. *Generate New Ideas*: Think of better ways to do the work in your area and outside of your area too, and tell your boss about it.
3. *Offer Your Help*: Your boss needs your support and help. Show him/her that you're there to provide full support.
4. *Ask Your Boss to Deligate*: Your boss might not be aware that you are ready to assume more responsibilities and take on new challenges. Ask the boss to delegate responsibilities you think you can take on.
5. *Offer Solutions*: Don't limit your contacts with the boss to the times you bring up a problem or a request for help. Bosses need to hear solutions, not just problems.
6. *Offer Compliments*: The boss is human. She needs to receive compliments when she does something truly outstanding, or when she helps you in a positive way. Don't worry that it might sound insincere. Compliments, done in good taste and for a good reason, are always appreciated as long as you don't overdo it.
7. *Show Commitment*: It's important for the boss to know that you care about your work, about the organisation, and about the boss. Show that you care, in words and in action. Go out of your way to provide good service and promote the company, and the department's name.
8. *Stay Positive*: Employees who talk and act in a negative way can depress people around them, including the boss. It's important for your own mental health and for that of others that you are positive and enthusiastic. Try saying, "Thank God, It's Monday" instead of the usual "Friday" reference. But it's a matter of your general attitude, not just what you say.

Recent Motivational Practices in Organisation

J. DHILIPAN AND KANNAN

MOTIVATION INTRODUCTION

The basic objective of a manager is to secure from his subordinates an optimum performance toward accomplishment of the predetermined objectives.

Performance = Ability × Effort × Opportunity

Variation in individual effort and performance is inevitable, even though people with similar capabilities are working in identical situations. Variation in individual effort and performance is attributable to the extent to which a person feels motivated to expend mental and physical effort to accomplish the given task.

Many contemporary authors have defined the concept of motivation. Motivation has been defined as the psychological process that gives behaviour purpose and direction. Motivation is operationally defined as the inner force that drives individuals to accomplish personal and organisational goals.

MOTIVATION THEORIES

Understanding what motivates employees and how they are motivated is the focus of different experts which has advanced different theories as to the nature of human needs as also the order in which he seeks to satisfy them.

According to Maslow, employees have five levels of needs: Physiological, Safety, Social, Ego and Self-actualizing. Maslow argues that lower level needs have to be satisfied before the next higher level need would motivate employees.

Herezberg's work categorizes motivation into two factors: Intrinsic factors such as achievement and recognition produce job satisfaction; extrinsic factors such as pay and job security produce job dissatisfaction.

Varoom's theory is based on the belief that employees effort will lead to performance and performance will lead to rewards. Rewards may be either positive or negative. The more positive the rewards, the more likely the employee will be highly motivated. Conversely, the more negative the reward, the less likely the employee will be motivated.

William Ouchi, in his integrated motivational model, provides an example of how management can transform the organisational environment and bring about close, co-operative and trusting relationships between managers and other groups.

FINANCIAL AND NON-FINANCIAL MOTIVATIONAL PRACTICES IN ORGANISATION

Armed with the psychological secrets of motivation, you will instantly learn how to eliminate the stumbling blocks of poor performance, boredom, time-keeping problems, lack of interest, poor attendance, inter-group conflicts, monotony, strikes, disputes and all aspects of communication problems with your employee motivation.

Identifying the needs of employees and meeting those needs in such a way that the employees reciprocate by doing whatever you require, you can have a team of highly motivated, highly knowledgeable, customer focused employees.

Some theorists like Herzberg believe that money is not a positive motivator. Getting employee pay right is a crucial task for a business. People feel strongly about it. Pay helps to satisfy many needs (Eg. Security, Esteem need and resources to pursue self-actualization). It helps attract reliable employees with the skills the business needs for success.

However, it is important to remember that pay is only one element of motivation and will work best where management also gives attention to:

- Developing good management and supervision
- Designing jobs and organizing work groups to make them as satisfying as possible
- Providing feedback to staff about their performance and training and development
- Making effective arrangements for communication and consultation.

Performance related pay is generally used where employee

performance cannot be appropriately measured in terms of output produced or sales achieved. Individual performance is reviewed regularly (usually once a year) against agreed objectives or performance standards. At the end of the appraisal, employees are categorized into performance groups which determine what the reward.

Piece-rate pay gives a payment for each item produced. It is therefore the easiest way for a business to ensure that employees are paid for the amount of work they do.

Time rates are used when employees are paid for the amount of time they spend at work. Commission is a payment made to employees based on the value of sales achieved. It can form all or part of a pay package; commission is, therefore, a form of "incentive pay."

Offering employees shares in a business is an increasingly popular part of pay packages. There are various schemes available which companies can use to offer shares as part of the remuneration:

- Employee share ownership plans
- Share option schemes
- Share save schemes

Both the employee and the employer contribute the amount under various schemes:

- Flat rate pension
- State earnings related pension supplement
- Occupational pension
- Personal pension
- Stakeholder pension

It involves the addition of extra, similar, tasks to a job. The employee needs to acquire new skills to carry out the additional tasks, and the motivational benefits of job enrichment are not usually experienced.

Many jobs are monotonous and unrewarding particularly in the primary and secondary production industries. Workers can feel dissatisfied in their position due to a lack of a challenge, repetitive procedures, or an over-controlled authority structure. Job enrichment tries to eliminate these problems, and brings better performance to the work place. Job rotation involves the movement of employees through a range of jobs in order to increase interest and motivation.

The world has proved the fact that "Happy workers are productive workers". A strained, tedious and boring corporate culture and work environment is the common de-motivating factor for the employees in an organisation. Realizing the value and advantages of fun at workplace, the HR professionals are taking special measures to incorporate the same in their organisational cultures.

- Arranging meeting over lunch and dinner which fosters the communication between the employees and the management
- Celebrating major festivals
- Arranging sports facilities within the organisation and sports events regularly
- Conducting events where the families of the employees can also participate
- Giving paid vacations to employees

CONCLUSION

As long as deadlines are met, targets are achieved, projects are successful and the results are leading to the achievement of the organisational goals, celebrating success and having fun at work is not wrong. Such culture promotes optimism, organisational values, team building and motivates employees to bring out the best in themselves. Hence, many organisations view motivation seriously.

All said and done, it is ultimately the values and attitudes of individual employees that will decide the success or failure of motivation. An individual's values and attitudes determine his outlook and behaviour. Values deals with what one regards to be right and wrong. Attitudes relate to modes of conduct. It is the manager's responsibility to promote positive attitudes among his subordinates and encourage them to perform better.

Motivation in Practice—Job Rotation

P. GEETHA

1. MEANING OF MOTIVATION

The objective of motivation is to give incentive, enthusiasm, and interest cause a specific action or certain behaviour. Motivation is present in every life function. A simple act such as eating is motivated by hunger. Education is motivated by the desire for knowledge. Motivators can be anything, from reward to coercion.

There are two main kinds of motivation: intrinsic and extrinsic. Intrinsic motivation is internal. It occurs when people are compelled to do something out of pleasure, importance, or desire. Extrinsic motivation occurs when external factors compel the person to do something. One of the methods of internal motivation is Job Rotation. The challenges of keeping a 21st century employee motivated at work are vast. Today, an organisation has very few options at hand in the increasing competition environment. Keeping an employee interested is not an easy job. Hence, employee retention is a major challenge that most HR teams face. This is where "Job Rotation" helps.

2. JOB ROTATION

Job rotation involves the movement of employees through a range of jobs in order to increase interest and motivation. Job rotation is the systematic movement of employees from job to job within an organisation. Rotation programs are a respected means for learning how other functions operate, and that such knowledge is essential to becoming a better business partner.

Job rotation can improve "multi-skilling" but also involves the need for greater training.

In a sense, job rotation is similar to job enlargement. This approach widens the activities of a worker by switching him or her around a range of work.

For example, an administrative employee might spend part of the week looking after the reception area of a business, dealing with customers and enquiries. Some time might then be spent manning the company telephone switchboard and then inputting data onto a database. Job rotation may offer the advantage of making it easier to cover for absent colleagues, but it may also reduce productivity as workers are initially unfamiliar with a new task.

3. IMPORTANCE OF JOB ROTATION

Job rotation is seen as a possible solution to two significant challenges faced by business:

(1) Skills shortages and skills gaps, and
(2) Employee motivation

Skills shortages occur when there is a lack of skilled individuals in the workforce.

Skills gaps occur when there is a lack of skills in a company's existing workforce which may still be found in the labour force as a whole.

4. ADVANTAGES OF JOB ROTATION

Job rotation has many advantages. One of them is that it keeps the employee interested in his work as he gets different job profiles and his work does not become monotonous. One of the other major advantages of job rotation is that it gives an employee a chance to learn a lot more than he normally would. He becomes multi-skilled and this is an asset that is always helpful.

For example, if an employee falls sick or is on leave and can't report to work and if there is a shortage of staff on a particular day, then thanks to the practice of job rotation, an organisation has enough skilled manpower to replace the employee temporarily and take up his job. Many organisations use job rotation as a tool to curb absenteeism. If an employee gets something new to learn, he would be more willing to report to work.

Job rotation ensures that an employee does not feel "stressed" out from the job, as this is a major issue that HR teams face today. To develop a good job rotation programme, the organisation must assess its needs and requirements. This kind of programme can be used either for promotion, sideward movements or succession planning. Whatever the need be, it should be clearly identified before making such a programme so as to help the organisation know in which direction it is moving.

Job rotation programmes are known to help an organisation develop management talent as well as help in improving its competitive advantage over its rivals. It is a known fact that for an organisation to succeed, it is of paramount importance to ensure that the top management is very skillful and is aware of the happenings in the industry.

With so much competition today, decisions made by the top management can change the fortunes of an organisation drastically. Thus, whatever training and advantage that can be given to them is an added bonus.

One of the most difficult issues that an HR team faces would be the criteria on which job rotation should be done. The amount of experience, education, leadership assessment and management preference has to be kept in mind. This makes it very complex as a lot of details need to be looked into before selecting the right employee.

Employees with a good amount of experience generally are preferred as their experience would help them adapt to different situations in a better manner compared to a fresher who's just joined the organisation. What further works in the favour of an old employee is the fact that he has been around for a longer time and thus is likely to feel cheated if a fresher is given a chance to learn something new before him.

Clearly job rotation has its advantages but making a fair policy for the same is not easy. However, if the organisation succeeds in doing this, then it surely will have long-term benefits in the end, a fact that every organisation needs to looks into.

5. BENEFITS OF JOB ROTATION

Some of the major benefits of job rotation are as follows:

- It provides the employees with opportunities to broaden the horizon of knowledge, skills, and abilities by working in different departments, business units, functions, and countries.
- Identification of knowledge, skills, and attitudes (KSAs) is required.
- It determines the areas where improvement is required.

It assesses the employees who have the potential and caliber for filling the position.

6. STEPS IN JOB ROTATION

6.1 Step 1

Typically, formal rotation programs offer customized assignments to promising employees in an effort to give them a view of the entire business. Assignments usually run for a year or more. Rotation programs can vary in size and formality, depending on the organisation.

There are many reasons for implementing a job rotation system, including the potential for increased product quality, giving employees the opportunity to explore alternative career paths, and perhaps most importantly, preventing stagnation and job boredom.

The best performing employees in organisations (those who receive the highest salaries and are promoted most rapidly) experience job rotation relatively early in their careers. People who rotate through a succession of jobs find it a valuable way for them to acquire a variety of skills they need to be successful.

6.2 Step 2

Sustaining employee interest in a single job is not easy, which is perhaps why retention poses such a big challenge for businesses, even in a slow economy. Employees outgrow their jobs quickly and it may not be possible for employers to provide enough diversity within a career path to maintain employee interest in the job.

This is where job rotation steps provide job enrichment from an employee's perspective. Employees who participate in job rotation programs develop a wide range of skills, are more adaptable to changes in jobs and career, and are generally more engaged and satisfied with their jobs when compared to workers who specialize in a single skill set or domain.

6.3 Step 3

As in everything, there is a downside to job rotation programs that cannot be ignored. Job rotation may increase the workload and decrease productivity for the rotating employee and for other employees who must take up the slack. This may result in a disruption of work flow and a focus by line managers on short-term solutions to correct these problems. In addition, line managers may be reluctant to allow high-performing employees to participate in job rotation programs. Finally, there are costs associated with the learning curve on new jobs, including time spent on learning, training costs and errors that employees often make while learning a new job

This is why preparation is a key to the success of any job rotation program. The successful implementation of a job rotation program requires an understanding of the costs and benefits of implementation, as well as agreement and teamwork from all parts of the organisation, including senior management, human resources and line managers.

7. CONCLUSION

Employees' motivation is very important to an organisation. Every large and small organisation must enhance employees' fulfilment through motivational techniques. It is a way to encourage employees in obtaining company's goals and achieving higher profits. As a result, many organisations will be able to expand their business markets from local to international markets. Eventually, these organisations will become more effective in doing business and will increase the economies of our country in the future.

References

WWW.Job rotation.com
WWW.Wikipedia.com

Motivation in Life Insurance Industry

A.L. Gowri

INTRODUCTION

Motivation is the core of every management. It is an act of energizing and activating people to satisfy their needs. Koontz and O'Donell are of the view that "Motivation is a general term applying to the entire class of drives, desires, needs, wishes and similar forces that induce an individual or a group of people to work."

Human motives are based on needs, whether consciously or subconsciously felt. Some are primary needs, such as the physiological requirements for water, air, food sleep and shelter. Other needs may be regarded as secondary such as self-esteem, status, affiliation with others, affection giving accomplishment and self-assertion. Naturally these needs vary in intensity and over time among different individuals.

KINDS OF MOTIVATION

Motivation is of two kinds:

(i) Intrinsic motivation occurs when people are internally motivated to do something; it either brings them pleasure or they feel what they are doing is sufficient.

(ii) Extrinsic motivation comes into play when an employee is compelled to do something or acts in a certain way because of factors external to him/her (like money or award).

WAYS TO MOTIVATE PEOPLE

The traditional ways to motivate people are simple—the carrot and the stick—reward and punishment method. The sense of fear that worked in earlier days has changed. Today we find that fear has lost much of its force at the workplace. Where fear does not work, money is used. But this also is not entirely satisfying. So in modern times, we have to look for something else to motivate people. Three motivating factors modern managers recognize as important are (a) a sense of identity, (b) a sense of importance, and (c) a sense of development. The employees are made to use these factors to identify themselves with the organisation and hence, they are motivated to achieve results.

MOTIVATION IN LIFE INSURANCE INDUSTRY

The life insurance company has 11 lakh agents and thousands of development officials who work for procuring business and around one lakh staff in all cadres who administer the entire volume of business in all departments which include new business, sales, office servicing, policy holders servicing, claims, salary savings schemes, etc.

Development Section

The agents are called the backbone of the organisation. These agents are motivated by giving suitable rewards in the form of money (commissions) and special prizes. Several competitions are floated by the organisation often. This will help the organisation to bring in new business and sequentially the organisation will achieve its goal.

Similarly, the development officers are motivated by appraising their work every year. Incentive Bonus is paid to them based on their performance. These development officials take control of their agents.

Agents are ranked based on their continuous business performance for some years. Special allowances and rewards are given to them depending upon the club in which they are placed.

Branch Managers and Assistant Branch Managers are called for a review meeting at the end of every month and the performances of their branch in all areas are discussed by higher officials.

Administrative Section

The administrative staff comprises clerical staff and officers who are in charge of the functioning of the office administration. Motivation given to this group is different from that of the development side. Promotions are given to them based on their eligibility, confidential report and performance in their interview.

Graduation allowances are given to the people in the clerical cadre for passing graduation. They are also given special allowance for clearing examinations conducted by insurance institutes. Special allowance is also paid when an employee completes his Master of Business Administration Degree from a recognized University.

Actuarial science examinations and Chartered Accountants examinations carry special allowance to all the employees irrespective of their cadres. Special incentive is given to the employees when they clear Hindi examinations conducted by Central Government.

From the above fact it is clear that the organisation encourages people to earn more knowledge. Knowledge gained by the employees will definitely improve the quality of working style among the employees which consecutively will improve the organisation's condition as a whole. In all the above referred cases, money is given as awards.

MOTIVATION BY TRAINING

Training programmes like Organisational Development/Human Resource Development are conducted for all staff almost every year. The training programmes explain the strengths and weaknesses of the organisation. It also explains the opportunities available and the threats faced by the organisation. This creates awareness among the employees to face the changing scenario in the world and to improve the working condition to compete with the other competitors in the field.

Meetings are conducted department-wise by Heads of Departments every month to analyze the variations that have occurred from the required performance. The reports of these meetings are submitted by Heads of Departments to higher officials.

Special Incentive is paid to all employees of the organisation based on the performance of the company at the end of the financial year and separate competitions are launched for the branches and due awards are given to the branches based on their achieving the targets.

MOTIVATION IN INFORMATION TECHNOLOGY

All Staff are given training in computers. The organisation has been at the forefront of Information Technology implementation in India. The entire jobs processed are computerized and all offices are connected through Wide Area Network.

From time to time the company has been integrating latest technology in its day to day working, thereby providing improved services to the policy holders. Staff are also gradually trained in computers to meet out the changing scenario. The latest addition to its technology has been the use of scanned images of policy dockets for policy servicing. This Electronic Document Management Systems (EDMS) project has taken up scanning of all 25 crore plus policy dockets and makes them available in branch offices in a phased manner. Now the company is in a position to analyze its entire data at a central location for analytical purposes and Management Information System (MIS) purposes.

Information technology has developed to such an extent that many sophisticated and efficient computer systems are available to increase managerial effectiveness. Client/Server architecture and liking of computers through Local Area Network (LAN), Wide Area Network (WAN) and Metro Area Network (MAN), Internet and Intranet facilities have enabled the personnel in an office to interact with the database and collect the desired output.

CONCLUSION

From the various steps taken by the management, it is clear that motivation is the core of management. The employees are given complete training to use the computers. The management has created and maintained an environment in which individuals work together in groups towards the accomplishment of its common objectives. The building of motivating factors into organisation roles and the entire process of leading people must be built on knowledge of motivation. By motivating its employees, the organisation has attained the objective by involving all people working to the best of their capabilities by providing efficient services with courtesy.

References

www.licindia.com

Human Resources Management, Insurance Institute of India.

Principles of Life Assurance, Insurance Institute of India.

Motivation and Organisational Commitment

R. Harini Hingnekar and Dr. A. Kalaimathi

INTRODUCTION

Organisational commitment is highly valuable. This paper highlights the importance of understanding the meaning organisational commitment. It is this factor which increases our job satisfaction, loyalty, and growth. The author has tried to explain her view of the concept of organisational commitment and its subsets.

Organisational commitment is vital for productivity, quality and good performance of an organisation. Numerous empirical evidences regarding job commitment and its relationship with job satisfaction have been offered. These findings reveal that the level of job commitment can also be influenced by various factors such as demography, pay, co-workers, work supervision, company's background and employee's job-satisfaction level.

In the last decade, there has been a steady interest in studying the organisational commitment of employees. Organisational commitment refers to "the relative strength of an individual's identification with and involvement in a particular organisation." (Mowday *et al.*, 1979, p. 226). Strongly committed employees are more likely to remain with the organisation than are those with weak commitment. Commitment may even be a better predictor of turn over than job satisfaction, because it is influenced less by day to day happenings than by job satisfaction. (Porter *et al.*, 1974).

EMPLOYEE COMMITMENT

The concept of employment commitment lies at the heart of any analysis of Human Resource Management. Indeed, the rationale for introducing Human Resource Management policies is to increase levels of commitment. Such is the importance of this construct. Yet, despite many studies on commitment, very little is understood of what managers mean by the term "commitment" when they evaluate someone's performance and motivation.

The literature defines commitment as an employee's level of attachment to some aspect of work. Various authors have been instrumental in identifying types of employee commitment as critical constructs in understanding the attitudes and behaviours of employees in an organisation. Meyer *et. al.* identify more than 25 employee commitment concepts and measures.

Arguing that conceptual redundancy exists across these, they group them into three foci, as commitment to work/job, commitment to career/ profession and commitment to organisation.

Though this study specifically addresses commitment to the organisation, or organisational commitment, it also considers work and career commitment towards clarifying the conceptual meaning.

Organisational Commitment

There are two dominant conceptualizations of organisational commitment in sociological literature. These are an employee's loyalty towards the organisation and an employee's intention to stay with the organisation. Loyalty is an affective response to, and identification with, an organisation, based on a sense of duty and responsibility.

One may use Herscovitch and Meyer's definition: "The degree to which an employee identifies with the goals and values of the organisation and is willing to exert effort to help it succeed." Loyalty is argued to be an important intervening variable between the structural conditions of work, and the values, and expectations, of employees, and their decision to stay, or leave.

Positive and rewarding features of work are expected to increase loyalty, which, in turn, will reduce the likelihood of leaving. Loyalty becomes stabilized with tenure, which partly explains the negative relationship typically found between tenure and turnover.

Intent to stay is portrayed as effectively neutral, and focuses on an employee's intention to remain a member of the organisation. It is much closer to economists' ideas on how weighing the costs of leaving versus staying, decides the employee to leave or stay. Hagen defines this form of commitment as the employee's expected likelihood of remaining employed in the same organisation. As with loyalty, intent to stay stabilizes with tenure, and helps explain the negative tenure and turnover relationship. Theoretically, it is viewed as an intervening response to structural conditions of work, as well as conditions of work elsewhere, or to not working at all.

Career Commitment

Career commitment refers to identification with, and involvement in, one's occupation. Much literature refers to similar or related concepts: occupational commitment, professional commitment, career salience, the cosmopolitan/local distinction and professionalism. Common to all these is the critical notion of being committed to one's career, or occupation, rather than to the organisation which employs one.

Work Commitment

Work commitment refers neither to the organisation nor to one's career, but to employment itself. Persons committed to work hard have a strong sense of duty towards their work, and place intrinsic value on work as a central life interest. This form of commitment relates terms like work motivation, job involvement, work as a central life interest and work involvement. Although work commitment is expected to be related to organisational commitment and career commitment, literature shows it to be empirically distinct from these two forms of commitment.

Organisational Commitment

The issue of organisational commitment within the private sector has generally received significant research focus over the past 25 years. This review further describes the past development of organisational commitment, and its relevance in future.

Development of Organisational Commitment

Two major theoretical approaches emerge from previous research on commitment:

Firstly, commitment is viewed as an attitude of attachment to the organisation, which leads to particular job-related behaviours. The committed employee, for example, is less often absent, and is less likely to leave the organisation voluntarily, than are less committed employees.

Secondly, one line of research in organisations focuses on the implications of certain types of behaviours on subsequent attitudes. A typical finding is that employees, who freely choose to behave in a certain way, and who find their decision difficult to change, become committed to the chosen behaviour and develop attitudes consistent with their choice.

Although the "commitment attitude behaviour" and "committing behaviour attitude" approaches emerge from different theoretical orientations, and have generated separate research traditions, understanding the commitment process is facilitated by viewing these two approaches as inherently interrelated.

Rather than viewing the causal arrow, between attitudinal and behavioural commitment, as pointing in one direction or the other, it is more useful to consider the two as reciprocally-related over time. It is equally reasonable to assume that (a) commitment attitudes lead to committing behaviours that subsequently reinforce and strengthen attitudes; and (b) committing behaviours lead to commitment attitudes and subsequent committing behaviours.

The important issue is not whether the commitment process begins with either attitude or behaviour. Rather, it is important to recognize that development of commitment may involve the subtle interplay of attitudes and behaviours over a period of time. The process through with commitment is developed may involve self-reinforcing cycles of attitudes and behaviours that evolve on the job, and, over time, strengthen employee commitment to the organisation.

Meyer and Allen present their three dimensional constructs as affective, continuance and normative commitment. These components of commitment have been identified in the literature:

1. *Affective Commitment*: The individual's affective or emotional attachment to the organisation (i.e. individuals stay with organisation because they want to);
2. *Continuance Commitment*: The perceived costs associated with leaving the organisation (i.e. the individual stays with the organisation because they need to); and
3. *Normative Commitment*: An individual's felt obligation to remain with the organisation (i.e., the individual stays with the organisation because they feel they caught to do so).

Affective Commitment refers to the employee's emotional attachment to, identification with, and involvement in, the organisation (based on positive feelings, or emotions, toward the organisation). The antecedents for affective commitment include perceived job characteristics (task autonomy, task significance, task identity, skill variety and supervisory feedback), organisational dependability (extent to which employees feel the organisation can be counted on to look after their interests), and perceived participatory management (extent to which employees feel they can influence decisions on the work environment and other issues of concern to them).

The use of these antecedents is consistent with the findings by researchers, such as Steers, Mottaz and Rowden, that these factors all create rewarding situations, intrinsically conductive to the development of affective commitment. In addition, age and organisational tenure are considered to be positively associated with affective commitment. It is hypothesized that employees with low affective commitment will choose to leave the organisation, while employees with a high affective commitment will stay for longer periods, as they believe in the organisation and its mission.

Continuance commitment refers to commitment based on the costs that the employee associates with leaving the organisation (due to the high cost of leaving). Potential antecedents of continuance commitment include age, tenure, career satisfaction and intent to leave. Age and tenure can function as predictors of continuance commitment, primarily because of their roles as surrogate measures of investment in the organisation.

Tenure can be indicative of non-transferable investments (close working relationship with co-workers, retirement investments, career investments and skills unique to the particular organisation). Age can also be negatively related to the number of available alternative job opportunities. Career satisfaction provides a more direct measure of career-related investments, which could be at risk if the individual leaves the organisation. In general, whatever employees perceive as sunk cost, resulting from leaving the organisation, are the antecedents of continuance commitment.

Normative commitment refers to an employee's feeling of obligation to remain with the organisation (based on the employee having internalized the values and goals of the organisation). The potential antecedents for normative commitment include co-worker commitment (including affective and normative dimensions, as well as commitment behaviours), organisational dependability and perceived participatory management are expected to instill a sense of moral obligation to reciprocate to the organisation.

Employees' attitudes toward their job and the organisation are expected to influence absenteeism indirectly through motivation to attend in the Steers and Rhodes model. For our study, we chose to focus on the role of organisational commitment. Recent advances in our understanding of organisational commitment suggest that the Steers and Rhodes model needs to consider type of commitment.

Organisational commitment originally focused on an individual's emotional attachment to an organisation (Mowday *et al.*, 1979). Based primarily on the measure developed by Mowday and his colleagues, a meta analysis by Farrell and Stamm (1988) found that organisational commitment was negatively related to absence frequency (r = -.23). However, organisational commitment has recently been expanded to a more comprehensive view. Meyer and Allen (1991, 1997) assert that organisation commitment is comprise affective, continuance, and normative components. Affective commitment relates to an individual's emotional attachment or identification with an organisation. It is akin to the traditional notions of organisational commitment. In other words, a person participates in an organisation because he/she "wants to." Continuance commitment relates to an individual's awareness that there are associated costs with withdrawing temporarily or permanently from an organisation. It may be that the person perceives that they have devoted too much time or energy to leave the organisation or may not be able to find another job. In other words, a person perceives that he/she "needs to participate." Finally, normative commitment is an employee's feeling of obligation to participate in an organisation. The employee believes it is the right thing to do or that he/she "ought to participate."

A variety of recent studies have examined the relationship between the different kinds of commitment and absenteeism. Overall, it appears that affective commitment has the strongest relation with absence behaviour (Meyer, 1997). The results for normative commitment are less consistent. Meyer *et al.* (1993) found that normative commitment was negatively related to absenteeism while Somers (1995) found no relationship between normative commitment and absenteeism. It should be noted that Meyer *et al.* (1993) used a self-reported measure of absences while Somers (1995) used organisational records to measure the total number of days absent per employee. Measurement issues of this type may account for some of the inconsistent findings in the area. Finally, continuance commitment has not found strong support in the absenteeism literature (e.g., Mayer and Schoorman, 1992). It should also be noted that the majority of these studies have been conducted on nurses in large hospitals. It seems justified to expand the study of organisational commitment and absenteeism to a non-professional sample.

Although organisational commitment and its various dimensions have been shown to be directly related to absenteeism, their effect is weak, accounting for less than ten percent of the variance explained in absenteeism. Thus, Meyer (1997) and Johns (1997) have suggested it may be advisable to see if these attitudes affect absenteeism indirectly. As Rhodes and Steers (1990) point out, one such intervening variable is motivation to attend. Affective, normative, and continuance commitment should all be positively related to motivation to attend but may differ in their relative strength. For example, it is expected that affective and normative commitment will be strongly related to a person's motivation to attend with continuance commitment relating to a lesser extent. It could be expected that if someone has high levels of affect toward their job or organisation (affective commitment), they would be more likely to be motivated to attend work everyday. In addition, if someone feels he or she ought to (normative commitment) go to work each day, this should be strongly related to motivation to attend. On the other hand, if someone feels he or she has to (continuance commitment) go to work, a weaker relationship with motivation to attend could be expected. In this case, economic conditions, personal finances, and other non-organisational factors are likely enter into the decision to attend. For the present study, we predict that the various dimensions of organisational commitment will indirectly influence the level of absenteeism through a person's motivation to attend.

Hypothesis: Motivation to attend will mediate the relationship between affective, normative, and continuance commitment and absenteeism.

Surveys were administered to customer service employees in the internet division of a large national retailer. Respondents completed the surveys during a 15-minute work break provided by the organisation. They completed the surveys in a conference room at individual tables without supervision. We guaranteed confidentiality to all respondents in a letter sent in advance of the survey. Two hundred and sixty-five employees completed the surveys, while the remaining 15 customer service representatives of this organisation did not, because they were either on leave or absent, yielding a response rate of 94.6 percent Twenty-two respondents did not self-identify. Consequently, for the analyses requiring matching data from the organisation, only 243 respondents were included.

The respondents who provided names did not appear to be different from respondents who did not in terms of gender ($t = -.67, p > .10$) or tenure with the organisation ($t = 1.25, p > .10$). All employees surveyed were at the same job level (customer service representatives). The average age of respondents was 28.43 years, 75 percent were female, and 19 percent were married. On average they had worked in their current position for 1.04 years and 1.49 years for the organisation. Fifty-one percent worked full time.

The organisation provided the number of absence incidents and the perceived cause of the absence event (as reported by an employee's supervisor). The organisation classified the perceived cause of the absence event according to the following categories: family situation, illness, notify (advance notice of illness), childcare issues, transportation, failure to report for work (no show), and other issues. Due to the similarity of several of the categories, we chose to combine several of the categories of absenteeism. Specifically, we chose to combine absenteeism attributed to family and childcare issues since we believe it is possible that managers may have coded an employee's absence as "family" even if the employee reported it as a childcare issue. In addition, absences attributed to illness and those classified as "notify" were combined because both deal with sickness as the cause of absence. Two Ph.D. students not affiliated with the current project were also asked to independently categorize the absence classifications given to us by the organisation. These two individuals were in 100 percent agreement in their categorization of absence behaviour at the organisation and in agreement with the combinations suggested above. Finally, we chose to eliminate absence due to "other" causes when examining the various dimensions of absenteeism, because we could not accurately determine the perceived cause of the absence event. Therefore, all analyses conducted in this study used the following categories: absence due to illness, absence due to family issues, absence due to transportation problems, and failure to report for work without notice (no show).

As in the case of the overall measure of absenteeism, the various categories of absenteeism were also subjected to a square root transformation. The transformation of absences attributed to illness exhibited a low skewness (.23) and kurtosis (-.07). A Kolomogoro-Smirnov test indicated that the transformation resulted in a normal distribution ($KS = 1.05, p > .10$). The square root transformation of the remaining absence categories differed significantly from normality. However, Hammer and Landau (1981) indicate that the magnitude of the deviation is more important than the level of significance. In particular, it has been suggested that researchers only need to be concerned with skewness values above 2 and kurtosis values greater than 5 (Kendall and Stuart, 1958). The square root transformations of absences attributed to family issues (skewness = 1.68, kurtosis = 2.42), transportation problems (skewness 1.67, kurtosis = 2.09), and no show (skewness = 1.69, kurtosis = 3.06) were within these requirements.

To establish the discriminant validity of the various absence categories, we examined the correlation between the different types of absence behaviours. Overall, we found that the absence categories were weakly correlated (r = .19). The magnitude of the individual correlations ranged from a low of .06 (family issues and no show) to a high of .35 (illness and no show). Although we cannot be completely sure if the employees gave their supervisors the true reason for their absence, the low correlations between the various categories of absences indicate that they represent different behaviours.

Motivation to attend was measured with three items assessing the degree to which participants felt motivated to go to work every day. These items were based on the work of Steers and Rhodes and obtained from Lee (1989). A sample item includes, "All in all, I usually feel motivated to come to work each day." A factor analysis with varimax rotation revealed that all items measuring motivation to attend loaded on one factor (alpha = .73).

Ability to attend was measured with four items designed to measure participant's beliefs on situations that limit their ability to attend work. The four items were, "Public transportation problems often are the reason why I am absent"; "When I am absent, it is because of illness"; "Child-care issues are most often the reasons why I miss a shift"; and "If I miss work, it is usually because of car problems." Brooke (1986) states that the ability to attend does not represent one underlying construct, but a label for the various categories listed above. Corroborating Brooke's observation, a factor analysis with varimax rotation revealed a two-factor solution for ability to attend (based on eigen values over 1 and observation of scree plot). This result is counter to what the Steers and Rhodes' model indicates but not unexpected based on past theoretical and empirical work in the field that has questioned the construct validity of the ability to attend measure. Therefore, based on the factor analysis and past theoretical work, we decided to sum (as opposed to average) the responses to the categories listed above. The logic behind this approach is that individuals who indicate more barriers to attendance should be less able to attend. It is important to note, like Brooke (1986), that ability to attend is not a traditional psychological construct. Instead, it is a summation of not-necessarily-correlated forces acting on attendance behaviour. Because there is no necessary correlation across these (summed) forces, measures of internal consistency are not appropriate. Aggregating these items into one measure offers a parsimonious solution and may best capture the true aspects of ability to attend.

Organisational commitment was measured with items from Meyer and Allen's (1991, 1997) expansion of the organisational commitment construct. Affective commitment (alpha = .87), normative commitment (alpha = .78), and continuance commitment (alpha = .79) were all measured with eight items.

Control Variables: Based on the nature of our sample and past empirical and theoretical work in absenteeism, we chose to control age, gender, tenure in the organisation, and level of education (Brooke, 1986). All of these variables have been shown to be related to absenteeism in past research and therefore need to be controlled in order to increase the internal validity of our study.

To test whether certain types of absenteeism are more related to motivation to attend and ability to attend in the Steers and Rhodes model of absenteeism, regression analyses were conducted examining absenteeism attributed to family issues, illness, transportation problems, and no show. Absenteeism coded as a "no show" and transportation problems failed to gain significant R^2 when the various absenteeism variables were regressed onto motivation to attend and ability to attend. However, motivation to attend and ability to attend explained a significant amount of incremental variance in absenteeism attributed to family issues [(delta) [R.sup.2] = .04, $p < .05$) and illness ([delta] [R.sup.2] = .03, $p < .05$). In support of hypothesis 1, when measures of ability to attend and motivation to attend were entered into an equation predicting absenteeism attributed to family issues, ability to attend became significant while motivation to attend did not. In support of hypothesis 3a, when motivation to attend and ability to attend were regressed onto absence due to illness, only motivation to attend was significantly related, thereby supporting the notion that absence attributed to illness may represent a voluntary absence behaviour.

> "Tests of mediation proposed in hypothesis 5 could not be conducted because motivation to attend was not significantly related to overall absenteeism (Baron and Kenny, 1986). However, the various dimensions of organisational commitment were strongly related to motivation to attend. Affective ($r = .49$, $p < .01$), normative ($r = .39$, $p < .001$), and continuance commitment ($r = .13$, $p < .05$) are positively related to a person's level of motivation to attend. Although strongly related, factor analyses demonstrate the discriminant validity of the items representing motivation to attend, affective, normative, and continuance commitment.

A factor analysis with varimax rotation indicated four separate factors (based on eigen values over 1 and observation of scree plot). Therefore, it appears that motivation to attend represents a different employee attitude than commitment. Regression analyses indicate that these three dimensions of organisational commitment explain approximately 26% of the variance in motivation to attend. In addition, although not directly hypothesized, but suggested in the discussion, affective ([beta] = .40, t = 6.49, p < .001) and normative commitment ([beta] = .20, t = 3.16, p < .01) had stronger relations with motivation to attend than continuance commitment ([beta] = -.02, t = -.43, p > .10).

Regression analyses were conducted to further test the suppressor effect of age on motivation to attend. When age is entered first into the equation, motivation to attend becomes significant and explains an additional 3.6 percent of the variance in overall absenteeism. Thus, a suppressor effect is suggested. A median split conducted on the sample demonstrated that motivation to attend is a significant predictor of overall absenteeism for younger workers (r = -.16, p < .10), but not for older workers (r = -.13, p > .10). In addition, we examined whether age moderated the relationship between motivation to attend and overall absenteeism.

Nunnally and Bernstein (1994) indicate a suppressor relationship exists where one independent variable (e.g., motivation to attend) is not related to the dependent variable, another variable (e.g., age) is significantly related to the dependent variable, and the two independent variables are correlated. As discussed earlier, motivation to attend is not significantly related to overall absenteeism (r = -.10, p > .10). However, age is significantly related to overall absenteeism (r = -.22, p < .01) and motivation to attend (r = - .35, p < .001).

CONCLUSION

There is progress in our understanding of commitment and organisational commitment, both conceptually, and, more practically, in terms of the positive consequences for organisations of having committed employees. Finding the relationship between human resource management practices, employee commitment and the financial performance of firms has important implications for improved integration of research across several business school disciplines.

Evidence clarifies that investment in employees can have positive financial consequences for firms and their shareholders, and may help broaden their narrow view of the world. From the literature review on organisational commitment, the authors identify that employee perception is the foundation of employee motivation, leading to higher organisation commitment, and that employee perception forms the antecedent of organisational commitment.

Positive employee perception leads to improved employee motivation, which in turn, leads to higher organisational commitment. As upbringing, race and religion are key factors influencing employee perception, a clear understanding of the meaning of organisational commitment among all persons concerned (such as researchers, respondents, practitioners and academicians) is vital.

Financial Motivation to Salesforce

DR. S. DHINESH BABU AND S. LALITHA BHUVANESWARI

INTRODUCTION

The function of remunerating salesmen includes determining the payment methods, such as commission or salary plus commission, etc. While fixing remuneration, certain important factors are kept in mind: (1) The remuneration to be paid should be adequate to meet the minimum requirement of the persons; (2) it would be motivating and justified; and (3) it should be flexible and easier to implement and understood by all.

Compensation must reflect the business strategy of the company. An employer, in general, awards compensation to an employee for the employee's services rendered to the employer. An employer's sales compensation program focuses on the employee's revenue production and other important job characteristics that are unique to the sales function.

Purpose of Compensation is to connect the individuals with the organisation. It must meet the needs and expectations of the salespeople, and be tied directly to performance. Here the major objectives are to attract, retain, and motivate talented sales employees.

Creating the perfect sales compensation plan is a struggle for companies of all sizes. Salespeople want to make the most money with the least effort. Business owners and managers want the most profits and the fewest hassles.

There's no one-size-fits-all recipe for sales pay plans. Within the sales profession, compensation packages vary widely. They can be based on straight salary or pure commission—or some combination of salary and commission. They can also involve bonuses, which can be based on personal sales, overall business profitability, group sales, product demonstrations, and other criteria. The rewards can also differ for various product lines or types of customers.

ESSENTIAL ELEMENTS OF A GOOD REMUNERATION PLAN

The amount of reward for the services rendered by a salesman has a great bearing on his efficiency. Payment of fair remuneration leads to high morale and increased productivity. A good scheme of remuneration must possess the following features:

- It must provide a certain minimum monthly income to the salesman.
- It must enable the hard-working salesman to exert his best and sell more so as to enable him to augment his income.
- It must be so devised that it does not require to be changed with the changing fortunes of the concern.
- It should not always be open to charges of favouritism and should be equitable both to the employer and the employee in good years and in bad years.
- The cost of administration of the plan for computing salesperson's income should be as low as possible.
- It must be simple enough to be understood by the salesman as to avoid all future disputes in the matter. Employees like to know how much more they can make on each wine or product sold in a specified time frame. A clear plan helps to eliminate arguments on who earns what. They also like commission structures that don't change mid-program or year-to-year.
- Setting up of realistic, achievable sales goals is very important. Salespeople want incentives based on factors that are in their control. They want to know how and when commissions will be paid, and don't like a ceiling or limit on potential income. If they earn it-they expect to get it. They also don't like a plan that penalizes them with unrealistic quotas or one that is limited by seasonal traffic.
- Provisions for frequent payments to the sales people should be made. Salespeople like to see quick results from their efforts and want to be paid right away.
- A plan competitive with others in the industry.
- The plan should enable the firm to attract, retain and develop a contented, efficient and loyal sales force.
- Provisions should be made in such a way to give extra benefits for doing duties other than selling.
- The plan should be in such a way that the managers to control the working hours of salesmen.
- It should be attractive and encouraging in such a way to retain the able salesmen.
- Before the implementation of remuneration plan, consultation should be done with the salesmen, sales supervisors and top managerial authority.

- The compensation rate must bear some relation with the 'going market price'.

BASIC SALES COMPENSATION TERMS

There are four sales compensation terms that are basic to plan design:

- Target cash compensation
- Mix of base and incentive pay
- Pay-at-risk leverage
- Selection of sales incentive goals

Target Cash Compensation

Target cash compensation is the amount of base pay plus incentive payments that are made available by the sales compensation plan for eligible employees who achieve expected performance results. Eligible employees are those that fulfil customer facing jobs that have a direct impact on sales results, and therefore, can be assigned a measurable sales quota. The amount of cash compensation to target for the purpose of attracting and retaining the caliber of sales talent needed to achieve company revenue goals is influenced by job content and scope of responsibility, competitive pay philosophy, portion of the sales and marketing budget allocated for sales compensation expenditures, and internal equity of payments to sales employees. Job content and scope pertains to understanding each sales role by the breadth of responsibility, degree of accountability, focus on customers, and influence over financial goals. Consider, for instance, how a sales manager's job may differ from a sales representative's job. For instance, a sales manager's job has more administrative responsibility. A competitive pay policy articulates an organisation's strategy for competing within targeted labor markets to recruit the employees it needs to achieve business success. Sales compensation plans must be designed to ensure that pay levels are commensurate with performance results. Assuming that goals are credible to the sales force and meaningful to the success of the business, internal equity occurs when top performing sales employees receive higher pay relative to average performers.

Mix of Base and Incentive Pay

Mix, in sales compensation, is the relationship of fixed and variable cash, where the fixed portion is base pay and the variable portion is incentive pay. Compensation mix is expressed as a percent of target cash compensation. In practice, mix represents the ratio between fixed and variable compensation in the targeted cash compensation value at expected (i.e., planned) performance. The ratio is expressed with the first value representing fixed compensation and the second representing variable. For example, a mix expressed as 25:75 means that target cash compensation is composed of 25% base salary and 75% incentive. For instance, a target cash compensation amount of $100,000 would be composed of $25,000 base salary and $75,000 incentive. The basis for incentive payment can vary. The incentive opportunity is typically expressed as a percent of base salary or target cash compensation for bonus plans. For commission plans, the incentive is typically expressed as a share of each occurrence such as for each profit dollar, each revenue dollar, or each unit sold. The extent to which a salesperson can influence the customer's decision to buy is the primary factor used to determine pay mix. Incentive opportunity tends to correlate with the role of the salesperson to impact the customers. Generally, the more a salesperson has to rely on influencing skills to produce a sale, the higher the incentive opportunity in the mix proportion.

Pay-at-risk Leverage

Leverage is the rate at which incentive compensation is enhanced for degrees of performance improvement. The maximum incentive opportunity is added to base salary to determine cash compensation at the established level of optimum performance.

Double leverage means that the target incentive for expected performance is twice that amount for optimum performance achievement. Triple leverage follows the same logic. Double or triple leverage are typically used to motivate the sales force to achieve optimum performance. Leverage is important because it defines the point at which optimum performance is achieved and rewarded. Leverage also links the value of additional sales over targeted goals to the amount of incentive opportunity. The extent to which incremental sales are valuable to the business determines the amount of leverage the company will offer its sales force.

Selection of Sales Incentive Performance Measures

The sales and marketing strategy plus the product distribution channels determine the suitable performance measures for sales compensation plans. All sales compensation plans should incorporate a production goal. Additional measures, such as product, customer, and milestone measures can be used in addition to the production goal. The following are the four categories of sales measures with sample goals:

- *Production (volume)*: Revenue: total, new, renewal, price, margin
- *Products (includes services)*: Units sold, product mix, up-selling
- *Accounts (customers, channels)*: New, retained, expanded, satisfaction
- *Milestones (events and activities)*: Threshold achievement, contract commitment

When designing sales compensation plans, selection of performance measures that support the organisation's business objectives should be done. Volume is commonly used since the core responsibility of most sales jobs is to expand the company's market share, develop new business, and grow the customer base. Changes in sales volume are the best way to measure the successful production of the business. Incentive goals must consider the accountability of the salesperson to impact the performance measure. The incentive goal must have a basis for being measured, and the number of different measures should be limited to three.

Several business factors must be considered to determine the fundamental strategy for sales compensation design:

Business Growth Stage

If the business is a new start, there may be zero cash to pay a sales representative a base salary. Product delivery may be dependent on influencing prospective customers to purchase a product to fund that product's development. In such a case, the sales representative would be paid purely by incentive (a 0/100 pay mix). If the business is more mature and established, then performance will be more predictable and target cash compensation may consist of a mix that includes a base salary and an incentive that is based on a quota.

Sales territories: Geographic territories must offer equivalent sales potential to the sales force. If designing a sales compensation plan around geography, study dimensions such as territory size and demographics.

Marketing focus: The plan and the selling role will have greater complexity if the company is concentrating its product to market efforts in many markets as opposed to fewer.

Application of thresholds: Thresholds are minimal levels of performance that must be achieved before an incentive is paid. Thresholds are used to cover the fixed costs of base salary, to establish a minimum performance standard, and to recognize a margin for quota-setting inaccuracies. At least 90% of sales personnel should meet or exceed the threshold performance level. Thresholds may be determined based on historical customer buying trends or breakeven volume.

Application of maximums: Maximums are total compensation that may be earned and are otherwise known as a cap. Generally, sales incentive plans are designed without a cap so as not to limit the performance capabilities of top producers. The rational for caps would be to limit earnings to profitable levels of sales volume, to control costs, and to overcome erroneous quota setting (e.g., windfalls).

Salesperson influence: The degree to which demand for company products must be created, versus satisfied, by the salesperson.

Quota allocation: The degree to which sales quotas can be reliably and accurately determined is compromised if the business is very dynamic such that setting quotas is difficult.

Sales event: An occurrence when a sale may be counted for compensation purposes. Management must consider the point at which sales credit is assigned because once the assignment occurs, the salesperson will no longer be concerned with the sale.

Windfalls: A major sales event may result outside of the salespersons normal influencing role. Maximums and other techniques are sometimes imposed to control for windfall events.

Shortfalls: A sales result significantly below expectations which are not influenced by the sales representative may be addressed by adjusting the quota downward, providing a guaranteed incentive payment, changing the mix to emphasize the base component, or adding a bonus component with a predetermined incentive goal.

Payment timing: A performance cycle is a period in which performance can be measured (i.e., monthly, quarterly, annually). Determining the timing of sales incentives depends on how the sale is made such as size of the sales transaction, number of transactions, length of the sales cycle, forecast accuracy (quota setting reliability), and the desired sales force behaviour.

Draws: A plan designed with a draw feature is for new salespeople who are accustomed to a relatively stable compensation cash flow. A draw is a compensation that is paid in advance of performance and is used to provide temporary cash flows to the salesperson until she begins earning incentive pay.

There are two types of draws:

- A recoverable draw provides for a minimum cash flow that is paid-back when actual earnings exceed the draw. Payback typically occurs at the next payment.
- A non-recoverable draw provides compensation guarantees to new salespeople that expire at a predetermined time. No compensation needs to be paid back if sales performance doesn't create earnings that meet or exceed the draw.

FORMAL COMPENSATION PROCESS

It is a continual process; it does not stop with the last step; it is constantly evaluated and revised.

1. Establish sales force objectives and plans

- Attain yearly sales volume and gross margins
- Attain monthly sales volume and sales volume of specific products
- Market penetration and exploiting the territories potential
- Call management and development of potential in key accounts as well as development of new accounts.
- Introduction of new products

2. Determine Major Compensation Factors

- *Wage level*—relate what salespeople are being paid as compared to those in other organisations
- *Wage structure*—pay differential among different sales levels within the organisation
- *Individual wage*
- *Administrative procedures*—when and how to give raises, criteria to use when giving raises, and how much to give so it is meaningful

3. Implement and Communicate Compensation Program

- Compensation message should contain what part the sales force is expected to take in reaching the organisations goals, a thorough discussion of what role the salesperson has in achieving the sales objectives, and the limitations and weaknesses of the program.

4. Relate Rewards to Performance

5. Measurement of Performance

- Determines whether the compensation program's goals are being met

6. Appraisal and Recycling

- Are the compensation objectives being met? Is the firm able to attract new salespeople with this plan? What is the relationship of compensation to turnover?

TYPES OF COMPENSATION PLANS

As companies are working harder to retain good salespeople, compensation plans are becoming more and more important. Sales compensation is extremely important in today's business environment, but is one of the most difficult tasks a sales manager must face. They don't want to offer a plan that is too comfortable but also don't want to make it so that it is so aggressive it turns people away. There are four basic methods of financial compensation: straight salary, commission, bonus, and a combination of any of these.

Straight Salary Plan

A sales force compensation plan that relies exclusively on salary as a financial reward for salespeople. A salary is a fixed sum of money paid at regular intervals. Straight salary is a fixed amount of money paid to a salesperson for their efforts over a period of time. Straight salary is based on anticipated performance and the needs of the salesperson. The amount paid to the salesperson is a function of the amount of time worked rather than any specific performance. Two sets of conditions favour the use of a straight salary compensation plan. These are (1) when management wishes to motivate people to achieve objectives other than short-run sales volume, and (2) when the individual salesperson's impact on sales volume is difficult to measure in a reasonable time. Straight salary is often found in the following situations: team selling situations, long negotiating periods, learning periods, and mixed promotional situations. There are a number of advantages for both the employee and the company when using a straight salary compensation plan.

Advantages

Sense of security for the salesperson since they will know what their monthly income will be.

Greater Sense of Loyalty to the Company

Increased flexibility in territorial assignments since there is not a feeling of attachment between the salesperson and customers.

Greater Control over the Salespersons Activities

Sometimes it is easier to recruit when they can assure the applicant of a steady income.

Salespeople are more likely to operate in the best interest of the firm.

Disadvantages

No financial incentive is offered to motivate the salesperson to put forth-extra effort.

Selling costs may increase because the salaries will continue to be paid when sales are down.

Income inequities, those who are least productive will be overpaid.

Leads to "adequate" performance, not superior performance.

Straight Commission Plan

Commission is the compensation paid to salespeople based on a fixed formula related to the salesperson's activity or performance. Straight commission plan is a sales force compensation plan that uses commissions as the sole basis for pay. A commission is payment for achieving a given level of performance. Salespeople are paid for results. Usually, commission payments are based on the salesperson's dollar or unit sales volume. However, they may be based on the profitability of sales so as to motivate the sales force to expend effort on the most profitable products or customers. Straight commission pays a salesperson based on a percentage of the sales or gross profits that they generate. This rewards the salesperson not for their time or efforts but more for their accomplishments. Straight commission plans are often used in industries such as real estate, car sales, door-to-door sales, or party based sales.

Advantages

Income is directly related to performance; there is no limit to earnings.

Easy to calculate; salesperson can keep track of their earnings

Salespeople realize their earnings are limited only by themselves

No sales costs to the company when there are no sales.

Salespeople have work freedom, when and how long they want to work.

Poor performing salespeople often quit.

Sales managers base income on accomplishments, not evaluations.

Disadvantages

Emphasis may be placed on sales volume rather than on profitable sales.

There is little loyalty to the company.

Uncertainty of earnings for salesperson.

Turnover of salespeople can be high when business drops.

Salespeople may overload customers with inventory, straining long-term customer relationships.

Salespeople are less flexible with having their territories divided, introducing new products and calling on new customers.

More difficult to recruit because of no guaranteed income.

Bonus

A bonus consists of a lump sum of money paid for some outstanding performance such as making a quota, obtaining a new account or selling a desired product mix. Most companies pay employees incentive earnings annually although there are some that pay semi-annually, quarterly or on a monthly basis. A bonus is always used in combination with a salary and/or commission.

Advantages

Flexibility

Quick, positive reinforcement

When offered in groups, will motivate a combined team effort

Disadvantages

Motivation may be broken if the company waits too long to pay out the bonus.

Sales manager must set realistic objectives and be able to evaluate quickly.

Groups may put all the work on one member.

COMBINATION PLANS

There are several different combination plans including the following:

Salary Plus Commission

Salary plus commission plan, under which a salesman is given some compensation besides fixed income. It is best used when management wants to get high sales without sacrificing customer service.

Salary Plus Bonus

Best for achieving long-run objectives; building long-run relationships with customers, or selling large installations.

Salary Plus Commission Plus Bonus

Best used when the company is subjected to strong seasonal sales, frequent inventory imbalances and when management wants to focus on certain products or customers.

Drawing Account and Commission Plan

Under which a salesman is enabled to pay recurring bills without taking recourse to borrowed money; and to help the salesmen in developing a new territory.

Commission Plus Bonus

Usually applied to group efforts, in which some salespeople call on central buyers or buying committees while others call on store managers.

Advantages

Provides the greatest flexibility and control over salespeople.
Provides security plus incentive.
Allows frequent, immediate reinforcement of desired sales behaviour.

Disadvantages

It can be complex and easily misunderstood.
It can be expensive.
The incentive portion may be too small to motivate.
It may fail to meet either the needs of salespeople or those of management.

OTHER PLANS

Sliding commission plan, which suggests payment of given commission on sales effected to a point "automatically increasing the commission rate as definite sales totals are reached".

Group commission plan which suggests payment of different commission at different rates to the salesman on different groups of articles sold.

Draw against Commission

The salesperson receives regular advances against future commissions. There is often an established limit to the total to be advanced. As you can see, the risk falls all on the company if the salesperson doesn't produce. While many companies have salesperson sign non-disclosures, non-competes and employee contracts, even if employment ends with a negative balance owed by the salesperson to the company, the deficit is usually not recoverable.

Guarantee against Commission

The salesperson receives a minimum periodic income even if commissions do not reach that level. This is similar to a draw but the money paid to the salesperson does not have to be repaid against future commissions.

Expenses Allowance Plan

According to the provisions of this plan, allowances to meet the expenses involved in travel, dining, lodging and entertaining are paid to the sales persons.

Profit sharing is a system by which employees receive a share of the profits of a business enterprise. It also refers to various incentive plans introduced by businesses that provide direct or indirect payments to employees that depend on company's profitability in addition to employees' regular salary and bonuses or an arrangement in which an employer shares some of its profits with its employees. The compensation can be stocks, bonds, or cash, and can be immediate or deferred until retirement. Profit sharing allows for changing contributions each year. Contributions are determined by a formula to allocate the overall contribution and distribution of accumulated funds after the retirement age.

How does Profit sharing work? The company contributes a portion of its pre-tax profits to a pool that will be distributed among eligible employees. The amount distributed to each employee may be weighted by the employee's base salary so that employees with higher base salaries receive a slightly higher amount of the shared pool of profits. Generally this is done on an annual basis.

Advantages

- Brings groups of employees to work together toward a common goal (the success/benefit of the company).
- Helps employees focus on profitability.
- The costs of implementing the plan rise and fall with the company's revenues.
- Enhances commitment to organisation goals.

Disadvantages

- The pay for each employee moves up or down together (no individual differences for merit or performance).
- Focuses only on the goal of profitability (which may be at the expense of quality).
- For smaller companies, these plans may result in drastic swings in earnings for employees, which the employees may find difficult to manage their personal finances.
- Adherence to the FLSA requires employers to recalculate each worker's "regular rate" of pay. To overcome this limitation, employers may restrict this type of compensation to exempt employees.

Sales compensation plans cover employees who are fulfilling sales jobs. Such plans have four fundamental elements: the range of cash compensation opportunity, the mix of base and incentive pay, the extent pay-at-risk, and the selection of pertinent incentive goals.

Quota-based Plan

The quota is the explicit limit (usually measured by volume or sometimes by value) on the amount of a particular product that can be imported or exported during a specified time period. A quota may be applied on a selective basis, with varying limits set according to the country of origin, or on a global basis, which only specifies the total limit and thus tends to benefit more efficient suppliers. In quota-based plan, each salesman is assigned with a certain fixed quota to be accomplished during a specified period of time. On attaining the given quota, commission at the fixed rate is given to each, along with the remuneration plan and if fails to attain the assigned quota, no commission is paid.

Fringe Benefits Plan

This plan can be implemented with any other remuneration plan. Fringe benefits are intended to provide security, morale and job satisfaction and which include retirement benefits such as pension, gratuity, provident fund, insurance, disability benefits and so on.

Non-Money Incentives

Not all incentive programs need to be paid out in cash. Performance-based recognition programs can be rewarded through: Free wine; large-format bottles, verticals or reserve wines; logo apparel or other non-wine merchandise; gift certificates for dinner, lodging or other local merchant offerings; or a personal day off-with pay.

Some companies offer employees incentive credits or vouchers that salespeople can earn and accumulate to "purchase" items already in their tasting room or towards specified items. This allows individual employees an opportunity to build their own wine collections or buy gifts for their CONSIDEA plan document must be written to state the terms and conditions of the plan. The plan document states the purpose of the plan in a way that avoids confusion should unexpected outcomes arise to protect both the company and the employee. The plan document specifies eligibility criteria, performance measures, and timing of awards, among other matters such as termination of the employee or the plan. Company leadership should review plan documentation with legal counsel before implementing the plan. Once the plan terms and conditions have been decided, communicating the compensation program to the salesforce may begin. The new plan must be communicated with positive influence over salespersons for a smooth transition to occur. Senior and field sales management must own the plan design and communicate it to the sales force. Face-to-face (superior-to-subordinate) communication is preferable. Communication must not stop after the initial plan introduction. Management will gain significant advantage through ongoing communications. Salespersons will gain advantage by monitoring their achievement toward established goals. Finally, testing the plan before initial communication and subsequently (after implementation) is critical to determining if a sales compensation plan is an effective one that is operating as planned. Annually evaluate the plan from two perspectives:

- The employer's perspective considers cost versus plan budget, observation of desired behaviours among the sales personnel, quota distribution against actual results, sales outcomes versus established goals, and competitiveness of earnings generated by the plan.
- The sales employee's perspective considers the equity of a pay-for-performance plan (e.g., do top performers earn the top awards), quota and goal attainment difficulty, total pay levels *versus* expected pay levels, and perceived competitiveness of the company's sales compensation plan.

CONCLUSION

Sales compensation designers should assess the current incentive plan to confirm and validate the following areas of interest:

Is the structural design of the plan appropriate; does it properly apply the principles of sound compensation design? Three areas to assess include:

1. Consistency with the job content and scope of responsibility.
2. Competitiveness with pay levels, mix and leverages (i.e., is the plan attracting and retaining the desired talent?)
3. Comparison with common plan practices to assess whether the calculation method, commission or bonus, is consistent with recruiting market competitors.

To determine whether the plan contributes to business success, assess the plan's alignment with business and human capital management objectives, pay-for-performance results, sales talent results (i.e., ability to retain top talent) and the competitiveness of sales compensation in the relevant recruiting markets.

References

S.L. Gupta, "Sales and Distribution Management", 1st ed., New Delhi, Excel Books, 1999.

Geoff Lancaster and David Jobber, "Selling and Sales Management", 3rd ed., Delhi, Macmillan India Ltd., 1997.

B.K. Acharya, P.B. Govekar, Prof. Bhanu Krishnan and Prof. Shailaja Ravindranath, "Field Sales Management", 3rd ed., Mumbai, Himalaya Publishing House, 1998.

Promod, K. Sahu and Kishore, C. Raut, "Salesmanship and Sales Management", 2nd ed., New Delhi, Vikas Publishing House Private Limited, 1993.

CHAPTER

12

Why 'P' Notes? Is this a Motivational Factor to Foreign Equity Investor?

M. JAISUN AND R. AYYAMPERUMAL

ABSTRACT

The international admittance to the Indian capital market is inadequate to Foreign Institutional Investors [FIIs]. The market has found a way to circumvent this by creating the device called participatory notes. This paper focuses on the use of Participatory notes [P-Notes] by foreign institutional investors and describes how it motivates the FIIs and how it focuses on our Indian capital market.

The broadening of India's foreign investor base in recent years has a bias towards hedge funds/unregistered foreign investors who invest primarily through Participatory notes. Financial instruments used by Hedge funds, which invest through participatory notes, borrow money cheaply from Western markets and invest these funds into stocks in emerging markets. The screw has, however, been tightened by making it mandatory for the P-notes issuing authority to ensure that the participatory notes are issued only to "regulated" entities and not just "registered" entities. This will make it difficult for unregulated hedge funds (though many hedge funds are regulated) to invest in the Indian equities through this route. So this paper explains the P-notes downside position and its crisis to our Indian stock market.

Keywords: Participatory notes, Hedge funds

INTRODUCTION

Foreign Institutional Investors have taken a keen interest in the Indian Stock Market since 1992, when they were allowed to invest in our markets after the balance of payments crisis, an offshore market for Participatory Notes [PNs] developed as a primary conduit for foreign investors to motivate and invest in India. The SEBI investigated P-Notes in 2001 stock scam and based on the recommendations of a joint parliamentary committee on the stocks scam, the government banned few overseas corporate bodies from operating in the primary and secondary markets. In 2003, a technical committee with representatives from SEBI, Reserve Bank of India and Finance Ministry was set-up to look into the P-Notes issue. Since international admittance to the Indian capital market is inadequate to Foreign Institutional Investors [FIIs], the market has found a way to circumvent this by creating the device called participatory notes. Securities and Exchange Board of India's [SEBI] proposal to tighten the rules for purchase of shares and bonds in Indian companies through the participatory note route took the breath away of the Indian stock market and it suffered its biggest fall in history. The hedge funds play an imperative role in P-notes because they invest through participatory notes, borrow money cheaply from Western markets and invest these funds into stocks in emerging markets. This gives them two-fold benefit: a chance to make a killing in a stock market where stocks are on the rise; and a chance to make the most of the rising value of the local currency.

Also it is true that FIIs issue PNs to funds/companies whose identity is not known to the Indian authorities. Though the P-Notes issue is an old one, the market has overreacted to it.

WHAT ARE P-NOTES?

- Participatory notes are instruments used by foreign funds/ investors, which/who are not registered with SEBI, but are interested in taking exposure in Indian securities.
- Participatory notes are generally issued overseas by the associates of India-based foreign brokerages. Brokers buy or sell securities on behalf of their clients on their proprietary account and issue such notes in favour of such foreign investors.
- Participatory notes are normally subscribed by investors who want to avoid as many regulatory processes as possible, so that they are adhered to minimum level of disclosure. But the FIIs with whom they are functioning are required to comply with "know your customer" [KYC] guidelines of SEBI.

FII and their Sub-accounts

- FII means an entity established or incorporated outside India which proposes to make investment in India. FII works in a very tight and scheduled environment and has to act in accordance with the guidelines framed by SEBI in 1995 and they also have to comply with the regulatory notifications of RBI, for matters specifically concerning foreign exchange. The following entities, proposing to invest on behalf of broad based funds, are also eligible to be registered as FIIs:

- o Asset Management Companies
- o Investment Manager/Advisor
- o Institutional Portfolio Managers
- o Trustees

- FII's sub-account includes those foreign corporates, foreign individuals and institutions, funds or portfolios established or incorporated outside India on whose behalf investments are proposed to be made in India by a registered FII.

Who gets P-Notes?

P-Notes are issued to the factual investors on the basis of stocks purchased by the FII. The registered FII looks after all the transactions, which appear as proprietary trades in its books. It is not obligatory for the FIIs to disclose their client details to the SEBI, unless asked specifically.

Eligible Persons to Invest through P-notes

- Any entity that is regulated, authorized or supervised by a central bank (Eg. Bank of England) or any other similar body provided that the entity must not only be authorized but also be regulated by the aforesaid regulatory bodies; and
- Any entity that is regulated, authorized or supervised by a securities or futures commission, such as the Financial Services Authority (UK), the Securities and Exchange Commission or other securities or futures authority or commission in any country, state or territory.

Estimation of Money in our Stocks through P-notes

According to one estimate, more than 30 per cent of foreign institutional money coming into India is from hedge funds. This has led SEBI to keep a close watch on FII transactions, and especially hedge funds. Hedge funds, which thrive on arbitrage opportunities, rarely hold a stock for a long time. With a view to monitoring investments through participatory notes, SEBI has decided that FIIs must report details of these instruments along with the names of their holders. SEBI has also proposed a ban on all PN issuances by sub-accounts of FIIs with immediate effect. They also will be required to wind up the current position over 18 months, during which period the capital markets regulator will review the position from time to time.

Regulations of P-notes

According to the statistics available at the SEBI web site, 109 registered FII's are there, of which 34 Issue P-Notes. FII's who issue/renew/cancel/redeem P-Notes need to report details about the P-Notes on a monthly basis not later than 7th of the following month. FII's investing/subscribing to the P-Notes are required to report on quarterly basis.

SEBI Guidelines about who can Invest through P-Notes

- Company incorporated according to the local laws in the country of registration
- Financial institution, such as bank which is monitored by a central bank
- Securities or future commission
- Member of a recognized stock exchange

Why P-notes are Dangerous?

The Participatory notes are a hit on the face of every citizen who is an investor. For a person to invest even in one share, several KYC (know your customer) forms have to be filled up, and PAN numbers and proof of address, etc. are provided. For the PN investor, the system is totally silent on even elementary information. The FIIs issue PNs to funds/companies whose identity is not known to the Indian authorities.

Hence, the participatory notes system is blatantly discriminatory and seems to favour ghost investors. Any self-respecting market, if it discriminates at all, does so against outsiders. But we have done the unthinkable.

We should recognize and internalize the fact that funds are in search of markets, and not the other way. Given the demographic shift in the developed markets (where pension funds have to locate markets to get returns for longer periods) and the lack of huge opportunities in long-term projects, it is natural that global funds are in search of markets.

PN Route

The PN route, through which a section of investors is participating in our markets, is a mystery wrapped in a puzzle, crammed inside a conundrum and delivered through a riddle. It is possible for the terror financiers, who could find this route attractive and simple, to enter and exit as per these calculations and are not shy about the greed for maximum returns. They pay the taxes applicable and laugh all the way to the bank with bonus incentives. So these are addressless funds that could be from doubtful sources and the glamour for it is interesting, if not absolutely suspicious.

CONCLUSION

P-notes are an important motivational factor to Foreign Investor in investing their money into India and also the FII money is certainly needed for the Indian stock markets. Without FII's one could not have thought about the Sensex reaching more than 20,000 points. With more FII's certainly the indices are poised to reach higher levels. However, the regulators' concern about the genuine inflow is certainly a valid one. SEBI has all the interest and authority to add, amend or modify regulations to the investing and trading procedures in Indian stock markets. So, their action, too, should be welcomed, since this will protect and motivate the interests of the Indian investors as well as foreign investors.

References

'SEBI reins in P-notes', from SBI Funds Management Private Limited.

Use of Participatory Notes' from International Monetary Fund Working paper by Dr. Manmohan Singh.

Foreign Institutional Investor from finance.indiamart.com

CHAPTER

13

A Journey from Touch of Motivation to Bond of Motivation*

JAYAPRAKASH JALA

The employee-employer relationship has taken new turns in the new global economy. The forces like money (or in other words, salary, bonus, incentives) and machinery, which used to run the mechanism well for decades, have started to fail as there are vast changes in the perspectives of the employees and the outlook of the employers. For several decades Indian market has been using motivation just as a momentary solution to boost the work process or as a tool to draw better performance in the process of production or accomplishment of targets. Motivation has been used with a limited scope as a tool to improve the work life effectiveness and thereby draw better financial results. Nowadays motivation has become a key link between the employees and the employers. This is not a short-term solution ar.y more, but it is the bond between the employees and employers. Previously, the investments and the employees were looked at as two different entities. The new perspective is that the expenditure incurred for employing and for the development employees is also looked at as investment. The new meaning of motivation demands for practicality apart from principles. Purposefully, the focus of this paper is set on education sector, because there is more scope for practicality in this sector and also the results can be seen within a semester or so. There is scope for asking people to validate the new practice, each time a change is made. Here the product also can speak apart from the producer and the consumer.

* (A research paper on motivational practices in education institutions as the bonding between employees and the employers)

AN INTRODUCTION TO EDUCATION SECTOR

This is one of the major sectors and this sector employs more in number than any other sector in the country. This sector is always in demand and the demand could never decrease as the value of education is well-established in the minds of the people. This is a sector where there is a lot to do with humans and their feelings more when compared to other sectors and no ERP solution can work effectively here as the human relationship element plays a predominant role in this sector. In the field of teaching, people (individuals) are very important and they are irreplaceable by their profession or skill. They receive their due respect for their skills and their roles. Making transitions smooth (to bring adaptability) is the key to any organisation and needs of employees and their families.

The current capital invested by the people into private education academics is officially estimated to be 40 billion dollars or close to INR 180 thousand crore and the investment into this market is expected to expand to a sum of 68 billion US$ (INR 306 thousand crore) each year according to the current market value of a dollar exchange rate in India) by the year 2012 (http://en.wikipedia.org/wiki/Education_in_India-dated 29th of July). So along with the growth of the capital being invested, the expected outcome will also be expected to be of high quality, especially when the competition is between the native and the foreign academic competencies.

Employees play an important role in the success of any organisation. Employees are engaged as long as they fulfil the objectives and the needs of the organisations. Employees also have got some expectations and they need to be fulfilled to retain employees over a period of time. These expectations of the employees keep changing from time to time along with the dynamics of the market. Once the role of teachers in academics was to impart knowledge, and nowadays the teacher is the source of inspiration for the student to mould himself to fit into a particular role and the knowledge is acquired from various other sources and the students are not dependant on the teacher alone. A teacher is expected to constantly update him or herself.

The Corporate Effect on Indian Academics

The corporate effect has brought about the beginning of new trends and approaches into Indian academics. Indian universities have started a trend of rewarding performance. This kind of a practice was just limited to corporates and commercial companies alone a decade ago. This kind of rewarding performance has brought in new HR practices like student feed back, (like customer feed back) and performance appraisals and performance incentives even in the field of academics. Universities like VIT are giving outstanding researcher awards. Institutes like IIT, Roorkee, is giving outstanding/best teacher of the year awards. Rewarding innovation is a way of staying ahead in motivating the employees. The perspective of the customers (Parents) and the consumers (students) has been turning service oriented as the market is slowly becoming service driven. Customers and consumers are also looking for guidance in the purchase decision-making and assistance through post-purchase service. The process has been extended as the parents are not looking at graduation (degree) as the finishing but they are also looking at the placement performance. The faculty is expected to adapt themselves to this new extension in the process. There are organisations today which conduct employee days to boost the morale and mood of the employees.

Change in the Approach of Employers

The 4A theory (acknowledge, affirm, assure, appreciate) that is often mentioned in the area of customer satisfaction is now slowly being turned into a principle of employee satisfaction. The employers are often concerned about how they can acknowledge, affirm, assure, and appreciate the work done by the employees and thereby increase the productivity and also lead to increased retention of employees. These four qualities have been identified as the psychological needs, and satisfaction of psychological needs like these four are applicable not to customers alone but also to employees.

The employees are getting better treatment than before. Those who are treated well will treat others well. It is a general principle of treatment and behaviour. Here is a sector where all the parties involved are human except for the infrastructure. So there is a greater need of escalating people into better human beings so that there will be no personality clashes between parties involved. Employees of other sectors are well aware that 50% of the people leave their jobs mostly due to boss and the treatment they receive from their higher ups. This ratio is not as high as 50% in the education sector and teachers have some other reasons for changing jobs.

Changing the Outlook of the Employees

Today's employees are not limiting themselves to the work assigned, but they are looking for opportunities to put their talents and ideas to use in their organisations. The employee wants to be recognized for his innovation and creativity. Employees are made a part of the decision-making process. There are organisations which have changed their policies to make their organisational decisions employee driven. In this kind of functioning, it is observed that the employees find themselves accountable to their performance levels. Institutes like IITs and central universities have given the complete liberty to the faculty/teachers to offer subjects of their choice and prove that those subjects enhance the performance levels of the students. Professors of IIT, Roorkee, say that the introduction of studies in Psychology (behavioural studies) in their Institute has drastically improved the performance of the students. The faculty thereby are expected to prove through researches that what they offer to the students actually contribute to the growth and better performance of the students when they enter the job market. Introduction of soft skills as a subject in all the colleges of ICFAI has given a great lift to the number of placements in all the affiliated colleges of the ICFAI University.

The employee-day kind of recent practices in the companies are used to build an emotional bonding of the employees to the organisation. This is taken as an opportunity to let the employees know that they are important in the function of that organisation. The companies take it as a way to expresse their gratitude and appreciation towards the work and support of the employees.

Families of brands have become a new fashion in the current market scenario. If the name of the institute is Somex, the employees when joining are invited to the family of Somex. Whenever they are addressed, they address by the name of that somex family member. This is a process of creating a sense of belongingness. With a turnover of 20,000 crores a year, according to the official records, this sector has a large market share to offer to a successful institute/organisation: Best fair play, best employee and most cooperative employee kind of awards. If a group of 10,000 students pay a 50,000 each for a higher education course, the total sum paid to the institute is 50,00,00,000 (fifty crores).

Looking at it from a Global View

As a result of the new changes to be brought in through the new HRD policy of the new union government, if we take an example of a university like MIT, (Massachusetts Institute of Technology), as an example to be established in India, (the current student population at MIT is 30,000) and the average academic expenditure of a student there is US$ 25,000 (dollars), on an average 11.25 lakhs a year. 30,000 students pay a total sum of (3712 crores an year in India), it is the 2% of the total expenditure of Indian academics

Employee empowerment is often defined as a training the employees to make them feel equipped and also feel empowered. In the education sector, it is taking new turns like training teachers for being able to use ICT (Information and communication technology) tools. Employee empowerment is a term used to express the ways in which non-managerial staff can make autonomous decisions without consulting a boss (wisegeek.com). Faculty empowering through various methods of training and re-training and updating and enabling them to use new methods and tools is a part of making them feel better or rather proud about the organisation they are working for.

Rewarding Innovation and Excellence

Make them Feel Better

The employees feel better in a place where there is scope to use their innovation and at times unleash their creativity through applying their new ideas. Faculty is given liberty to frame a syllabus and decide on the methods of teaching and they are highly acceptable to the employees. IITs,

IIMs and many other universities like SRM (Tamilnadu), VIT (Tamilnadu), Thapar (Punjab), etc. have given freedom to the staff to frame the syllabus as well as to decide on the methods of teaching.

Providing the basic needs is another way of keeping an employee motivated and satisfied. According to Moslow's theory of hierarchy of needs, apart from the needs mentioned by him, like self-actualization needs, esteem needs, social needs, safety needs and physiological needs, there is a new dimension which people are looking for, and the needs of the 21st century employees are psychological needs such as security.

Privacy, Infrastructure and Facilities

Organisations are forced to go beyond the 3 F based facilities like fun (1) like LTC (leave travel concession) and office tours, family benefits (2) like coverage of medical and education expense apart from accommodation in quarters. Many of the IITs and IIMs have given residences to their employees along with families on the campus and their employee retention is high when compared to other large sized institutes, and these large institutes have started housing them under the banner of employee welfare. MANUU (Moulana Azad National Urdu University) and the HCU Hyderabad Central University are trying to provide permanent residences in a land of 60 acres on their massive campus. This brings a sense of settlement and belongingness to the employees. VIT University has also allotted houses to 350 employees through a housing society to their employees. Thapar University of Punjab is making all efforts to provide furnished accommodations to their employees and this too is a step in the process of motivating the employees.

Developing Ownership in the Employees

The constant struggle of the employers is to develop accountability in all the acts of the employees. If an employee catches the vision of the top management and also adapts his vision to that of the management, he will develop ownership towards the organisation. The managements have understood that high salaries alone cannot tie the bond between the employees and the organisation, but it takes more to keep the bonding alive.

Training and Development of Academic Staff

There are 45,000 colleges (http://www.indiastudycenter.com/univ/list.htm) and 379 Universities (http://en.wikipedia.org/wiki/List_of_universities_in_India) in India and we do not have sufficient training centers to update the skills our faculty members. There are only 57 UGC recognized academic staff colleges in India, and a dozen of training bodies like NITTTR, and a dozen of QIP Centres (all IIT's) which can train 60,000 to 70,000 academic staff each year to keep them abreast or updated with the new changes in the subjects and teaching methodologies. There are many other institutes which are also working alongside for teacher development. For example, the CEDBEC (centre for education beyond curriculum) of Christ University and the self-funded academic staff college of VIT University are examples of the other such efforts.

Private and Corporate Partnerships

Taking external help and using cross-functional methods have become the preferred fashion or style of work. A faculty/teacher today is expected to send a finished good (a student with skills required to hit the road running). Educational institutes are taking the help of corporate to train and develop the teachers of their colleges. The best example comes from INFOSYS which conducts Campus Connect training programs for the faculty members of various colleges both at the technical front and in teaching skills. The INFOSYS private limited is also extending soft skills development programme for faculties and the students through campus connect programme. The WIPRO private limited is conducting a special teacher training programme called Mission 10X, which aims at training 10,000 engineering teachers by the year 2010, and trains teachers in various skills including teaching skills and technical skills with the help of international certification bodies like Cambridge and Dale Carnegie certification institutes in quality teaching.

There is still a great need to motivate teaching community to draw better results in the academic performance of India. There is a great need to organize the Indian Higher education sector and divide into sectors or areas, which will enable ease in administration. Better administration will certainly bring additional motivation in the teachers. There needs to be a teacher registration body and also that body should ask the teachers to update themselves and earn continuum education credits from the teacher training centers. There is an immediate need to establish criteria for teacher quality assessment and also start more higher education—teacher training centers. For all this to happen, teachers need to be paid better than ever in the past and the same opinion was expressed by the 8th knowledge commission headed by Mr. Sam Pitroda. More care for the employees is possible in a more organized environment. The teachers will create blogs, websites, webcasts, podcasts etc. and they will go to the next level when this motivation works as a bond.

References

http://web.mit.edu/sfs/afford/undergraduate_expenses.html (29-07-09).
http://en.wikipedia.org/wiki/Education_in_India (29-07-09).
http://www.wisegeek.com/what-is-employee-empowerment.htm (28-07-09).
http://www.indiastudycenter.com/univ/list.htm (28-07-09).
http://en.wikipedia.org/wiki/List_of_universities_in_India (29-07-09).

CHAPTER

14

Motivational Factors Influencing Job Satisfaction of the University and College Teachers

DR. U. JERINABI AND MRS. T. LALITHA DEVI

INTRODUCTION

"Motivation is like food for the brain. You cannot get enough in one sitting. It needs continual and regular top ups" —*Peter Davies*

Motivation is the condition that energizes, direct and sustains work behaviour. Motivation has been defined in numerous ways. One of the best is "motivation is the forces acting either on or within a person to initiate behaviour." In the field of psychology, human motivation has long been studied as a way to explain an individual's behaviour. In reality, motivation is inferred rather than measured. The inference is made due to behavioural changes that result from external stimuli. It is also a performance variable because changes in a person's motivation are frequently of a temporary nature; with many people, what is high priority today may become singularly unimportant tomorrow.

Satisfaction is another interesting work-related phenomenon. According to the great management theorist Frederick Herzberg, job satisfaction and job dissatisfaction are caused by total different sets of factors. In that regard Herzberg presents the following factors: achievement, recognition, responsibility, growth, and the nature of the work. He classifies these factors as motivators, and claims that these are the factors that will enhance job satisfaction. He found that job dissatisfaction is caused by factors such as poor supervision, bad working conditions, unpleasant colleagues, low salaries, objectionable work policies or procedures, and low job security.

JOB SATISFACTION

The term "Job satisfaction" refers to the amount of over all positive effort of feelings that individuals have towards their job and it is a pleasurable or positive emotional state resulting from the appraisal of one's job experience. It is the difference between the amount of rewards the workers receive and the amount they believe they should receive. Job Satisfaction has been considered as a state of condition where people are:

- Induced to do work efficiently and effectively
- Convinced to remain in the enterprises
- Prepared to act efficiently during contingencies
- Prepared to welcome the changes without resistance
- Interested in promoting the image of the organisation
- More happy and satisfied with their job

COMPONENTS OF JOB SATISFACTION

Philip Apple has tested five major components of Job Satisfaction as follows:

- Attitude towards work group
- General working condition
- Attitude towards company
- Monetary benefits and
- Attitude towards supervision

FACTORS INFLUENCING JOB SATISFACTION

There are number of factors that influence Job Satisfaction. However the main influences can be summarized as follows:

1. Opportunity

Employees are more satisfied when they have challenging opportunities at work. This includes participating in interesting projects, jobs with a satisfying degree of challenging and opportunity for increased responsibility.

2. Fair Rewards

Employees are satisfied when they feel that they are rewarded fairly for the work they do. Consider employees responsible, the effort they have put forth, the work they have done well and the demand for their jobs.

3. Adequate Authourity

Employees are more satisfied, when they have adequate freedom and authority to do their job.

4. The Work Itself

The content of the work itself is a major source of satisfaction. For example, research related to the job characteristics approach to job design, covered in this chapter. It shows the feedback from the job itself and autonomy are two of the major job related motivational factors. Recent research has found that such job characteristics and if the creative requirement of employee's job is net, then they tend to be satisfied.

5. Pay, Wages and Salaries

The pay, wages and salaries are recognized to be a significant but cognitive complex and multidimensional factor in job satisfaction. Money not only helps people attain their basic needs but is also instrumental in providing upper level need satisfied. Employees often see pay as a reflection of how management view their contribution to the organisation. Fringe benefits are also important, but they are not as influential, one reason undoubtedly is that most employees do not even know how much they are receiving in benefits.

6. Promotion

Promotional opportunities seem to have a varying effect on Job Satisfaction. This is because promotions take a number of different forms and have a variety of accompanying rewards. For example, individuals who are promoted on the basis of seniority often experience job satisfaction but not as much as their who are promoted on the basis of performance. Additionally, a promotion with a 10% salary raise is typically not as satisfying as one with a 20% salary raise. These differences help explain why execution promotions may be more satisfying than promotions that occur at the lower levels of organisations.

7. Supervision

Supervision is another moderately important source of job satisfaction. For now, however it can be used than there seem to be two dimensions of supervisory style that affect job satisfaction. One is employee centeredness, which is measured by the degree to which supervision takes a personal interest and cares about employees. It commonly manifested insistence to the individual, and communicating with the associate on a personal as well as on official level.

8. Work Group

The nature of the work group or team will have an effect on Job Satisfaction. Friendly, co-operative co-workers or team members are a modest source of Job Satisfaction to individual employees. The work groups, specially a "right" team, serves, as a source of support, comfort, advice and assistance to the individual members. A "good" work group or effective team makes the job more enjoyable. However, this factor is not essential to job satisfaction. On the other hand, if the reverse conditions exist the people are difficult to get along with this factor, may have a negative effect on job satisfaction.

9. Working Condition

Working condition has a modest effect on job satisfaction. If the working conditions are good (clean, effective, surroundings). For instance, the persons will find it easier to carry out their job. If the working conditions on job satisfaction is similar to that of the work group. If things are good, there may or may not be a job satisfaction problem, if things are poor, there very likely will be.

DETERMINANTS OF JOB SATISFACTION

According to Abraham A. Karnan, there are three types of variables which determine the job satisfaction of an individual:

1. Organisation variables
2. Personal variables
3. Situational variables

ORGANISATIONAL VARIABLES

1. Occupational Level

The higher the lead of the job, the greater the satisfaction of an individual. This is because higher level jobs carry greater prestige and self-control.

2. Job Content

Greater the variation in job content and less the receptiveness with which the task must be performed, the greater the satisfaction of the dividual involved.

3. Considerate Leadership

People like to be treated with consideration. Hence considerate leadership results in higher Job Satisfaction than considerate leadership.

4. Pay and Promotional Opportunities

All other things being equal, these two variables are positively related to job satisfaction.

5. Interaction in the Work Group

Interaction is most satisfying when if results in the cognition that other persons attitudes are similar to one's self. It results in being accepted by others and it facilitates the achievement of goals.

PERSONAL VARIBALES

1. Age

This is generally a positive relations between age and job satisfaction up to the pre-retirement years and then there is a sharp decrease in satisfaction.

2. Educational Level

With occupational level help constant there is a negative relationship between educational level and the job satisfaction.

3. Role Perception

Different individuals hold different perceptions about their role in kind of activities and behaviour they should engage into perform their job successfully, job satisfaction is determined by this factor also.

4. Sex

There is as yet no consistent evidence as to whether women are more satisfied with their job then men holding such factors as job and occupational level constant. One might predict this to be the case considering the generally lower occupational aspiration of women.

SITUATIONAL VARIABLE

(a) Experience

Several investigations have indicated that job satisfaction is relatively high at the start drops slowly to the fifth or eight years, then rises again with more time on the jobs.

(b) Working conditions

There seems to be a tendency for working conditions to be ranked lower, perhaps because they have been improved. It seems plausible that the prestige value applied to the white-collar occupations is the result of more desirable conditions of work.

(c) Welfare Facilities

Welfare facilities can satisfy different needs. It motivates the employees. So it will increase job satisfaction.

(d) Union-Management relationship

Union-Management relationship also positively related to job satisfaction.

(e) Working Hours of the Organisation

Working hours more than 8 hours or 8 hours without proper intervals will badly affect the health of the workers. This may cause job dissatisfaction.

(f) Grievance Redressal Procedure

A healthy problem-solving method was help to solve the problems easily and in time. It will increase job satisfaction.

JOB SATISFACTION AMONG TEACHING STAFF

Teaching is the noblest of all professions. It is most rewarding too, not in terms of luxuries but in terms of it's being the dispenser of human destinies. Kothari Education Commission rightly opined in its report with the words that "The destiny of India being in its class room." No wonder that the teacher occupies the centre stage in the grand opera of learning, which is almost daily played in the classroom of India.

Education as we know the back bone of a progressive nation and the teacher is the pirot of any education system, as he plays a key role in its whole process. So the success of the education programs depends to a great extent upon character and ability of the teacher who is the cornerstone of each of education since teaching is the organisation of learning. So teacher is essentially an organizer.

A teacher is the embodiment of honesty, equanimity, justice, nobility and wisdom. Above all he is a karmayogi, who believes in purity of thought and action, who believes means to be as important as end. It is university agrees that the quality of an educational programme is determined to a large extent by the teaching of the teacher. The document challenge of education—A Policy perspective (1985) has highlighted teacher performance is the most crucial impact in the field of education. No development has been reached the three should be of the development of new technology which are likely to revolutionize the class room teaching. Unless capable and committed teachers are in service, the education system cannot utilize them, for becoming a suitable and potential instrument of national development.

On the other hand, the teaching of a teacher largely depends upon the level of job satisfaction, involvement and profession or if his status as internal, personal factors as feel helplessness. This helplessness will lead to a state that in some ways to resemble the depression, low self-concept and lack of confidence, inferiority complex, anxiety and passive. These negative characteristics will hamper the day-to-day life and also will fall in dissatisfaction. Another way of a person not fully involves into an activity, he will perceive dissatisfaction with that activity. So it can be said that job involvement and leaned helplessness both are closely related to a person's satisfaction. Teacher can be treated in the same way.

The big news from the academic is that nobody wants to teach any more neither young man nor young woman and it is just teaching in a school that is looked upon, even teaching in a college pass and figures very low in the priority of our youth. When any youngster does not get any access in to any other lucrative profession he/she opts for teaching profession, eventually it lessen their job involvement and create learned helplessness. So to attract the youngsters, to satisfy them with their job, to expect a high job involvement and for developing a high self-concept among them something must be done. Therefore, teachers must be declared endangered species not for any humanitarian reasons but as reason of that they are so pirota to the whole business of education, without its progress of even the economic brand is not possible.

NEED FOR THE STUDY

Man is used to be dissatisfied as his needs are insatiable. So a human being satisfied into can be, hardly cited. The desires and needs are directly proportion to his growth. If his needs are not fulfilled or made available, he feels frustrated and thus feels uneasy and disturbed. As far as this aspect is concerned, the industrial world is no exception.

The working personnel are the blood stream of every organisation. It is the workers who bring prosperity to their organisation satisfaction or contentment is the secret of success of every organisation. Job satisfaction gives shape to his mind and inculcates loyalty, morale, gratitude, responsibility and other positive aspects in him.

In every organisation, the management is responsible to provide its personnel with the requisites of job satisfaction. This is easily told than brought in to practice.

Job satisfaction is one of the most crucial but commercial issues in industrial psychology. It has many definitions, most of which are neither easily acceptable nor irrelevant. Many management experts have expressed it in their own way, but have hardly arrived at a conclusion.

OBJECTIVES OF THE STUDY

1. To bring out a profile of the university and college teachers and their progress and welfare facilities provided to the teachers.
2. To determine the job satisfaction of both the college and university teachers.
3. To find out the various demographic factors which influence the job satisfaction of the teachers.

SIGNIFICANCE OF THE STUDY

Education is perceived to be universal phenòmena. It is adequately organized and regulated through formal institutions like schools and colleges. There are different factors which determine the quality of education and its contribution to national development. The quality competence and character of teachers are undoubtedly very significant.

In a developing society teacher has assured a great responsibility to bring out good citizens who could carry out the profession in a dignified and productive manner. Teachers of modern day are looked up as the main guide to prepare the students. To achieve their objectives and aspirations, nothing is more important than to secure a sufficient and high quality teaching profession, providing them with best possible professional preparation and to locate for them satisfactory condition of work to make their teaching more effective. In order to perform their role effectively teacher should be emotionally and professionally satisfied.

Job satisfaction is of great significance for effective functioning of an organisation. Satisfaction leads to effective functioning of the system. If better services are expected from a teacher and if it is desired to effect and hold better talent in the profession, then there is an immediate need to know the causes of dissatisfaction among teachers and suggest remedies for them. So teachers' job satisfaction is an issue of interest as it related to productivity, as a social concerned as an indicator for organisational job commitment.

While extensive job satisfaction, job involvement, researches have been conducted in industrial settings and learned helplessness has been conducted in only abnormal psychology, the field of education has only recently begun to consider these aspects of organisational life. Although a number of studies have been carried out on job satisfaction and job involvement of teachers working at different levels, these studies do not lead to any final conclusions because the result-related studies are quite contradictory.

RESEARCH METHODOLOGY

Both the primary and secondary data were collected for the purpose of the study. The primary data were collected through a structured Questionnaire. The sampling size was 300 staff based on Random sampling and Convenience sampling methods. The sample respondents were the staff working in the various universities and colleges located in Coimbatore District. Considerable data has also been tapped from secondary sources such as Journals, Newspapers, Magazines and Internet to make highlights on the staff working both in colleges and universities. The data so collected were properly analysed using the statistical tools like percentage, mean, standard deviation, Chi-square test and Likert scaling analysis.

LIMITATIONS OF THE STUDY

1. As the study has been conducted only on 300 respondents. This may reveal approximate result.
2. Findings of the study are influenced by personal bias of the respondents.

3. Behaviour of the respondents is subject to frequent changes. So the result of the study may also be subject to changes in time.

SUGGESTIONS

Based on the study following are the suggestions were made

- The career advancement should be purely on merit.
- The information sharing in the department should be free and frank.
- They should be provided with sufficient large office space.
- They should be provided with secretarial support for their research work.
- They should get salary equal to their effort.
- The retirement benefit scheme should be satisfactory.

RESULTS AND DISCUSSION

I. Percentage analysis was used to analyse the profile of the selected University and College teachers (Table I)

- Majority of the respondents (43%) belongs to the age group between 41 years to 50 years, Female respondents constitute 58 percent and the remaining 42 percent were female. Majority of the respondents were married and have small family size. Classification based on education showed 51 percent of the respondents were Research Scholars, 31 percent of the respondents were Doctorates and 18 percent of the respondents were postgraduates.
- The income level classification of respondents showed that 32 percent of the respondents fall into the income group of below 10,000 per month, 28 percent of the respondents fall into the income group of Rs. 10,000-Rs. 20,000 per month, 21 percent if the respondents fall into the income group of Rs. 20,000-Rs. 30,000 per month and 19 percent of the respondents fall into the income group of above Rs. 30,000 per month.
- The years of experience shows that 62 percent of the respondents were below 10 years of service, 21 percent of the respondents were below 11 years—20 years of service and 17 percent of the respondents were above 20 years of service.
- The working place of the respondents shows that 50 percent of the respondents were university staff and 50 percent of the respondents were college staff.
- The position of respondents shows that 42 percent of the respondents were Lecturers, 32 percent of respondents were Professors, 15 percent of the respondents were Senior grade staff, 11 percent of the respondents were Readers.

TABLE I

Profile of the Respondents

Variables		*No. of respondents (300)*	*Percentage*
Age in years	Up to 40 Years	74	25
	41-50 Years	128	43
	Above 50 Years	98	32
Gender	Male	127	42
	Female	173	58
Marital status	Married	187	62
	Unmarried	113	38
Education	Postgraduate	53	18
	M.Phil.	152	51
	Ph.D.	95	31
Annual income	Below Rs. 10,000	94	32
	Rs. 10,000-Rs. 20,000	85	28
	Rs. 20,000-Rs. 30,000	58	19
	Above Rs. 30,000	63	21
Year of service of the Respondents	Below 10 Years	187	62
	11 Years-20 Years	62	21
	Above 20 Years	51	17
Working place of the Respondents	University	150	50
	Govt. College	43	14
	Aided College	42	14
	Self-Financing College	65	22
Position of the Respondents	Professor	97	32
	Reader	33	11
	Senior Grade	44	15
	Lecturer	126	42

Source: Field Survey.

2. Percentage analysis and Likerts Scaling Technique were used to Analyse the Level of Job Satisfaction of the Respondents (Table 2)

The level of satisfaction of the respondents shows that 45 percent of the respondents agreed that they found real enjoyment in their job, 35 percent of the respondents agreed that they like their job better than the average person, 62 percent of the respondents neither agreed nor disagreed that they were seldom bored with their job, 54 percent of the respondents neither agreed nor disagreed that they would not consider taking another kind of job, 42 percent of the respondents agreed that most of the days they were enthusiastic about their job, 31 percent of the respondents agreed that they felt fairly well satisfied with their job, 33 percent of the respondents

TABLE 2

Job satisfaction of the Respondents

Particulars	Strongly Agree (5)			Agree (4)			Neutral (3)			Disagree (2)			Strongly Disagree (1)			Total	Total	Total	Rank
	No.	r S.V.	%	No.	r S.V.	%	No.	r S.V.	%	No.	r S.V.	%	No.	r S.V.	%	No.	r S.V.	%	
1	2						3			4			5			6		7	8
I Find real enjoyment in my Job	52	260	17	133	532	45	67	201	22	32	64	11	16	16	5	300	1073	100	4
I like my job better than the average person	72	360	24	105	420	35	83	249	28	27	54	9	13	13	4	300	109	100	3
I am seldom bored with my job	15	75	5	54	216	18	185	555	62	28	56	9	18	18	6	300	920	100	8
I would not consider taking another kind of job	29	145	9	47	188	16	162	486	54	39	78	13	23	23	8	300	920	100	8
Most days I am enthusiastic about my job	43	215	14	127	508	42	77	231	26	32	96	11	21	21	7	300	1071	100	5
I feel fairly well satisfied with my job	79	395	26	92	368	31	52	156	17	45	90	15	32	32	11	300	1041	100	6
The work I do is very important to me	67	335	22	97	388	33	44	132	15	52	104	17	40	40	13	300	999	100	9
My job activities are personally meaningful to me	38	190	13	115	460	38	99	297	33	25	50	8	23	23	8	300	1020	100	7
I am confident about my ability to do my job	85	425	28	147	588	49	53	159	18	15	30	5	-	-	-	300	1202	100	1

(Contd.)

TABLE 2 (*Contd.*)

1		*2*						*3*			*4*			*5*		*6*		*7*	*8*
I have mastered the skills necessary for my job	74	370	25	123	492	41	62	186	21	27	54	9	14	14	5	300	1116	100	2
Total NOR	554			1040			884			322			200			3000/ 3000			
Total Score Value		2770			4160			2652			676			200			10458/ 10458		
Total Percentage			184.6			346.6			294.6			107.3			66.6			1000/ 1000	
Rank		2			1			3			4			5					

agreed that the work they were doing was very important to them, 38 percent of the respondents agreed that their job activities were personally meaningful to them. 49 percent of the respondents agreed that they were confident about their ability in doing their job, and 41 percent of the respondents agreed that they have mastered the skills necessary for their job.

3. Chi-square Test was used to Test the Association between Different Demographic Factors of the Respondents (Table 3)

It is inferred that the personal factors like age and monthly income, educational qualification and monthly income has no significant influence on the respondents job satisfaction. The study shows that the age of the respondents and their job position has significant influence on their job satisfaction. Educational qualification and job position has influence on the respondents job satisfaction. It also reveals that the respondents monthly income and years of service has significant influence on their job satisfaction.

TABLE 3

Demographic Factors of the Respondents

Variables	*Calculated Value*	*Table Value*	*Level of Significance*	*Result*
Age and Monthly Income of Respondents	10.8796	12.6	5%	Not Significant
Educational Qualification and Monthly Income of Respondents	15.91	16.9	5%	Not Significant
Age and Position of the Respondents	21.8	12.6	5%	Significant
Education Qualification and Position of the Respondents	60.31	16.91	5%	Significant
Service and Monthly Income of the Respondents	72.28	12.59	5%	Significant

CONCLUSION

It may conclude from the studies that unmarried female or male is more satisfied with their jobs. Some studies shows that age, sex and experience has no impact on a person's job satisfaction. On the other hand, studies conclude that sex, age, salary and experience had positive correlation with job satisfaction. There is also concluded double employments, self-esteem, extraversion, neuroticism, job burn-out, job stress, martial status, locus of control and level of teaching are positively correlated with job satisfaction of staff. Some studies revealed that primary teachers are less satisfied than secondary teachers and secondary teachers have same level of satisfaction of college teacher. Extra qualification is also correlated to job satisfaction. Thus there are many contradictions and similarities among researchers on these variables which affect job satisfaction.

References

Wegge, J., Schmidt, K., Parkes, C., and van Dick, K. (2007). 'Taking a sickie': Job satisfaction and job involvement as interactive predictors of absenteeism in a public organisation, *Journal of Occupational and Organisational Psychology*, 80, 77-89.

Wright State University. "Personality more important than job satisfaction in determining job performance success, WSU psychologist says." Press release. Published May 2, 2007. Last accessed May 26, 2007.

Mount, M., Ilies, R., and Johnson, E. (2006). Relationship of personality traits and counterproductive work behaviours: The mediating effects of job satisfaction. *Personnel Psychology*, 59, 591-622.

Mount, M., Ilies, R., and Johnson, E. (2006). Relationship of personality traits and counterproductive work behaviours: The mediating effects of job satisfaction. Personnel Psychology, 59, 591-622.

Saari, L.M., and Judge, T.A. (2004). Employee Attitudes and job Satisfaction. *Human Resource Management*, 43, 395-407.

Rode, J.C. (2004). Job satisfaction and life satisfaction revisited: A longitudinal test of an integrated model. *Human Relations*, Vol. 57(9), 1205-1230.

Cranny, Smith and Stone, 1992 cited in Weiss, H.M. (2002). Deconstructing job satisfaction: separating evaluations, beliefs and affective experiences. *Human Resource Management Review*, 12, 173-194, p. 174.

Brief, 1998 cited in Weiss, H.M. (2002). Deconstructing job satisfaction: separating evaluations, beliefs and affective experiences. *Human Resource Management Review*, 12, 173-194, p. 174.

Weiss, H.M. (2002). Deconstructing job satisfaction: separating evaluations, beliefs and affective experiences. *Human Resource Management Review*, 12, pp. 173-94.

Motivation at Work Place

Dr. Kalpana

Motivated staff is essential to productive and pleasant environment. Everyone is motivated by something. When you go to hotel, you are motivated by hunger. When you go for gym, then you are motivated to be fit and healthy. So what motivates a person is not just work, but efficient and loyal work. That depends on individual's personality.

The modern concept of Human resources is that employees are the internal customers of an organisation. You should strive to make your employees feel that their job is the best, the most fulfilling work environment they've ever had.

HOW TO MOTIVATE EMPLOYEES?

Keep Asking: It should be the habit of the employer to ask frequently, "How do they feel in the job?" and this type of question in informal way will help the employees to come closer to you and they will be able to address issues in a comfortable manner.

Basically a leader has to ask following questions to himself in any organisation:

- o Will I be able to play with possibilities?
- o Do I have basic technique to influence people?
- o Can I be an empowered leader in a challenging business environment?
- o Can I be a transformational leader for market recovery?
- o How can I retain my customers through my employees?
- o How can I prevent my employees from causing collateral damage in the labor-management battle?

When a leader could answer the above questions, then he has to adopt certain motivational methods in his organisation which are discussed below:

Listen to them with Involvement

Don't just hear them talking. Active listening is a vital skill for the survival of any workplace. An employer should make them feel that employees are listened to with involvement. Listening brings new ideas from employees to the organisation.

Recognise Regularly

Show them that you notice their hard work. Let them know that you appreciate what they've done, and do it a hand in shaping the team's environment. It also raises the bar for the rest of the team. This will bring everyone in the team to perform well.

Gift Them

Buy them something. It doesn't have to be expensive; lunch will do in a pinch or doughnuts and coffee in the morning. If they perform well, get them a gift certificate to the local mall or some cute gifts, etc.

Little Fun at Work

Don't lock your ability to have fun behind your suits. Let them play around a little. If it starts to get out of hand, you are there. Bring it back to being productive fun. Working with fun will bring more productivity. Enjoy yourself; you spend more time at work than you do awake in your own home. If you find a job you love, you will never work a day in your life. At the same time see that you work at the time you work and play at the time you play. In many organisations, they play music for the employees to have fun at work. It is also good example for making people work enthusiastically.

Friendly Competition

We need to compete against one another, to prove to ourselves and everyone out there that we can do it, and do it the best. But the competition should be friendly and it should not affect the team at any cost. Competition should not bring any rivalry among others.

Be Friendly with Everyone, But don't become Friends

Whenever you get closer to someone, it will bring favour to one and not to others. Favouritism is a hard accusation to live down, especially if it's true. Don't put yourself in a position that could result in an environment of favouritism. Giving preferential treatment to a person, on a non-work-related basis, is unfair. Unfairness in the workplace leads to turn-over.

Share the Necessary Information

Don't keep all the information to yourself. Let them know where they stand often; this will keep them in the loop. Here again another important concept that an employer should keep in mind is that he can share not 100% information but the needed one for that moment can be shared, and sharing everything also will not bring interests in the minds of the employees. One of the most common downfalls of any organisation is lack of communication. It's tough trying to be motivated in the face of goals that you can't measure

Coach, and Accept Coaching

Coaching people alone is not the important job of an employer, but being along with them during the coaching is more important. Whenever any training takes place, it could be best when the employer also participates in that training. Sometimes it could employee coaching the employer and employer should have the mind set of accepting when any employee could be a good trainer than his boss.

Kindling Positive Thoughts

Negative feeling causes depression. Psychologists refer to this phenomenon as convergent thinking. Here energy flow should be created in a positive manner and environment to be created by employer which always gives positive feeling to the employees.

Clarity in Thoughts

Basically the employer should not be a confused person; only positive emotions attract people, and while communicating to the employees, the employer should be clear in his thoughts and should tell the employees what he wants and which process the employees have to follow to attain that. Most of the employees get job satisfaction when their boss is clear in his correspondence.

Apart from that, an employer should think what shifts focus that he can do to motivate employees, it becomes necessary to question the following for the organisation:

- How has the job changed and what are the new responsibilities?
- Why is the job restructured. Is it part of a longer overhaul?
- How will their performance be evaluated and by whom?
- Do they need to learn new skills?
- Can the old responsibilities be delegated?
- How will their career benefit from this transition?
- What new skills or training do they need to perform successfully?
- Will this make them more marketable in the future?

Without making changes often in the work place, it would be difficult to get things done; even in our home, we can see happiness when we could make changes in our interior or moving furniture from one place to another, etc. The same methodology applies to the organisation also.

References

Dr. Christopher Johnson (2002); Walden university; www.essortment.com

Dr. E.J. Sharma; Workplace Motivation; www.itpeopleindia.com

K.B. Madsen (1961); Theories of Motivation.

Beekman (2000); Employee Motivation and the Psychological Contract.

Richard M. Steers, Lyman W. Porter (1991); Motivation and Work Behaviour.

CHAPTER

16

Employee Motivation in the Present Economic Scenario

DR. P. KAMESWARA RAO AND DR. N.R.V. PRABHU

ABSTRACT

We have understood that one of the vital problems faced by organisations is that despite recruiting highly competent employees, the output is not satisfactory. We have therefore understood that competency alone is not sufficient to deliver results unless he/she is continuously motivated. Motivated employees are able to deliver both efficiency and effectiveness to achieve goals. Normally any training aims at providing basic understanding of motivation needs with practical and effective motivational techniques for employees. This paper attempts to understand motivation, discuss the need for motivation, ways to motivation, expectations of employees, and what they don't want from the HR professionals.

Key words: Motivation

INTRODUCTION

In order to remain successful in this globally competitive business environment, organisations need human resource that would deliver their full potential to achieve organisational goals. But many say, "Don't undo what you cannot redo". It is true in our day-to-day as well as in professional life. For example, if we cannot motivate people around us, we cannot motivate our employees and even we cannot motivate our children in the present society. Therefore, we are not the persons to de-motivate them. Generally if we cannot appreciate anybody, we shouldn't discourage or criticize anyone. It is a corollary that there is a "Positive Side" of all incidents and of all acts and actions of every experience. Let us accept the fact that none of us is perfect. We all have space for improvement. We all need support to grow and excel in life and career.

Let us also accept that Human Resource Professionals are very poor in "Human Behaviour" and "Human Psychology." Let us understand that "One size does not fit all". Most companies have it all wrong. They don't have to motivate their employees. They have to stop de-motivating them.

REVIEW OF LITERATURE

Motivation Concepts

(1) Intrinsic and extrinsic motivation
(2) Intrinsic motivation

Intrinsic motivation comes from rewards inherent to a task or activity itself—the enjoyment of a puzzle or the love of playing basketball, for example. One is said to be intrinsically motivated when engaging in an activity "with no apparent reward except for the activity itself". This form of motivation has been studied by social and educational psychologists since the early 1970s. Research has found that it is usually associated with high educational achievement and enjoyment by students. Intrinsic motivation has been explained by Fritz Heider's attribution theory, Bandura's work on self-efficacy, and Ryan and Deci's cognitive evaluation theory.

Intrinsic Motivation and the 16 Basic Desires Theory

Stating from a studies involving more than 6,000 people, Professor Steven Reiss has proposed a theory that finds 16 basic desires that guide nearly all human behaviour.

The desires are:

(1) Acceptance, the need for approval
(2) Curiosity, the need to think
(3) Eating, the need for food
(4) Family, the need to raise children
(5) Honor, the need to be loyal to the traditional values of one's clan/ethnic group
(6) Idealism, the need for social justice
(7) Independence, the need for individuality
(8) Order, the need for organized, stable, predictable environments
(9) Physical Activity, the need for exercise
(10) Power, the need for influence of will
(11) Romance, the need for sex
(12) Saving, the need to collect
(13) Social Contact, the need for friends (peer relationships)
(14) Status, the need for social standing/importance

(15) Tranquility, the need to be safe
(16) Vengeance, the need to strike back

In this model, people differ in these basic desires. These basic desires represent intrinsic desires that directly motivate a person's behaviour, and not aimed at indirectly satisfying other desires. People may also be motivated by non-basic desires, but in this case this does not relate to deep motivation, or only as a means to achieve other basic desires.

In the earlier days many employers considered the employees as just another input into the production of goods and services. What perhaps changed this way of thinking about employees was research, referred to as the Hawthorne Studies conducted by Elton Mayo from 1924 to 1932 (Dickson, 1973). This study has found that employees are not motivated solely by money, and employee behaviour is linked to their attitudes (Dickson, 1973). The Hawthorne Studies began the human relations approach to management, whereby the needs and motivation of employees become the primary focus of managers (Bedeian, 1993).

Motivation Defined

Many contemporary authors have also defined the concept of motivation. Motivation has been defined as the psychological process that gives behaviour purpose and direction (Kreitner, 1995); a predisposition to behave in a purposive manner to achieve specific, unmet needs (Buford, Bedeian, and Lindner, 1995); an internal drive to satisfy an unsatisfied need (Higgins, 1994); and the will to achieve (Bedeian, 1993). For this paper, motivation is operationally defined as the inner force that drives individuals to accomplish personal and organisational goals.

Motivation Theories

We need to understand what motivate employees and how they are motivated. Five major approaches that have led to our understanding of motivation are Maslow's need-hierarchy theory, Herzberg's two-factor theory, Vroom's expectancy theory, Adams' equity theory, and Skinner's reinforcement theory. According to Maslow, employees have five levels of needs (Maslow, 1943): physiological, safety, social, ego, and self-actualizing. Maslow argues that lower level needs have to be satisfied before the next higher level need would motivate employees. Herzberg's work categorizes motivation into two factors: motivators and hygienes (Herzberg, Mausner, and Snyderman, 1959). Motivator or intrinsic factors, such as achievement and recognition, produce job satisfaction. Hygiene or extrinsic factors, such as pay and job security, produce job dissatisfaction. Vroom's theory is based on the belief that employee effort will lead to performance and performance will lead to rewards (Vroom, 1964). Rewards may be either positive or negative. The more positive the reward, the more likely the employee will be highly motivated. Conversely, the more negative the reward, the less likely the employee will be motivated.

Adams' theory states that employees strive for equity between themselves and other workers. Equity is achieved when the ratio of employee outcomes over inputs is equal to other employee outcomes over inputs (Adams, 1965).

Skinner's theory simply states that those employees' behaviours that lead to positive outcomes will be repeated and behaviours that lead to negative outcomes will not be repeated (Skinner, 1953). Managers should positively reinforce employee behaviours that lead to positive outcomes. Managers should negatively reinforce employee behaviour that leads to negative outcomes.

The Role of Motivation

It is very interesting to answer the question, "why do we need motivated employees?" The answer is survival (Smith, 1994). Motivated employees are needed in our rapidly changing workplaces. Motivated employees help organisations survive. Motivated employees are more productive. To be effective, managers need to understand what motivates employees within the context of the roles they perform. Of all the functions a manager performs, motivating employees are arguably the most complex. This is due, in part, to the fact that what motivates employees changes constantly (Bowen and Radhakrishna, 1991). For example, research suggests that as employees' income increases, money becomes less of a motivator (Kovach, 1987). Also, as employees get older, interesting work becomes more of a motivator.

Understanding Employee Motivation

The employees who work for your company are naturally motivated. All you need to do is to utilize their natural ability, which you can do without spending a time. That's right. No money. In fact, money can actually decrease an employee's motivation and performance. The first step in utilizing your employees' natural abilities is to eliminate your organisation's negative practices that zap away their natural motivation. The second step your organisation can take is to develop true motivators, which can spark all your employees into being motivated. By decreasing negative zapping de-motivators and by adding true motivators, you will tap into your employees' natural motivation. Your employees' natural motivation relies on the fact that all people have human desires for affiliation, achievement, and for control and power over their work. In addition, they have desires for ownership, competence, recognition, and meaning in their work. But there are several ways that management unwittingly de-motivates employees and diminishes their enthusiasm.

Many companies treat employees as disposable. At the first sign of business difficulty, employees, who are usually routinely referred to as "our greatest asset", become expendable. Employees generally receive inadequate recognition and reward: About half of the workers in our surveys report receiving little or no credit, and almost two-thirds say management is much more likely to criticize them for poor performance than praise them for good work. Management inadvertently makes it difficult for employees to do their jobs. Excessive levels of required approvals, endless paperwork, insufficient training, failure to communicate, infrequent delegation of authority, and a lack of a credible vision contribute to employees' frustration.

Clearing up Common Myths about Employee Motivation

The job of motivating employees is extremely important to managers and supervisors. But several myths persist, especially among new managers and supervisors. Before looking at what management can do to motivate employees, it's important first to clear up these common myths.

Myth 1: "I can motivate people". Not really—they have to motivate themselves. You can't motivate people anymore than you can empower them. Employees have to motivate and empower themselves. However, you can set-up an environment for motivating themselves.

Myth 2: "Money is a good motivator." Not really. Certain things like money, a nice office and job security can help people from becoming less motivated, but they usually don't help people to become more motivated. A key goal is to understand the motivation of each of your employees.

Myth 3: "Fear is a damn good motivator". Fear is a great motivator for a very short time. That's why a lot of yelling from the boss won't seem to "light a spark under employees" for a very long time.

Myth 4: "I know what motivates me, so I know what motivates my employees." Not really. Different people are motivated by different things. I may be greatly motivated by earning time away from my job to spend more time with my family. You might be motivated much more by recognition of a job well done. People are not motivated by the same things. Again, a key goal is to understand what motivates each of your employees.

Myth 5: "Increased job satisfaction means increased job performance." Research shows this isn't necessarily true at all. Increased job satisfaction does not necessarily mean increased job performance. If the goals of the organisation are not aligned with the goals of employees, then employees will not effectively work toward the mission of the organisation.

Myth 6: "I can't comprehend employee motivation—it's a science". Not true. There are some very basic steps you can take that will go a long way toward supporting your employees to motivate themselves toward increased performance in their jobs.

Principles of "Employee Motivation"

1. Motivating employees starts with motivating yourself: It's amazing how, if you hate your job, it seems like everyone else does, too. If you are very stressed out, it seems like everyone else is, too. Enthusiasm is contagious. If you're enthusiastic about your job, it's much easier for others to be, too. Also, if you're

doing a good job of taking care of yourself and your own job, you'll have much clearer perspective on how others are doing in theirs.

A great place to start learning about motivation is to start understanding your own motivation. The key to helping to motivate your employees is to understand what motivates them. So what motivates you? Consider, for example, time with family, recognition, a job well-done, service, learning, etc. How is your job configured to support your own motivation? What can you do to better motivate yourself?

2. Always work to align goals of the organisation with goals of employees: As mentioned above, employees can be all fired up about their work and be working very hard. However, if the results of their work don't contribute to the goals of the organisation, then the organisation is not any better off than if the employees were sitting on their hands—maybe worse off! Therefore, it's critical that managers and supervisors know what they want from their employees. These preferences should be worded in terms of goals for the organisation. Identifying the goals for the organisation is usually done during strategic planning. Whatever steps you take to support the motivation of your employees (various steps are suggested below), ensure that employees have strong input to identifying their goals and that these goals are aligned with the goals of the organisation. (Goals should be worded to be "SMARTER". More about this later on below.)
3. Key to supporting the motivation of your employees is to understand what motivates each of them: Different things motivate each person. Whatever steps you take to support the motivation of your employees, they should first include finding out what it is that really motivates each of your employees. You can find this out by asking them, listening to them and observing them (More about this later on below).
4. Recognize that supporting employee motivation is a process, not a task: Organisations change all the time, as do people. Indeed, it is an ongoing process to sustain an environment where employees can strongly motivate themselves. If you look at sustaining employee motivation as an ongoing process, then you'll be much more fulfilled and motivated yourself.
5. Support employee motivation by using organisational systems (for example, policies and procedures)—don't just count on good intentions: Don't just count on cultivating strong interpersonal relationships with employees to help motivate them. The nature of these relationships can change greatly, for example, during times of stress. Instead, use reliable and comprehensive systems in the workplace to help motivate

employees. For example, establish compensation systems, employee performance systems, organisational policies and procedures, etc. to support employee motivation. Also, establishing various systems and structures helps ensure clear understanding and equitable treatment of employees.

PROCESS OF EMPLOYEE MOTIVATION

(A) *Personalized Motivation*: Sullivan, a professor of management at San Francisco State University, observes that the need to identify employees' critical motivators is important because most managers are terrible at motivating their employees. When managers don't know what motivates an individual, they mistakenly assume that all workers want the same thing, or they make random guess about what motivates an individual. Both are serious errors. If we expect managers to successfully motivate their individual employees, human resources professionals must accept the responsibility of providing managers with a list of what motivates and frustrates a new or recently transferred employee. I have found that even "bad" managers, when they are educated about what excites and challenges an individual worker, can become "good" managers in as short as a month. Just ask your employees the following questions:

(a) What would you like less of?

(b) What are the elements of any job that frustrate you or inhibit your productivity?

(c) What would you like more of?

(d) What are the elements of any job that excite, challenge and motivate you to be more productive?

(e) How would you like to be managed?

(f) Why did you quit your last few jobs?

(B) *Admit to Yourself (and to an appropriate someone else), if you don't like an Employee*: Managers and supervisors are people. It's not unusual to just not like someone who works for you. That someone could, for example, look like an uncle you don't like. In this case, admit to yourself that you don't like the employee. Then talk to someone else who is appropriate to hear about your distaste for the employee, for example, a peer, your boss, your spouse, etc. Indicate to the appropriate person that you want to explore what it is that you don't like about the employee and would like to come to a clearer perception of how you can accomplish a positive working relationship with the employee. It often helps a great deal just to talk out loud about how you feel and get someone else's opinion about the situation. As noted above, if you continue to focus on what you see about employee performance, you'll go a long way toward ensuring that your treatment of employees remains fair and equitable

(C) *Have one-on-one Meetings with each Employee*: Employees are motivated more by your care and concern for them than by your attention to them. Get to know your employees, their families, their favourite foods, names of their children, etc. This can sound manipulative—and it will be if not done sincerely. However, even if you sincerely want to get to know each of your employees, it may not happen unless you intentionally set aside time to be with each of them.

(D) *Instill an Inspiring Purpose*: A critical condition for employee enthusiasm is a clear, credible, and inspiring organisational purpose, in effect, a "reason for being" that translates for workers into a "reason for being there" that goes above and beyond money.

Every manager should be able to state a strong purpose for his unit. What follows is one purpose statement we especially admire. It has been developed by a three-person benefits group in a midsize firm. Benefits are about people. It's not whether you have the forms filled in or whether the checks are written. It's whether the people are cared for when they're sick, helped when they're in trouble. Stating a mission is a powerful tool. But equally important is the manager's ability to explain and communicate to subordinates the reason behind the mission. Can the manager of stockroom workers do better than telling her staff that their mission is to keep the room stocked? Can she communicate the importance of the job, the people who are relying on the stockroom being properly maintained, both inside and outside the company? The importance for even goods that might be considered prosaic to be where they need to be when they need to be there? That manager will go a long way toward providing a sense of purpose.

(E) *Reward it when you see it*: A critical lesson for new managers and supervisors is to learn to focus on employee behaviours, not on employee personalities. Performance in the workplace should be based on behaviours toward goals, not on popularity of employees. You can get in a great deal of trouble (legally, morally and interpersonally) for focusing only on how you feel about your employees rather than on what you're seeing with your eyeballs.

(F) *Reward it soon after you see it*: This helps to reinforce the notion that you highly prefer the behaviours that you're currently seeing from your employees. Often, the shorter the time between an employee's action and your reward for the action, the clearer it is to the employee that you highly prefer that action.

(G) *Cultivate strong skills in Delegation*: Delegation includes conveying responsibility and authority to your employees so they can carry out certain tasks. However, you leave it up to your employees to decide how they will carry out the tasks. Skills in delegation can free up a great deal of time for managers and supervisors. It also allows employees to take a stronger role in their jobs, which usually means more fulfilment and motivation in their jobs, as well.

(H) *Celebrate Achievements*: This critical step is often forgotten. New managers and supervisors are often focused on a getting "a lot done." This usually means identifying and solving problems. Experienced managers come to understand that acknowledging and celebrating a solution to a problem can be every bit as important as the solution itself. Without ongoing acknowledgement of success, employees become frustrated, skeptical and even cynical about efforts in the organisation.

(I) *Promote Teamwork*: Most work requires a team effort in order to be done effectively. Research shows repeatedly that the quality of a group's efforts in areas such as problem solving is usually superior to that of individuals working on their own. In addition, most workers get a motivation boost from working in teams.

Whenever possible, managers should organize employees into self-managed teams, with the teams having authority over matters such as quality control, scheduling, and many work methods. Such teams require less management and normally result in a healthy reduction in management layers and costs.

(J) Creating teams has as much to do with Camaraderie as core Competences. A manager needs to carefully assess who works best with whom. At the same time, it is important to create the opportunity for cross-learning and diversity of ideas, methods, and approaches. Be clear with the new team about its role, how it will operate, and your expectations for its output.

(K) Let Employees hear from their Customers (Internal or External): Let employees hear customers proclaim the benefits of the efforts of the employee. For example, if the employee is working to keep internal computer systems running for other employees (internal customers) in the organisation, then have other employees express their gratitude to the employee. If an employee is providing a product or service to external customers, then bring in a customer to express their appreciation to the employee.

(L) *Implement at least the Basic Principles of Performance Management*: Good performance management includes identifying goals, measures to indicate if the goals are being met or not, ongoing attention and feedback about measures toward the goals, and corrective actions to redirect activities back toward achieving the goals when necessary. Performance management can focus on organisations, groups, and processes in the organisation and employees.

(M) *Be an Expediter for your Employees*: Incorporating a command-and-control style is a sure-fire path to de-motivation. Instead, redefine your primary role as serving as your employees' expediter: It is your job to facilitate getting their jobs done. Your reports are, in this sense, your "customers." Your role as an expediter involves a range of activities, including serving as a linchpin to other business units and managerial levels to represent their best interests and ensure your people get what they need to succeed.

(N) How do you know, beyond what's obvious, what is most important to your employees for getting their jobs done? Ask them! "Lunch and schmooze" sessions with employees are particularly helpful for doing this. And if, for whatever reason, you can't immediately address a particular need or request, be open about it and then let your workers know how you're progressing at resolving their problems. This is a great way to build trust.

(O) *Coach your employees for improvement.*

(P) A major reason so many managers do not assist subordinates in improving their performance is, simply, that they don't know how to do this without irritating or discouraging them. A few basic principles will improve this substantially. First and foremost, employees whose overall performance is satisfactory should be made aware of that. It is easier for employees to accept, and welcome, feedback for improvement if they know management is basically pleased with what they do and is helping them do it even better.

Space limitations prevent a full treatment of the subject of giving meaningful feedback, of which recognition is a central part, but these key points should be the basis of any feedback plan:

A. Performance feedback is not the same as an annual appraisal. Give actual performance feedback as close in time to the occurrence as possible. Use the formal annual appraisal to summarize the year, not surprise the worker with past wrongs.
B. Recognize that workers want to know when they have done poorly. Don't succumb to the fear of giving appropriate criticism; your workers need to know when they are not performing well. At the same time, don't forget to give positive feedback. It is, after all, your goal to create a team that warrants praise.
C. Comments concerning desired improvements should be specific, factual, unemotional, and directed at performance rather than at employees' personally. Avoid making overall evaluative remarks

(such as, "That work was shoddy") or comments about employees' personalities or motives (such as, "You've been careless"). Instead, provide specific, concrete details about what you feel needs to be improved and how.

D. Keep the feedback relevant to the employee's role. Don't let your comments wander to anything not directly tied to the tasks at hand.

E. Listen to employees for their views of problems. Employees' experience and observations often are helpful in determining how performance issues can be best dealt with, including how you can be most helpful.

F. Remember the reason for feedback--you want to improve performance, not prove your superiority. So keep it real, and focus on what is actually doable without demanding the impossible.

G. Follow-up and reinforce. Praise improvement or engage in course correction—while praising the effort—as quickly as possible.

H. Don't offer feedback about something you know nothing about. Get someone who knows the situation to look at it.

TOOLS FOR EMPLOYEE MOTIVATION

For any setup in any industry, HR works within boundary and parameters with a mix of activity involved may vary from industry to industry; the trends go like this for a HRD Head: 40% HR activity, 30% IR and 20% Admin. activity, 10% Academics (Training and Learning), Others like Safety and Security, Estate Management, Housing, Residential Accommodation, Clubs, School and so on. Since one can not singularize employee's behaviour in general which is not the same at any level, the mind composition of every employee varying to a large extent poses a big challenge before HR professional to set a uniform regulation to motivate all the employees equally. Every single employee produces different reaction match to their culture, adaptability, flexibility, organisation environment and typically their EQ, required to be used while making interpersonal relation.

In the workplace, motivation is a primary factor when it comes to getting work done. No matter how skilled the workers in any specific department are, the goals of the supervisor will not reach the desired level of success and timeliness if the proper employee motivation is not in place. Let me share with you all as how to get your employee's motivation going: Save expenses while implementing these tips!

There are some parameters that will instil in the workforce as how exactly motivations suppose to be in an organisation.

- Is employee's eagerness to get the job done a natural quality?
- Is he relied upon support? Or motivation is structurally "imposed" upon?
- Is he requiring enforcement under specific supervision?

These are the questions that deserve a solid understanding of how to proceed in order to find the answer that best fits your human resource management scenario. In any capacity, to answer these fundamental questions related to human resources is not easy; hence, the task of any human resources specialist or team of consultants becomes a bit complex.

And the very reason is that not every employee is the same. While some have a Self-Starting Approach to every job at hand, other employees may need an Extra Nudge in the right direction before results can be expected from the lot.

It has been approved by many HR specialists in India that employee motivation is proven to work in nearly every case.

- o The right stimuli are added to the mix (employees of week/ small interval).
- o The fast-acting techniques that are known to motivate employees are to be introduced - (short breaks, buzz training, pep talk).
- o Higher stimuli can be used for those who require higher levels of motivation in order to get work done of higher order by enriching job (vertical).
- o Well-administered incentive can be introduced (show the end results).
- o *Objective—Producing incentive* enhancement is for inherent motivation (Simultaneous benefits—rewards).

The results are surprising even for self-motivated and natural go-getters as they respond well to motivation techniques.

Unfortunately, when HR unknowingly applies these techniques, often it has been observed that self-motivated employees feel neglected as human resources departments focus more on those with lower levels of motivation. And as a result the outcome has been increased frustration among those who give it their all but end up feeling as if they've been given the short end of the stick in return—low attention like elder disciplined son in a family.

RESEARCH STUDY

It is common for corporate to talk of employee recognition being one of the important tools for motivation. But in actual practice it is not widely prevalent in the corporate work environment. These are the initial inferences of a survey conducted by the Ahmedabad-based Consultant for Organisational Solutions.

Commenting on the survey, says Consulting for Organisational Solutions managing partner Savita Rajendran, "Although corporate do accept the need for acknowledgement and recognition being an integral part of employee motivation, very few have the genuine conviction to implement it."

This is partly because there are a lot of power equations and cultural barriers among the top management that leads to hassles in implementing human resource initiatives that acknowledge employee commitment.

The other major challenge is ineffective reward management initiatives in the organisations, thereby hindering such programmes. The prevalence of traditional mindsets amongst the top management professionals is also another factor that leads to such initiatives not gaining widespread acceptance in the corporate environment.

Further, according to the survey, although certain corporate do have strong communication systems in acknowledging win-win performances, they are not adequately backed up with independent and challenging assignments for the professionals.

Ms Rajendran observes: "Among the major drawback identified are inhibitions regarding age and gender which are still quite dominant in several establishments."

There are no clear-cut solutions that the survey outlines to tide over such gaps in the HR system. "All one can do is to enable the decision-makers to introspect on their internal inadequacies and create self-development plans to overcome such limitations," says Ms Rajendran.

CONCLUSION

We conclude that motivated employees are crucial to a company's success—this has never been truer than today, when margins are thin and economic recovery remains elusive. It is quite interesting to note that these hard bottom-line realities may also mean that managers can't rely as much as they might have in the past on using financial incentives to drive employee engagement. But, if the company has a solid approach to talent management, a bad manager can undermine it in his unit. The most important thing is to provide employees with a sense of security, one in which they do not fear that their jobs will be in jeopardy if their performance is not perfect and one in which layoffs are considered an extreme last resort, not just another option for dealing with hard times. However, the best-applied motivation policy is universal. By creating a uniform standardized incentive-based system of rewards for job performance every employee will respond equally well and perceive motivation for high-level goals set by the management or HRD.

REFERENCES

Smith, K.L. (1990). The future of leaders in Extension. *Journal of Extension*, 28 (1) Skinner, B.F. (1953). Science and Human Behaviour. New York: Free Press Harvard Management Update, "Stop Demotivating Your Employees", Vol. 11, No. 1, January 2006.

Kovach, K.A. (1987). What motivates employees? Workers and supervisors give different answers. *Business Horizons*, 30, 58-65.

Harpaz, I. (1990). The importance of work goals: an international perspective. *Journal of International Business Studies*, 21, 75-93.

http://www.bpoindia.org

http://blogs.siliconindia.com

Deci, E. (1972), "Intrinsic Motivation, Extrinsic Reinforcement, and Inequity", *Journal of Personality and Social Psychology,* 22(1): 113-20.

Bandura, A. (1997), Self-efficacy: The exercise of control, New York: Freeman, pp. 604, ISBN 9780716726265.

Reiss, Steven (2000), Who am I: The 16 basic desires that motivate our actions and define our personalities, New York: Tarcher/Putnam, p. 288, ISBN 1-58542-045-X, http://books.google.fr/books?id=EbOjA5oAsEUC

Reiss, Steven (2004), "Multifaceted nature of intrinsic motivation: The theory of 16 basic desires", *Review of General Psychology,* 8(3): 179-193, doi:10.1037/1089-2680.8.3.179

http://www.financialexpress.com

Motivation and Organisational Commitment

P.N. KANCHANA

ABSTRACT

Motivation refers to efforts exerted toward any goal. Three key elements of motivation are efforts, organisational goals, and needs. These drives lead to a search behaviour to find particular goals that, if attained, will satisfy the need and reduce the tension...actor which increases our job satisfaction, loyalty, and growth. The author has tried to explain her view of the concept of organisational commitment and how it is attainable through motivation.

This helps to increase the organisational commitment, job involvement, job satisfaction and feels the organisation as their comfort zone.

The Drive to acquire, Drive to bond, Drive to comprehend, Drive to defend are the drives that motivates employees and the indicators of motivation are measured by engagement, satisfaction, commitment and intention to quit. The organisational levers of motivation are the reward. Managers are using different motivation for diverse workforce like flexible refers to effort exerted toward to organisational goals because our focus is on work-related behaviour. Three key elements can be seen in this definition: effort, organisational goals, and of intensity or drive. A motivated person tries hard. But high levels of effort are unlikely to lead to favourable job performance unless the effort is channeled in a direction that benefits the organisation. Therefore, we must consider the quality of the effort as well as its intensity. Effort that is directed toward, and consistent with, organisational goals is the kind of effort that we should be seeking. Finally, we will treat motivation as a need-satisfying process.

THE MOTIVATION PROCESS

A need refers to some internal state that makes certain outcomes appear attractive. An unsatisfied need creates tension that stimulates drives within an individual. These drives lead to a search behaviour to find particular goals that, if attained, will satisfy the need and reduce the tension.

MOTIVATION AND ORGANISATIONAL COMMITMENT

Organisational Commitment is highly valuable. This paper highlights the importance of understanding the meaning of organisational commitment. It is this factor which increases our job satisfaction, loyalty, growth. The author has tried to explain her view of the concept of organisational commitment and how it is attainable through motivation. Organisational commitment is vital for productivity, quality and good performance of an organisational commitment is viewed as an attitude of attachment to the organisation, which leads to particular job-related behaviours. The committed employee, for example, is less often absent, and is less likely to leave the organisation voluntarily, than are less committed employees.

The motivation helps to increase the organisational commitment, job involvement, job satisfaction. We can say that motivated employees are in a state of tension. To relieve this tension, they exert efforts. The greater the tension is, the higher is the effort level. If this effort leads to need satisfaction, it reduces tension. Because we are interested in work behaviour, this tension-reduction effort must also be directed toward organisational goals. Therefore, inherent in our definition of motivation is the requirement that the individual's needs be compatible with the organisation's goals. When the two don't match, individuals may exert high levels of effort that run counter to the interests of the organisation. Incidentally, this isn't all that unusual. Some employees regularly spend a lot of time talking with friends at work to satisfy their social need. There's a high level of effort but little being done in the way of work.

One of the most important employee motivation factor is treating people fairly and with respect. As a manager if you do not respect your employees, you will never be able to motivate them. Furthermore, they will not respect you. You can show that you respect your employees by assigning them tasks that they are best suited for. Everyone has a unique set of skills and talents. These skills and talents are a huge resource for a savvy manager. By accentuating your employees' strong points, you make them feel good, and they are motivated because they can accomplish tasks best suited for them.

MOTIVATIONAL FACTORS

Performance is considered to be a function of ability and motivation, thus:

Job performance = f(ability)(motivation)

Ability in turn depends on education, experience and training and its improvement is a slow and long process. On the other hand, motivation can be improved quickly. There are many options and an uninitiated manager may not even know where to start. As a guideline, there are broadly seven strategies for motivation:

- Positive reinforcement/high expectations
- Effective discipline and punishment
- Treating people fairly
- Satisfying employees' needs
- Setting work-related goals
- Restructuring jobs
- Base rewards on job performance

These are the basic strategies, though the mix in the final 'recipe' will vary from workplace situation to situation. Essentially, there is a gap between an individual's actual state and some desired state, and the manager tries to reduce this gap.

Motivation is, in effect, a means to reduce and manipulate this gap. It is inducing others in a specific way towards goals specifically stated by the motivator. Naturally, these goals as also the motivation system must conform to the corporate policy of the organisation. The motivational system must be tailored to the situation and to the organisation.

In one of the most elaborate studies on employee motivation, involving 31,000 men and 13,000 women, the Minneapolis Gas Company sought to determine what their potential employees desire most from a job. This study was carried out during a 20 year period from 1945 to 1965 and was quite revealing. The ratings for the various factors differed only slightly between men and women, but both groups considered security as the highest rated factor. The next three facts are advancement, type of work, and the company proud to work for.

Surprisingly, factors such as pay, benefits and working conditions are given a low rating by both groups. So after all, and contrary to common belief, money is not the prime motivator.

Using these talents wisely leads us to another set of employee motivation factors. Managers need to develop the leaders around them. Building on an individual's strengths also allows them the motivation to work on areas they are not strong in. Correctly combining tasks for employees that focus on their strengths but also challenge them to do better in their weaker areas build a great employee base. Now the employees are starting to take on more and more challenging projects with confidence. This leaves a manager to do what they need to do—manage. It also builds employee self-esteem and confidence. A confident employee is one who is easily motivated. Also, by allowing them to develop into very productive individuals you are showing respect for their talents. This in and of itself is motivating. It starts a cycle of self-motivation and confidence that continually builds upon its own momentum leads to increase in organisational commitment, employee engagement, job satisfaction and each employee feels the organisation as comfort zone. This leads to a very strong and loyal employee base. Companies with this type of management get things done.

The best advice on employee motivation factors is to start a cycle of self-confidence and motivation by developing each individual's strengths. This becomes a can-do situation for everyone. The really great thing about this, it builds positive energy within the company. Positive energy always breeds more positive energy. What better way to motivate employees than from within themselves!

Organisational Commitment and Changing Employment Relationships

Much of the research on employment relationships has viewed these relationships as falling under one of two umbrellas: contractual and relational relationships. Drawing from work on psychological contracts in organisations (MacNeil, 1985; and Rousseau, 1989), these types of relationships can be described according to the extent to which employees view their employment relationship as a long-term proposition where the relationship takes precedence over a more immediate tally of what is given by employers and employees (relational) or the extent to which the relationship is viewed as a short-term proposition, where items that form a more tangible exchange (e.g., salary) take precedence (contractual). With increasing globalization, the current trend is away from relational employment relationships where there is a mutual investment on the part of the organisation and the employee toward employment relationships that emphasize strong performance for the duration of the task rather than commitment on the part of employees (Tsui and Wu, 2005).

While this trend may be seen globally, it is especially noticeable in countries such as India that have traditionally placed a strong value on loyalty. Shah (2000) points out that "promise and fulfilment of promise have immense significance in the Indian society, as indicated in Indian mythology and religious Hindu and Islamic texts" (p. 104), and that the concept of "Gandhian Trusteeship" (p. 110) is a key factor in traditional Indian approaches to the employment relationship. This trusteeship emphasizes social justice issues and promotes organisational practices such as secure employment and an emphasis on the training and development of employees. In return, employees are expected to remain committed to the organisation.

CIRCULAR FLOW OF MOTIVATION AND ORGANISATIONAL COMMITMENT

Organisational Commitment

Organisational commitment is defined as 'the degree to which an employee identifies with a particular organisation and its goals, and wishes

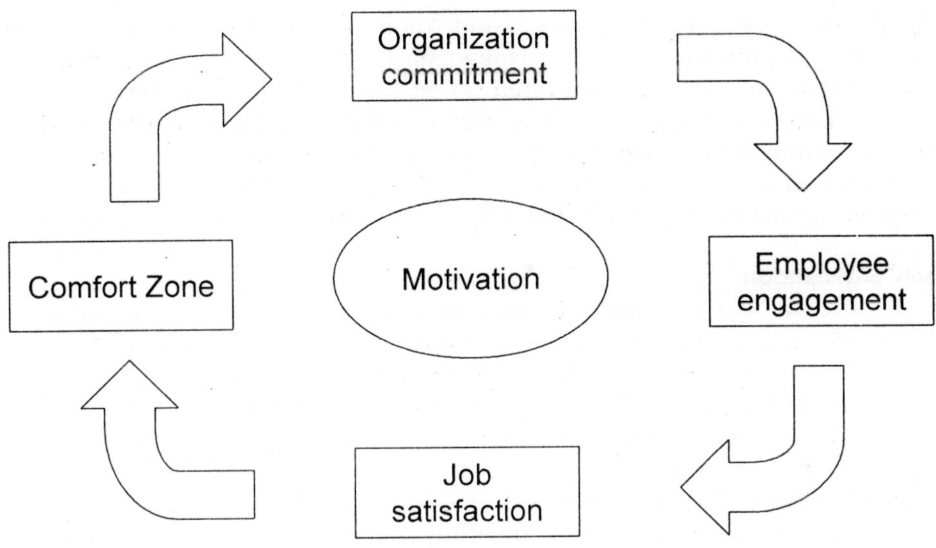

to maintain membership in the organisation' (Robbins, 2005). More or less a similar definition is proposed by Michinsky (2007) who says that it is the extent to which an employee feels a sense of allegiance to his or her employer. OC, thus, reflects a sense of loyalty and a physiological like towards one's employer. Though a strong relationship is found between satisfaction and commitment, researches have treated both of them differently and have established that commitment may lead to satisfaction. According to Muchinsky (2007), "the general pattern of results reveals that job satisfaction, job involvement and organisational commitment are substantially correlated with each other." Meyer and Allen (1991) have proposed three components to the construct of organisational commitment which include the affective, the continuance and the normative components. The affective component is the employee's emotional attachment to and identification with the organisation. The continuance component refers to commitment based on the costs that the employee associates with leaving the organisation and normative component refers to the employee's feelings of obligation to remain with the organisation.

Employee Engagement

Employee engagement, according to Tripathy (2007), refers to the level of commitment and involvement an employee has towards its organisation and values. It is defined as the degree of commitment towards the job, which an employee performs and till how long the employee remains with the organisation as a result of this commitment. It is also said to be a state wherein employees are emotionally attached, in addition to intellectually committed to the job (Hewitt Associates, 2004). To put it simply, employee engagement is developing a happy and loyal workforce, and it is a two way relationship between employees and their organisation. It is vital to business organisation as it retains and increases the performance, commitment, involvement, and dedication level of the employees.

Employee engagement has been defined as "a positive attitude held by the employee towards the organisations and its values." An engaged employee is aware of the business context, and works with colleagues to improve performance within the job for the benefit of the organisation.

Job Satisfaction

In the earlier days, it was considered that a highly satisfied workforce will facilitate organisations to achieve better level of performance, thus evolving the concept of job satisfaction (JS). Job satisfaction is defined by Locke as "a pleasurable or positive emotional state resulting from the appraisal of one's job or job experience." It is also mentioned that job satisfaction is a result of employee's perception of how well their job provides those things which they view as important. Research studies regarding JS have established conflicting results. For example, Smith *et. al.* have opined that the work itself, pay, promotion opportunities, supervision and co-workers had major influences on job satisfaction. JS is generally considered more the result or job performance than its cause. The reasoning is that high performance usually leads to rewards, such as recognition, higher pay and promotion. It is these subsequent rewards that are considered cause of job satisfaction. JS reportedly plays an important role for an organisation in term of its productivity, efficiency and employee in terms of health and well-being.

Comfort Zone

Comfort zone refers to the set of environments and behaviours with which one is comfortable, without creating a sense of risk. A person's personality can be described by his or her comfort zones. Highly successful persons may routinely step outside their comfort zones, to accomplish what they wish. A comfort zone is a type of mental conditioning that causes a person to create and operate mental boundaries that are not real. Such boundaries create an unfounded sense of security. Like inertia, a person who has established a comfort zone in a particular axis of his or her life, will tend to stay within that zone without stepping outside of it. To step outside a person's comfort zone, they must experiment with new and different behaviours, and then experience the new and different responses that then occur within his environment.

An example could be a recognized need to leave an unsatisfactory job but the fear of doing so as it would result in losing the sense of security the individual derives from the job. The sense of security the individual perceives could be attributed to the mental conditioning zone may result when the mental concept that (a) person(s) has/have about something and not congruent with one another.

The motivation helps to increase the organisational commitment, job involvement, job satisfaction and feels the organisation as their comfort zone.

ORGANISATIONAL COMMITMENT, INTELLECTUAL CAPITAL AND ORGANISATIONAL COMPETITIVENESS

Organisational commitment has received considerable attention as a result of its ability to produce desirable outcomes for organisations. High rates of employee turnover results in greater inefficiencies in organisations as they must bear the costs associated with hiring and training new employees, as well as the costs of lost productivity when experienced workers leave. This is especially true in organisations where the organisational capital is primarily intellectual, that is, where employee knowledge, skills, and abilities form the basis for the services and deliverables of the organisation, and high rates of turnover may lead to reduced productivity (Balfour and Neff, 1992) and reduced competitiveness.

The consequences of organisational commitment go beyond turnover decisions by employees. The empirical literature supports the notion that higher levels of organisational commitment result in lower turnover, but also lead to increased job effort, increased job performance, increased organisational citizenship behaviours, and improved attendance and productivity (see, for example, Meyer *et al.*, 2002; Vandenberghe *et al.*, 2002; Kwantes, 2003; and Gellatly *et al.*, 2006).

Designing Motivating Jobs

Managers should design jobs deliberately and thoughtfully reflect on the demands of the changing environment as well as the organisation's technology, skills and abilities, and preferences of its employees. When jobs are designed with those things in mind, employees are motivated to reach their full productive capabilities. The following are the ways the managers can motivating the employees.

Job Enlargement

When jobs are narrow in focus and highly specialized, motivating employees is a real challenge. Thus, many organisations have looked at other job design options. One of the earliest efforts at overcoming the drawbacks of job specialization involved the horizontal expansion of a job through increasing job scope. The number of different tasks required in a job and the frequency with which these tasks are repeated. For instance, a dental hygienist's job could be enlarged so that in addition to dental cleaning, he or she is pulling patients' files, refilling them when finished, and cleaning and storing instruments. This type of job design option is called job enlargement.

Job Enrichment

Another way to designing motivating jobs is through the vertical expansion of a job by adding planning and evaluating responsibilities is job enrichment. Job enrichment increases job depth, which is the degree of control employees have over their work. In other words, employees are empowered to assume some of the tasks typically done by their managers. Thus, the tasks in an enriched job should allow workers to do a complete activity with increased freedom, independence, and responsibility. These tasks should also provide feedback so that individuals can assess and correct their own performance. For instance, in an enriched job, dental hygienist, in addition to dental cleaning, could schedule appointments and follow-up with clients. Although job enrichment can improve the quality of work, employee motivation, and satisfaction, the research evidence on the use of job enrichment programs has been inconclusive.

Drives that Motivates Employees

Paul R. Lawrence and Nitin Nohria in their book "How Human Nature Shapes Our Choices" (2002) mention four drives that underlie Motivation:

1. *The drive to acquire*: Drive to acquire scarce goods that bolster our sense of belonging
2. *The drive to bond*: Form of connections with individuals and groups. At work the drive to bond accounts for the enormous boost in motivation when employees feel proud of belonging to the organisation.
3. *The drive to comprehend*: Satisfy our curiosity and master the world around us. Employees are motivated by jobs that challenge them and enable them to grow and learn.
4. *The drive to defend*: Protect against external threats and promote justice. We all naturally defend our property, accomplishments, our family and friends, and our ideas and beliefs against external threats.

The authors completed two major studies aimed to measure the overall motivation. The surveyed 385 employees in the financial service giant and a leading IT services firm and other 300 employees from Fortune 500 companies. The four commonly measured workplace indicators of motivation are focused:

1. *Engagement*: It represents the energy, effort, and initiative employees bring to their jobs.
2. *Satisfaction*: It reflects the extent to which they feel that the company meets their expectations at work and satisfies its implicit and explicit contracts with them
3. *Commitment*: It captures the extent to which employees engage in corporate citizenship.
4. *Intention to quit*: It is best proxy for employee turnover.

The studies show that an organisation's ability to meet the four fundamental drives explains, on average, about 60% of employees variance on motivational indicators. It is also found that certain drives influence some motivational indicators more than others. Fulfilling the drive to bond has the greatest effect on employee commitment, whereas meeting the drive to comprehend is most closely linked with employee engagement. But a company can best improve overall motivational scores by satisfying all four drives in concert.

The Organisational Levers of Motivation

The reward system: The drive to acquire is most easily satisfied by an organisational reward system—how effectively it discriminates between good and poor performers, ties rewards to performance, and gives the best people opportunities for advancement.

Organisational culture: The most effective way to fulfil the drive to bond—to engender a strong relationship—is to create a culture that promotes teamwork, collaboration, openness, and friendship.

Job design: The drive to comprehend is best addressed by designing jobs that are meaningful, interesting, and challenging.

Performance-management and resource-allocation processes: Fair, trustworthy and transparent processes for performance management and resource allocation help to meet people's drive to defend.

This table explains and matches each drive with its corresponding lever and its specific actions the company can take to make most of the tools at its disposal:

Drive	*Primary Level*	*Actions*
Acquire average	Reward System	• Sharply differentiate good performers from and poor performers • Tie rewards clearly to performance • Pay as well as your competitors
Bond	Organisational culture	1. Foster mutual reliance and friendship among co-workers 2. Value collaboration and teamwork 3. Encourage sharing of best practices
Comprehend	Job design	1. Design jobs that have distinct and important roles in the organisation 2. Design jobs that are meaningful and foster a sense of contribution to the organisation
Defend	Performance-Management and Resource-Allocation Processes	1. Increase the transparency of all processes 2. Emphasize their fairness 3. Build trust by being just and transparent in granting rewards, assignments, and other forms of recognition

Employees don't expect their superiors to be able to substantially affect company's overall reward system, culture, job design, or management systems. Managers can, for example, link rewards and performance in areas such as praise, recognition, and choice assignments. They can also allocate a bonus pool in ways that distinguish between top and bottom performers. Likely, even in a cutthroat culture that does not promote relationship, a manager can take actions that encourage team work and make jobs more meaningful and interesting. Many supervisors are regarded well by their employees precisely because they foster a highly motivating local environment, even if the organisation as a whole falls short.

Motivating a Diverse Workforce

To maximize motivation among today's diverse workforce, managers need to think in terms of flexibility. For instance, studies tell us that men place more importance on having autonomy in their jobs than do women. In contrast, the opportunity to learn, convenient and flexible work hours, and good interpersonal relations are more important to women. Managers need to recognize that what motivates a single mother with two dependent children who is working full time to support her family may be very different from the needs of a single part-time employee or an older employee who is working only to supplement his or her retirement income. Employees have different personal needs and goals that they are hoping to satisfy through their job. A diverse array of rewards is needed to motivate employees with such varied needs.

Flexible Working Schedules

Many of the so-called family-friendly benefits that organisations have implemented are a response to the varied needs of a diverse workforce. In addition, many organisations have developed flexible working schedules that recognize different needs. What are some of these types of flexible working schedules?

A *compressed workweek* is a workweek in which employees work longer hours per day but fewer days per week. The most common form is four 10-hour days (a 4-40 program). However, organisations could design whatever schedules they wanted to fit employees' needs. For example, employees at ChevronTexaco's headquarters work nine hours every Monday through Thursday, eight hours on a Friday, and zero hours the next Friday. This compressed workweek provides employees with time off for running errands, pursuing hobbies, or taking care of family problems.

Another alternative is *flexible work hours* (also popularly known as *flextime*), which is a scheduling system in which employees are required to work a specific number of hours a week but are free to vary those hours within certain limits. In a flextime schedule, there are certain common core hours when all employees are required to be on the job, but starting, ending, and lunch-hour times are flexible. Flextime is one of the most desired benefits employees want from their employers. And employers have responded, according to a survey, indicating that 57 percent of employers were offering flextime in 1999.

Another job scheduling option that can be effective in motivating a diverse workforce is *job sharing*, the practice of having two or more people split a full-time job. This type of job schedule might be attractive, for example, to individuals with school-age children or retirees, who want to work but do not want the demands and hassles of a full-time position.

Another alternative made possible by information technology is *telecommuting*. Here, employees work at home and are linked to the workplace by computer and modem. Many jobs can be done at home, and this approach might be close to the ideal job for some people because there is no commuting, the hours are flexible, there is freedom to dress as you please, and there are little or no interruptions from colleagues. However, keep in mind that not all employees embrace the idea of telecommuting. Some workers relish the informal interactions at work that satisfy their social needs as well as being a source of new ideas.

Application of Employee Motivation Theory to the Workplace

Management literature is replete with actual case histories of what does and what does not motivate people. Presented here is a tentative initial broad selection of the various practices that have been tried in order to draw lessons for the future.

'Stick' or 'Carrot' Approach

The traditional Victorian style of strict discipline and punishment has not only failed to deliver the goods, but it has also left a mood of discontent amongst the "working class".

Punishment appears to have produced negative rather than positive results and has increased the hostility between 'them' (the management) and 'us' (the workers). In contrast to this, the 'carrot' approach, involving approval, praise and recognition of effort has markedly improved the work atmosphere, leading to more productive work places and giving workers greater job satisfaction.

Manager's Motivation 'Toolkit'

The manager's main task is to develop a productive work place, with and through those he or she is in charge of. The manager should motivate his or her team, both individually and collectively so that a productive work place is maintained and developed, and at the same time employees derive satisfaction from their jobs.

This may appear somewhat contradictory, but it seems to work. The main tools in the manager's kitbag for motivating the team are:

- approval, praise and recognition
- trust, respect and high expectations
- loyalty, given that it may be received

- removing organisational barriers that stand in the way of individual and group performance (smooth business processes, systems, methods and resources—see outline team building program)
- job enrichment
- good communications
- financial incentives

These are arranged in order of importance and it is interesting to note that cash is way down the ladder of motivators. Let's look at a couple of examples taken from real life situations.

The Swedish shipbuilding company, Kockums, turned a 15 million dollar loss into a 100 million dollar profit in the course of ten years due entirely to a changed perception of the workforce brought about by better motivation. At Western Electric, there was a dramatic improvement in output after the supervisors and managers started taking greater interest in their employees.

Don't Coerce—Persuade!

Persuasion is far more powerful than coercion, just as the pen is mightier than the sword. Managers have a much better chance of success if they use persuasion rather than coercion. The former builds morale, initiative and motivation, whilst the latter quite effectively kills such qualities. The three basic components in persuasion are:

- suggest
- play on the person's sentiments
- appeal to logic

Once convinced, the person is so motivated as to deliver the 'goods'. The manager will have achieved the goal quietly, gently and with the minimum of effort. It is, in effect, an effortless achievement.

More contemporary "persuaders," used by advertising and marketing people, include the following:

- Faster talk is found to be more effective, since it is remembered better.
- Brain emits fast beta waves when a person is really interested in a particular presentation. These waves can be detected by an instrument.
- Subliminal approach using short duration presentation, whereby the message is transmitted below the level of awareness.

Can these findings be used in actual work conditions? AT&T (The American Telephone and Telegraph Co.) recognizing the importance of hidden needs, at one time succeeded in promoting long distance calls by use of the simple phrase: 'Reach out, reach out and touch someone'. Managers will need to adapt this persuasion/motivation technique to their own situation.

CONCLUSION

Motivating high levels of employee performance is an important organisational consideration. Both academic researchers and practicing managers have been trying to understand and explain employee motivation for years. The concept of employment commitment lies at the heart of any analysis of Human Resource Management. Indeed, the rationale for introducing Human Resource Management policies is to increase levels of commitment, so positive outcomes can ensue. Such is the importance of this construct. Yet, despite many studies on commitment, very little is understood of what managers mean by the term "commitment" when they evaluate performance and motivation.

Motivating and rewarding employees are one of the most important and one of the most challenging activities that managers perform. Effective managers who want their employees to put forth maximum effort recognize that they need to know how and why employees are motivated and to tailor their motivational practices to satisfy the needs and wants of those employees. Of all the resources available, the human resource is clearly the most significant, but also the most difficult to manage. Excellence can only be achieved through excellent performance of every person, rather than by the high-pitched performance of a few individuals.

CASE APPLICATION

Is This Any Way to Motivate Employees?

Click Commerce's offices are similar to other dot-com businesses—casual attire, white boards everywhere for employees to write or sketch on, and an entertainment room with three pinball machines and six Daytona 500 simulators. The company is a leading provider of business-to-business software that manufacturing companies use to manage relationships with business partners and customers. It also offers software for managing accounting, inventory, marketing, and ordering. The Chicago-based company was originally founded in 1996 as Click Interactive, Inc., but changed its name to Click Commerce in December 1999 to better reflect its focus on the business-to-business e-commerce market. CEO Michael Ferro (photo left), one of the "Top 40 Entrepreneurs Under 40," has led the company through the difficulties of an Internet start-up to a successful initial public offering of stock in June 2000. However, his approach to motivation can be described as a bit unusual because it involves taking employees out of their normal work environment and requiring them to do something completely different as a form of "punishment."

Ferro believes that an occasional kick in the pants is good for employee motivation. He has created what he calls "the penalty box" for his programmers who are burned out or who act overly cocky. In actuality, this is a temporary assignment—from a few weeks to a few months—in the company's sales department. While those chosen may see such a stint as a penalty, Ferro focuses on the positive—it gives isolated programmers new experiences and broadens their responsibilities.

The "punishment" part of the box is that all salespeople, including programmers on temporary assignment, are required to wear professional business attire at all times. For programmers who are used to wearing the more typical jeans and T-shirt, wearing suits and ties is somewhat humiliating. In addition, most programmers, who enjoy their insulated lifestyle, don't relish giving up the cloistered existence of working full-time on their computer and instead of writing software they have to call on customers. This isn't easy for people who are used to interacting with a computer and who have chosen this profession to a large degree because of the job's independence and isolation.

Although there is a stigma attached to being temporarily assigned to sales, some of the programmers do acknowledge the value of the assignment. Jim Heising (photo right), for example, admits he gained some valuable insights into customers while forced to make sales calls. Now the company's chief technology officer, Heising says that although sometimes customers' requests are far-fetched, other times they come up with great ideas that can actually be implemented.

Questions

1. Explain the advantages and disadvantages of Ferro's motivational approach using Maslow's hierarchy of needs theory, reinforcement theory, and expectancy theory.
2. If you were a Click programmer, what would you think about being assigned to the penalty box?
3. Log on to Click Commerce's Web site and find the information on Careers. Click on two of the job titles listed there and assess these jobs according to the job characteristics model.
4. At a time when most managers are encouraged to be nice to their employees, would you suggest to Ferro that he change his motivational approach? Explain your answer.

Bringing Positive Behavioural Changes in the Employees

M. Manikandan and Dr. T. Ramachandran

The term motivation derives from the Latin word "movere" meaning "to move".

INTRODUCTION

Effective employee's motivation has long been one of management's most difficult and important duties. Motivation represents "those psychological processes that cause the arousal, direction and persistence of voluntary actions that are goal-directed".

In this age, any company that wants to get ahead needs to have motivated workers. Traditional incentive programs have been based upon extrinsic motivators such as salary and benefits. Intrinsic motivation, however, is needed in order to arouse a person's passion or commitment to the job. Shared vision, leadership, teamwork, training, increased capability, and goal accomplishments are powerful motivators which can be encouraged, embedded, or "designed in" to create a high performance culture.

In this paper we analyze the motivational practices of the company: Motivation through Goal setting.

Motivation through Goal Setting

Regardless of the nature of their specific achievements, successful people tend to have one thing in common. Their lives are goal-oriented. Through goal setting, we can see how the simple behaviour of setting goals activates a powerful motivational process that leads to sustained, high performance.

GOALS

Edwin Locke, a leading authority on goal setting, defines a Goal as "What an individual is trying to accomplish; it is the object or aim of an action". The motivational effect of performance goals and goal-based reward plans has been recognized for a long time.

GOALS SETTING MODEL

Goal Setting Model

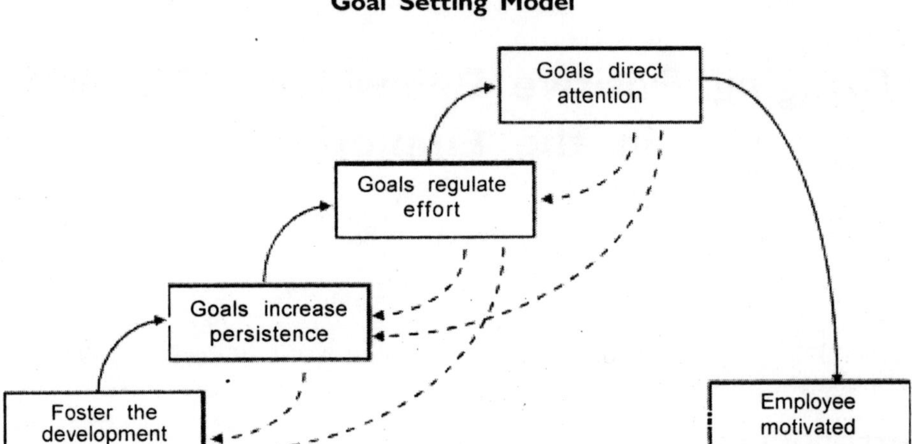

GOALS DIRECT ATTENTION

Goals direct one's attention and effort toward goal-relevant activities and away from goal -irrelevant activities. If you have a term project due in a few days, your thoughts and actions tend to revolve around completing that project. Robert Ruffolo, CEO of drug maker Wyeth, used the power of goals to direct the attention of the company's research and development operation. The company now sets the goals for how many drug compounds must be produced by each scientist. Prior to instituting this goal setting program, Wyeth averaged the development of only four drug compounds per year. Since establishing the research and development goals, the company has averaged 12 per year with no increase in revenue.

GOALS REGULATE EFFORT

Not only do goals make us selectively perceptive, they also motivate us to act. The instructor's deadline for turning in your term project would prompt you to complete it. As opposed to going out with friends, watching television, or studying for another course. Generally the level of effort expended is proportionate to the difficulty of the goal.

GOALS INCREASE PERSISTENCE

Within the context of goals setting persistence represents the effort expended on a task over an extended period of time. It takes effort to run 100 meters; it takes persistence to run a 26 mile marathon. Persistent people tend to see obstacles as challenges to be overcome rather than as reasons to fail. A difficult goal that is important to an individual is a constant reminder to keep exerting effort in the appropriate direction. Annika Sorenstam is a great example of someone who persisted at her goal of being the best female golfer in the world. She has won 69 tournaments since starting the LPGA tour in 1994.

Just like Tiger Woods, major titles and a single-season Grand Slam have become her focus. "Nobody else has done it, so I think that says it all," she said, "but I like to set high goals, I like to motivate myself. If you believe it in your mind, I think you can do it".

GOALS FOSTER THE DEVELOPMENT AND ACTION PLAN

If there is a gap between your potential and the goal you want to achieve, you face the problem of getting from here to there. For example, the person who has resolved to lose 20 pounds must develop a plan for getting from "here" to "there." Goals can help because they encourage people to develop strategies and action plans that enable them to achieve their goals. By virtue of setting a weight-reduction goal, the dieter may choose a strategy of exercising more, eating less, or some combination of the two.

LESSONS FROM GOALS SETTING

Research also consistently supports goal setting as a motivational technique. Setting performance goals increases individuals, group, and organisational performance. Further the positive effects of goal setting were found in many other countries or regions: Australia, Canada, The Caribbean, England, West Germany and Japan also. Goal setting works in different culture. Reviews of the many goals setting practices have given four practical insights:

1. Specific goals lead to greater performance.
2. Feedback enhances the effect of specific, difficult goals.
3. Participative goals, assigned goals, and self-set goals are equally effective.
4. Goals commitment and monetary incentives affect goal setting outcomes.

Understanding and predicting employee motivation continues to be one of the most popular areas in management research. Several significant workplace issues are important to look at in understanding motivation.

To maximize motivation among today's diversified work force, managers need to think in terms of being flexible. Many of the so-called family-friendly programmes and flexible working schedules that organisations have developed are a response to the varied needs of a diverse workforce.

Use goals since the literature on goal setting suggests that managers should ensure that employees have hard, specific goals and feedback on how well they are doing in pursuit of those goals.

Ensure that goals are perceived as attainable. Employees who see goals as unattainable will reduce their level of effort.

OTHER MOTIVATIONAL PRACTICES

- A compressed workweek is a workweek comprising four 10-hour days.
- Flexible work hours (also known as flextime) describes a scheduling system in which employees are required to work a number of hours a week, but are free, within limits, to vary the hours of work.
- Job sharing is the practice of having two or more people split a forty-hour-a-week job.
- Telecommuting allows employees to do their work at home through the linking by computer and modem of the employee and the office.
- Cultural differences also play a role in motivating a diverse workforce. Managers need to be aware of cultural differences in developing appropriate motivation programmes.
- Pay-for-performance programs are compensation plans that pay employees on the basis of some performance measure.
- Employee stock ownership plans (ESOPs) is a compensation program in which employees become part owners of the organisation by receiving stock as a performance incentive.
- Motivating minimum-wage employees is one of the toughest motivation challenges a manager faces. Since money typically can't be used as a reward, managers look for other types of rewards such as employee recognition programs. But managers can also look to job design and expectancy theories of motivation to find some help in motivating these workers.
- Recognize individual differences in terms of needs, attitudes, personality, and other important individual factors.
- Match people to jobs by identifying what needs are important to individuals and trying to provide jobs that allow them to fulfil those needs.
- *Individualize rewards*: Because employees have different needs, what is a reward and reinforcer to one may not work for another.

- Link rewards to performance by making rewards contingent on desired levels of performance.
- *Check the system for equity*: Employees should perceive that the rewards or outcomes are equal to the inputs given.
- *Don't ignore money*: The allocation of performance-based wage increases, piecework bonuses, and other pay incentives is important in determining employee motivation.

CONCLUSION

The essence of Motivation management is confidence, trust and satisfaction. The cost of neglecting motivation can lead to declined performance of the employee which in turn leads to reduced productivity. Performance either declines or the propensity to leave increases, when motivational levels drop. When poor-performing employees are not motivated to improve, they drag results down, reduce productivity among their team members and, worse, seldom leave because they have no place to go.

The crux of motivation management is to understand that employees are motivated by what they believe is going to happen, not by what managers' promise will happen. Managers can motivate employees by setting in motion the three conditions required for motivation—confidence, trust and satisfaction—and by creating an environment that reinforces those conditions.

Managers also cannot assume that each employee will be satisfied if the three "big outcomes"—money, advancement and job security—are fulfilled. Another outcome, such as praise, recognition, openness or honesty, may be more of a motivating factor to some employees. Another interesting point is that when the work itself is satisfying, employees tend to be very forgiving when there is a shortfall in rewards. The reason is that employees are getting something that is highly prized by most people in today's work environment—enjoyment from their work.

REFERENCES

M. Haire, E.E. Ghiselli, and L.W. Porter, Managerial thinking : An International Study, Wiley, New York, 1966.

Banerjee, Abhijit V., 1992, A simple model of herd behaviour. *The Quarterly Journal of Economics*, 107(3), 797-817.

David Whitsett, "Where are your Enriched Jobs?", *Harvard Business Review*, January-February 1975, pp. 74-80.

The World of Motivation

H. MUTHU GANESH

INTRODUCTION

Motivational practices in the organisation have become one of the important and mostly seen topics because of the hectic recession we have faced after three decades. Due to this recession both the employee and employer are affected. The employee is affected mainly by depression and stress which lead to the decline in productivity which in turn affects the employer.

Now, to compensate this, extra motivational support is given by the organisation. Companies mainly focus on bringing various motivational theories to satisfy the employees and increase productivity.

Motivation is very important to all decisions you have to make. Without the ability to define motivation and how you can make it work for you, your life will be an endless drama going around in circles.

When there is motivation for the employees in a firm, they become satisfied and hence, productivity, revenue and profit of the organisation also increase, attracting investors and shareholders towards them.

In the current situation, the overall economy has faced a great slowdown and the many companies' revenue and profit have gone down. To balance the slowdown and to survive in the economy, companies are mainly following the cost cutting method.

Directly affected, due to recession, are investors and shareholders. Many industries announced salary reduction, long leave for their employees and permanent job loss. In the current situation, we can't expect promotion and increments. Also money circulation has got reduced and the general business has realized the slowdown. To balance this situation in India, RBI has increased Liquidity by reducing CRR 5%, SLR 24% and REPO 4.7%, and Reverse REPO 3.25%.

Even though the government is taking corrective measures, the public (employee) are depressed and stressed. The employees also face stress-related problems due to over load in their job, i.e., an employee is utilized to do multiple works and, facilities like food allowance and travel allowance are either reduced or waived-off. When the employee is affected by stress, his health too becomes worse and which in turn affects the productivity of the company. Hence, motivation is indispensable to the survival any organisation.

By formal and informal communication with the employees, the company can make them understand the present situation of the organisation and the economic status of the country, and the employees themselves will involve in cost reduction in company activities.

The company is offering more in house training to their employees to improve their personality, passion and balanced working culture. The employees will be revealed from stress, productivity will be increased and the firm can overcome the present environmental situation.

Negative and positive motivational forces could include coercion, desire, fear, influence and need. Depending on how coercion, fear and influence are framed, they could be either negative or positive forces that act as actuators. For instance, a fear (negative force) of bodily injury could be a motivation to implement the use of safety equipment (positive force).

Companies offer basic pay scale instead of job termination. The employee will increase his productivity through part-time work or through self.

Organisation is changing its structure. Some positions are closed and the employee in that position is redirected to other position, which may create stress to the employee but later this helps the organisation to improve its productivity and revenue. Simultaneously the employee's growth too will be improved.

Basically, in order to keep employees motivated, 7 strategies that can be adopted

Providing positive reinforcements for the tasks accomplished and setting higher goals to be achieved—

- Setting down certain effective rules and regulations to be followed in the office.
- Seeing that fair rules are set in the office.
- Looking into employees' needs and seeing that they are comfortable in their work environment.
- There should be work-related goals set from time to time.
- There should be regular appraisals and platforms where employees can share their job experiences.
- There should be consistency and constancy on the job rewarding and incentives.

Experience turns Storm into Lift

Do you know that an eagle knows when a storm is approaching long before it breaks?

The eagle will fly to some high spot and wait for the winds to come. When the storm hits, it sets its wings so that the wind will pick it up and lift itself above the storm. While the storm rages below, the eagle is soaring above it.

The eagle does not escape the storm. It simply uses the storm to lift itself higher. It rises on the winds that bring the storm.

When the storms of life come upon us—and all of us will experience them—we can rise above them by setting our minds and our belief toward God. The storms do not have to overcome us. We can allow God's power to lift us above them.

God enables us to ride the winds of the storm that bring sickness, tragedy, failure and disappointment in our lives. We can soar above the storm.

Remember, it is not the burdens of life that weigh us down; it is how we handle them.

—Alexander Fleming

His name was Fleming, and he was a poor Scottish farmer. One day, while trying to eke out a living for his family, he heard a cry for help coming from a nearby bog. He dropped his tools and ran to the bog. There, mired to his waist in black muck, was a terrified boy, screaming and struggling to free himself. Farmer Fleming saved the lad from what could have been a slow and terrifying death.

The next day, a fancy carriage pulled up to the Scotsman's sparse surroundings. An elegantly dressed nobleman stepped out and introduced himself as the father of the boy Farmer Fleming had saved.

"I want to repay you," said the nobleman. "You saved my son's life."

"No, I can't accept payment for what I did," the Scottish farmer replied, waving off the offer. At that moment, the farmer's own son came to the door of the family hovel.

"Is that your son?," the nobleman asked. "Yes," the farmer replied proudly.

"I'll make you a deal. Let me take him and give him a good education.

If the lad is anything like his father, he'll grow to a man you can be proud of."

And that he did. In time, Farmer Fleming's son graduated from St. Mary's Hospital Medical School in London, and went on to become known throughout the world as the noted Sir Alexander Fleming, the discoverer of Penicillin. Years afterward, the nobleman's son was stricken with pneumonia.

What saved him? Penicillin. The name of the nobleman? Lord Randolph Churchill.

His son's name? Sir Winston Churchill.

Someone once said, "What goes around comes around."

Many people work all their lives and dislike what they do for a living. In fact, I was astounded by a statistic in a USA Today survey that said 53 percent of people in the American workplace are unhappy with their jobs. It is amazing that the majority of people don't like their jobs. How can you be productive and dedicated to something you don't like to do? Loving what you do is one of the most important keys to living a "true and real" life.

What Doesn't Motivate: Money

We all need money to support our families and ourselves. It's definitely an incentive. But compensation, which includes pay and benefits, doesn't motivate; it normally activates employees to do the minimum that is required in their job descriptions.

Competition: Whether in the form of sales contests, piecework incentives, or close supervision, competitive methods may seem to increase motivation and productivity. The perception is that they can do for a little while anyway. The down side is that even with this perceived increase in motivation and productivity, the desire of the individual to engage in the activity for its own sake is depleted. You see, with intrinsic motivation, the reward is the activity itself!

Recognition: Praise and rewards are excellent ways to say, "The Job is well done." They are necessary in a consistent way for employees to gauge their performance, but should not be used as motivator. Such contingent use of rewards and praise makes employees wonder what your motives may be. In other words, the employee says, "Now what does she want from me?"

Disciplinary Action: Negative feedback can be disastrous, if employees are made to feel incompetent and controlled. While we cannot ignore poor performance, we can be autonomy--supportive in our manner of approach. This simply means that we try to see things from the employee's perception and we offer an opportunity for self-direction.

What Does Motivate?

Since intrinsic motivation is the key to an employee's performance and fulfilment on the job, create an environment where intrinsic motivation can flourish! Here's how: Make sure employees have the expertise and tools they need to be, and feel competent to do the job entrusted to them. This may be in the form of physical tools, office equipment, skills training, or certain communication strategies. Seek to understand their point of view by trying to see things from the employee perspective. Don't know what it is? Ask them. Conduct an anonymous survey if need be. Talk to your customers, too.

Allow employees to make their own choices. Let them choose the ways and methods to get the results you are looking for. Let them have a say in how things get done and what the outcome is expected to be. Be responsive to employees. Show employees that you see them as human beings with a set of personal values and principles that they bring to the job.

Let them discover their own authenticity, which in turn leads them to act out of self-direction (autonomy). Assist them in their search to discover their destinies, both on the job and off, and you will have employees realizing personal fulfilment. Then, explore the ways that employees values, principles and destiny line up (align) with those of your company—and wow! Synergy!

Investing in employees will provide high returns in ways you will see, hear, and feel, including increased productivity and innovation, creative problem-solving, reduced turnover and lower absenteeism.

Motivational Thoughts

Challenges can be viewed in two different ways, either as problems or as gateways.

"There exist limitless opportunities in every industry. Where there is an open mind, there will always be a frontier"—(Charles Kettering).

"Never believe what the lines of your hand predict about your future because people who don't have hands also have a future. Believe in yourself"—(Author unknown).

"Don't see others as doing better than you. Beat your own records daily because success is a fight between you and yourself"—(Mohammad Monish).

References

www.personal-development-course.com
www.selfgrowth.com
www.evancarmichael.com
www.howtomotivateemployeesnow.com
www.timesofindia.com

CHAPTER

20

Employee Motivation and Organisational Environment

B. Poongodi

THE PREFACE

"Motivation is defined as an urge in an individual to perform goal-directed behaviour."

Motivation practice and theory are difficult subjects, touching on several disciplines. In spite of enormous research, basic as well as applied, the subject of motivation is not clearly understood and more often than not poorly practiced. The job of a manager is to get things done through employees. The manager should be able to motivate employees. To understand motivation one must understand human nature itself. And there lies the problem! Happy workers are productive employees has been a part of our organisational thinking for so long that many just take for granted that it has to be true. It started with managers beginning their efforts of making their employees happier by engaging in practices such as *laissez-faire* leadership, granting and expanding employee benefits, improving working conditions, and adding events such as company picnics, seniority based award events, and other gatherings. These were paternalistic practices and they were based on findings that hadn't withstood the tests of time. Productive workers do seem to be happier though so perhaps that is where the confusion is coming from. Simply put, this means that productivity leads to satisfaction and happiness, not the other way around. People who do a good job tend to feel intrinsically good about it. Productive employees tend to get more recognition for a job well done, more pay raises, and more opportunities for promotion and career development.

MANAGEMENT'S ROLE IN MOTIVATION

Managers apply the appropriate (to their workplaces) mix of theories in a common sense approach that engages the needs and aspirations of the people who they seek to motivate.

The intention is to provide a resource-set on how such variables can be viewed and approached in terms of improving those business processes thereby improving the work productivity that are impacted on or by employees.

Following is a conceptual model of the Relationship between productivity and employee motivation.

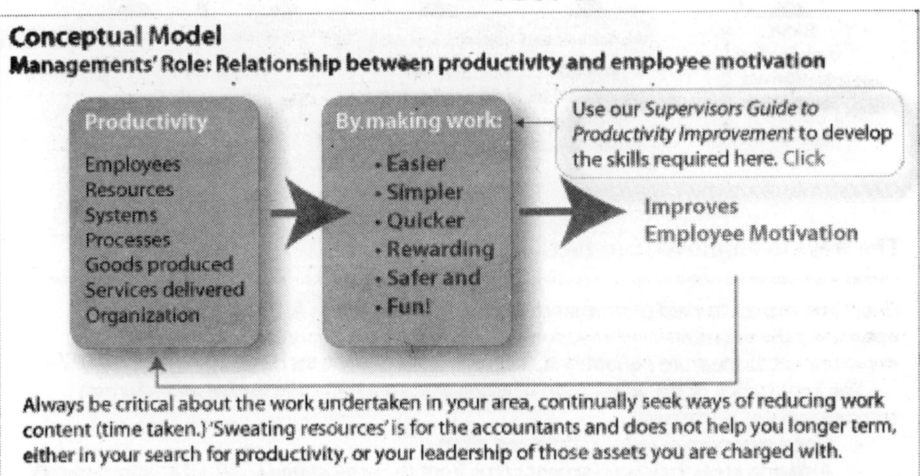

Human nature can be very simple, yet very complex too. An understanding and appreciation of this is a prerequisite to effective employee motivation in the workplace and therefore effective management and leadership. These articles on motivation theory and practice concentrate on various theories regarding human nature in general and motivation in particular. Included are articles on the practical aspects of motivation in the workplace and the research that has been undertaken in this field, notably by Douglas McGregor (theory y), Frederick Herzberg (two factor motivation hygiene theory) Abraham Maslow (theory z, hierarchy of needs), Elton Mayo (Hawthorne Experiments) Chris Argyris Rensis Likert and David McClelland (achievement motivation.)

The Need to Study and Apply the Principles of Employee Motivation

Quite apart from the benefit and moral value of an altruistic approach to treating colleagues as human beings and respecting human dignity in all its forms, research and observations show that well motivated employees are more productive and creative. The inverse also holds true. The schematic below indicates the potential contribution the practical application of the principles this paper has on reducing work content in the organisation.

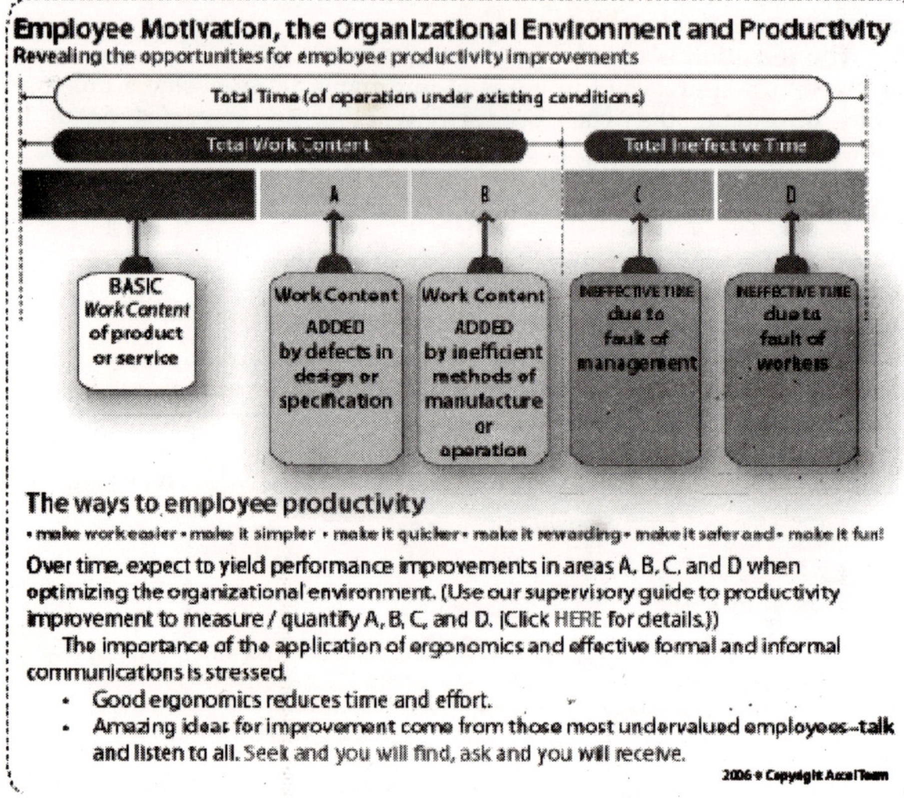

Motivation is the Key to Performance Improvement

There is an old saying you can take a horse to the water but you cannot force it to drink; it will drink only if it's thirsty—so with people. They will do what they want to do or otherwise motivated to do. Whether it is to excel on the workshop floor or in the 'ivory tower' they must be motivated or driven to it, either by themselves or through external stimulus.

Are they born with the self-motivation or drive?

Yes and No.

If no, they can be motivated, for motivation is a skill which can and must be learnt. This is essential for any business to survive and succeed. Performance is considered to be a function of ability and motivation, thus:

Job performance = f(ability)(motivation)

Ability in turn depends on education, experience and training and its improvement is a slow and long process. On the other hand motivation can be improved quickly. There are many options and an uninitiated manager may not even know where to start.

As a guideline, there are broadly seven strategies for motivation.

1. Positive reinforcement/high expectations
2. Effective discipline and punishment
3. Treating people fairly
4. Satisfying employees needs
5. Setting work-related goals
6. Restructuring jobs
7. Base rewards on job performance

These are the basic strategies, though the mix in the final 'recipe' will vary from workplace situation to situation. Essentially, there is a gap between an individuals actual state and some desired state and the manager tries to reduce this gap. Motivation is, in effect, a means to reduce and manipulate this gap. It is inducing others in a specific way towards goals specifically stated by the motivator. Naturally, these goals as also the motivation system must conform to the corporate policy of the organisation. The motivational system must be tailored to the situation and to the organisation.

In one of the most elaborate studies on employee motivation, involving 31,000 men and 13,000 women, the Minneapolis Gas Company sought to determine what their potential employees desire most from a job. This study was carried out during a 20 year period from 1945 to 1965 and was quite revealing. The ratings for the various factors differed only slightly between men and women, but both groups considered security as the highest rated factor. The next three factors were:

1. advancement
2. type of work
3. company-proud to work for

Surprisingly, factors such as pay, benefits and working conditions were given a low rating by both groups. So after all, and contrary to common belief, money is not the prime motivator. (Though this should not be regarded as a signal to reward employees poorly or unfairly.)

CONCLUSION

Motivation therefore, though a dominant intrinsic urge in an individual, the leader of the team can guide the ways and means by which the followers can satisfy their needs. It is obviously difficult to motivate an individual since he is guided by expressed motivation or unconscious motivation and multiplicity of motivational sequences. It is easy to introduce a team motivation or group motivation where the individual idiosyncrasy looses importance and the group goal becomes the target. It is then not motivation per se but a group morale - an "espirit de corps", i.e. a sense of group activity with desire for high achievement of the group goal where an individual can comfortably ignore his personal goals or needs. Such morale is mostly psychological in nature and not physiological. A leader's job is, therefore, to inculcate the extirpation of the group morale if he proposes to achieve the target through his follows where equal weight is given to performance of task and welfare of the followers, a stage of suspended pendulum or middle of the road method.

CHAPTER

21

Managing Global Organisations—Issues, Challenges, and Strategies

DR. N.R.V. PRABHU AND DR. P. KAMESWARA RAO

ABSTRACT

Sourcing and outsourcing have become common practices all over the world. Doing business globally is no more a distant dream but a reality that can not be neglected even by small size enterprises if they have to survive the intense competition in almost all segments of businesses. Being global however does not mean just doing business abroad (Rhinesmith). In a true Global Company there is harmony between different cultures and resources and materials move seamlessly across different countries (Zinnov). What really distinguishes truly global organisations? Are they different from local organisations? The paper takes a critical strategic look at these aspects and suggests strategies to tackle the challenges.

Keywords: Global Sourcing, Culture, Harmony, Strategies, Culture Sensitivity

1. INTRODUCTION

Sourcing and outsourcing of business processes is now a common practice in almost all the business segments. This has made present day businesses Global in nature with the operations spread all over the world and organisations that are truly multinational. Managing such organisations is not a simple task and it demands its own strategies and policies. There are, hence, many issues and questions which need serious considerations in the management of such organisations. Being global however does not mean just doing business abroad (Rhinesmith). In a true Global company there is harmony between different cultures and resources and materials move seamlessly across different countries (Zinnov). So, the real issues in management of such organisations essentially are of two types, viz.: (a) Issues of Strategic nature, and (b) Issues of Cultural nature. We can also say that the issues are of two types: hard issues and soft issues. It would. however, be too simplistic to assume that the division is so clear cut and there could be issues of more complex nature which not only call for a different approach but also are of nature which could not necessarily be defined by the above mentioned typology. As defined by Ansoff Strategy is more about decision-making than anything else (Ansoff I., 1988). Again if one considers other approaches to strategy as that of Henry Mintzberg than it is not just decision-making alone, but also about the pattern, position and other P's as given by him. One may argue that it is simply the obsession with P's that has influenced Mintzberg to take this view of Strategy but the question remains and that is whether the definitions hold true even when one is dealing at not just local level but on much large scale of Global level. Then again is the competitive view of Strategy as given by M. Porter and its relevance at managing of Global organisations (Porter, M., 1994). Porter also gives his model of management of Global organisations based on his competitive advantage theory. As is evident managing of strategy itself would first need clear definition of what is intended by the concept.

As regards to culture there seems to be divided opinion on what exactly constitutes 'culture' and its being such a soft issue there are far too many issues that fall under the definition of what constitutes really the culture of an organisation. The diversity in life styles, way of thinking, national character, religion and many other factors play an important role in deciding the cultural character of an organisation.

There are hundreds of national and regional cultures that affect the style of doing business at Global level. R.D. Lewis (When Cultures Collide: Managing Successfully Across Cultures, 2000) and C.M. Hampden *et al* (Building Cross Cultural Competence, 2000), have dwelt upon these issues in detail.

2. GLOBAL SOURCING AS A STRATEGY

In order to remain competitive organisations need to out source a no. of their products and services offshore. The earlier make or buy choice now has one more dimension and that is whether to buy locally or globally and whether to make it locally or out source it to offshore production units. Ricardian concept has been fully stretched and no company would like to involve in activities that are not worth engaging in from the point of value addition. The same stands true for services too where companies would only like to retain those services which call for real worth value addition by them. Rest of the functions is being shifted to countries like India, Philippines, China, and Malaysia, etc. One of the researches (Forrester) in the U.S.A. predicts the migration of 3.3 million service and knowledge-based jobs overseas by the year 2015, 70% of them to India alone.

Another trend that is forcing the world organisations to adopt a global outsourcing approach is the complete replacement of national economies by global economies with politics relegated to a second position. As pointed out by Robert Rich, a former Harvard Professor, in his book 'The Work of Nations', "We are all living through a transformation that will rearrange the politics and economics of the coming century". As a matter of fact the most of the companies today must resort to the strategy of being, 'global', i.e. thinking globally and acting locally.

The trend of outsourcing has had an impact on the value chain of an organisation and today it may stretch over a no. countries or regions. This involves managing a multinational, multilingual, and more crucial, multicultural organisational structure. Without doubt this calls for a high degree of specialization in managing the highly complex set of demands of such organisations. Outsourcing as a strategy as such involves many issues which are not just strategic in nature but also are behavioural, philosophical and more important, psychological in nature.

Outsourcing as a strategy as such must take care of these complex issues if efficiency and effectiveness are to be achieved in such organisations. We can identify following main issues of strategic nature in the management of such organisations:

(a) Issues and Challenges pertaining to Global Strategy and Structure
(b) Issues and Challenges pertaining to Global Business management
(c) Issues and Challenges pertaining to Global People management
(d) Issues and Challenges pertaining to Global Self-Management

3. ISSUES AND CHALLENGES OF GLOBAL STRATEGY AND STRUCTURES

Global strategy definition—Effective global strategy can only be designed by a thorough understanding of the environment in which the business is proposed to be carried out. Global Macro environment is extremely complex and too volatile and hence will need a team of experts on many countries and regions of the world. A geographic classification of world markets is the easiest but not necessarily the best way to define world markets for environmental analysis. The world market can be defined geographically into following categories:

(a) North American and Canadian markets
(b) European and Scandinavian markets
(c) Middle East and Pan Islamic markets
(d) Russian and other related countries' markets
(e) Asian and South Asian markets
(f) Chinese markets

(g) Japanese and far-east markets
(h) Australian and island markets
(i) African markets
(j) South American markets

This list off course can be made more elaborate and in no way is exhaustive but a suggestive effort for the sake of ease of understanding. A truly global organisation then will need experts in these geographic areas who have a thorough understanding of the geo-climatic, economic and socio-cultural peculiarities of these regions and of the customers therein. In addition to these, strategic analysis based on regional trade blocks will have to be considered too. Some of the major such blocks are, NAFTA, SAFTA, ASEAN, EUROPEAN Common markets, etc.

While basic strategies of competence may hold true for all these world regions yet the way they are implemented will require a more thorough analysis of the various cultural and other religio-political aspects that differentiate these regions. It is beyond the scope of this paper to go into the detailed strategic issues of each of these regions and their impact on business as that specifically will be the job assigned to the business experts on these regions. Books and theories may appear on these very issues giving guidelines on these strategic and other issues specific to these regions. This is not to say that presently such literature does not exist but from management specialization point of view the next generation of managers may have to have such specific specializations in view of the Global nature of present day businesses.

Competitive Advantage—the issue of gaining competitive advantage has been dealt in detail by M. Porter in his book 'Competitive Advantage of Nations'. As per Porter, there are four attributes of a nation that contribute to create national competitive advantage in International markets viz. Factor conditions, demand conditions, related and supporting industries, and firm strategy, structure and rivalry. In a Global strategic perspective a company will have to analyze the various competencies of a nation based on these factors and study the national 'diamond' (a term used by Porter to refer to the basic four determinants as a system forming four corners of a diamond when represented schematically). In evolving a global competitive strategy the choice of a region or nation for a particular segment or industry will be the outcome of the strategic analysis of that nation from these factorial conditions. A company then has the following strategic alternatives to consider and select from:

(a) Exporting—In a truly globalized environment, exports need to be global too, to include sourcing of finance, material and managerial inputs based purely on business considerations. For a truly global company national identities have only strategic business meaning and nothing else. A company will have to decide its exporting strategy with a view to increase its export

earnings in three areas viz.—
(i) Value added exports, (ii) increase the quantity of exports, and (iii) export new products.

(b) Foreign investment—In order to have a physical presence and the feel of the market global companies must resort to offshore investments. These are essential from the point of view of cost advantage, trade barriers and the demand for the local content by being a local producer in that country. Many Indian companies now have started offshore production, assembly, as well trading activities in a big way.

(c) Mergers, acquisitions and Joint ventures—these are the main strategic tools for a company to expand its business overseas and becoming global. The recent acquisition of foreign companies by such Indian companies as the Tata group, the Reliance group, the U.B. group is only indicative of their coming of age and becoming truly global. Similarly mergers and Joint ventures too are strategically necessary measures for a company to expand offshore.

Structural issues of global companies are mainly governed by the strategy adopted and must stick to the old dictum 'structure follows strategy'. Requirements of the business segment, nature and character of the local and global market in question will also govern the type of structure the company should adopt. Strategic Business Units of course is a choice considering the need for flexibility, quick deployment and re-structuring capabilities.

The following figure highlights a few essential differences between global and non-global organisation structures—

Non-Global Global

Non-Global		Global
Centralization	Hierarchy of Authority	Decentralization
Narrow	Division of Labor	Wide
Precise	Span of Control	Open

Source: Zinnov LLC, 2006, 'Global Organisations: An Analysis', article on internet).

As can be seen, Global Organisations have a distinct set of needs in terms of structure which are completely different from the traditional local or non-global organisations.

4. ISSUES OF AND CHALLENGES OF GLOBAL BUSINESS MANAGEMENT

Doing business on a global level again needs different approaches compared to those of non-global businesses. A new class of management thinkers is emerging who view the global business strategies in new light altogether. The traditional view of business management considers beating the competition as the main ideological basis of all business whether global or non-global. However, this style of business is considered by many as no longer effective due to a number of reasons. Some of these are as below:

(a) Over crowded industries—Most of the industries have too many players vying for the market share, thus reducing the returns and making entry and survival both extremely difficult.
(b) Due to proliferation of various brands at global level, differentiation is becoming quite difficult.
(c) With trade barriers between nations and regions being dismantled, and with instant availability of information regarding products and prices, even niche markets are disappearing.
(d) Due to accelerated technological advances, industrial productivity has increased multifold resulting in unprecedented array of products and services. The result is supply far exceeds demand in a number of industries.
(e) Population decline in developed nations/markets has resulted in stagnant demands in these markets, thus reducing demand in these parts.

Result of all these changes is that—

(a) There is accelerated commoditization of product/services world-wide,
(b) Price wars have increased, and
(c) Profit margins have further shrunk.

What all of this means is that it is becoming exceedingly difficult for global companies to do business based on established norms and practices of business? This was probably first spelt out by Tom Peters in his path breaking book, 'Liberation Management', in which he went to the extent of calling the present day business environment 'crazy' and thus called for 'crazy' strategies to deal with them. More recently authors, W.Chan Kim and Renee Mauborgne in their book, 'Blue Ocean Strategies'. (Kim and Mauborgne, 2005), highlight many of these points and call for doing business with what they term as 'Blue Ocean strategies'. They term the old methods as Red Ocean Strategic which they feel is outdated. In their case for Blue Ocean Strategies, they propose 'Value Innovation' and not 'Competitive benchmarking' as the main strategic logic of doing business. The Blue Ocean philosophy can be stated thus, 'Focus not on beating the competition but on making the competition irrelevant by creating a leap in value for buyers and your company'.

As the things stand today, Value creation which may be incremental is not enough, but Value innovation is the necessity where the value is added in quantum leap. The two elements which allow this leap in value are cost minimization and value maximization thus creating value innovation.

Global companies, hence, need to be both cost effective as well as value effective. Premium quality delivered at minimal cost is the new success mantra in doing global business and any company which can not do this may as well quit and be satisfied to be a local player if at all there is any such category of business.

5. ISSUES AND CHALLENGES OF PEOPLE MANAGEMENT

The present trend in global business is that of migration of jobs and services overseas and as predicted by Forrester Research in the U.S., from U.S. alone more than 3.3 million service and knowledge-based jobs will be outsourced 70% of them to India by the year 2015. In addition to the trend of outsourcing at the workplace too, more diversity in terms of nationality, ethnic and cultural factors, and styles of working are the major changes that are already evident and will be more so, in future. Global businesses need professionals with different backgrounds, cultures, styles and motivations. All this will increase the possibility of increased misunderstandings and more serious cultural blunders.

In case of countries like India which already have large diversity in all these aspects in the domestic businesses addition of global diversity will only lead to a more complex work place management.

Most of the issues in People management are really issues in Cultural diversity and its management in global corporate. Global companies need to develop and manage a right global culture. Global culture can be defined as 'a worldwide system of shared goals, values, and behaviours'. A truly global and diversified company needs to develop a right corporate culture for its businesses. Zinnov *et. al.* define a nation's culture as consisting of—

(a) *Material culture*—Understanding the inventions, scientific achievements, Entrepreneurship.
(b) *Legal factors*—Common laws and regulations, intellectual property laws, anti-trust regulations.
(c) *Language*—spoken, written, official languages.
(d) *Social set-up*—Understanding the religion, social strata (social set-up), belief systems, sacred objects, type of prayers, taboos, religious holidays, social interests.
(e) *Political environment*—Knowing the ideologies, Nationalism, Sovereignty, and the political risks involved.
(f) *Education and values*—Understanding the Educational system (formal and non-formal) and the values, attitude to time, perfection, etc.

Success or failure of Global Company depends as much on building a truly global corporate culture as on following sound strategies. Culture and its related issues are of soft nature and more difficult to implement than the hard issues of strategy and structure. Many years ago Tom Peters and others working in Mackinsey, while designing their world famous 7 S's model, made it amply clear the importance of such soft factors as style, shared values, etc. in shaping the strategy of a company. Later Hickman and Silva (C. Hickman and Silva, M., 'Creating Excellence') highlighted the role played by corporate culture in success or failure of a company's strategy. In case of global companies, this aspect assumes even more importance as there are a number of cultures to understand depending on the country of operation and unless there is a harmonious fusion of the various cultures involved, the company can not implement any strategy successfully.

Building Global Corporate Culture needs constant and on going efforts. It is not a one time task. Some of the key elements in this task are:

(a) A clear Global vision that is shared by all the cultural and national diverse groups of the company employees. This vision should be able to inspire these diverse groups.
(b) Proper training and sensitizing of the human resources—it is imperative to impart carefully designed workshops and interactive training sessions where managers can express their concerns and opinions and are educated about the global vision and their responsibility in spreading this.
(c) Cultural integration and acceptance of the global strategy and other programs.
(d) There should be a healthy respect and regard for diverse views and decision-making should be decentralized and not done from one country alone.
(e) Movement of resources particularly, human resources across the borders to different locations should be encouraged to create a sense of real global belonging with tolerance and understanding of diverse cultures and work styles.
(f) In the end a completely transparent performance reward and appreciation system will go a long way in ensuring faith and confidence amongst the employees.

Leadership issues in global companies—Indeed to manage truly global teams there would be requirement of specially trained team leaders. John Heller elaborates the qualities required of such leaders (Heller, 'Criteria for Selecting International Mangers'). "Ideally, it seems he (she) should have the stamina of an Olympic Swimmer, the mental agility of an Einstein, the conversation skills of a Professor of Languages, the detachment of a judge, the tact of a diplomat, and the perseverance of an Egyptian pyramid builder—and if he is going to measure up to the demands of living and working in a foreign country, he should have a feeling of culture, his moral judgment should not be rigid and he should show no signs of prejudice". This may sound to be truly a tall order indeed! Yet, at the bare minimum a global manager must have is the clear understanding that people are not the same all over.

Effective management of global companies hence is a balance of the hard issues of strategy and structure along with soft issues of culture and people management.

World cultures, according to Richard Lewis (when Cultures Collide: Managing Successfully across Cultures, 2000), can be divided into three groups viz.—

(a) *Linear-active*—These are the task oriented planners such as the Germans, Swedes, Swiss Americans and the Dutch. These people like to concentrate on one thing at a time and are more time conscious.
(b) *Multi-active*—These are people more focused on interactions and dialogues, such as the Italians, French, Spanish, Mexicans, Portuguese and Arabs. They are not time conscious and meetings may run long. Relationships are valued more than anything else.
(c) *Re-active*—These are the more introverted cultures, respect-oriented and value listening more. They are the Japanese, Chinese, Finns and the South-east Asians.

Each of these groups calls for specific ways of doing business with them and any ignorance of their cultural traits can spell disaster. Leadership Status and time are viewed differently by different cultural groups as given below:

Time Consciousness—Anglo-Saxons Germanic and Scandinavian culture value time and are time dominated. Asian cultures view time as cyclic needing due course to unfold. The Japanese value properness, tradition and respect more than time and could be time consuming in their tasks.

Leadership styles—There are two dominant styles viz. Task and Network orientation. A task-oriented leader is more concerned about, solving problems, task management, and efficiency. A Network-oriented leader on the other hand is more concerned about soft issues such as motivation, hierarchy, status, etc.

Traits—American managers can be assertive, aggressive, goal oriented and quick in decision-making. German and British managers value, tradition, punctuality, orderliness and tend to be stiff lipped. Asian managers value culture, religion and inspire by prestige and reputation of the group.

Global managers must understand that 'One size does not fit all' here is no universal right or wrong way of doing things.

6. ISSUES AND CHALLENGES OF SELF-MANAGEMENT

"Physician heal thyself": This dictum applies to managers too, who seem to be adept at managing others but are ineffective when it comes to managing themselves. This gives rise to issues concerning the self management of mangers by themselves. Global management makes very hard demands on global managers and unless they learn how to manage 'Self", early burn outs and failures on this front can be the result.

There are many dimensions to this aspect of global management but some of the major issues which need attention are:

(a) *Time management*—With space shrinking due to fast means of travel all over the world, managers will be strutting around the globe all the time. Unless they learn to manage their personal time well by prioritizing their commitments they will not have time for many an important things main being their own kith and kin. This can often lead to unsatisfactory family life and loss of love and nearness of their family members. Global managers will have to devote some of their time qualitatively to their family members and friends.

(b) *Health and fitness management*—A hectic Global work style can take its toll on the health and physical fitness of the managers. They need to devote time for this aspect in their busy schedule.

(c) *Mental and Spiritual fitness*—Physical fitness alone is not sufficient and Global managers who are exposed to so many diverse types of physical, mental and behavioural environments will need mental and spiritual counseling if they have to maintain their efficiency levels high. Stress at work place is the outcome of such lifestyle and effective means of stress management are necessary to take care of this element. Meditation is one of the most effective ways of countering stress due to jet-lag and other work-related factors. Training of managers in meditation is strongly advocated.

(d) *Ethical and Social issues*—Business ethics is as much a personal requirement as it is a social one. Managers must be made aware of their responsibility in this regard and must consciously develop these dimensions of their personality in global business management.

Self-management probably is the most neglected dimension of managerial training not only in global business management but also domestic management.

7. CULTURAL SENSITIVITY AND GLOBAL STRATEGY

A company needs to assess itself in terms of cultural sensitivity before embarking on any Global venture. Here again a simple policy of satisfying the cultural needs will not give it the much needed competitive advantage over the competitors. The concept of Blue ocean strategy can be used in this context too, where a quantum leap in terms of cultural needs satisfaction is aimed at with the objective of making competitors 'irrelevant'. The concept of customer delight needs to be redefined to take into consideration the cultural needs of the customer. A company which can send a culturally strong message to its customers will have much better brand positioning than other companies. This has been made amply clear by some strategic failures in India of such global brands as McDonald and KFC, etc. in few Indian cities. Their repositioning and redesigning of product lines to suit the local needs also speaks volumes for the necessity of being culture sensitive in Indian markets which are highly sensitive in this respect.

One should not forget that the 1857 revolt against the British had a cultural reason too. A normal SWOT Analysis is not sufficient to evaluate a company's strength and weaknesses. Hence, an assessment of the cultural match of the company with the requirements of the specific market region is necessary. Cultural sensitivity of the market region hence must be understood by any company which is trying to venture into it. The cultural sensitivity of the market can be evaluated and then a scale of sensitivity can be developed between 'not so sensitive culturally' to 'very highly sensitive culturally' markets. The Linear active markets are not culturally as sensitive as Reactive markets. A company must also develop a sort of evaluation matrix to match its cultural profile with that of the market needed profile and then make efforts to develop its local strategy. In a market that is high on the scale of cultural sensitivity a company must try and differentiate itself in a quantum manner to gain competitive advantage or 'blue ocean advantage'.

Some of the factors that need to be assessed for judging the cultural sensitivity of a market are:

(a) Religious beliefs and dogmas,
(b) Heritage symbols and associated rituals and systems,
(c) Social values and related issues,
(d) Historical profile and important symbols,
(e) Cultural systems and habits,
(f) Lifestyles and factors related to these, and
(g) Any other miscellaneous factors such as traditions, provincial laws.

In order to create blue ocean strategies 'cultural differentiation' along with cost minimization could be a very good global strategy. This has made Chinese goods popular in India, where even statues of Gods and other religious products are being manufactured in China at a very competitive cost and being marketed in India. Even festival products required in India are being imported from China. It only shows sensitivity of the Chinese manufacturers to Indian markets' cultural needs. The same is not the case with the Indian manufacturers. There is a vast rural market in India which still remains unexploited.

8. CONCLUSION

In conclusion it can be said that management of global organisations is both a challenging and complex task. Conventional management principles and concepts need not always be of help in creating the necessary results. The scale of operation and the nature are quite different from managing local or domestic organisations.

Strategy and culture both play a crucial role in deciding on the effectiveness of such organisations. The peculiar nature of today's Global business demands all together different approaches in both strategic as well as cultural matters. 'Blue Ocean strategies' based on 'quantum differentiation' and cost minimization and a sensitivity to cultural diversity and needs arising out of them are tools that can help tackle the challenges posed in the management of global organisations. Developing a 'culture sensitivity' index of the target markets and a 'culture sensitivity' profile of the organisation to match the needs can be an effective strategy to deal with the multiple challenges in managing the global organisations. A model based on this concept is given in Figure 1. As per the model we get four combinations viz, HH, HL, LH and LL. Suggested strategies for these are: Blue ocean for a company high on profile and in markets high in culture sensitivity, Glocal, i.e. think global act local for HL combination, Glocal export orientation for LH combination and local strategies for LL combination. A company should evaluate both the market and its own sensitivity to culture and select appropriate strategies or a combination of them.

FIGURE 1

Culture Sensitivity Matrix
Culture Sensitivity Index of Market

	High	*Low*
Culture Sensitivity Profile of the Company	Blue Ocean Strategies (Global differentiation)	Red Ocean (Global) Strategies
	Global Export-oriented Strategies	Local Strategies

References

Ansoff, H.J., "The New Corporate Strategy", New York, John Wiley and Sons,1988.

Heller, Jean E., "Criteria for Selecting an International Manager", *Personnel*, 57, No. 3 (May-June 1), 1980.

Jauch, L.R. and Glueck, W.F., "Strategic Management and Business Policy", New York, McGraw Hill Book Co., 1989.

Lewis Richard L., "When Cultures Collide: Managing Successfully Across Cultures", 2000.

Porter, M., "Competitive Advantage of Nations", London, Macmillan, 1994.

Ohmae Kenichi, "The Borderless World", New Delhi, Prentice Hall of India, 1994.

Reich, Robert, "The Work of Nations: Preparing Ourselves for 21st Century Capitalism", New York, Alfred A. Knopf, 1991.

Rhinesmith, Dr. Stephen, H., "A Manager's Guide to Globalization: Six Skills for Success in a Changing World", Chicago, Irwin, 1996.

Zinnov, L.L.C., "Global Organisations: An Analysis", Article on internet.

CHAPTER

22

Motivation: Concepts and Theory

DR. KALAIMATHI AND R. RAJALAKSHMI

INTRODUCTION TO MOTIVATION

At one time, employees were considered just another input into the production of goods and services. What perhaps changed this way of thinking about employees was research, referred to as the Hawthorne Studies, conducted by Elton Mayo from 1924 to 1932 (Dickson, 1973). This study has found that employees are not motivated solely by money and employee behaviour is linked to their attitudes (Dickson, 1973). The Hawthorne Studies began the human relations approach to management, whereby the needs and motivation of employees become the primary focus of managers (Bedeian, 1993).

MOTIVATION DEFINED

Motivation has been defined as the psychological process that gives behaviour purpose and direction (Kreitner, 1995); a predisposition to behave in a purposive manner to achieve specific, unmet needs (Buford, Bedeian, and Lindner, 1995); an internal drive to satisfy an unsatisfied need (Higgins, 1994); and the will to achieve (Bedeian, 1993). For this paper, motivation is operationally defined as the inner force that drives individuals to accomplish personal and organisational goals.

THE ROLE OF MOTIVATION

Why do we need motivated employees? The answer is survival (Smith, 1994). Motivated employees are needed in our rapidly changing workplaces. Motivated employees help organisations survive. Motivated employees are more productive. To be effective, managers need to understand what motivates employees within the context of the roles they perform. Of all the functions a manager performs, motivating employees is arguably the most complex. This is due, in part, to the fact that what motivates employees changes constantly (Bowen and Radhakrishna, 1991). For example, research suggests that as employees' income increases, money becomes less of a motivator (Kovach, 1987). Also, as employees get older, interesting work becomes more of a motivator.

MOTIVATION—BASIC CONCEPTS AND THEORIES

It intends to give a very brief overview on the most important concepts and theories of motivation.

According to Arnold, there are 3 *components* of motivation:

- *Direction*—what a person is trying to do?,
- *Effort*—how hard a person is trying?, and
- *Persistence*—how long a person keeps on trying?

Furthermore, literature distinguishes 2 *types of factors* that influence motivation:

- *Intrinsic*—self-generated factors (responsibility, freedom to act, scope to use and develop skills and abilities, interesting and challenging work, opportunities for advancement)—they have a deeper and longer-term effect.
- *Extrinsic*—what is done for people to motivate them? (rewards, promotion, punishment)—they have an immediate and powerful effect, but won't necessarily last long.

Most influential is the *Needs (content)* Theory

- The underlying concept is the belief that an unsatisfied need creates tension and a state of disequilibrium. To restore balance, a goal is identified that will satisfy the need and a behaviour pathway to this goal is selected.
- All behaviours are motivated by unsatisfied needs.
- People will be better motivated if their work experience satisfies their needs and wants.

Maslows Hierarchy of Needs

- Self-fulfilment
- Esteem
- Social
- Safety

- Physiological
- If a lower need is satisfied, the next higher one becomes dominant
- Higher-order needs provide greatest motivation
- Different people may have different priorities.

Alderfer's ERG Theory

- Subjective states of satisfaction and desire
- Three primary categories of human needs:
- *Existence needs*—need for material and energy exchange
- *Relatedness needs*—transactions with human environment, process of sharing or growth needs—people make creative or productive efforts for themselves mutually.

McClelland's Needs

- Based mainly on studies of managers
- Three most important needs:
- *Achievement*—need for competitive success measured against a personal standard of Excellence
- *Affiliation*—need for warm, friendly relationships with others
- *Power*—need to control and influence others.

Herzberg's Two-factor Model

- *Motivators*—factors that really motivate people
- *Hygiene factors*—dissatisfiers; their absence would de-motivate people, but their presence not necessarily improves motivation.

Process Cognitive Theory

- Emphasis on psychological processes that effect motivation and on basic needs.
- Concerned with people's perception and the way they interpret and understand it.
- People will be highly motivated if they can control the means to attain their goals.

Expectancy Theory by Vroom

- Value instrumentality (belief that if we do one thing, it will lead to another) and expectancy (probability that action or effort will lead to an outcome)
- Strength of expectations may be based on past experiences.
- Motivation is only likely when a clearly perceived relationship

exists between performance and an outcome that is seen as a means of satisfying needs

- Porter and Lawler: two factors determining the effort people put into their jobs:
- Value of rewards to individuals in so far as they satisfy their needs
- Probability that rewards depend on effort, as perceived by individuals, their expectation about relationships between effort and reward
- Two additional variables:
- *Ability*—individual characteristics and skills
- *Role perceptions*—what he wants to do or thinks he is required to do, good if they correspond with the viewpoint of the organisation.

Goal Theory

- Latham and Locke
- Motivation and performance are higher when individuals set specific goals
- Goals have to be difficult but accepted
- Feedback on performance
- Participation in goal setting is importantgoals need to be agreed
- As long as they are accepted demanding goals lead to better performance than easy goals.

Reactance Theory by Brehm

- Individuals are not passive receivers but responders
- They seek to reduce uncertainty by seeking control about factors influencing rewards.

Equity Theory by Adams

- Perceptions people have about how they are being treated as compared with others
- Involves feelings and perceptions; it is always a comparative process
- People will work better if they are treated equitably
- Two forms of equity:
- *Distributive*—fairness people feel they are rewarded in accordance with their contribution and in comparison with others
- *Procedural*—perceptions of employees about fairness of company procedures
- We hope/expect that the inputs we give into our job equal the outputs we get.

Other Theories

- *Behavioural theory (Skinner)*: behaviour is learnt from experience; learning takes place mainly through reinforcement
- *Social learning theory (Bandura)*: significance of reinforcement as a determinant of future behaviour, importance of internal psychological factors, esp. Expectancies
- *Attribution theory (Guest)*: explanation of performance after we have invested considerable effort and motivation in a task; four types of explanations: ability, effort, task difficulty, and luck; motivation depends on the factor used to explain success or failure.

CONCLUSION

Thus, the article describes concepts and theories of motivation. The employees should be motivated by the following ten motivating factors in hierarchy of importance: (a) job security, (b) sympathetic help with personal problems, (c) personal loyalty to employees, (d) interesting work, (e) good working conditions, (f) tactful discipline, (g) good wages, (h) promotions and growth in the organisation, (i) feeling of being in on things, and (j) full appreciation of work done. By following these motivating factors, the organisations can reach a tremendous growth level.

Motivation and Organisational Commitment

REENA

INTRODUCTION

Motivation is defined as an urge in an individual to perform goal directed behaviour. Therefore, motivation cannot be from outside but it is an intrinsic desire in a man to achieve the goal through performance or activity.

Motives are expressions of person's need. Hence, they are personal and internal. Incentives on the other hand are external to the person. They are made part of work environment by management in order to encourage workers to accomplish a task. The motivational model indicates that a sense of felt deprivation generates needs and such needs create tension in an individual. The individual perceives and makes cost benefit analysis on the ways and means of releasing such tension. Once such perception is cleared, individual pounces upon the activities and achieves some results. If it is success, he feels rewarded and falls in the cycle of motivation again. If it is failure, he feels punished and once again, after due modification of ways and means, pounces back on the cycle or feels frustrated. Therefore, motivation leads to a goal directed behaviour.

If organisations recognize that people are the most valuable fundamental asset in any business, then they must also recognize that 'motivation' is the most critical activity for organisational success.

Organisational Commitment is highly valuable. It is this factor which increases our job satisfaction, loyalty, and growth. Organisational commitment is vital for productivity, quality and good performance of an organisation. Numerous empirical evidences regarding job commitment and its relationship with job satisfaction have been offered. These findings reveal that the level of job commitment can also be influenced by various factors such as demography, pay, co-workers, work supervision, company's background and employee's job-satisfaction level. This article highlights the importance of understanding the meaning of organisational commitment and motivation for effective research. As we mostly base our concepts on our own perceptions, the meaning of organisational commitment and its importance differs from one person to another, especially when we originate from different religious and cultural backgrounds.

The management of people at work is an integral part of the management process. To understand the critical importance of people in the organisation is to recognize that the human element and the organisation are synonymous. A well-managed organisation usually sees an average worker as the root source of quality and productivity gains. Such organisations do not look to capital investment, but to employees, as the fundamental source of improvement. An organisation is effective to the degree to which it achieves its goals. An effective organisation will make sure that there is a spirit of cooperation and sense of commitment and satisfaction within the sphere of its influence. In order to make employees satisfied and committed to their jobs, there is need for strong and effective motivation at workplace.

MOTIVATION

Motivation is defined as an urge in an individual to perform goal directed behaviour. Therefore, motivation cannot be inflicted from outside but it is an intrinsic desire in a man to achieve the goal through performance or activity. Motivation begins with a keen insight into the role of a leader in an organisational context. Each leader in the organisation should view himself as a coach, with the responsibility to guide their team toward success. An important part of being an effective coach means focusing on creating learning opportunities for individuals, rather than on training them. It means empowering individuals and teams to leverage the best of their skills, and giving them the opportunity to fail and try again. Many of the most powerful learning experiences come from failure.

The way in which organisations communicate their vision and their future is critical. Shared information is powerful. Open and honest communication, in itself, can be a motivator. Employees feel engaged when they are trusted with information about the direction of the organisation. Leaders that are the most open and insightful with their team create the highest level of loyalty with team members because they feel part of a valued inner circle.

Introduction to Motivation Theory

Motivation theories which were popular in the 1950's include David McClelland's needs theory, which relates to "management by objectives" and Frederick Herzberg's description in Motivation to Work of motivation based upon empowerment and self-esteem . Probably the most well known motivation theory is Maslow's Hierarchy of Needs, in which higher level needs include affiliation and recognition, as well as self-respect and competence. Later, Douglas McGregor described an authoritarian and traditional Theory X contrasted with a holistic and participative Theory Y.

A. Hierarchy of Needs

According to Maslow, human needs are organized in a series of levels--a hierarchy of importance.

At the lowest level are the physiological needs. These needs, when satisfied, cease to become motivators of behaviour. On the other hand, when basic physiological needs are not satisfied, they become important to the exclusion of everything else.

- When the physiological needs are satisfied, needs at the next higher level begin to motivate behaviour. These are the safety needs, for protection against danger, threat, and deprivation. As long as we feel we are being treated fairly, our safety needs will be satisfied. If we become uncertain and confused about management actions which we do not understand, we will feel insecure and our safety needs will begin to dominate our behaviour.
- Once physiological and safety needs are satisfied, social needs become important motivators of behaviour. These include the need to belong, to associate with, and to be accepted by one's fellows. While tightly knit, cohesive work groups may be far more effective than an equal number of separate individuals in achieving organisational goals, management actions often tend to divide employees by encouraging competitive behaviour, rewarding individual performance, and discouraging discussion with fellow workers. As a consequence, people become resistant to working together.

B. McGregor's Theory Y

One outdated management philosophy is based on the assumption that people are basically lazy and therefore require constant monitoring. The more current philosophy stems from an underlying belief that, given a choice between success and failure, most people would rather succeed—and almost everyone has the potential to be successful.

This second philosophy is well-illustrated in McGregor's "Theory Y" in The Human Side of Enterprise. Theory Y is based upon the following:

1. "The expenditure of physical and mental effort in work is as natural as play or rest.
2. External control and the threat of punishment are not the only

means for bringing about effort toward organisational objectives. Man will exercise self-direction and self-control in the service of objectives to which he is committed.

- Commitment to objectives is a function of the rewards associated with their achievement. The most significant of such rewards, e.g., the satisfaction of ego and self-actualization needs, can be direct products of effort directed toward organisational objectives.
- The average human being learns, under proper conditions, not only to accept but to seek responsibility. Avoidance of responsibility, lack of ambition, and emphasis on security are generally consequences of experience, not inherent human characteristics.
- The capacity to exercise a relatively high degree of imagination, ingenuity, and creativity in the solution of organisational problems is widely, not narrowly, distributed in the population.
- Under the conditions of modern industrial life, the intellectual potentialities of the average human being are only partially utilized.

Theory Y leads to the conclusion that positive results can be achieved by setting up the right conditions, including creating the right atmosphere, that allow for achievement. If these conditions are not met, however, the negative consequences will occur. "If employees are lazy, indifferent, unwilling to take responsibility, intransigent, uncreative, uncooperative, Theory Y implies that the causes lie in management's methods of organisation and control."

II. TYPES OF MOTIVATION

A. Extrinsic Motivation

More on the Carrot and Stick Philosophy

According to Levinson, the carrot and stick approach leads to a kind of self-fulfilling prophecy—the more one tries to drive people by manipulating their behaviour with rewards and punishment, the more they will try to resist by doing things like forming unions and sabotaging management efforts. "When employees sense that they are being viewed as jackasses, they will automatically see management's messages as manipulative, and they will resist them, no matter how clear the type or how pretty the pictures".

Cash: The Ultimate Reward

"The first thing management thinks about as a way to reward employees is money, but the last thing it does with money is to use it as an effective reward for anything but attendance". The literature tends to agree that the primary motivation of the paycheck is to get one to show up on the job every day, and little more, especially in any long-term sense. "There is no firm basis for the assumption that paying people more will encourage them to do better work or even, in the long-run, more work". According to Schneider in Winning the Service Game, paychecks and other cash incentives fail the following motivation tests.

1. *Availability*—the company may not have cash available for this purpose
2. *Flexibility*—paychecks cannot easily be varied from week to week according to performance
3. *Reversibility*—once given, cash cannot be taken away
4. *Performance*—level of pay is a better predictor of management level or seniority than performance
5. *Visibility*—cash transactions are one-to-one only
6. *Timeliness*—bonuses do not immediately follow the performance of desired behaviours
7. *Durability*—the impact on motivation is short-term at best.

"Just because too little money can irritate and de-motivate does not mean that more and more money will bring about increased satisfaction, much less increased motivation."

Work as Punishment

While Alfie Kohn's research methods and conclusions may be controversial, it is true that many of the rewards we receive at work cannot actually be utilized at work. We can't spend our paychecks there, and we have to wait until retirement to collect on our pensions and other accrued benefits. Work, then, is the penalty we have to pay to enjoy these benefits. "It is not surprising, therefore, that for many wage earners work is perceived as a form of punishment which is the price to be paid for various kinds of satisfaction away from the job" (McGregor, p. 40).

So What Really Matters

In addition to concrete rewards, Schneider identifies three additional rewards that may give rise to more effective extrinsic motivators:

1. The content of the job itself
2. Recognition and feedback from coworkers, supervisors, and customers
3. Accomplishing goals that are challenging and meaningful.

In relative terms, research tends to agree that there are other factors besides concrete rewards which are more important in determining employee satisfaction. In a study involving hundreds of employees, "the results showed that...confusion, politics, and conflicting goals on the job—inhibiting factors that made it tough to do good work—were more consequential than issues like pay and supervisory style, which organisations often assume to be the problem."

B. Intrinsic Motivation

"Intrinsic motivation, then, is motivation which comes from the inside of a person. "It is an emotional preference for a task that gives us pleasure and enjoyment." Intrinsic motivation arises from having "a strong emotional interest in an activity and a sense of freedom and autonomy related to it".

Intrinsic motivations tend to be deeper and more personal than extrinsic motivations. And self-motivations are, by definition, intrinsic. The following motivations are likely to be intrinsic:

- Enjoyment of the work itself for its own sake
- Desire to have a "piece of the action," such as sharing visions, missions, leadership, authority, and responsibility
- Pride in performing excellently
- Need to prove some secret point to oneself
- Achievement of a deep-seated value (such as helping another person)
- Having a deep and abiding belief in the importance of the work one is doing
- The excitement and pleasure of a challenge
- Desire to exceed one's previous level of job performance (being self-competitive).

MOTIVATIONAL TECHNIQUES TO GET YOU WHERE YOU WANT TO GO

Learning how to take action, get motivated and stay that way is the key that will drive you to succeed and these simple motivation techniques will help you get what you want out of life.

Plan to Succeed

Successful people are goal oriented. They plan their goals, and then work in incremental steps to achieve those goals. Your goals need to be specific, realistic and achievable. Visualize your goals so that they become real, and then write them down and keep them somewhere as a daily reminder of what it is you're aiming for.

- To stay motivated, you need to feel inspired and excited about what you are aiming to achieve. If you can't get excited about your success goals, you'll never find the inspiration and motivation you need to take action to change your life.

- If your goals don't excite you, then you've chosen the wrong goals. Go back to the drawing board and think about what it is that inspires and excites you, then you'll have a goal you can work towards.
- The longest journey begins with a single step, so plan on adding one new positive step to your daily routine each day to move you towards your goal. Adding one positive step each day will help you take control of your future and rid you of past negative habits.
- Set aside 15 minutes each day to review your goals and the progress you have made. Measuring your progress will keep you inspired to achieve the results you want and help you recognize problem areas that may need work. Acknowledging your achievements is a way of patting yourself on the back for a job well done.
- Believe in the possibilities. Don't allow your fears to stand in the way of your future success. Acknowledge the fact that everyone feels fear when they step outside their comfort zone. As the old adage says, "Feel the fear, and then do it anyway!"

Thinking your Way to Success

Successful people believe in themselves and their ability to succeed, despite the setbacks, obstacles and failures they will encounter along the way. The road to success is littered with those who fall at the first hurdle and don't have what it takes to get up again.

Accept the fact that you will fail, maybe more than once, and in many different ways. Believing that you will achieve your goals without a setback is unrealistic. Successful people turn the negative events that are sure to occur into learning experiences, and then they adjust accordingly and move on. To be motivated you have to be positive.

Being positive puts you in control of your own destiny, so when you understand that only YOU can control your future you also understand that only YOU can control the present.

On those days when it all seems too hard, simply focus on what it is you're aiming for and imagine how exciting it will be when you achieve your goals.

Let the excitement of realizing your dreams fuel your imagination, and from that you can power into your day.

- *Learn something new every day*: The more you know, the closer you'll get to achieve your goal in the time you've set yourself. Information can help you gain confidence, dispel fear and give you the inspiration and motivation you need to lead a better, more fulfilling life.
- *Get your life right*: Staying motivated and achieving your goals is a whole lot easier if you can keep your focus.

Aim to rid yourself of the clutter that prevents you from staying focused.

- *Organize your workspace* so that it creates a positive, stimulating environment. A cluttered workspace creates a cluttered mind, so take the time to clean up around you.
  Make your workplace a happy place to be by pinning your favourite quotation to the wall where you can see it or adding a vase of fresh flowers to a table nearby—whatever brings a smile to your face will keep you in a positive frame of mind and dispel any negative thoughts that may try to creep in.
- An active mind requires an active body and an active body requires a healthy lifestyle. You can't expect to operate at your peak if you don't have the physical stamina to maintain the momentum. That means eating a healthy diet, getting regular exercise and getting enough sleep. Feeling positive about your physical well-being has a tremendous impact on how you feel about achieving your goals.

Helping or Hindering

Surround yourself with people who inspire and motivate you to succeed. Ask yourself if the people in your life are helping or hindering you on your path to success, then make any changes necessary.

You don't have to go it alone—share the excitement of what you are aiming to achieve with those around you who will root for you every step of the way.

Take time out each day to relax. *Switch off* and spend time doing an activity you enjoy (other than work!)—go for a walk, take a bike ride or simply spend quality time with your family. Balancing work and play is an important part of staying healthy, happy and motivated.

Learn to live your life with *passion*. Appreciate all that you have around you and how great it feels simply to be alive at this particular moment in time.

Recent Trends in Motivation

What top employees want and what their employers think they want are often two different things, according to a recent survey by Watson Wyatt (www.watsonsyatt.com). The Washington, D.C.-based human resources consulting firm asked 410 North American companies and 3,600 of their top performers to name the perks most likely to keep them happy.

"There is a gap between what employers think is important for attracting high-performing employees and what those employees think," says Rick Beal, an architect of the study. "Financial reward is not the number-one motivator. These people are more motivated by things that help enrich their career."

The three most prized non-monetary perks were advancement opportunities (76 percent), flexible work schedules (73 percent), and opportunities to learn new skills (68 percent).

"One of the things we've looked at for years is the perception of whether performance or merit pay works. Most companies say they are tired of differentiating performance," says Beal. "But employees say performance rewards work for them."

However, only 24 percent of respondents said that they view rewards as a means of engaging workers to improve performance. This is a mistake, says Beal. "Notwithstanding the current slowdown, the tight labor market demands that employers be more aggressive and creative with their rewards". High performers don't just want money, learning opportunities, or whatever. The truth is, they want it all.

Organisational Commitment

Organisational commitment refers to "The relative strength of an individual's identification with and involvement in a particular Organisation.

Organisational Commitment is an attitudinal or emotive dimension of work motivation, manifesting its form in members' behaviour. Organisational Commitment is a subset of employee commitment, which comprises work Commitment, Career Commitment and Organisational Commitment.

Strongly committed employees are more likely to remain with the organisation than are those with weak commitment. Commitment may even be better predictor of turn over than job satisfaction because it is influenced less by day to day happenings than is job satisfaction.

Employee Commitment

The concept of employment commitment lies at the heart of any analysis of Human Resource Management. Indeed, the rationale for introducing Human resource Management policies is to increase levels of commitment so positive outcomes can ensue. Such is the importance of this construct. Yet, despite many studies on commitment, very little is understood of what managers mean by the term 'commitment' when they evaluate someone's performance and motivation.

The literature defines commitment as an employee's level of attachment to some aspect of work. Various authors have been instrumental in identifying types of employee commitment as critical constructs in understanding the attitudes and behaviours of employees in an organisation.

Though this study specifically addresses commitment to the organisation, or organisational commitment, it also considers work and career commitment towards clarifying the conceptual meaning.

Arguing that conceptual redundancy exists across these, they group them into three foci, as commitment to work/job, commitment to career/ profession and commitment to organisation.

Organisational Commitment

There are two dominant conceptualizations of organisational commitment in sociological literature. These are an employee's loyalty towards the organisation and an employee's intention to stay with the organisation. Loyalty is an affective response to, and identification with, an organisation, based on a sense of duty and responsibility.

Loyalty is argued to be an important intervening variable between the structural conditions of work, and the values, and expectations, of employees, and their decision to stay, or leave.

Positive and rewarding features of work are expected to increase loyalty, which, in turn, will reduce the likelihood of leaving. Loyalty becomes stabilized with tenure, which partly explains the negative relationship typically found between tenure and turnover.

Intent to stay is portrayed as effectively neutral, and focuses on an employee's intention to remain a member of the organisation.

Hagen defines this form of commitment as the employee's expected likelihood of remaining employed in the same organisation. As with loyalty, intent to stay stabilizes with tenure, and helps explain the negative tenure and turnover relationship. Theoretically, it is viewed as an intervening response to structural conditions of work, as well as conditions of work elsewhere, or to not working at all.

Career Commitment

Career commitment refers to identification with, and involvement in, one's occupation. Much literature refers to similar or related concepts: occupational commitment, professional commitment, career salience, the cosmopolitan/local distinction and professionalism. Common to all these is the critical notion of being committed to one's career, or occupation, rather than to the organisation which employs one.

Work Commitment

Work commitment refers neither to the organisation nor to one's career, but to employment itself. Persons committed to work hard have a strong sense of duty towards their work, and place intrinsic value on work as a central life interest. This form of commitment relates terms like work motivation, job involvement, work as a central life interest and work involvement. Although work commitment is expected to be related to organisational commitment and career commitment, literature shows it to be empirically distinct from these two forms of commitment.

Development of Organisational Commitment

Two major theoretical approaches emerge from previous research on commitment:

Firstly, commitment is viewed as an attitude of attachment to the organisation, which leads to particular job-related behaviours. The committed employee, for example, is less often absent, and is less likely to leave the organisation voluntarily, than are less committed employees.

Secondly, one line of research in organisations focuses on the implications of certain types of behaviours on subsequent attitudes. A typical finding is that employees who freely choose to behave in a certain way, and who find their decision difficult to change, become committed to the chosen behaviour and develop attitudes consistent with their choice.

One approach emphasizes the influence of commitment attitudes on behaviours, whereas the other emphasizes. Although the 'commitment attitude behaviour' and 'committing behaviour attitude' approaches emerge from different theoretical orientations, and have generated separate research traditions, understanding the commitment process is facilitated by viewing these two approaches as, inherently, inter-related.

Rather than viewing the causal arrow, between attitudinal and behavioural commitment, as pointing in one direction or the other, it is more useful to consider the two as reciprocally-related over time.

It is equally reasonable to assume that—

(a) Commitment attitudes lead to committing behaviours that subsequently reinforce and strengthen attitudes; and
(b) Committing behaviours lead to commitment attitudes and subsequent committing behaviours.

The important issue is not whether the commitment process begins with either attitude or behaviour. Rather, it is important to recognize the development of commitment which may involve the subtle interplay of attitudes and behaviours over a period of time.

The process through which commitment is developed may involve self-reinforcing cycles of attitudes and behaviours that evolve on the job, and over time, strengthen employees' commitment to the organisation.

Meyer and Allen present three approaches, and define their three dimensional constructs as affective, continuance and normative commitment.

1. *Affective Commitment*: The individual's affective or emotional attachment to the organisation. (i.e. individuals stay with organisation because they want to).
2. *Continuance Commitment*: The perceived costs associated with leaving the organisation (i.e. the individual stays with the organisation because they need to).
3. *Normative Commitment*: An individual's felt obligation to remain with the organisation (i.e., the individual stays with the organisation because they feel they caught to do so).

Affective Commitment refers to the employee's emotional attachment to, identification with, and involvement in, the organisation [based on positive feelings, or emotions, toward the organisation]. The antecedents for affective commitment include perceived job characteristics [task autonomy, task significance, task identity, skill variety and supervisory feedback], organisational dependability [extent to which employees feel the organisation can be counted on to look after their interests], and perceived participatory management extent to which employees fell they can influence decisions on the work environment and other issues of concern to them.

It is hypothesized that employees with low affective commitment will choose to leave an organisation, while employees with a high affective commitment will stay for longer periods, as they believe in the organisation and its mission.

Continuance commitment refers to commitment based on the costs that the employee associates with leaving the organisation [due to the high cost of leaving]. Potential antecedents of continuance commitment include age, tenure, career satisfaction and intent to leave. Age and tenure can function as predictors of continuance commitment, primarily because of their roles as surrogate measures of investment in the organisation.

Tenure can be indicative of non-transferable investments [close working relationship with co-workers, retirement investments, career investments and skills unique to the particular organisation]. Age can also be negatively related to the number of available alternative job opportunities. Career satisfaction provides a more direct measure of career-related investments, which could be at risk if the individual leaves the organisation.

In general, whatever employees perceive as sunk cost, resulting from leaving the organisation, are the antecedents of continuance commitment.

Normative commitment refers to an employee's feeling of obligation to remain with the organisation [based on the employee having internalized the values and goals of the organisation]. The potential antecedents for normative commitment include co-worker commitment [including affective and normative dimensions, as well as commitment behaviours], organisational dependability and perceived participatory management are expected to instill a sense of moral obligation to reciprocate to the organisation.

HRM refers to the overall philosophy about the organisation and how people should be Managed, and is not merely limited to certain specific functions. HRM focuses on congruence and commitment instead of compliance and control. In the present day turbulent reality, there is a need to develop industry specific HRM policy and practices to remain competitive and to develop committed workforce.

CONCLUSION

There is progress in our understanding of motivation and organisational commitment, both conceptually, and, more practically, in terms of the positive consequences for organisations to have committed employees. Finding the relationship between human resource management practices, employee commitment and the financial performance of firms has important implications for improved integration of research across several business school disciplines. Evidence clarifies that investments in employees can have positive financial consequences for firms and their shareholders, and may help broaden their narrow view of the world. Employee perception is the foundation of employee motivation, leading to higher organisational commitment, and that employee perception forms the antecedent of organisational commitment. Positive employee perception leads to improved employee motivation, which, in turn, leads to higher organisational commitment.

References

Armenakis, A., 1999. Ethnics program Pose Potential Threats. Internal Auditor.

Bard, K., 2002. Employee ownership and affective Organisational Commitment: Employee perceptions of fairness and their preference for company shares over cash. *Scandinavian Journal of Management.*

Meyer, J.P. and Lynne, H., 2001. 'Commitment in the workplace—Toward a general model'. *Human Resource Management Review.*

Meyer, J.P. and Allen, J.N., 1997. Commitment in the workplace—Thousand Oaks, CA: Sage Publications.

Singh, V. and Vinnicombe, S., 2000. What does 'commitment' really mean? Views of UK and Swedish engineering managers'. *Personnel Review,* Vol. 29(2).

Rajendra Muthuveloo and Radvan Che Rose, 2005, TYPOLOGY of organisational commitment—*American Journal of Applied Science,* 2(6): 1078-81, 2005.

Grossman, S.P. (1988). Motivation. In Adelman, G. (Ed.), Encyclopedia of Neuroscience, pp. 60-65. Birkh¨auser, Boston.

Chamberlin, J., "Reaching 'flow' to optimize work and play," American Psychological Association, Vol. 29, No. 7, Available at: http://www.apa.org/monitor/jul98/joy.html.

Chan, T.S., and Ahern, T.C., "Targeting motivation—adapting flow theory to instructional design," *Journal of Educational Computing Research,* 21(2), 152-63.

Csikszentmihalyi, M. Flow. The Psychology of Optimal Experience, New York: Harper and Row, 1990.

Best Practices for Motivating Bank Employees

E.V. Rigin and K. Sankar Ganesh

ABSTRACT

The term Motivation is a commonly read or at least heard about by every employee. However, many employers, when they really want to motivate their employees, are not aware of or familiar with the right techniques and strategies by which they can motivate their employees. It is simple to understand that even optimistic employees come with a lot of factors which de-motivate them or unfulfilled factors which may motivate them. In our daily life we can see millions of people are not motivated in their jobs. Now it is the need of the hour to cautiously study and understand that employees of different segments have different motivational factors, and based on them the bankers have to design an appropriate strategy to motivate the employees. This article sees the means and ways to motivate the bank employees.

Key Words: Motivation, banking sector, job design, morale, strategies, work performance, communication, organisational structure, training and development, work culture.

INTRODUCTION

The global scenario and the economic down turn has created an alarming situation denoting that it is really a tough task to motivate the bank employees by providing monetary benefits. The corporate are restructuring to cut down their cost to the maximum extent. In this situation, the employers shall understand that money is not the only factor which motivates the employees. It is very obvious that people spend more time at work than the time spent with their families. Hence, their morale should positive and a state of self-motivation is necessary. People are confused with that it is an employee's job to motivate oneself or the employer is responsible to motivate employees. In such an extremely competitive banking environment, the bank employees are to be motivated with effective motivational strategies.

As person's motivation is combination of desire and energy directed in achieving the target. Influencing employees means making them behave in a desired manner and thereby marching towards the mission. People are motivated by their beliefs, values, and interests, worthy causes, fear and other similar forces. Some of the forces are internal, such as needs, interests, and beliefs. Other forces are external, such as the environment or pressure from a loved one. The simple formula for motivation is that there must an open viewpoint on human nature. It is important to understand that people react differently for the same situation at the same time.

There are a few challenges the Banks are facing today:

(a) Investors demand for drastic growth rate of the bank by increasing the market share.
(b) The bottom line of the branches should acquire and retain profitable customers.
(c) Heavy competition to differentiate its products and services from other competitors.
(d) To build greater brand image and brand value in the market.
(e) To attract the right talent and to motivate and retain them.

If the employees in an organisation are demotivated, the total performance of the organisation will go down. Hence, the employer has to identify the employee's satisfactory level towards the organisation policy and towards job-related factors very often. Some of the symptoms to identify the low level of satisfaction of the employees are

- Employees Consistently late to reach the organisation
- Performing lower than the actual caliber
- Fail to follow the instrument and policy
- Poor performance or factors indicating low morale
- Absenteeism
- Stress and frustration and more......

If these situations prevail in any bank, then it is an alarming situation to be viewed seriously.

Economic Crisis

The global crisis has created great implications for the banking industry. The world has been facing the worst economic crisis since the Great Depression. Effects of the crisis have spread far and wide due to excessive debt, deflationary conditions, financial closures and unjustified money hoarding. The world economic crisis has not affected India badly like US and other countries. Statistics states that only 16% of the Indian companies are going for pay freezing. But the employment opportunities are affected and the economic crisis has created a tough time for the new entrants.

Challenging Work Culture in Banks

The culture represents the set of behaviour and practices prevailing in an organisation. The business scenario in India shows the companies are going for pay cuts and removal of employees as cost cutting strategy. The non-performing employees are removed. This situation has increased the pressure among the employees and the banks are managing the task with a limited number of staff. The employees have to perform multitasks and as a result, work burden has also increased. Many banks are giving marketing targets to employees or the target of opening new accounts. These situations indicate that the banks have challenging work culture.

Factors Demotivating Employees

Generally it is very difficult to see employees highly motivated. They find faults and mistakes even for small issues. There are few factors where employees can be easily de-motivated.

Employees Expect Employees to Win all the Time

It is impossible to win all the time. But the employer pressurizes the employees to win all the time. Moreover, adequate encouragement is essential to minimize the faults and weakness. This encouragement may avoid de-motivation of employees.

Failure to Express Gratitude

The employers should express their gratitude and thankfulness for every success. Expressing gratitude will give a feeling in the mind of the employees that that the management is recognizing their efforts and understanding the dedication and performance. If gratitude is not properly expressed, it may be a de-motivating factor.

Not Listening to Employee's Idea

Good ideas may come at any level of employees; listening to the employees may help in the organisational improvement and even grievances can be easily solved. In banks the employees are handling customers of different types. The experience with the customers should be shared and hence it is vital to listen to the employees.

Avoiding Gossips and Avoiding Firing in front of other Employees

Gossips should be avoided. This may create bad image in the mind of the employees. The top level employee's activities are watched and their words are observed keenly. Moreover, every individual are expecting self-respect. If they are fired in front of others, they are very much affected. The employees' mistakes shall be explained in person.

Share the Victory and not to Own it

Of course majority of the Banks are celebrating their victory with their employees. The sharing of victory should be cautiously done. Sharing of rewards and praises may motivate the employees. But when such things are absent, they act as a de-motivating factor.

Grate Motivators

Motivation enhances the employees to behave in a desired manner. The purpose of motivation in Banks is to make the employees behave in a desired manner. Banks with highly motivated employees are highly successful. Motivation helps the employees to shine with high order of performance. Their morale towards the bank will be great.

Counseling

Banking should create a designation for counseling their staff. As the employees are dealing with the customers of different attitude, they should not be mentally affected. In counseling, both the personal and official problems can be discussed employees not performing up to their ability may be identified and given counseling for the betterment of the bank performance.

(1) Challenging and Exciting Job

The banks are motivating their employees by giving challenging and exciting job. Challenging job avoids boredom and the employees get involved. The young generation love challenging jobs. This helps the employees to improve their ability.

(2) Involving the Employees in Problem Solving and Planning

Problem can be easily solved, when the employees participate. Moreover when the employees involve in planning, the execution of the plan is easier and it encourages the employees to understand the plan; thus, their involvement in accomplishing their goal will increase to a great extent.

(3) Develop Morale and Unity

The Banker has to create positive morale among the employees. They should be proud of working in the bank. The morale of the employees determines the involvement they show in the job. The employer should also create a feeling of unity among the employees. Only the strong team can make the employees feel secured and increase the productivity.

(4) Develop Ethical Value and Moral Beliefs

Ethical value and morality make the employees feel what is right and what is wrong and the value of what is good and bad may be felt. This helps the bank to have highly valued people who have strong ethical values.

(5) Rewarding Good Behaviour and Celebrating Accomplishment

Rewarding good behaviour makes it occur again and again. Celebration of accomplishment energizes them to restart with full enthusiasm. Rewarding employees highly motivates them. Nowadays all banks are rewarding their employees, and this has to be implemented with full vigor. Customers feedback shall be used for rewarding the employees.

(6) Role Clarity and Job Security

The duties and responsibilities should be very clear without overlapping. This facilitates the employees to perform their task without any confusion. If the role of an individual is not clear, then bottleneck in performance of the work may happen. Another most basic factor which motivates the employee is job security. Only when the employees feels that they are secure, their fear will be removed and they can concentrate more on their work.

(7) Top Level Employees being Effective Leader

Top level managers should also be effective leaders. Only leaders highly influence the employees than the managers in achieving their targets. Only a good leader can understand their employees and motivate them.

(8) Effective Training

Learning changes the behaviour of the employees permanently and training helps them to become specialists in their area of work. Hence, learning and training are long-term process and the banker should provide them to their employees continuously. It is also understood that highly trained employees are highly motivated and, hence, for effective motivation, effective training is essential. It helps the employees to perform their task more efficiently.

(9) Effective Performance Appraisal System

Performance appraisal aims for effective evaluation of the employee performance and thereby motivates their employees by rewarding, providing hike in salary and by promoting. The non-performers should be rightly identified and they should be trained. The effective performance appraisal system ensures unbiased evaluation.

(10) Cafeteria Benefits

Employees' preferred benefits are to be optional and this helps the employees to identify their interested benefits and to get satisfied. When this privillage is given to employees, they understand the importance given to them. The compensation for the employees overtime shall be given option to avail monetary benefits or to avail work time reduction. Many employees may need free hour for their overtime instead of monetary benefit.

(11) Transparent Career Path and Promotion

The career path gives idea about the entrance and exit of employees' career. If the path is clear and transparent, the employees know the means to grow to the top position. Similarly, promotion is very essential for the employees to be motivated permanently.

(12) Periodic Stress Removal

Due to personal and official reasons, employees get stress. Stress affects the performance and it leads to burnout. Hence, stressed employees should be identified and they should be treated psychologically, to reduce their stress and keep them highly motivated.

CONCLUSION

Motivation is a psychological process; it is directly related to the performance of the employees and the successfulness of the bank. Bank employees perform both clerical and administrative jobs. Hence, evaluating and motivating them on a regular basis are very essential.

REFERENCES

Kostova, T. (1999). "Transnational transfer of strategic organisational practices: A contextual perspective," *Academy of Management Review*, 24(2): 308-24.

Ritter, J. and Taylor, L. (1997). 'Economic Models of Employee Motivation'. Working Paper Series. Federal Reserve Bank of St. Louis. Retrieved 7 March 2008.

Quality of Work Life and its Impact on Employees

Dr. S. Sakthivel Rani

INTRODUCTION

Quality of work life is playing an important role in the human resource management. Quality of work life is a philosophy, a set of principles, which holds that people are the most important resource in the organisation as they are trustworthy, responsible and capable of making valuable contribution and they should be treated with dignity and respect. The elements that are relevant to an individual's quality of work life include the task, the physical work environment, social environment within the organisation, administrative system and relationship between lives on and off the job. Quality of work life consists of opportunities for active involvement in group working arrangements or problem solving that are of mutual benefit to employees or employers, based on labor management co-operation. People also conceive of quality of work life as asset of methods, such as autonomous work groups, job enrichment and high involvement aimed at boosting the satisfaction and productivity of workers. It requires employee commitment to the organisation and environment in which this commitment can flourish. Thus, quality of work life is a comprehensive construct that includes an individuals job-related well-being and the extent to which work experiences are rewarding, fulfilling and devoid of stress and other negative personal consequences.

Accordingly, the rising number of two-income households is heightening the concern for employee's quality of work life. Given that female participation at work is increasing, it is apparent that males and females independently will need to take care of both work and home. There, quality of work life experience rather than work per se becomes the focus of attention and workplace wellness is crucial in promoting healthier working environments. The evolution of quality of work life began in late 1960's emphasing the human dimensions of work by focusing on quality of the relationship between the worker and the working environment.

BACKGROUND

This article reviews literature on quality of work life (QWL) in terms of its meaning and its constructs. As the work culture changes drastically in the recent years, the traditional concept of work to fulfil humans' basic needs are also facing out. The basic needs are continued to diversify and change according to the evolution of the work system and standards of living of a workforce. Thus, a definition by Suttle (1977) on the QWL as'the degree to which work are able to satisfy important personal basic needs through their experience in the organisation is no longer relevant. Generally, jobs in the contemporary work environment offer sufficient rewards, benefits, recognition and control to employees over their actions. Although to some extent contemporary workforce are compensated appropriately, their personal spending practices, lifestyles, leisure activities, individual value systems, health and so forth can affect their levels of need. It is similar to the argument posted in the Maslow's hierarchy of needs in which each individual has different level of needs because in reality what is important to some employees may not be important to others although they are being treated equally in the same organisation. This definition, focusing on personal needs, has neglected the fact that the construct of QWL is subjective and continuously evolves due to ever-growing needs of each and every employee.

Hackman and Oldhams (1980) further highlight the constructs of QWL in relation to the interaction between work environment and personal needs. The work environment that is able to fulfil employees' personal needs is considered to provide a positive interaction effect, which will lead to an excellent QWL. They emphasize that the personal needs are satisfied, when rewards from the organisation, such as compensation, promotion, recognition and development meet their expectations. Parallel to this definition, Lawler (1982) defines QWL in terms of job characteristics and work conditions. He highlights that the core dimension of the entire QWL in the organisation is to improve employees' well-being and productivity. The most common interaction that relates to improvement of employees' well-being and productivity is the design of the job. Job design that is able to provide higher employee satisfaction is expected to be more productive. However, he accepted the fact that QWL is complex, because it comprises physical and mental well-being of employees. Later definition by Beukema (1987) describes QWL as the degree to which employees are able to shape their jobs actively, in accordance with their options, interests and needs. It is the degree of power an organisation gives to its employees to design their work. This means that the individual employee has the full freedom to design his job functions to meet his personal needs and interests. This definition emphasizes the individual's choice of interest in carrying out the task. However, this definition differs from the former which stresses on the organisation that designs the job to meet employees' interest. It is difficult for the organisation to fulfil the personal needs and values of each employee. However if the organisation provides the appropriate authority to design work activities to the individual employees, then it is highly possible that the work activities can match their employees' needs that contribute to the organisational performance.

In the same vein, Heskett, Sasser and Schlesinger (1997) define QWL as the feelings that employees have towards their jobs, colleagues and organisations that ignite a chain leading to the organisations' growth and profitability. A good feeling towards their job means the employees feel happy doing work which will lead to a productive work environment. This definition provides an insight that the satisfying work environment is considered to provide better QWL. Proceeding to previous definitions of Lau, Wong, Chan and Law (2001) operationalised QWL as the favourable working environment that supports and promotes satisfaction by providing employees with rewards, job security and career growth opportunities. Indirectly the definition indicates that an individual who is not satisfied with reward may be satisfied with the job security and to some extent would enjoy the career opportunity provided by the organisation for their personal as well as professional's growth.

The recent definition by Serey (2006) on QWL is quite conclusive and best meet the contemporary work environment. The definition is related to meaningful and satisfying work. It includes: (i) an opportunity to exercise one's talents and capacities, to face challenges and situations that require independent initiative and self-direction; (ii) an activity thought to be worthwhile by the individuals involved; (iii) an activity in which one understands the role the individual plays in the achievement of some overall goals; and (iv) a sense of taking pride in what one is doing and in doing it well. This issue of meaningful and satisfying work is often merged with discussions of job satisfaction, and believed to be more favourable to QWL.

This review on the definitions of QWL indicates that QWL is a multi-dimensional construct, made up of a number of interrelated factors that need careful consideration to conceptualize and measure. It is associated with job satisfaction, job involvement, motivation, productivity, health, safety and well-being, job security, competence development and balance between work and non-work life as is conceptualized by European Foundation for the Improvement of Living Conditions.

To summarize, QWL is viewed as a wide-ranging concept, which includes adequate and fair remuneration, safe and healthy working conditions and social integration in the work organisation that enables an individual to develop and use all his or her capacities. Most of the definitions aim at achieving the effective work environment that meets with the organisational and personal needs and values that promote health, well being, job security, job satisfaction, competency development and balance between work and non-work life. The definitions also emphasize the good feeling perceived from the interaction between the individuals and the work environment.

OBJECTIVES OF THE STUDY

The objectives of the study are as follows:

- To identify the impact of quality of work life among the employees.
- To find out the level of career satisfaction among the employees.
- To determine the degree of career achievement attainted by the employees.
- To make a suggestion for improvement in quality of work life.

RESEARCH METHODOLOGY

The researcher has adopted "Descriptive Research" for this study. It includes surveys and fact-finding enquiries of different kinds. A complex enumeration of all items in the population is known as census inquiry. Here census survey is used and a total of 230 respondents in HCL peripherals were taken for survey. A pilot study was initiated among 30 respondents for the purpose of identifying and eliminating the potential problems. Final questionnaire was arrived at after making necessary corrections. The data were collected through a well-defined questionnaire with a 5 point scale, where 5 is rated as strongly agree and 1 is rated as strongly disagree. The reliability of the data was also tested through alpha test and correlation. Alpha value is more than 0.6 and the correlation values shows positive correlation among the factors considered for the study. Secondary sources wee used to identify the related variables considered for the study.

The questionnaire consists of 44 statements and the various statements are grouped into various constructs. The various constructs used for this study are learning new things, job satisfaction, utilization of employee skills and abilities, safety, health conditions, bonus or pay increment, trade unions, chances for promotions, fringe benefits, welfare, job security, and training opportunities.

DEMOGRAPHIC PROFILE OF THE RESPONDENTS

An analysis of the gender of the respondents reveals that 92% of the respondents are male and 8% are female. Details regarding the distribution of respondents based on age group reveal that 26% of the respondents are between 21-25, 63% between 26-30, 11% between the age group of 31-35. Information regarding experience is that around 72% have an experience of 1-5 years, 28% have an experience of 10 years.

Table 1 represents the mean scores of the quality of work life measures among different respondents. It clearly explains that except the role of trade unions, all the other factors like learning new things, job satisfaction, utilization of employee skills and abilities, safety, health conditions, bonus or pay increment, chances for promotions, fringe benefits, welfare, job security, and training opportunities are reasonably favourable for the employees. It indicates that the environment is favourable for the employees to increase their work performance. The percentage scores on Quality of Work Life are as follows:

TABLE I

Percentage Scores on Quality of Work Life

Sl. No.	*Dimensions*	*Mean*	*Percentage score*	*Favourableness*
1.	Learning new things	3.521	63	Reasonable
2.	Job satisfaction	3.512	63	Reasonable
3.	Utilization of employee skills and abilities	3.547	63.675	Reasonable
4.	Safety	3.350	63.25	Reasonable
5.	Health conditions	3.504	62.25	Reasonable
6.	Bonus or pay increment	3.504	65.25	Reasonable
7.	Trade unions	4.186	79.65	Highly Favourable
8.	Chances for promotions	3.586	64.65	Reasonable
9.	Fringe benefits	3.413	60.325	Reasonable
10.	Welfare	3.534	63.35	Reasonable
11.	Job security	3.390	73.35	Reasonable
12.	Training opportunities	3.482	62.05	Reasonable

HYPOTHESIS TESTING

Chi-Square test is based on chi-square distribution and as a parametric test, it is used for comparing sample variance to a theoretical population variance. As a non-parametric test chi-square can be used as a test of goodness of fit and test of independence. In the goodness of fit it is used to test how well assumed theoretical distribution fit to the observed data. In case of independence, it is used to test whether or not the two attributes are associated.

The hypotheses were framed to find out whether there exists any relation between the factors like Experience vs. Promotions, Gender *vs.* Promotions and Age *vs.* respect for employees.

TABLE 2

Variables	*Sig. of P Value*	*Level of*	
Experience *Vs.* Promotions	.293	.05	S
Gender *Vs.* Promotions	.582	.05	S
Age *Vs.* respect for employees	.076	.05	S

The chi-square test reveals that there is no significant association between the variables like experience *vs.* Promotions, Gender *vs.* Promotions and age *vs.* respect for employees at the 95% confidence level.

ANOVA

One-Way ANOVA is used when there is only one categorical independent variable and one dependent (metric) variable. Each category of an independent variable is called a level. An F-test under the ANOVA to test the null hypothesis that the mean values of the dependent variable are not significantly different from each other, at different levels of the independent variable. The F-test shows a significant level (p-value) of less than .05 on the ANOVA table, and the null hypothesis is rejected. If the p-value from the F-test is greater than or equal to .05, the null hypothesis is accepted. Thus, if the p-value from the F-test is less than .05, it proves at the 95 per cent confidence level that the variation in the independent variable is to cause significant variation in the dependent variable.

ANOVA has been conducted to explore if there are differences between age and job satisfaction, age and promotions, age and use of skills and abilities.

TABLE 3

Factors	*Mean*	*F*	*Sig.*
Age *Vs.* Job Satisfaction	5.462	5.919	.001
Age *Vs.* Promotion	5.331	5.539	.001
Age *Vs.* Skills and abilities	4.964	4.640	.004

Results indicate that there are no significant relations between the various factors like Age *vs.* Job Satisfaction, Age *vs.* Promotion and Age *vs.* Skills and abilities.

CAREER SATISFACTION AND CAREER ACHIEVEMENT

The KMO value in this research is greater than .9; it is considered as sampling adequacy. Communalities indicate the level of variance in the variables and have been accounted for the extracted factors. From the component matrix, 2 components are extracted namely career satisfaction and career achievement. The two major factors have been identified: The QWL are developing special abilities and handling promotions.

TABLE 4

KMO and Bartlett's Test

Kaiser-Meyer—Olkin Measure of Sampling Adequacy		.964
Bartlett's Test of sphericity	Approx. Chi Square	10850.567
	df	946
	sig	.000

ANALYSIS AND DISCUSSION

It is observed that on gender wise classification the male members are majority. 63 per cent of the respondents belong to the age group of 26-30. 33 per cent of the respondents are working as Jr Engineer/Executives. 71 per cent of the respondents are having one to five years of experience. Reliability analysis of theresearch shows that the cronbachs alpha is .986, and hence, the factors included in the questionnaire have internal consistency. Positive relationship exists between the variables like experience and promotion, gender and promotions, age *vs.* respect for employees. In ANOVA test, it is revealed that there exists a relationship between age and various factors like job satisfaction, promotion and utilization of skills and abilities.

Without doubt, the most important determinant of quality of work life is career achievement followed by career satisfaction and career balance. Age, education, total tenure years of employment and tenure with current employer correlate positively with quality of work life. Similarly the increase in the total tenure years of employment and tenure with the current employer also indicate the increase in the level of quality of work life. It also indicates that older respondents have been long in their career than are younger executives.

Fair compensation and job security drive the employees to take up more responsibilities, improvement in the individual skills, performance and accomplishments. Since the company is providing a good healthy working environment for the employees, the employees are more satisfied with their jobs. Since the organisation is providing opportunities for personal/professional development to their employees, the employees are ready to accept responsibilities at higher levels.

CONCLUSION

Organisations in many developing countries such as India are experiencing tremendous challenges in meeting the employment market demand. A good human resource practice would encourage the professionals to be more productive while enjoying their work. Therefore, quality of work life is becoming an important human resource issue in all organisations. Effective strategic human resource policies and procedures are essential to govern and provide excellent quality of work life among the employees. Conversely, poor human resource strategic measures that are unable to address these issues can effectively distort the quality of work life, which will eventually fail the organisations' vision of becoming competitive globally. Thus, this analysis attempts to suggest the meaning and what makes up the quality of work life from the perspective of the employees within the organisation. It is pertinent to have a better understanding of the changes in the components of quality of work life. By knowing the constructs of quality of work life, organisations are able to identify ways and means to improve the approach in minimizing the adverse impact of changes in work environments pertaining to quality of work life.

References

Allen, T.D., D.E., Herst, C.S., Bruck, and M., Sutton, 2000. "Consequence Associated With Work-to-Family Conflict: A Review and Agenda for Future Research". *Journal of Occupational Health Psychology*, No. 5, pp. 278-308.

Aminah, A., 2002. "Conflict between Work and Family Roles of Employed Women in Malaysia". In: Proceedings of the 17th Annual Conference of the Society for Industrial and Organisational Psychology, Toronto, Ontario, Canada.

Asakura, R., and Y. Fujigaki, 1993. "The Impact of Computer Technology on Job Characteristics and Worker Health". In: M.J. Smith and G. Salvendy (ed.) Human Computer Interaction: Applications and Case Studies, New York: Elsevier, pp. 982-87.

Bagnara, S., M., Mariani, and O. Parlangeli, 2001. "Quality of Working Life in Services". In: G. Bradley (ed.) Humans on the Net: Information and Communication Technology, Work Organisation and Human Beings. Stockholm, Sweden: Prevent, pp 139-54.

Beukema, L., 1987. "Kwaliteit Van De Arbeidstijdverkorting [Quality of reduction of working hours]. Groningen: Karstapel". In: Suzanne, E.J. Arts, Ada Kerkstra, Jouke Van Der Zee, and Húda Huyer Abu Saad, (eds.) (2001). Quality of Working Life and Workload in Home Help Services: A Review of the Literature and a Proposal for a Research Model. *Scandinavian Journal of Caring Society*, 15, pp. 12-24.

Evans, P., and T.S., Wurster, 2000. "Blown to Bits: How the New Economics of Information Transforms Strategy". Boston, Mass: Harvard Business School Press.

Grzywacz, J.G., and N.F. Marks, 2000. "Reconceptualising the Work-Family Interface: An Ecological Perspective on the Correlates of Positive and Negative Spillover between Work and Family". *Journal of Occupational Health Psychology*, 5, pp. 111-26.

Hackman, J.R., and G.R. Oldham, 1980. Work Redesign. Reading, M.A: Addison-Wesley.

Heskett, J.L., Sasser, W.E., Jr and L.A. Schlesinger, 1997. "The service profit chain". New York: The Free Press.

Lau, T., Y.H. Wong, K.F. Chan, and M. Law, "Information Technology and the Work Environment—Does it Change the Way People Interact at Work". *Human Systems Management*, 20(3), pp. 267-80.

Lawler E.E., 1982. "Strategies for Improving the Quality of Work Life". *American Psychologist*, 37, pp. 486-693.

Serey, T.T., 2006. "Choosing a Robust Quality of Work Life". *Business Forum*, 27(2), pp. 7-10.

Suttle, J.L., 1977. "Improving Life at Work: Problem and Prospects". In: H.R. Hackman and J.L Suttle (eds.) Improving Life at Work: Behavioural Science approaches to organisational change (pp. 1-29). Santa Barbara, CA: Goodyear.

Traut, C.A., R. Larsen, and S.H. Feimer, 2000. "Hanging on or Fading Out?: Job Satisfaction and the Long-Term Worker". *Public Personnel Management.*, 29, pp. 343-51.

Watson, I., J. Buchanan, I. Campbell, and C., Briggs, 2003. "Fragmented Futures: New Challenges In Working Life", Sydney, New South Wales: The Federation Press.

CHAPTER

26

Motivational Practices in Family-oriented Businesses to the Successors

S. SEKAR SUBRAMANIAN AND DR. P.C. SEKAR

ABSTRACT

Motivation is, in fact, pressing the right button to get the desired human behaviour. It is a process of stimulating people to action to accomplish goals. The management follows various practices to motivate people. Motivational practices differ from company to company. The family-oriented businesses also follow various motivational practices to motivate the employees and the successors. The successors of family business are of different types and of different characters. Very few successors have real interest to participate in the family business. Others are hesitating to take part in family business. The leaders of family business or kartas have to bring all the successors into the family business with real interest. Therefore, they follow different types of motivational practices for the successors. This article focuses on various recent motivational practices followed by the leaders of family business to bring their successors into the business with real interest.

Key words: Family Business—Kartas—Successors—Real interest successors, Easy going successors and Hesitating successors—Theory "X" and Theory "Y"—Recognition—Appreciation—Counseling—Training inside the business and outside the business-Rotation of assignments—Team-building exercises—Trusted mentors—Outside exposure.

FAMILY BUSINESS

Family Businesses include all enterprises that are owned, managed or significantly influenced by a family. In family firms, family has the final say in whoever is responsible for managing it. Family businesses are a blend of change and continuity, emotion and rationality and loyalty and competence. It makes the **family** business unique in composition.

- Family culture and values define business culture and values.
- Family membership usually entitles entry and ownership in the family business.
- Top positions are usually reserved for family members.
- Most of the family leaders have long tenure lasting till their lifetime or till their health permits.
- Family name is the corporate identity.

These are the important features of family-oriented business. The kartas of family business are very much interested in motivating the successors to take part in family business with real interest. So, the discussion of importance of succession is essential.

SUCCESSION

Succession means the transition of family business leadership and ownership from one generation to the next. Broadly speaking, however, succession is a lifelong process of planning and management that encompasses a wide range of steps aimed at ensuring the continuity of the business through the generations.

It includes:

- Factors as diverse as exposing your children to the business at an early age.
- Developing teamwork among sibling successors.
- Preparing for your own financial security in retirement.
- Drawing up an estate plan.

We make an important assumption that you and your family have already decided to keep the business in the family. We know this isn't a decision that can be taken lightly. It requires serious reflection and a strong commitment by the owner-manager and other family members. In order to keep the business within the family, the interest of next generation plays a vital role. To get clear idea, the successors of family business can be divided into various categories.

SUCCESSORS

Generally the successors of well known and well established family business concerns grow in a sophisticated social set-up. Only very few of them have real interest and involvement in family business while others do not.

We can divide the others who do not have real interest and involvement in family business into two categories. They are easy going successors and hesitating successors.

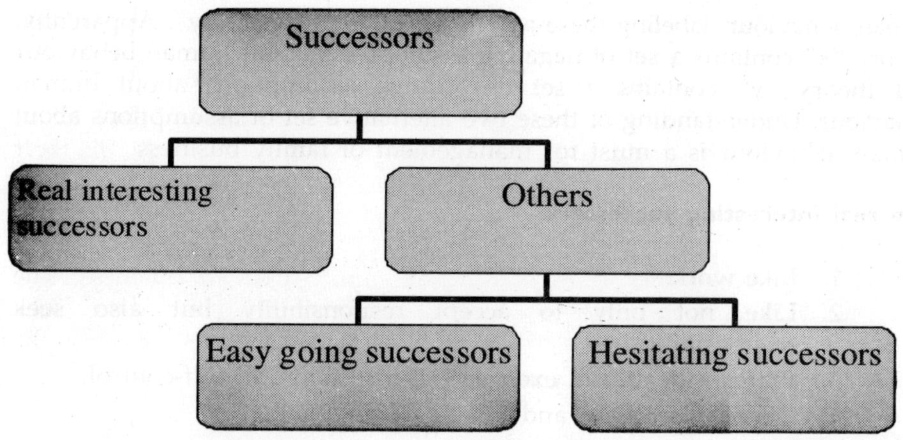

Easy going successors do not bother about their family business and even about their own future life. The leaders of the family business have to educate them to take part in the business. To bring the real interest and involvement among this type of successors, the leaders can make arrangement for counseling.

The hesitating successors hesitate to take part in the family business due to lack of technical knowledge about the business. In that case training is essential for the successors to bring out the real interest and involvement.

Recent motivational practices in family business include both counseling and training to the successors.

MOTIVATION

Motivation may be defined as a planned managerial process, which stimulates people to work to the best of their capabilities for the most effective and efficient realization of the common objectives of the enterprise; by providing them with motives to work for-based on their unfulfilled needs.

Motivation may be:

(1) Positive, or
(2) Negative

A positive motivation promises incentives to people and a negative motivation threatens the enforcement of disincentives.

In family oriented businesses, only positive motivation is possible to the successors, because they are sons and daughters of the owners.

THEORY "X" AND THEORY "Y"

Douglas Mc Gregor has developed two sets of assumptions about human behaviour, labeling these as Theory "x" and theory "y". Apparently, Theory "x" contains a set of negative assumptions about human behaviour and theory "y" contains a set of positive assumptions about human behaviour. Understanding of these two alternative set of assumptions about human behaviour is a must for management of family business.

The real interesting successors

1. Like work.
2. Like not only to accept responsibility but also seek responsibility.
3. Prefer to lead and exercise self-direction and self-control.
4. Possess creativity and imagination.
5. Have commitment to objectives.
6. Are not much self-centered and are interested in organisational goals.
7. Have unlimited potential of capabilities.

The other successors (Easy going and Hesitating successors)

1. Have a dislike for work and like to avoid work.
2. Wish to avoid responsibility.
3. Prefer to be directed by or led by others.
4. Lack creativity and imagination.
5. Do not have commitment to objectives.
6. Are self-centered and indifferent to organisational goals.
7. Have limited potential of capabilities.

The management of family business has to adopt the following steps to deal with the real interesting successors:

1. Democratic leadership.
2. Two way communication.
3. Flexible control.
4. Decentralization of authority.

The management of family business has to adopt the following steps to deal with the easy going and hesitating successors:

1. Autocratic leadership.
2. One way communication.
3. Rigid control.
4. Centralization of authority.

MOTIVATIONAL PRACTICES

The motivational practices followed in FOBs are shown in the following diagram:

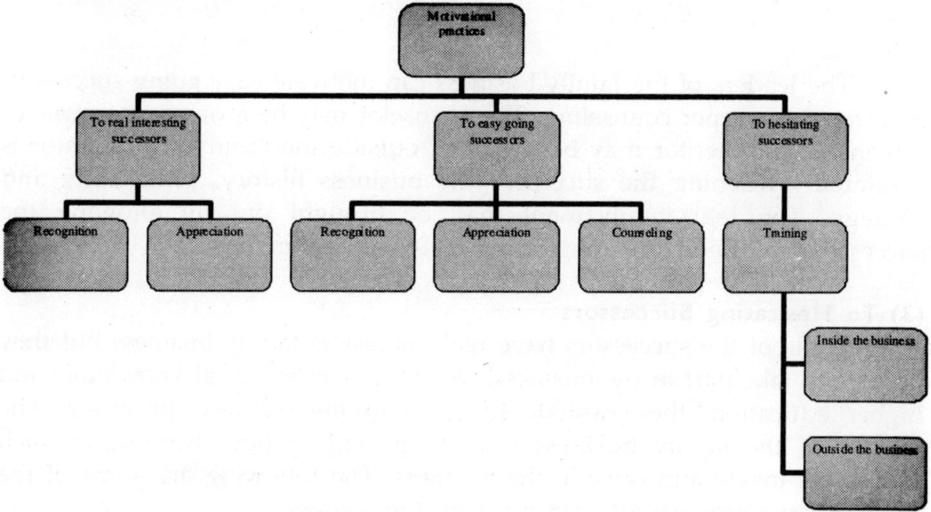

(1) To Real Interesting Successors

Only very few successors of family business have real involvement in business. From the childhood they have interest in business. They should be encouraged to participate in the business activities. They should be associated with the decision-making process. They can be encouraged in the following ways.

(a) Recognition

The leaders of the family business should give proper recognition to the interest shown and the work done by the successors. The performance of successors increases manifold when there is a positive reinforcement among the successors by the leaders of the family business.

(b) Appreciation

Sometimes, praise of work is a great motivator for a successor. Successors should be encouraged to participate in the decision-making process. They should have a hand in setting their goals so that they have a feeling of personal responsibility for their task. They should be given more latitude in deciding about certain routine things. Giving of a fine status also act as a motivator.

(2) To Easy-going Successors

The successors who do not bother about anything are called easy going successors. They spend more time and money towards entertainment. The leaders of the family due to more love and affection do not care about the personal life of their heirs.

Apart from the recognition and appreciation to the work done by the successors as we discussed earlier, the leaders of the family business should take one more step to create interest among such successors which is counseling.

(a) Counseling

The leaders of the family business can motivate easy going successors by arranging proper counseling. The counselor may be a owner-manager or a mentor. The mentor may be inside or outside the family. The mentor is continually teaching the successor the business history, philosophy and strategy. The real involvement may be brought out by allowing the successors to attend the company socials and ceremonies, etc.

(3) To Hesitating Successors

Some of the successors have real interest in family business but they hesitate to take part in the business. Due to lack of technical knowledge and higher education, they hesitate to come to the business premises. The leaders of the family business have to provide proper training to such successors inside and outside the business. The following are some of the training programs usually arranged by the leaders:

(a) Inside the Business

- Rotation of assignments and Gross-training within the company.
- Job assignments that offer the development of specific skills such as sales, marketing, finance, manufacturing, etc.
- Team-building exercises such as a take force assignments or joint travel with other managers.
- Involvements in business processes (board meetings, strategic planning sessions, etc.)

(b) Outside the Business

- Coaching by trusted mentors from outside the family and perhaps outside the business.
- Minimum years of work experience outside the family business.
- Outside exposure-visits to other companies.
- Giving additional education including technical education to the successors relating to their family business.

The above training programs are usually followed in the family businesses to motivate the hesitating successors.

CONCLUSION

The leaders of the family business follow a number of motivational practices to bring their heirs into the business with real interest and involvement. This is more important because the second part of the life of the leaders (after retirement) fully dependent on the success of their successors.

References

Rajesh Jain, Governance of family firms.
Craig E. Aranaft, Stephen L. McClure and John L. Ward; Family Business Succession.
Harold Koontz and Heinz Weihrich, Essentials of Management.
Dr. P.C. Sekar, Principles of Management.
R.N. Gupta, Principles of Management.

CHAPTER

27

Motivational Practices in Hotel Industry in Tirunelveli City

DR. K. SUBRAMANIAN AND S.M. ASYED MOHAMED KHAJA

INTRODUCTION

Motivation is the key to the success of any organisation: Service undertakings/manufacturing concerns/trading undertakings. Every organisation has its own goals to achieve. These goals can be achieved only through the employees. The basic problem is to identify what makes the people act.

Motivation can be defined as a process of stimulating people to act for the purpose of achieving the goals. Motivation can be defined as "a willingness to expand energy, to achieve a goal or reward."

BASIC NEEDS OF THE WORKERS

Better facilities, more pay, recognition, and more opportunities for promotion are some of the needs of the people. Drives are called motives and they represent the behaviour in the process of motivation.

Physiological Needs in the Workplace

They include the first necessities of life including air, water, food and sleep. This is the first reason that motivates people to work hard. It also depends on the degree of the need. If losing a job means the possibility of starving or losing a home, most people will naturally be inclined to work harder.

Safety Needs in the Workplace

Once biological needs are met, employees may continue to work hard to maintain job security. However, for most of the employees, motivation ends there. After job security is established, lack of motivation becomes related to higher and deeper needs.

Social Needs in the Workplace

Co-worker compatibility is important. If relationships are sour or there is a lack of, it can lead to boredom with unmotivated workers taking extra long lunch breaks or reaching work spot late.

Esteem Needs in the Workplace

Many managers and bosses subconsciously overlook this important need. To create happy and motivated workers, it is necessary to make them feel important and appreciated. When employees do a good job on a project, reward them with bonuses or other perks and benefits. Having an employees-of-the-month program is a cost-friendly idea that will inspire workers.

Self-Actualization Needs in the Workplace

Offerings that challenge the minds of employees and providing opportunities for growth are also great workplace motivation strategies. Opt for an employee incentive program where workers are able to receive commission, and job title shouldn't matter. It can also be an opportunity to discover the hidden talent. Second, give greater responsibilities to employees. It makes them feel important and allows them to take ownership of the company.

No matter what idea one puts into use, it's important to think about all the needs that are not being met. Keep in mind that when the "whys" in working are deeper, more enthusiasm and motivation will be produced.

USEFUL TIPS TO MOTIVATE THE EMPLOYEES

Show employees that the organisation is interested in the success of the employees.

60 to 70 per cent of workers do not feel that their companies help them to develop their career. Managers of successful companies are acutely aware that even the most brilliant business model will not work without skilled individuals motivated by a culture of management concern.

Allow employees to develop their skills

Many employees find themselves trapped in a narrow job function. Frustrated employees, unable to satisfy their need for growth, resign, leaving holes that affect the company's workflow in the short-term. The company also loses strong performers who could concentrate on more important roles over the long-term.

Give Employees a Clear Idea of the Long-term Goals of the Company

Three quarters of unhappy employees do not believe that their company knows where it is going. Companies should endeavour to change their perceptions by communicating effectively to employees the direction they want to take.

Reduce Labour Turnover with Good Training Programmes

Two principles can help companies score big retention wins through training. Firstly, keep it relevant. Some firms act as though any training is better than none. From the employees' perspective, that is not true. If training is not relevant to their jobs, they feel it is a waste of time. Secondly, use training to broaden experience. Companies too often provide training that merely reinforces old skills instead of building new ones.

Celebrate Birth Day of Employees

Just prepare a list of employees whose B'day can be celebrated with a big cake according to your team strength, and conduct a small session on weekends with all the employees.

Implementation of "Employee of the Month" Award

Collect rating of employees from their seniors and put a column for senior person and HR person also. Then after filling in all the columns, the person who has secured highest points will be the "Employee of The Month" of that particular month.

Money is good motivation

This is true in many situations as far as the employees are concerned. Money is the basic motivator of all employees as the primary needs are to be met only with money. However, money is not an end. It only serves as a means for achieving the minimum standard of living. To meet the sky high inflation, employees need a decent salary or wages. If it is provided by the employers, it acts as a good motivation. In some cases, it may be an individual financial incentive and when the task is done by a group, then collective incentives may be provided.

Stability of job

When the workers are provided stability in their job, then they feel safe and their level of satisfaction will be more, which will have an impact on the productivity of the organisation. Increased job satisfaction leads to increased performance.

Intimacy with the work force

To motivate the employees, one should understand that the employees should feel that the management has a deep concern for them: Ask their wards' name, their education and the lifestyle they are leading and the like.

No bias

Performance in the work place should be based on the performance of the employees and not on the popularity of the employee.

Delegation of work

When the management follows the practice of delegating the work to the subordinates, naturally skill development is possible and second line managers are trained, which will avoid brain drain in the organisation.

The environment of the work place should be in such a way that the employees feel happy and empowered by themselves.

The management should take the shortest time to reward the employee after the worker performed the job. The delay in payment of reward should be avoided.

The management may follow a policy to appreciate the good work of a worker in the presence of others and criticize the bad work privately.

A sound management always believes that participation of subordinates in decision-making enhances the motivational level of the employees.

When everything is kept as secret then it will create frustration in the minds of the employees which may be avoided as far as possible.

A prudent management will always aim at getting voluntary co-operation from their employees.

Workers' participation in setting the goals of the management is essential so that they will have a feeling of personal responsibility for their task.

Guidance by the management from time to time enhances the vitality and efficiency of the workers in the organisation.

High morale and low morale are directly related to higher production and lower production respectively.

Experienced managers acknowledge and celebrate the solutions to the problem; it is also a step to motivate the employees who have contributed in getting the solutions to the problems.

A manager who discourages and irritates his employees will never improve his subordinates' performance.

MOTIVATIONAL STEPS IN HOTEL SECTOR IN TIRUNELVELI CITY

Hotel industry is one of the important industries where workers and employees are more in number. This industry provides more employment opportunities and has a good contribution in inviting the tourists. This tourism directly and indirectly creates revenue for the respective zones. Proper attention by the employees is one of the factors which determine the success of the hotels. Erratic behaviour of the workers creates dissatisfaction to the customers which in turn affects the reputation and even sometimes the survival of the hotel. Only motivated employees of the hotels will attend the customers properly. Satisfied customers' voice is more powerful than advertisement and sales promotional measures.

More number of B grade hotels is functioning in Tirunelveli city and the city comes under Tirunelveli Municipal corporation limit. Tourist movement to the nearby Trichendur, a temple city, and Kanyakumari, which is one of the sacred places, makes many hotels profitable in the study area.

OBJECTIVES

The study aims at the following objectives:

(A) To analyse the motivational practices followed in the hotel sector.
(B) To analyse the satisfaction of the workers in the hotel sector.

SAMPLE

Ten hotels were selected at random which provides both boarding and lodging. In the lodges also sufficient numbers of employees are working. None of them is Star status hotel. A few of them are "A" grade hotels and a few come under "B" category. A questionnaire was prepared and distributed among the employees in the hotels. The observation technique was also followed to get first hand information. Few web sites were consulted to get secondary data for the study

FINDINGS

- 60% of the employees are working on temporary basis. However, they are also provided free clothing and shelter by the administration of the management.
- More than 85 percent of the employees are men.
- More than 70% of the workers have expressed that tips provided by the customers are one of the additional remunerations to the employees. Such income is encouraged by the managements of the hotels. The workers also express that if the administration prefers to restrict these tips, and then there will be demand from the workers' side to enhance the salary for them.
- Accommodation is provided by the management for many of the employees whose residence is other than Tirunelveli. Most of the employees have expressed that it is one of the major motivations provided by their management.
- Washing allowance is provided by the management.
- Many have expressed that not less than one month bonus is paid to the workers in the hotel industry in the study area during festive occasion (Deepavali function).
- Most of the workers have expressed that overtime is encouraged by the management and adequate remuneration is paid to them.

- In many cases the relationship with the supervisor is not cordial. Conflict is a matter of regular scene.
- From the view point of many respondents, salary structure is not attractive to the employees of hotels.
- Those employees who show their talents in attending the customers precisely during their visit to the hotel are given promotion to a better status in the same hotel or they are asked to join the sister concerns with increased pay and allowances. Many workers have expressed that even though all employees are treated equally, promotion is based on the performance of the individual.
- In many cases, the workers are not allowed to avail the leave facilities due to the increased work load during summer holidays and weekends. Under these situations, many workers prefer to take leave without informing the management. This sometimes leads to conflict between the workers and the management.
- There is no feedback collected by the management to assess the performance of the employees.
- While fixing the shift duties for the workers, the management makes it a practice to consult the workers concerned or their representatives. This attitude is welcomed by the workers in the study area.
- In the study area in this industry, workers are expected to cater to the needs of customers for a prescribed area only (one or two tables with maximum seating capacity of 6 at a table). For the value they have serviced, the workers are provided incentives by the management. Such incentives are paid at the weekends. The rate of incentive changes from one hotel to another. Some of the employees resign from services in the hotel for the reason that they are provided better incentives in the nearby hotels in the same area.
- It goes without saying that the workers are provided free food in the hotels where they are working. It is one of the major attractive factors for less educated people who are unable to get the job elsewhere. In the study area it is noticed that many people from the rural areas prefer a job in the hotel for this reason.
- In many hotels there is voluntary co-operation among the employees.
- Free trips to the nearby areas once a year, and a longer trip to places like Kodaikanal, Ooty and Mysore are arranged by the management. This step is one of the receptive factors that motivate the employees.
- Bringing co-ordination is one of the heavy tasks for the management.

- In the study area in some situations, disobedience on the part of the employees is the major reason for terminating the employee from the organisation.
- Like that labour turnover due to resignation is also recorded due to lower pay offered by the management.
- In almost all the organisations, minimum wages are offered to the employees.
- In the study area it is found that qualified persons (catering technology) are also provided jobs in the hotels. They are offered a better pay depending upon their contributions to the organisation.
- It is observed that the employees need a continuous direction and control from the management through supervisors and wing leaders.
- Separate independent houses on rental basis are arranged by the management to its employees. They are provided with basic facilities and enough provisions are made for recreation and time passing entertainments.

CONCLUSION

Even though the salary is not attractive and in some hotels only the minimum wages are paid, the management is able to get manpower. The reason is the velocity of unemployment problem. The management must come forward to improve the quality of work environment and to increase the salary to their employees. When this is provided, labour turn over may be reduced to a greater extent.

Building Motivation in Today's Workplace

DR. R. SHOBANA DEVI AND DR. P. SUNDARA PANDIAN

Motivation is the activation of goal-oriented behaviour. Motivation may be internal or external. The term is generally used for humans but, theoretically, it can also be used to describe the causes for animal behaviour as well. In many of today's work environments, employees' primary goal is quitting time and payday. Leaders' priorities are power, control and maintaining the *status quo*. Getting the job done is down the list. Once needed skills are mastered and employees follow established procedures, the job offers little or no challenge. The unwritten law is "accept the way things are or leave."

"Change equals challenge" is the source of motivation, workplace efficiency and job security. Because of fast changing trends and technology, work environments are evolving into continuous challenges. Responsibility is moving to the front line where it becomes the workers' responsibility to find the best way to get the job done, not management alone. For this to succeed, the front line must have continuous learning opportunity, be in a continuous learning mode and be continuously adapting to new environments.

Without motivation, employees will function at the lowest level possible and the results of the business will always be mediocre. Here are some ideas that can change that feeling in the office.

MOTIVATION TECHNIQUES

Certainly motivation is important to retain the quality staff and to make them put in their best efforts. In most workplaces, the atmosphere is gloomy and sluggish. Workers come in and do the least work possible to earn their salary and to keep their job. No one feels as if they want to be at the office. In this type of scenario, how could anyone expect to produce high quality results?

Link Pays and Perks to Performance

Rewards should go to those who achieve the most, based on a fair system. Employers can provide continuous opportunities to learn and to grow, even without promotions. Employees like that because they know that they have more marketable skills, so that if their job does end, they'll be able to find another one more easily.

Praise those who Perform Well

Managers sometimes forget to do "the simple things that cost nothing: letting [employees] know how much we appreciate what they are doing on an individual basis. That can be very motivating.

Take Employees' own Goals into Account

How do we keep our best people when we don't have a lot of resources? One of the ways is to make sure we are talking to them, finding out what's important to them. Keep job evaluations, such as annual performance reviews, separate from the personal-developmental discussions.

Make Pay and other Decisions as Equitable as Possible

Employees take tough news (such as no pay increase) in stride if they understand why the action has been taken, and if they feel it is being handled fairly. If people think they are being treated unfairly, their motivation will evaporate completely. Managers need to take the time to really explain to people the business challenges the company faces and why that's forcing some tough decisions.

Negotiate for Perks other than Pay Raises

These might include more training, travel, or a more flexible schedule. Employees are always looking for more decision-making authority, more of a say in how they do their work, and also more control of their own time and space—flexibility. Those are the kind of things that not a lot of employers provide, but are very important to employees these days because they're trying to get better balance in their lives, and they want to feel like they are respected.

Praise Achievement

Many workers feel disconnected and unimportant in their jobs. They do their daily tasks but it doesn't matter whether they excel in them or just keep them done. If there's no difference, most employees will end up gravitating toward the latter end of the quality spectrum. For this reason, we want to praise workers who do great work. Not only will our praise encourage them to keep working harder, but it will inspire the rest of the office, too.

Set High Expectations

Think back to when we were in school. Did we know the kids whose parents expected them to get high marks on their report cards? Did we also know the kids whose parents were satisfied as long as they weren't flunking? Now think about how those kids compared in terms of motivation.

Children whose parents set high expectations for them are more likely to achieve great things than those whose parents expect the minimum. The same is true of motivation in the workplace. We have to set a higher bar for quality, so our workers know we believe they can do better.

Know the Employees

If we are the Bosses or the Managers, getting to know our employees might seem like a bad idea. But it's actually great for motivation in the workplace. The employees can get to know us and that can make a huge difference in their motivation. It's a lot harder to let someone down when we know they'll be coming to talk to us first in the morning. If they feel comfortable with us, they'll have an easier time approaching us with problems and concerns that might also be interfering with their motivation.

Learn their Motivations

Another effective idea for motivation in the workplace is simply to find out what works for our employees and provide it to them. For example, some employees may be motivated by financial rewards. If they excel in their job, for example, we could offer them a gift card. We could bring in food for lunch as a surprise for the workers, or we could offer a contest for top performers. The important thing is that we learn enough about our workers to figure out the best way to motivate them to do the best job possible.

CONCLUSION

Financial rewards only play a little role in motivating employees. Money undoubtedly is a good motivator, but not always. Psychological rewards too play a significant part in boosting employees' morale. Just make sure we know every aspect of motivating our employees so that they can achieve the best rewards not only for themselves but for the company as well. Make sure we value our workforce contributions. Do not ever take away benefits from them. Remember that withdrawing benefits or downgrading the working conditions can really turn off our employees badly, so better avoid this. Also, harsh treatment, lack of trust and equality between different employees and rudeness create disharmony in the working environment. So make sure that the working environment itself is a source of motivation.

References

Brown, J.S., Duguid, P. (1991), "Organisational learning and communities of practice", Vol. 2 No. 1, pp. 40-57.

Jensen, M., Nielson, W., Kerns, R. Toward the development of a motivational model of pain self-management. *The Journal of Pain*. 2003; 4:477-92.

Miller, W., Rollnick, S. Motivational Interviewing: Preparing people for change, 2, New York: NY: Guilford Press; 2002.

Novy, D., Nelson, D, Francis, D., Turk, D. Perspectives of chronic pain: An evaluative comparison of restrictive and comprehensive models. *Psychological Bulletin*. 1995; 118:238-47.

http://www.accel-team.com/motivation/intro.html

http://EzineArticles.com/?expert=Tracy_Brinkmann

Motivation and Employee Retention in Indian ITES Industry

M. SHUNMUGA SUNDARAM AND P. SUMATHI

ABSTRACT

The ITES industry in India is gaining momentum and promises to add 3.3 million jobs in a country where productive employment is scarce. The nascent IT industry in India has come a long way in a very short time. Just a decade back, it all started as an activity in resetting password, making address changes and transcribing medical records and other such tasks. Today it has graduated to serve that call for expert knowledge and decision-making. There are numerous openings for job-seekers in the IT industry. The industry is estimated to grow into a $301 billion industry by 2010, and it is a sheer pleasure for the aspiring workforce in India. Indians have tactfully managed to produce quality assurance in different areas. Though there are so many benefits and privileges associated with IT industry, yet employees moving from job in less than a year, the multi-billion-dollar industry is confronting with the problem of retaining talent. Hence, it is the need of the hour to give strategic importance to the problem of retaining talent by the IT industry. It is to be recognized what tempts the employees to move out from the job. Motivation would be one of the points for consideration to face the problem of retaining talents boldly. In the present paper, an attempt has been made to see what motivates employees to join the ITES industry and why they are leaving the job. Moreover, an attempt has also been made to provide some suggestive framework by using motivational tool to retain employees.

INTRODUCTION

The business world is always dynamic and ever changing. The history of business world provides many examples of empowering some individual, group or nations, while excluding others. Outsourcing industry, the new entrants in the business lexicon a few decades ago, is now one of the most emerging sectors in the business world. With economic liberalization and service globalization, India too opens up its avenue for the outsourcing players. A few years ago, when outsourcing started out its journey in India to become the back office of the world, the path was fraught with uncertainty, but now, a significant portion of India's GDP has been contributed from the outsourcing industry. India still continues to be rated as the most preferred destination for outsourcing. Genpact, American Express, Citibank, British Airway, Dell, HP, Standard Chartered Bank, Deutche Bank, and Philips are among the companies taking advantage of India's capabilities. Despite conflicting accounts, the first documented practice of outsourcing appeared in the area of information system when General Electric contracted with Arthur Andersen and UNIVAC in 1954. The highlights of evolution of outsourcing industry are summarized in Chart 1.

CHART I

Evolution of Outsourcing Industry

Year	*Forms of Outsourcing*
1960	Time sharing
1970	Contract programming
1980	In sourced/in house
1990	Trigger effect
2000	Business process outsourcing and offshoring

In practice organisations use different approaches in outsourcing and typically in a hybrid fashion. There are primarily three approaches that are used both effectively and efficiently at different times over the last decade:

Big Bang approach is one where a significant portion of all activities is outsourced at one time; reported often in the media but less used in practice. The strengths of this approach are more interest from supplier due to potential revenue, centralized program and lower co-ordination cost. The weakness of this approach is greater risk; supplier may not have adequate skills. The piece meal approach is outsourced independently overtime and a variety of suppliers are used. The strength of this approach is the best supplier and price for each outsource activity over time. Third is the incremental approach where one or more suppliers are selected for pilot project with planned escalation of outsourcing; escalation occurs if preceding outsourcing is successful. The strength of this approach is to meet the immediate need through pilot.

BUSINESS PROCESS OUTSOURCING: A CONCEPTUAL OVERVIEW

ITES is a long-term contracting out of non-niche business process to an outside service provider to achieve better synergies in the organisational functioning. Business process outsourcing may be defined as the buying of component sub-assembly, finished product and services from outside suppliers rather than by supplying them internally. The scope of ITES sector is being expanded day by day. The nature of activities carried out by this is varied and complex. The major areas of ITES operations are database for recruitment and selection; insurance claims; processing of loan application; handling customer complaint; after sales service; telephone service; training activity; payroll system; appraisal system; customer complaint; human resource information system; market research, etc.

The resources like human, physical, finance and others playa key role in competitive economy, decide success or failure of business and the organisation is required to procure these resources at cheaper price to produce goods and services with quality to get competitive advantage over competitors. This is possible through business process outsourcing because ITES facilitate business community to get required resources at cheaper price in order to get competitive advantages over the competitor. The success of outsourcing business depends on improvement of quality workforce, strengthening infrastructure, proper people management, enhanced customer interaction and problem solution. Despite the tremendous growth, the ITES industry also confronts the problem of retaining the talent. People have been the backbone of ITES industry. Yet the very factor that has been industry's strength could turn into its enemies. ITES attrition rates are officially pegged by the industry at 46%, but informally it is as high as 70 percent.

LITERATURE REVIEW

The human resource arena is fast changing with the advent of the dynamic, volatile and employee-oriented ITES industry. The challenge of effective human resource management haunts every business process outsourcing managerial executive. The ITES industry has closed the gaps of geographical and national diversities and thus adopted a global business environment with an international standard. This cross-national approach has resulted in a paradigm shift in the trends of managing human resources of the ITES industry. The global approach with the diverse of work culture, workforce, international standards and intense competition intensifies the challenges of effective human resource management. The future of the ITES industry lies in the effective blending of the concept of human resource and evolving best suited strategies in human resource management and development (Nakkiran and Franklin).

Despite the fast growth in the ITES industry, players in India still have not reached a stage where they truly handle an entire business process. Apart from the regular HR functions, every HR manager has to rethink on the human resource strategies involved in identifying skilled personnel, to motivate, retain, develop and elevate the employees. The fact that though entry-level recruitment has not been a problem for the HR manager with the fresh graduates in the labor pool readily available with language skills, the industry has been facing a fast rate of labor turnover in this category. Attrition signifies not only the loss of talent but also includes the cost of training the new recruits. The attrition rate is reported around 35%, which is high for any industry. The employees though young with huge salary soon realize that the job characteristic has the side effect of psychological and physical burden. Many ITES centers demand nearly 10 hours of night shift, which damages the natural body clock of the employees and compounds in the form of social stress and health problems (Madhumathi and Sujatha).

Another problem has been the acute shortage of skilled CSR in an industry that suffers from a high rate of attrition. There is no creditable and independent institution for the formal training and certification of CSR competencies (Sanket). In a study Nitin Aggarwal, reveals that with employees moving to jobs in less than a year, the multi-billion dollar Indian ITES industry is confronting gnawing problems like productivity loss, training cost to name a few. The "Business World-ITES Industry Report" views that "it is difficult to pick which is the more serious problem-the outsourcing backlash or attrition. People have been the backbone of the Indian ITES industry-no other offshore location offers the unique combinations of volume and skills base that India does. Yet, the very factor that has been the industry's strengths could turn into its enemies. ITES attrition rates are officially pegged by the industry at 46%, but informally companies, even those among the top 10, admit that the attrition rates often scale as high as 70%. Along with attrition rates, salaries have also shot up drastically over the last couple of years. And there's a third problem. The huge talent resource base that has been the pride of the Indian ITES industry is fast depleting (Sengupta *et. al.*).

People, processes, and technologies are the key elements of the ITES business. Meanwhile, the industry has more to worry about than just reckless start-ups. Another major problem is the high rate of attrition and growth aspiration of the workforce. High attrition and growth aspiration of the workforce are the major problems faced by the Indian ITES firms. At least 60,000 of the 1,71,000 workforce change jobs every year. About 80% of them look for better prospect within the industry, as for example, agents want to become team leaders, who want to be upgraded as supervisors, or quality professionals or operations heads.

The labor cost is rising because voice based laborers are paid 10% to 15% more wages than the non-voice based employees because of the odd working hours and as a compensation for the resultant stress that is created. As far as training these employees Rs. 45,000 to Rs. 50,000 is spent on training and when the employee turnover rate rises, the overall cost of operation is also on the rise (Vijayalakshmi). It is not worth mentioning that in most of the literature that has been collected, more contemplation has been given to the narrative overview of the problems rather than providing the key to solve the problems. As the industry is growing and producing a lot of openings for the Indian youth, where productive employment is scarce, it is justified to conduct a study on the different human resource problems in the ITES industry with a special attention on retaining talent.

OBJECTIVES

The objectives of the study are:

1. To examine what motivates employees to join the ITES industry
2. To identify what tempts the employees to move out from the job.
3. To provide some suggestive framework by using motivational tool to retain employees.

METHODOLOGY

The paper is based on both secondary and primary data. Methodology adopted for the study is both descriptive and analytical. For collecting primary data Mail Questionnaire is used. The sample size is 30 and the process of convenient sampling is used. The average/percentage method has been used to analyze the data.

FINDINGS

From the analysis of the data it is found that the following are the key factors for which people join the ITES industry—

- *Age group*: When we look at the age group, all these respondents are in the age range of 21-25, with average age of 23.5 years. This shows that this sector is chosen by the younger people as their initial job.
- *First time jobs*: For most of the respondents, the current job is the first or second job. No respondents join the present job from other industries.
- *High salary*: The starting salary for these respondents is above Rs. 10,000. This is above most of the remuneration received in starting of a career without any professional degree. So it can be safely predicted that the starting salary has attractive attribute for joining the industry.
- *Group Mediclaim insurance scheme*: Unlike many start up jobs, ITES offers many HR benefits starting from the day one to the employee. Mediclaim, PF and other facilities are such examples.
- *Flexi time*: Because of the flexi timings a class of people opts for the ITES jobs.
- *Getting in hand experiences*: As the entry is easy, a lot of youngsters join the industry to gain industrial experience. This could be a basis for shaping their career with some experiences and helps them to determine their skills.

- *Scope for enhancement*: It is seen that the students also enter the industry in a big way to earn money during their holidays or night. These employees are always working temporarily.

The study also finds the following factor that tempts the employees to move out from the job. The stress level in the ITES is quite high according to the respondents. Though the work timings change from day and night, there are no or little compensatory benefits for working in night. The growth is slow. Time taken to grow up from the preliminary to a higher level is longer. Promotions are rare and they cannot raise quickly enough in the preliminary level. Need for educational enhancement is told by employees. As mentioned earlier, peers join this sector to earn and save money so that they continue with their dreams. The industry also doesn't provide any facility to enhance their qualification in the work period. Since the scope for enhancing the career is limited, people tend to shift their job in the early days.

SUGGESTIONS

It is clear from the study that though ITES employees are provided many facilities, they are not fully motivated to stay in one organisation. It is timely for all the employers to consider motivating employees as their present philosophy. But here the question is how to motivate them for retaining them in the same organisation because the basic fact is that most of us are considering our growth rather than the organisational growth. Let us see what we can do to retain the employees:

- *Give Employees much control over their work*: This might be one of the suggestive frameworks for motivating employees to stay in their job. One should try to give the employees the utmost level of control over their job by the means of putting creative element in the process of doing job, at least some degree of freedom in making decision, , etc.
- *Challenge them to improve the operation*: The more control and autonomy employees have over their work, the more they will be able to take better decisions in their work. Opportunities should be given to take challenges in improving their operation and using creative talent in the different aspects of their job.
- *Get to know every employee*: It is important to know every employee to have him or her motivated. It's important to have deployed team-building measures. Starting from the day one, the manager should have one to one meeting to know the employees better.
- *Give respect*: This is important to acknowledge every employee and his work. He should know that the company truly values his place and his contribution to the company. And he is an inseparable part of the future company.

- *Appreciate when employees do the right thing*: It is also important to show appreciation when something good happens to the company because of the team or individual actions. Such appreciation and acknowledgement in front of others boost employee confidence and these are good tools for motivating the employees.
- *The Great Idea Award and Implementation of the Idea*: There should be provision for acknowledging the most innovative employees and their ideas. These ideas should also be converted into regular day-to-day practice to make the employees take ownership of the success.
- *Opportunity for Study Leave*: As it is seen that most of the employees leave their job to enhance their educational qualification, it is therefore timely for the employer to have provision for the study leave, so those employees can get an opportunity to enhance their educational qualification.
- *Job Rotation*: In most of the interviews it has been seen that employees leave their job due to repetitive nature of the job. There should be provision for job rotation to avoid the repetitive nature of the job
- *Clear Career Path*: The new entrants in the organisation is not clear about their career path. Therefore it is important for the manager to make clear the career goal of the employees who have joined recently.

CONCLUSION

Managing the retention of talent in ITES is the necessary glue needed to build a supportive climate to implement a successful business process transformation. Retention of employees is critical to the long-term health and success of any organisation. Effective employee retention requires a systematic effort by the employee to create and foster an environment that encourages current employees to remain employed, by having policies and practices in place that address their diverse needs. Indeed most of the employers are busy with tracking information not on controlling people but on to creating and developing innovative and powerful solution to retain talent. The organisations are trying to have something innovative in their hands to retain talent to make a difference. But in real sense, this is not a very easy task. Here one has to think of how to engage employees in their work so that the problem of retention can be solved. As from the study it has been clear that "as employees' income increase, money become less of a motivators. Also as employees get older, interesting work becomes motivators."

In the above figure an attempt has been made to establish a framework to retain talent in the industry. As the Figure 1 shows, one has to use the "motivation mix" to solve such problems, where "motivation

FIGURE 1

Relation between Motivation Mix and Retention of Talent

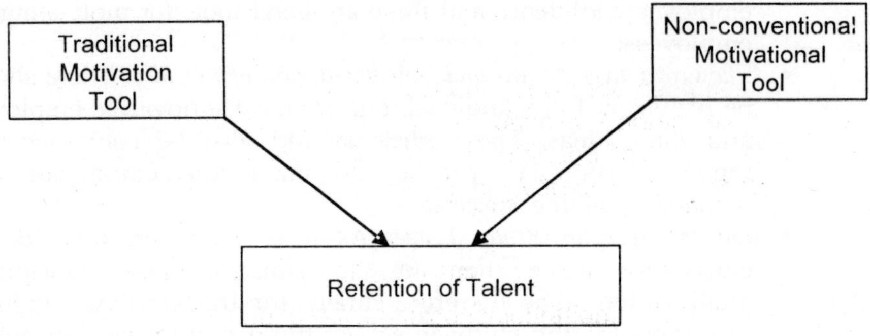

mix" implies combination of traditional motivational tools (like money, insurance benefits other fringe benefit, etc.) and the non-conventional ones (like involvement, appreciation, recognition, implementation of ideas and so on). The traditional motivational tool must be used with the non-conventional one to motivate the employees not to change their job. In the times ahead, if the organisation can use the "motivation mix" in proper manner, it can retain talent boldly.

REFERENCES

Aggarwal, Nitin (2005). Making the Right Call. *Indian Management,* 40-42.

Madhumita, R. and R. Sujatha (2005). Effectiveness in Outsourcing. *Indian Accounting Review,* 9(1), 64-66.

Nakkiram, S. and Franklin D. John. HRM and Development in ITES; ITES Concept, Current Trend, Management and Future Challenges. Deep and Deep Publication Pvt. Ltd., New Delhi, 289-99.

Sanket, Vij (2005). Call Centres: The House Keepers of the World. *Synergy,* 3(2), 91-110

Sengupta, Singdha; Singh Shelly and Moses Nelson Vinod. Business World ITES Industry Report, ABP Pvt. Ltd, New Delhi, 75-76.

Vijayalakshmi, D. Indian Manufactured Product Outsourcing—Trends and Trap. ITES Concept, Current Trend, Management and Future Challenges. Deep & Deep Publication Pvt. Ltd., New Delhi, 243-42.

Motivational Practice in Leading Private Sector Company

DR. B. SENTHIL ARASU AND DR. P. SUNDARA PANDIAN

PREAMBLE

Nearly all-conscious behaviour of human being is motivated. The internal needs and drives lead to tensions, which in turn result in actions. The need for food results in hunger and hence, a person is motivated to eat.

A manager requires creating and maintaining an environment in which individuals work together in groups towards the accomplishment of common objectives. A manager cannot do a job without knowing what motivates people. The building of motivating factors into organisational roles, the staffing of these roles and the entire process of leading people must be built on the sound knowledge of motivation. It is necessary to remember that level of motivation varies both between individuals and within group at different times. Today, in the increasingly competitive environment, maintaining a highly motivated workforce is the most challenging task. The art of motivation starts by learning how to influence the behaviour of the individual. This understanding helps to achieve both the individual as well as organisational objectives. Motivation is a powerful tool in the hands of leaders. It can persuade, convince and propel people to act.

WHAT IS MOTIVATION?

It is a general tendency to believe that motivation is a personal trait of every individual. Some people have it and the others don't. In practice, some are labeled to be lazy because they do not display an outward sign of motivation. However, individuals differ in their basic motivational drives. It also depends upon their areas of interest. The concept of motivation is situational and its level varies between different individuals, at different times. If you understand what motivates people, you have at your command the most powerful tool for dealing with them.

DEFINING MOTIVATION

Motivation is to inspire people to work, individually or in groups such as to produce the best of results. It is the will to act by exerting high level of efforts towards achieving organisational goals, conditioned by smart and efficient working and the ability to satisfy some individual needs.

Motivation is getting somebody to do something because they want to do it. It was once assumed that motivation had to be injected from outside, but it is now understood that everyone is motivated by several differing forces.

Motivation is a general term applied to the entire class of drives, desires, needs, wishes and similar forces. To say that managers motivate their subordinates is to say that they act in such a manner so as to satisfy drives and desires and induce the subordinates to act in a desired manner. Motivation is the most important of management tasks. It comprises the abilities to communicate, to set an example, to challenge, to encourage, to obtain feedback, to involve, to delegate, to develop and train, to inform, to brief and to provide a just reward.

PROCESS OF MOTIVATION

In the initial stage, a person starts feeling the lack of something. There is an arousal of need so urgent, that the bearer has to venture in its search to satisfy it. This leads to creation of tension, which makes the person forget everything else and start work in order to satisfy the same. This tension also creates attitudes and drives and regarding the type of satisfaction that is desired. Then it leads a person to venture in search of information. Eventually it leads to evaluation of alternatives where the best alternative is chosen. After choosing the alternative, necessary action is taken. Because of the performance of the activity, satisfaction is achieved which then relieves him of his tensions.

TYPES OF MOTIVATION

(1) Achievement Motivation

It is the drive to pursue and attain goals. An individual with achievement motivation wishes to achieve objectives and advance up the ladder of success. Here, accomplishment is important and not for the rewards that accompany it. It is similar to 'Kaizen' approach of Japanese Management.

(2) Affiliation Motivation

It is a drive to relate people on social basis. Persons with affiliation motivation perform work better when they are complimented for their favourable attitudes and co-operation.

(3) Competence Motivation

It is the drive to be good at something, allowing the individual to perform high quality work. Competence motivates people to seek job mastery, take pride in developing and using their problem-solving skills and strive to innovate when confronted with obstacles. They learn from their experience.

(4) Power Motivation

It is the drive to influence people and change situations. Power motivates people who wish to create an impact on their organisation and are willing to take calculated risks to do so.

(5) Attitude Motivation

Attitude motivation is how people think and feel. It is their self-confidence, belief in themselves, and attitude to life. It is how they feel about the future and how they react to the past.

(6) Incentive Motivation

It is where a person or a team reaps an award performing an activity. It is "You do this and you get that," sort of attitude. It is the types of awards and prizes that drive people to work a little harder.

(7) Fear Motivation

Fear motivation and coercions are acts against the will of the person. It is instantaneous and gets the job done quickly, but helpful only for a short-run.

KEYS TO MOTIVATION

Motivation, in and of itself, is little more than a feeling, an urge to move ahead. It cannot bring you the success and happiness you desire. It is the key to motivation that moves you from where you are now, to where you want to be. Without each element taking its place, you will have a difficult time trying to improve your life. But all hope is not lost! When you know the keys, you are ahead of the game. No longer will you wait for motivation to come to you, you'll go out there and get it!

1. DESIRE

This is the most misunderstood step in the entire process. When I work with individuals and businesses to increase their motivation, the source of the problem usually comes to this: they don't really want what they are working towards. It may sound obvious that you have to want something in order to achieve it, but it is the degree to which you desire that differentiates those who get what they want and those who are left wondering why. The first step is to honestly ask yourself how much you actually want to reach your target. In some cases, you may realize that the objective you thought you wanted was actually far from the real target.

2. BELIEF

The next step in the equation is belief. Do you believe in yourself and your abilities? Do you believe that you can do it? If not, then you must stop at this point for a personal Q and A. You must list why you don't think you can do it, and then work to fix those weaknesses. You must be confident of your ability to make it happen. Those who do not understand this step bang their heads against the wall in confusion at their futile attempts at success. When you truly believe in yourself, there is little that you cannot accomplish. A confident mind finds a way around every obstacle, or it simply runs through it. Each problem becomes an opportunity, and each minute that you are awake is fertile ground for new ideas, thoughts, and angles to approach the challenge.

3. GOALS

This is where you get the thoughts out of your mind and turn them into a working plan of action. A goal is a concrete and manageable blueprint for success. If you do not start with a specific goal in mind, you will be starting with a great disadvantage. Simply stating and committing your goal to paper brings you one important step closer to achievement. There is no magic in a goal. It is merely a focused view of where you want to head. It adds a bold red line on the map, and points you to the destination. But a goal is like everything else that is worthwhile in life; it only works if you do.

4. ATTITUDE

Throughout your trip to improvement and success, there will be ups and downs. There has to be. No road is completely smooth and free of obstacles. The way to make this work for you is to bring a positive and winning attitude with you. With the right attitude, you can be handed a failure, see it for what it is, a learning experience, and move on. I have seen the greatest of intentions fall flat because of a negative attitude. I have also seen the greatest of accomplishments because of a positive attitude. The choice is yours. The power of a positive attitude has been demonstrated again and again in our world. Choosing to be positive is choosing to be successful.

MOTIVATIONAL PRACTICE IN LEADING PRIVATE SECTOR COMPANY

The Private Sector Company is a Leading Indian engineering, construction and manufacturing company. It has diverse interests such as hydraulic equipment, electrical and electronic power services, fertilizer projects, medical electronics, financial services and information technology. The motivation practices followed in the leading private sector company are worth examining.

RECOGNITION AND MOTIVATION

They believe that their people are their greatest assets and that they are not just employees but strategic partners in their journey to achieve organisational objectives. In furtherance of their stated philosophy, their well-developed policies help them to recognize performance at work.

RECOGNIZING INDIVIDUALS AND TEAMS

They understand the crucial role recognition plays in motivating employees to demonstrate superior performance. There are many ways in which they acknowledge and appreciate good performance--from a sincere sharing of an "I Appreciate" note for a specific job well done to granting honors through an established formal "Employee Award Plans."

So if you're an achiever with a passion for setting and attaining goals, you'll find many opportunities for being recognized at the company. The 'Employee Motivation' Plan is another success story—a unique experiment to empower the line managers to recognize and give spot rewards to individuals and team in pursuit of excellence.

RECOGNIZING COLLECTIVE EXCELLENCE

In addition to the above, they have mechanisms to recognize collective excellence at an organisation level, on an annual basis. One such initiative is 'CE's Award for Best Managed Project'. The award recognizes excellence in the management of projects and encourages a competitive spirit amongst the Business Units to achieve better performance through higher standards in project management.

To encourages and foster the growth of a customer-oriented culture in the organisation and within a business unit in particular, the 'Rolling Trophy for the SBU with Best Customer Orientation' has been institutionalized. This award encourages a competitive spirit amongst the business units to achieve better performance through higher standards in customer service.

HR

The leading private sector company recognizes that people give the company its competitive edge. And through its people, the company delivers total customer satisfaction and enhanced shareholder value. The private sector company goes through a process of continuous learning, assisted by training programmes. Apart from on-the-job training and technical training, about 200 programmes on general management and behavioural topics (such as creativity, interpersonal skills, conflict management, achievement motivation and empowerment) are conducted each year. The private sector company always believes in experimentation with and implementation of new ideas and systems in HR, such as the performance appraisal system and career development. A unique experiment done in HR department, of self-directed teams, has brought about a significant change in creativity and customer service. Interactive CD-ROM-based programmes have enabled employees to learn at their pace. The company central library regularly evaluates and incorporates new training packages and assists other departments in procuring these self-learning packages.

The private sector company has its own Management Development Centre (MDC) at Lonavala (a hill-station around 100 km from Mumbai) with facilities to run multiple training programmes simultaneously. Most of company core development programmes and some behavioural training programmes are conducted here. MDC offers employees the opportunity for knowledge enhancement and learning through self-study and introspection. The faculty is drawn from India's finest management institutions.

An extensive and rigorous recruitment process ensures quality induction. The private sector company Graduate Engineer Trainee recruitment process covers India's major engineering colleges and institutions. Programmes, plant visits and comprehensive information-sharing facilitate induction.

TOTAL QUALITY MANAGEMENT

The private Sector Company started its change-management journey using TQM as a major initiative. Employees went through intensive training that emphasized enhanced teamwork, a structured approach to problem-solving, sharper focus on customer satisfaction and the creation of an empowered culture. Several improvement projects have been completed through Cross-Functional Teams. The Company has a talented pool of 500 trainers, and is in a position to cascade training initiatives. The change-management journey has helped the company to tap the potential of its people, and the company is now poised for a quantum leap.

EMPLOYEE FOCUS

The Employees Suggestion Scheme triggers the creativity of employees and motivates them to suggest measures to upgrade quality, enhance productivity, reduce cost and fine-tune safety practices. It acts as a powerful tool in moulding the value system of employees in line with the company's vision. Annual awards like Bachatvir and Suchanavir and awards in interdepartmental competitions promote participation. So far, 48 employees have won the Vishwakarma Rashtriya Puraskar instituted by the Ministry of Labour, Government of India.

WELFARE

Medical services of the company include preventive measures, promoting occupational health, curative treatment handling emergencies and accidents, periodic check-up of employees working in hazardous conditions and those with coronary risk factors, as well as periodic follow-up of tuberculosis, leprosy, cancer, diabetic and hypertensive cases. The company trains employees in first aid and organizes cancer check-ups, blood donation drives, hypertension and diabetic surveys and health education talks. The company has received several awards for its medical services and the prestigious NASEOH awards for employing the largest number of disabled persons at its Powai Works. The company has full-fledged medical clinics at its factories in Awarpur, Kansbahal, Hazira, Bangalore and Hirmi.

The company extends its medical services to the community through its Andheri Health Centre where consultants provide integrated health care to promote physical well-being and timely treatment through early diagnosis. Maternal and pediatric care is an important activity at the Centre. It is also a government-recognized institute for family planning and immunization. Trained counselors offer guidance to employees and their families in coping with personal and interpersonal problems at home and at work. They conduct programmes for employees' spouses and children to enhance their social awareness.

CONCLUSION

Motivation is necessary for any human activity. We generally don't realize it and don't observe it. Motivation is necessary in our day-to-day activities. It is as important in business as anywhere else.

It is just that in business the goals are set by someone else and the employees are expected to achieve them. The employees need to be motivated enough. This is done by offering many rewards and facilities. Many researches have been conducted on motivation in business or in other words motivation in the workplace. The organisations are always looking after introduction and implementation of new techniques to motivate their employees.

CHAPTER

31

Recent Motivational Practices and Quality of Work Life in a Successful Organisation

T.S. Uma Rani

ABSTRACT

Work is an integral part of our everyday life, as it is our livelihood or career or business. On an average we spend around twelve hours daily in the work place; this is one-third of our entire life; it does influence the overall quality of our life. It should yield job satisfaction, give peace of mind, fulfilment of having done a task, as it is expected without any flaw and having spent the time fruitfully, constructively and purposefully. Even if it is a small step towards our lifetime goal, at the end of the day, it gives satisfaction and eagerness to look forward to the next day. Quality of Work Life is a multi-dimensional construct, made up of a number of interrelated factors that need careful consideration to conceptualize and measure. Thus, QWL is a comprehensive construct that includes an individual's job-related well-being and the extent to which work experiences are challenging, rewarding, fulfilling and devoid of stress and other negative personal consequences.

INTRODUCTION

Work is an integral part of our everyday life, as it is our livelihood or career or business. On an average we spend around twelve hours daily in the work place; this is one-third of our entire life; it does influence the overall quality of our life. It should yield job satisfaction, give peace of mind, fulfilment of having done a task, as it is expected without any flaw and having spent the time fruitfully, constructively and purposefully. Even if it is a small step towards our lifetime goal, at the end of the day, it gives satisfaction and eagerness to look forward to the next day. Thus, Quality of Work Life is a multi-dimensional construct, made up of a number of interrelated factors that need careful consideration to conceptualize and measure.

Quality of Work Life (QWL) is a philosophy, a set of principles, which holds that people are the most important resource in the organisation as they are trustworthy, responsible and capable of making valuable contribution and they should be treated with dignity and respect. The elements that are relevant to an individual's quality of work life include the task, the physical work environment, and social environment within the organisation, administrative system and relationship between on and off the job.

Warr and colleagues, in an investigation of quality of working life, considered a range of apparently relevant factors, including work involvement, intrinsic job motivation, higher order need strength, perceived intrinsic job characteristics, job satisfaction, life satisfaction, happiness, and self-rated anxiety.

CONCEPT AND MEANING

Quality of work life is a process by which an organisation responds to employees needs for developing mechanism to allow them to share fully in making the decision that designs their lives at work. QWL consists of opportunities for active involvement in group working arrangements or problem-solving that are of mutual benefit to employees or employers, based on labor-management cooperation. People also conceive of QWL as a set of methods, such as autonomous work groups, job enrichment, and high-involvement aimed at boosting the satisfaction and productivity of workers. It requires employee commitment to the organisation and an environment in which this commitment can flourish.

MOTIVATION AND QUALITY OF WORK LIFE

Sirgy *et. al.* (2001) suggested that the key factors in quality of working life are need satisfaction based on job requirements, need satisfaction based on work environment, need satisfaction based on Supervisory behaviours, need satisfaction based on ancillary programmes, and organisational commitment. They define quality of working life as satisfaction of these key needs through resources, activities, and outcomes stemming from participation in the workplace. Maslow's needs are seen as relevant in underpinning this model, covering Health and safety, economic and family, social, esteem, actualization, knowledge and aesthetics, although the relevance of non-work aspects is played down as attention is focused on quality of work life rather than on the broader concept of quality of life.

Jerome M. Roscow, President of the Work in American Institute, has identified four critical and motivating factors, which affect the quality of work life during the year ahead. These are pay, employee's benefit, job security and alternative work schedule.

Pay

Quality of work life is built around equitable pay program. In future more workers may want to participate in the profit of the firm.

Employees Benefit

Since workers are now better organized and educated, they demand more from the employers all over the world apart from the pay--in the form of social security and welfare benefit as matter of right which were once considered a part of the bargaining process.

Job Security

Condition in the work environment must be created by the employer, which will give all the employees freedom from the fear of losing their jobs. A system must be created for optimum financial security. These alone are essential to improve the quality of work life in the organisation.

Alternative Work Security

With view to tackle job boredom, modern organisations have been experimenting with several forms of alternate work schedule such as four day work week, flextime and part-time week.

THE FACTORS THAT INTERACT QUALITY OF WORK LIFE IN ANY ORGANISATION

Career and Job Satisfaction (CJS)
Working Conditions (WCs)
General Well-Being (GWB)
Work Life Balance (WLB)
Stress at Work (SAW)
Control at Work (CAW)

Career and Job Satisfaction (CJS)

Career and Job Satisfaction is a very important factor in the overall quality of working life. Career and Job satisfaction reflects an employee's feelings about, or evaluation of, their satisfaction or contentment with their job and career and the training they receive to do it.

Working Conditions (WCs)

This includes aspects of the work environment such as noise and temperature, shift patterns and working hours, pay, tools and equipment, safety and security. Working Conditions assess the extent to which the employee is satisfied with the fundamental resources, working conditions and security necessary to do their job effectively. It is perhaps obvious that physical working conditions that influence perceptions of employee health and safety would affect employee QWL. Less obvious may be the link between the resources you get to complete your job, so-called work hygiene and QWL

General Well-Being (GWB)

General well-being (GWB) assesses the extent to which an individual feels good or content in them, in a way which may be independent of their work situation. GWB both influences, and is influenced by work. Mental health problems, predominantly depression and anxiety disorders, are common, and may have a major impact on the general well-being of the population and on the use of health service resources. General feelings of well-being may make the difference between positive or negative evaluations of work. The GWB factor is concerned with issues of mood, depression and anxiety, life satisfaction, general quality of life, optimism and happiness.

Work Life Balance (WLB)

Work Life Balance reflects the extent to which the employer is perceived to support family and home life. This factor explores the interrelationship between home and work life domains. It examines how these two life contexts influence one another. Issues that influence employee WLB include adequate facilities at work, flexible working hours and the understanding of managers.

Stress at Work (SAW)

Stress at Work is determined by the extent to which an individual perceives they have excessive pressures and feel stressed at work. The Stress at Work factor is assessed through items dealing with demand and perception of stress and actual demand overload. It is possible to be pressured at work and not be stressed at work (indeed some authors argue that lack of pressure at work can lead to stress), but in general high stress is associated with high pressure.

Control at Work (CAW)

Control at Work reflects the level to which employees feel they can control their work through the freedom to express their opinions and being involved in decisions at work. Perceived control at work is being increasingly recognized as a central concept in the understanding of relationships between stressful experiences, behaviour and health. Control at work within the current QWL model is influenced by issues of communication at work, decision-making and decision control.

FOR THE EFFECTIVE FUNCTIONING OF AN ORGANISATION

For the effective functioning of an organisation, every employee must be

treated equally, educated and motivated with the following concepts that influence and decide the quality of work life.

Career Prospects: Every job should offer career development. That is an important factor, which decides the quality of work life. Status improvement, more recognition from the management, and appreciation are the motivating factors for anyone to take keen interest in his job. The work atmosphere should be conducive to achieve organisational goal as well as individual development. It is a win-win situation for both the parties; an employee should be rewarded appropriately for his good work, extra efforts, sincerity and at the same time a lethargic and careless employee should be penalized suitably; this will motivate to work with more zeal and deter the latter from being so and strive for better performance.

Challenges: The job should offer some challenges at least to make it interesting; that enables employees to upgrade their knowledge, skills and capabilities, whereas the monotony of the job makes employees dull, non-enthusiastic, dissatisfied, frustrating, complacent, initiativeless and uninteresting. Challenging is the fire that keeps the innovation and thrill alive. A well-accomplished challenging job yields greater satisfaction than a monetary perk; it boosts the self-confidence also.

Growth and Development: If an organisation does not give chance for growth and personnel development, it is very difficult to retain the talented personnel and also to find new talent with experience and skill.

Risk Involved and Reward: Generally reward or compensation is directly proportional to the quantum of work, man-hours, nature and extent of responsibility, accountability, delegated powers, authority of position in the organisational chart, risk involvement, level of expected commitment, deadlines and targets, industry, country, demand and supply of skilled manpower and even political stability and economic policies of a nation. Although risk is involved in every job, its nature and degree varies in them; all said and done, reward is the key criterion to lure a prospective worker to accept the offer.

Regular assessment: Regular assessment of Quality of Working Life can potentially provide organisations with important information about the welfare of their employees, such as job satisfaction, general well-being, work-related stress and the home-work interface. Most people recognize the importance of sleeping well, and actively try to enjoy the leisure time that they can snatch. But all too often, people tend to see work as something they just have to put up with, or even something they don't even expect to enjoy.

Attitude: The person who is entrusted with a particular job needs to have sufficient knowledge, required skill and expertise, enough experience, enthusiasm, energy level, willingness to learn new things, dynamism, sense of belongingness in the organisation, involvement in the job, inter-personnel relations, adaptability to changes in the situation, openness for innovative ideas, competitiveness, zeal, ability to wok under pressure, leadership qualities and team-spirit.

Environment: The job may involve dealing with customers who have varied tolerance level, preference, behavioural pattern, and level of understanding; or it may involve working with dangerous machines like drilling pipes, cranes, lathe machines, welding and soldering machines, where maximum safety precautions have to be observed which need a lot of concentration, alertness, presence of mind, quick with involuntary actions, synchronization of eyes, hands and body, sometimes high level of patience, tactfulness empathy and compassion and control over emotions.

Opportunities: Some jobs offer opportunities for learning, research, discovery, self-development, and enhancement of skills, room for innovation, public recognition, exploration, celebrity-status and loads of fame. Others are monotonous, repetitive, dull, and routine, with no room for improvement and in every sense boring. Naturally the former ones are interesting and very much rewarding also.

Nature of job: Some jobs need soft skills, leadership qualities, intelligence, decision-making abilities, abilities to train and extract work from others; other jobs need forethought, vision and yet other jobs need motor skills, perfection and extreme carefulness.

People: Almost everyone has to deal with three sets of people in the workplace. Those are namely boss, co-workers in the same level and subordinates.

Stress Level: All these above mentioned factors are inter-related and interdependant. Stress level need not be directly proportional to the compensation. Stress is of different types—mental stress/physical stress and psychological or emotional stress. Among these mental stress and emotional stress cause more damage than physical stress.

TEN IMPORTANT WAYS TO IMPROVE QUALITY OF WORK LIFE

An organisation must motivate the employees to follow the ten important ways to improve quality of work life. The ways that are recently used in all the organisation are as follows:

(1) Have a personal vision of who you want to be and what you want to do—keep in mind that if you do not have one for yourself, you will likely become part of someone else's vision!

(2) Test out your own personal vision with that of your organisations—in how many ways do they support each other? Ask questions to better understand your organisation's mission, vision and values.

(3) Learn, and keep on learning—go to training sessions and in-services, enrol in college courses, read books, know why, not just how.

(4) Buddy-up—find ways to share the load with other team members. Sharing the load makes work easier to manage and less stressful.

(5) Share your successes—this allows you to learn from the success of others, as well as giving you a boost when you need.
(6) Get it off your chest—talk things over with your buddy, friend, supervisor when things trouble you; don't keep it bottled up inside.
(7) Find joy in being of service to others—think about how the person you are serving is better off as a result of your work, and rejoice in that knowledge.
(8) Take time for breaks—pay particular attention to the need to refresh body, mind and spirit.
(9) Try out new ideas—to innovate is to grow. By using your creativity and innovation, life becomes exciting and fulfilling.
(10) Have fun at work—laughter is the best medicine, but use only appropriate humor. Damaging someone else's self-esteem for the fun of it is no laughing matter.

CONCLUTION

Other things seem to be more likely to make people feel good about their work, once the basics are OK at work. Challenging work (not too little, not too much) can make them feel good. Thus, QWL is a comprehensive construct that includes an individual's job-related well-being and the extent to which work experiences are challenging, rewarding, fulfilling and devoid of stress and other negative personal consequences.

References

Kothari, C.R., "Research Methodology", New Delhi, Vikram Publishing House Pvt. Ltd.

Gupta, S.P., "Statistical Methodology", New Delhi, Sultan Chand and Sons, Publishers, 2002.

Rao, T.V. (1991), 'Readings in Human Resources Development', Mohan Primlani for Oxford and IBH Publishing Co., Pvt. Ltd., New Delhi.

WEBSITE:
www.google.com
www.hlipl.com
www.managementparadise.com

Recent Motivational Practices in the Organisation

DR. G. VANISHREE

Motivation is the acceptance of high level of effort towards an end, the end being need, satisfaction. Motivation is an effort made for certain performance. Motivation makes a person energetic to satisfy organisational needs through which his personal needs also get accomplished. Since 1950 motivational concepts have been developed: *Maslow's* hierarchy of needs, theory X and theory Y of *Douglas Mc Gregor, Frederick Herzberg's* hygiene theory, ERG (Existence relatedness and growth) of Clayton Alderfer, 3 needs of *David Mc Clelland* in the form of achievement, power, and need.

Some of the organisations follow certain methods to motivate their employees:

- Appreciation.
- Leisure.
- Rewards.
- Having good sense of humor.
- Organizing social get together.
- Celebrating *before he becomes frustrated.*
- Encourage *"a lot done"*; then *"what you did"*.
- Making them participate.
- Maintaining suggestion box.
- Inviting people to set goals.
- Keeping alive the team spirit.
- Coaching, monitoring, rewarding.
- Internal exchange of job to be considered.
- Financial and non-financial benefits to be enhanced as

incentives (non-financial includes status, need, recognition, inspiration, etc).

- Maintaining high morale.
- Maintaining quality circle.

Some of the recent practices of motivations are:

- Create a mind set *(top executives also wear Company's uniform and eat in the same canteen as done in Bangalore international airport).*
- British airway's 40,000 staff members were put together for a 2 day program called "putting people first".
- Leaders stand as examples of motivators *(as is done in the case of L&T).*

Financial incentives which are given will definitely work, but non-financial incentives like social status, need, recognition, inspiration will also work to retain an employee in the organisation for a long time. Team spirit is maintained as all work for common goal. Doing right things at right time improves the outcome of resources to relish best quality output and fetch more profits.

Globalization has made most of the corporate sectors to go beyond total quality management named as re-engineering, which is concerned in the field of thought, design, cost, speed, service, quality, quantity, etc. Idle work belongs to management which has shown benchmarking effect in the field of corporate outstanding performance, which in turn mobilizes people to create challenging tasks and follow different adaptive factors suitable for the organisation.

Few corporate sectors, for motivating its staff, follow reduction of negative implication on employees, 3600 feedback and collect data of their performance and capabilities. Existing skills are enhanced according to the needs. When people are meant to do, it is the enterprise which should involve all in conversation and make to do list.

People are put in charge for doing more just by trusting them; this itself is the biggest motivation to build his personal and professional needs. Once loyalty is earned, employees believe that they are trusted. Team leaders are generally persuading and influencing others to comment on doing certain courses of action. If an employee is emotionally built, it makes him realize the importance of success by which the head creates a platform continuously creating value of corporate transformation. If the culture of the organisation teaches *every one can and will,* this makes everybody to move a step forward and make the difference. Motivation of working staff creates benchmarking outcome of what corporate sectors need today for competitive global environment.

Make the employees a major stake holder and see that they accomplish the set goals of the organisation. Employee motivation has become a challenge to improve their performance which in turn influences the good will of companies and leaves no option then to motivate them through internal letters of appreciation or through in news letters. Some corporate sectors award gifts and vouchers to the winners, best performers, best team and some outstanding jobs. Well, incentives which are given financially will surely workout but now the latest strategies adopted by corporate sectors are non-financial benefits which include social status, recognition, inspiration, appraisal and fulfilment of their required needs.

Personality development programs are taken up as in the case of *Indian Institute of Management, Calcutta*, which is conducting a programme for managers having experience of 10 years or above to undergo training for one year, and the fee is 2.25 lakhs. Such steps taken by institutions reap good results. It motivates the person who is under training through corporate and at the same time fetches more output which makes him a best leader as the present skills are enhanced in technical and on technical field. Another example of *JNTU* can be highlighted as it has come out with a programme, *train the trainer;* here professors are trained who in turn train the associates and assistant professors to give best of their knowledge to students--in building an image of oneself and the organisation. Among highlighted examples a founder of *Sony* company in Japan *Akoi* Moriter creates family like relation in his organisation, shares feeling of belongingness and comes personally to encourage people whereever he finds them putting more efforts. Yes this is a kind of motivation which makes people put their best efforts as they are recognized.

Atlantic and Pacific Tea Company is following compensation based on performance; 25% of its sales revenue is returned as cash bonus for their employees, which motivates them to put more efforts and have the feeling of belongingness. A toy company in America follows piece rates pay plans and no base salary is mentioned. The senior corporate executives receive large benefits regardless of their company's profit or loss. Some companies in 1990's started giving more real wages in the form of *fly first class on official work, child care, elderly care, free uniforms, educational benefits, hi-tech communicative devise, and company's car* for employees. Hence, they are in the same organisation and fetch good results and get specialized to reap economies of specialization.

Jet airways recruited fresh pilots and adopted two-tire pay system. Experienced pilots were paid more pay and fresh pilots were comparatively paid less. This was followed by other airlines and motivated people to join as pilots with less experience. Such attractions help in building environment to change the scenario of society and organisations. In fact, it is nothing but changing old culture according to the needs of the present. Some CEO's of a company enjoy their birthday with top executives holidaying; this brings them both enjoyment and leisure. Beyond these practices flexible working hours of employees put up more quality with the same existing staff and we find in general employees demand more time for other responsibilities. It can be fulfilled because the ultimate aim of man is not only to satisfy his boss but also to satisfy himself as a member of family.

Designing the job as and when required is essential rather than follow the same structure and culture of old gives an advantage of competitive strategy and swim easily in global market.

Someone has pointed out that *the tip of doorman is directly proportionate to his attitude towards customers.* Yes a kind of motivation related to psychology in which each individual finds his own ways and means of motivation again depends upon thought, need, and time, as inspiration depends on deed and need.

CHAPTER

33

Quality of Work Life and Motivation

DR. S. VARADARAJ

The most important resource of any organisation is often said to be its people. The growth, development, prosperity and progress of any organisation depend on the strength of its potential human resources. Such people have to make things happen to aid in the achievement of the organisational objectives. Human resources harness all other resources effectively, whereas all other resources undergo the process of depreciation. A machine's maximum value reaches, the day it starts producing. Man never reaches an ultimate value through the life-time at work but is able to change, grow and enrich his value. Success of an organisation mainly depends on the quality of its manpower and its performance.

An employee is a worker in the factory and the bread-winner of his family. The happiness of the family depends upon the health and well-being of the worker. Safe and healthy working conditions ensure good health, continuity of services, and decreased bad labour-management relations. A healthy worker registers high productivity. He is cheerful, confident and may prove an invaluable asset to the organisation. Therefore, importance of environmental factors in working life cannot be ignored.

Quality of Work Life is very significant in the context of commitment to work motivation and job performance. It is the degree to which members of a work organisation are able to satisfy important personal needs through their experiences in the organisation. Managerial expectations are strongly linked with the organisational Quality of Work Life and it is a means to facilitate the gratification of human needs and goal-achievement.

It is not only monetary benefits, though monetary benefits still occupy the first place in the list of elements of Quality of Work Life, but also other elements like physical working conditions, job reconstructing and job-redesign, career-development, promotional opportunities, etc. are gaining importance rapidly. As such, the worker expects the management to improve all these facilities which thereby improve quality of work life.

If good Quality of Work Life is provided, employees concentrate more on their individual and group development. The management can get their attention with their high motivation and morale which paves way for rapid and smooth Human Resource Development.

Quality of Work Life refers to the level of satisfaction, motivation, involvement, and commitment individuals experience with respect to their lives at work. It is the degree to which individuals are able to satisfy their important personal needs while employed by the firm. Companies interested in enhancing employees' Quality of Work Life generally instills in employees the feeling of security, equity, pride, family democracy, ownership, autonomy, responsibility and flexibility.

This article, based on the study conducted in Textile and Engineering industries in Coimbatore District, Tamil Nadu, focuses on the various aspects of Quality of Work Life and its impact on motivation of employees in industries.

REVIEW OF LITERATURES

It is noteworthy that a number of studies were conducted regarding Quality of Work Life in various industries. The following are some of the observations and inferences made by various researchers regarding Quality of Work Life and the factors contributing to it.

Yousuf (1996) says that Quality of Work Life is a generic phrase that covers a person's feelings about every dimension of work including economic rewards, benefits, security, working conditions, organisational and interpersonal relations. To sum up, it can be said that Quality of Work Life denotes all organisational inputs which aim at improving the employees' satisfaction and enhancing organisational effectiveness.

McGarg and Bhatia (1997) say that Quality of Work Life is the basis for human resource development. It is important to have a conducive atmosphere. Quality of Work Life is one of the most important factors which lead to such conducive atmosphere. Good quality of work life leads to an atmosphere of good interpersonal relations and highly motivated employees who strive for their development.

Noble (1984) presents a detailed description of a Quality of Work Life experiment to improve worker motivation at a General Electric plant after the introduction of expensive numerical-control technology. Noble drew insightful connections between Quality of Work Life programs and the enhancement of productivity. He concludes that management is prone to revert to traditional authoritarian controls, if Quality of Work Life is perceived as a threat to its control over the labour process.

Buchanan and Boddy (1982) suggest that work should be organized to develop human skills and motivation is required for overall system effectiveness. Emphasizing on human beings in the organisation, Buchanan and Boddy (1983) discuss that human force is more important than economic and market forces. It is, therefore, important that work is organized to develop the human skills and motivation for organisational effectiveness.

Tannenbaum (1983) observes that sense of identification with the company contributes to motivation and to the success of the enterprise. He suggests that supportive egalitarian and participative climate have implications on Quality of Work Life.

The study conducted by Singh (1984) indicates that the overall perceived Quality of Work Life in the Indian industries is considerably poor. While this finding is common to all the work dimensions studied, the Quality of Work Life is perceived to be the poorest in the area of democratization of work culture leading to a state of mismatch between motivational profile and the existing Quality of Work Life.

Various studies invariably admit the role of Quality of Work Life in increasing productivity and improving job satisfaction and motivation.

OBJECTIVES OF THE STUDY

The present study is undertaken with the following objectives:

1. To identify the Quality of Work Life factors that influence the motivation of employees in the industries;
2. To study the opinion of the employees with regard to the factors of motivation among the categories of employees classified according to demographic variables; and
3. To suggest measures to improve the Quality of Work Life and thereby improve the level of motivation of employees.

RESEARCH INSTRUMENT

The factors of the study were drawn out from the related studies and the statements of the schedule were framed representing the factors. The Quality of Work Life factors considered for the study were Nature of job, Pay and compensation, Development and encouragement, Human relations and social integration, Workers' participation in management, Working conditions, Occupational stress, Alternative work schedule, Grievance procedure and Promotion policy.

The specific factors that contribute to the motivation of employees are as follows: Status of the organisation, Matching of job and skill, Fair and adequate wage, Adequate training, Opportunities for development, Promotion of human relations, Encouragement to offer suggestions, Introduction of novel ideas, Provision of quality equipments, Efforts to reduce monotony, Stress reduction programmes, Flexible working hours, Machinery for grievance-redressal and Fair promotion policy.

A structured, non-disguised interview schedule was prepared for the purpose of collecting the data. The extents of agreement on the statements were measured using five point Likert Scale. The various levels of agreement ranging from strongly agree to strongly disagree on the Likert Scale were assigned a numerical value. The survey was preceded by a pilot study, conducted by interviewing a sample of 50 respondents.

POPULATION AND SAMPLE PROFILE

In the industrial sector, Textile and Engineering industries are the major players which not only account for huge production and export but also they are the big employment providers. The study of Quality of Work Life in these two sectors is of great relevance which may help understand the overall Quality of Work Life in Indian industry.

The present study is confined to Coimbatore District of Tamil Nadu. This district is selected, keeping in mind that it is well-endowed with human resources. For the purpose of the study, five concerns from each textile and engineering industries were selected. It was decided to collect the necessary information from 500 employees of each industry. These employees were drawn from five concerns according to the number of employees. A Non-probability, proportionate quota sampling was used for the study.

COLLECTION OF DATA

For collecting the data, the respondents were contacted individually and given a brief description about the nature and purpose of the study. For the convenience of the respondents the statements were translated into Tamil and the questions were asked in a very simple manner with explanation to questions wherever necessary.

ANALYSIS AND INTERPRETATION

The data collected from the primary sources were analyzed using SPSS 11.0 package. Mean and Standard Deviation scores on motivation with respect to the demographic variables were calculated. Analysis of Variance on the opinion of the respondents regarding motivation was worked out. Analysis of significance of difference between the opinions of the respondents was also worked out with respect to each demographic variable.

For the purpose of analysis, the respondents are categorized according to their demographic characteristics: Gender, Marital Status, Age, Experience, Monthly Income, Educational Status and Level of Skill.

The following sections exhibit the classification of respondents and their mean scores and standard deviation. To test the significance of difference in the opinion scores, Z-test is worked out for the categories of respondents with respect to nature of industry, gender and marital status.

TABLE 1

Significance of Difference in Opinion Regarding Motivation

S. No.	Particulars	N	Mean	Std. Deviation	Z-Value	Level of Sig.
1.	**Nature of Industry**					
	Engineering	500	3.4361	0.3433		
					14.184	0.000
	Textiles	500	3:1199	0.3615		
2.	**Gender**					
	Male	818	3.2984	0.3873		
					3.555	0.000
	Female	182	3.1865	0.3689		
3.	**Marital Status**					
	Married	675	3.3030	0.3672		
					2.957	0.003
	Unmarried	325	3.2262	0.4189		
	Total	1000	3.2780	0.3863		

As far as motivation is concerned, the highest mean score is found in the case of the respondents of engineering industry and the lowest mean score is found in the case of the respondents of textile industry (refer Appendix I). It is found that the male respondents show more favourable opinion than the female respondents regarding motivation. The Z-value indicates that the married respondents show more favourable opinion regarding motivation than the unmarried respondents.

Analysis of variance is carried out to see the difference in opinion regarding motivation among the various categories of the respondents classified according to age, experience, monthly income, educational qualification and level of skill with the following null hypothesis:

Ho: There is no significant difference in the perception regarding motivation among the various categories of the respondents classified according to demographic characteristics.

TABLE 2

Significance of Variance in Opinion Regarding Motivation

S. No.	Categories compared	df (v_1;v_2)	F-value	Level of Sig.
1.	Age	2;997	3.793	0.023
2.	Experience	2;997	0.962	0.382
3.	Monthly Income	2;997	0.432	0.649
4.	Education	3;996	22.097	0.000
5.	Level of skill	3;996	2.927	0.033

The above table shows that there are significant differences at 1 per cent level in the opinion of the respondents classified on educational qualification regarding motivation. As far as age and level of skill of the respondents are concerned there is significant difference in opinion at 5 per cent level among the categories. However, there is no significant difference in opinion of the respondents belonging to various categories classified on the basis of experience and monthly income.

(i) Age

As far as age is concerned the respondents whose age is up to 25 years are grouped under 'low age category'; the respondents whose age is between 26 and 40 years are grouped under 'middle age category' and the respondents whose age is more than 40 years are grouped under 'high age category'. The following table shows the significance of difference in opinion regarding motivation between the respondents classified on the basis of age.

TABLE 3

Significance of Difference in Opinion Regarding Motivation between Categories Based on Age

Categories Compared	*Z-Value*	*df*	*Level of Sig.*
Low and Middle Age	-2.697	799	0.007
Low and High Age	-1.479	466	0.140
Middle and High Age	0.832	729	0.406

The Z-values indicate that the respondents of middle age category show more favourable opinion regarding motivation than the respondents of low age category at 0.01 level. But in the case of other categories of the respondents there is no significant difference of opinion is found.

(ii) Experience

As far as experience is concerned, the respondents who are in the experience of up to 5 years are brought under 'low experience category'; respondents with 6 to 10 years of experience are brought under 'medium

TABLE 4

Significance of Difference in Opinion Regarding Motivation between Categories Based on Experience

Categories Compared	*Z-Value*	*df*	*Level of Sig.*
Low and Medium Experience	-1.148	769	0.251
Low and High Experience	-1.109	675	0.268
Medium and High Experience	-0.067	550	0.947

experience category' and the respondents with more than 10 years of experience are brought under 'high experience category'. The following table shows the significance of difference in opinion regarding motivation between the respondents classified according to their experience.

It is observed that there is no significant difference of opinion regarding motivation between the various categories of the respondents classified with respect to experience.

(iii) Monthly Income

The respondents are classified on the basis of their monthly income in to three categories namely, low, moderate and high. The respondents whose monthly income is up to Rs.3,000 are grouped under 'low income category'; respondents whose income ranges between Rs. 3,000 and Rs. 5,000 are grouped under 'moderate income category' and the respondents whose monthly income exceeds Rs.5,000 are grouped under 'high income category'. The following table shows the significance of difference in opinion regarding motivation between the respondents classified on the basis of monthly income.

TABLE 5

Significance of Difference in Opinion Regarding Motivation between Categories Based on Monthly Income

Categories Compared	*Z-Value*	*df*	*Level of Sig.*
Low and Moderate Income	-0.656	743	0.512
Low and High Income	-0.913	471	0.362
Moderate and High Income	-0.398	780	0.691

It is observed that there is no significant difference in opinion regarding motivation between various categories of the respondents classified according to monthly income.

(iv) Education

Since the education decides the level of skill and the nature of work to be performed in the particular organisation, it is important to classify the respondents according to their education. Based on education, the respondents are classified into four categories viz., primary education, secondary education, higher secondary education and degree/diploma. The following table shows the significance of difference in opinion regarding motivation between the respondents classified according to their education.

The Z-values for this factor confirms that the respondents with higher secondary and degree/diploma education reveal more favourable opinion regarding motivation than the respondents with primary and secondary education at 0.01 level. However, in the case of other categories it is found that there is no significant difference of opinion.

TABLE 6

Significance of Difference in Opinion Regarding Motivation between Categories Based on Education

Categories Compared	*Z-Value*	*df*	*Level of Sig.*
Primary and Secondary	-1.280	537	0.201
Primary and Hr. Secondary	-6.705	579	0.000
Primary and Degree/Diploma	-3.866	206	0.000
Secondary and Hr. Secondary	-6.516	790	0.000
Secondary and Degree/Diploma	-3.044	417	0.002
Hr. Sec. and Degree/Diploma	-0.300	459	0.764

(v) Level of Skill

Based on the level of skill, the respondents are classified into four categories, namely, supervisors, skilled, semi-skilled and unskilled respondents. The following table shows the significance of difference in opinion regarding motivation between the respondents classified on the basis of level of skill.

TABLE 7

Significance of Difference in Opinion Regarding Motivation between Categories Based on Level of Skill

Categories Compared	*Z-Value*	*df*	*Level of Sig.*
Supervisors and Skilled	1.560	428	0.120
Supervisors and Semi-skilled	-0.642	494	0.521
Supervisors and Unskilled	1.244	382	0.214
Skilled and Semi-skilled	-2.625	614	0.009
Skilled and Unskilled	-0.107	502	0.915
Semi-skilled and Unskilled	2.189	568	0.029

The Z-values indicate that the respondents of semi-skilled category show more favourable opinion regarding motivation than the skilled respondents at 0.01 level and the respondents of semi-skilled category show more favourable opinion than unskilled at 0.05 level. However, in the case of other categories it is found that there is no significant difference of opinion.

SUGGESTIONS

This study is able to pinpoint some grey areas with respect to the factors of Quality of Work Life, which have close association with motivation, need special attention. These involve both hygienic and motivational factors such as training and development, human relations, work environment, work schedule and counseling. The researcher recommends the administrators of these industries to take steps to address the problems by enacting the recommendations with suitable modifications that fit their organisations.

(i) Effective Training and Development

Employees in engineering industry are normally more educated and skilled than the textile industry and it is quite natural that the more enlightened employees expect the management to take some measures for their development. As the technology grows in rapid pace it is imperative for the engineering industry to keep the employees acquainted with development and train them appropriately.

(ii) Good Human Relations and Social Integration

The complex nature of production processes and the heterogeneous nature of employees are the reasons for the not so healthy human relations and social integration in textile industry. Hence, the management has to take some special efforts to improve this factor. It is suggested that at least once in a month, meeting at departmental level may be arranged by the supervisors where the employees could put forward their opinion and speak out their problems.

(iii) Conducive Work Environment

It is quite understandable that the very nature of textile industry is such that the administrators work overtime and spend huge resources to create and maintain good working condition. It is suggested that the management may take steps to replace the old machineries and equipments with modern ones, so that the employees may feel more comfortable, more variety and less fatigue in their jobs. It is a fact that introduction of novel ideas and equipments would make the employees excited, active, feel proud and motivated towards their work.

(iv) Flexible Work Schedule

The tight and rigid work schedule will always keep the employees under pressure. The employees of textile industry are not happy regarding work schedule practised in the industry. Hence, it is suggested that a weekly or monthly schedule, which is flexible in nature may be evolved with the help of supervisors.

(v) Comprehensive Induction Training

It is suggested to both the industries to arrange for induction training which would help the new entrants to fully acquaint with the job, co-workers and organisation.

(vi) Effective Employee Counseling

It is also suggested that both the industries may give special attention on employee counseling. These industries normally attract many young unmarried men and women. Their lack of exposure to realities of work life and social life make them more emotional and problematic.

CONCLUSION

Going through the various findings of the study, the general impression one would get is that the motivation in engineering industry, by and large, is better than in textile industry. As both industries are in the forefront of the industrial growth and accommodate the major chunk of the work force of the country, concerted and concrete efforts for enhancement of quality of work life would do a lot to improve the morale and motivation of the employees, and as a result there would be improvement in the health of our Indian industry.

References

Buchanan, D.A. and Boddy, D.A. (1982), Advanced Technology and the Quality of Working Life: the Effects of Word Processing on Video Typist, *Journal of Occupational Psychology*, March, Vol. 55(1), pp. 1-11.

Buchanan, D.A. and Boddy, D.A. (1983), Advanced Technology and the Quality of Working Life: the Effects of Computerized Controls on Biscuit-making Operations, *Journal of Occupational Psychology*, June, Vol. 56(2), pp. 109-19.

De, N.R. (1976), Some Dimensions of Quality of Working Life, in Proceedings of National Seminar of Quality of Working Life, Bombay.

McGarg and Bhatia, B.S. (1997), Quality of Work Life: Basis for Human Resource Development, Deep & Deep Publications.

Noble, David F. (1984), Forces of Production: A Social History of Industrial Automation, New York: Alfred A. Knopf.

Singh, P. (1984), Motivational Profile and Quality of Corporate Work Life: A Case of Mismatch, *Indian Management*, Vol. 23, No. 2, February, pp. 13-20.

Tannenbaum, A.S. (1983), Employee-owned Companies, Research in Organisation Behaviour, Vol. 5, pp. 235-68.

Yousuf, S.M.A. (1996), Evaluating the Quality of Working Life, *Management and Labour Studies*, Vol. 21(1).

APPENDIX

MEAN AND SD SCORE OF RESPONDENTS CLASSIFIED ON THE BASIS OF DEMOGRAPHIC VARIABLES

S. No.	*Particulars*	*N*	*Mean*	*Std. Deviation*
1.	**Age**			
	Up to 25 Years	269	3.2251	0.4111
	26 to 40 Years	532	3.3045	0.3840
	Above 40 Years	199	3.2786	0.3505
2.	**Experience**			
	Up to 5 Years	448	3.2592	0.4103
	6 to 10 Years	323	3.2924	0.3748
	Above 10 Years	229	3.2945	0.3521
3.	**Monthly Income**			
	Up to Rs. 3000	218	3.2583	0.4584
	Rs. 3001 to Rs. 5000	527	3.2799	0.3856
	Above Rs. 5000	255	3.2909	0.3143
4.	**Education Qualification**			
	Primary	164	3.1578	0.3602
	Secondary	375	3.2042	0.3984
	Higher Secondary	417	3.3792	0.3576
	Degree/Diploma	44	3.3963	0.3755
5.	**Level of Skill**			
	Supervisor	155	3.2972	0.3631
	Skilled	275	3.2414	0.3523
	Semi-skilled	341	3.3209	0.3905
	Unskilled	229	3.2451	0.4270
	Total	1000	3.2780	0.3863

CHAPTER

34

Employee's Motivational Factors: An Overview

S. VENKATESAN

INTRODUCTION

One of the important human activities is managing. Ever since people began forming group to accomplish aims they could not achieve as individual, managing has becomes entail to ensure the co-ordination of individual efforts. As the society has to rely increasingly on group efforts and has many organized group have become large the task of managers has been raising the importance.

Basically, every organisation consists of purpose, structure, technology and environment. This lack of something creates tension in the mind of the individual; the individual tries to overcome by engaging himself in a behaviour through which he satisfies his needs.

Motivation is necessary for performance. If people do not feel inclined to engage them in work behaviour they will not put in necessary effort to perform well. However, performance of an individual in the organisation depends on other factors too besides his level of motivation. There are so many intricacies in motivation. Performance relationship, relationship was reward and motivation, and the most important, how an individual can be motivated for better performance.

MOTIVATION—AN INTRODUCTION

Motivation is one of the most important factors affecting human behaviour and performance. This is the reason why managers attach great importance to motivation in organisational setting. Lip Kert has called motivation as the core of management. Effective directing leads to effectiveness, both at organisational and individual levels. This requires the understanding of what individuals want from the organisation. However, what individuals want from the organisation has not been fully identified there.

Concept of Motivation

Today, virtually all people—lay people and scholars—have their own concept of motivation and they include various terms like motives, needs, wants, drives, desires, wishes, incentives, etc. in defining motivation. Technically, the term motivation can be traced to the Latin word movere, which means "to move." In order to understand the concept of motivation, we have to examine three terms: motive, motivating and motivation and their relationship.

Motive

Based on the Latin word movere, motive (need) has been defined as follows:

"A motive is an inner state that energises, activates, or moves (hence motivation), and·that directs behaviour towards goals."

Motive has also been described as follows

"A motive is restlessness, a lack, a yen, a force. Once in the grip of a motive, the organism does something to reduce the restlessness, to remedy the lack, to alleviate the yen, to mitigate the force."

Here, we can differentiate between needs and wants. While needs are more comprehensive and include desires—both physiological and psychological, wants are expressed in narrow sense and include only those desires for which a person has money and also the desire to spend the money to satisfy the wants. As we shall see later in this discussion, there are many psychological needs, like social needs, recognition needs, etc. which do not fall under the category of wants.

Motivating

Motivating is a term which implies that one person, in the organisational context, a manager, induces another, say employee, to engage in action (work behaviour) by ensuring that a channel to satisfy the motive becomes available and accessible to the individual.

In addition to channelising the strong motives in a direction that is satisfying to both the organisation and the employees, the manager can also activate the latent motives in individuals and harness them in a manner that would be functional for the organisation.

Motivation

While a motive is energizer of action, motivating is the channelisation and activation of motives, motivation is the work behaviour itself. Motivation depends on motives and motivating, therefore, it becomes a complex process. For example, Dubin has defined motivation as follows: "Motivation is the complex forces starting and keeping a person at work in an organisation. Motivation is something that moves the person to action, and continues him in the course of action already initiated".

Motivation is a process that starts with a physiological or psychological need that activates a behaviour or a drive that is aimed at a goal. Every employee is expected to show increased and qualitative productivity by the manager. To achieve this, the behaviour of the employee is very important. The behaviour of the employees is influenced by the environment in which they find themselves. Finally, an employee's behaviour will be a function of that employee's innate drives or felt needs and the opportunities he or she has to satisfy those drives or needs in the workplace.

If employees are never given opportunities to utilize all of their skills, then the employer may never have the benefit of their total performance. Work performance is also contingent upon employee abilities. If employees lack the learned skills or innate talents to do a particular job, then performance will be less than optimal. A third dimension of performance is motivation.

"Motivation is the act of stimulating someone or oneself to get desired course of action, to push right button to get desired reactions."

The following are the features of motivation:

- Motivation is an act of managers
- Motivation is a continuous process
- Motivation can be positive or negative
- Motivation is goal-oriented
- Motivation is complex in nature
- Motivation is an art
- Motivation is system-oriented
- Motivation is different from job satisfaction

NEED AND IMPORTANCE OF MOTIVATION

Motivation offers several importances to he organisation and to the employees:

- Higher efficiency
- Reduce absenteeism
- Reduces employee turnover
- Improves a corporate image
- Good relations
- Improved morale
- Reduced wastages and breakages
- Reduced accidents
- Facilitates initiative and innovation

It is normally believed that money acts as a motivator. In general the role of money as a motivator depends upon certain factors which are explained as follows:

Money fails to motivate people, when there is no direct relationship between reward and effort. Economic conditions of people influence the Importance of money. For poor person, the value of certain amount of money is quite high as compared to rich.

Money is a significant motivator at lower level of employees' level however money may not be a significant factor for senior executives who have already fulfilled their lower level needs. Employees are concerned not only wish the amount of money paid to them, but it should be fair and equitable as paid to that of other employees of same level or status. Social attitudes towards money and wealth also decide the motivation to earn more and more.

Nature of Motivation

Based on the definition of motivation, we can derive its nature relevant for human behaviour in organisation. Following characteristics of motivation clarify its nature:

1. Based on Motives

Motivation is based on individual's motives which are internal to the individual. These motives are in the form of feelings that the individual lacks something. In order to overcome this feeling of lackness, he tries to behave in a manner which helps in overcoming this feeling.

2. Affected by Motivating

Motivation is affected by way the individual is motivated. The act of motivating channelises need satisfaction. Besides, it can also activate the latent needs in the individual, that is, the needs that are less strong and somewhat dormant, and harness them in a manner that would be functional for the organisation.

3. Goal-directed Behaviour

Motivation leads to goal-directed behaviour. A goal-directed behaviour is one which satisfies the causes for which behaviour takes place. Motivation has profound influence on human behaviour; in the organisational context; it harnesses human energy to organisational requirements.

4. Related to Satisfaction

Motivation is related to satisfaction. Satisfaction refers to the contentment experiences of an individual which he derives out of need fulfilment. Thus, satisfaction is a consequence of rewards and punishments associated with past experiences. It provides means to analyze outcomes already experienced by the individual.

5. Person Motivated in Totality

A person is motivated in totality and not in part. Each individual in the organisation is a self-contained unit and his needs are interrelated. These affect his behaviour in different ways. Moreover, feeling of needs and their satisfaction is a continuous process. As such, these create continuity in behaviour.

6. Complex Process

Motivation is a complex process; complexity emerges because of the nature of needs and the type of behaviour that is attempted to satisfy those needs. These generate complexity in motivation process in the following ways:

(i) Needs are internal feelings of individuals and sometimes, even they, themselves, may not be quite aware about their needs and the priority of these. Thus, understanding of human needs and providing means for their satisfaction becomes difficult.

(ii) Even if needs are identified, the problem is not over here as a particular need may result into different behaviours from different individuals because of their differences. For example, the need for promotion may be uniform for different individuals but all individuals may not engage in similar type of behaviour; they may adopt different routes to satisfy their promotion needs.

(iii) A particular behaviour may emerge not only because of the specific need but it may be because of a variety of needs. For example, hard work in the organisation may be due to the need for earning more money to satisfy physiological needs, or may be to enjoy the performance of work itself and money becomes secondary, or to get recognition as a hardworking person.

(iv) Goal-directed behaviour may not lead to goal attainment. There may be many constraints in the situation which may restrain the goal attainment of goal-directed behaviour. This may lead to frustration in an individual creating lot of problems.

Motivation by Needs

There are many needs which an individual may have and there are various ways in which these may be classified. The basic objective behind classification of needs into different categories is to find out similarity and dissimilarity in various needs so that incentives are grouped to satisfy the needs falling under one category or the other. From this point of view, a meaningful classification of needs is based on the sources through which needs emerge.

Needs may be a natural, biological phenomenon in an individual, or these may develop over the period of time through learning. Since these two types of needs emerge from two different sources, these may be satisfied by different types of incentives. Besides, there are certain needs which are neither purely biological nor these are completely learned but fall in between the two.

Therefore, a separate category has to be provided for these. Thus, needs may be grouped into three categories:

1. Primary needs
2. Secondary needs
3. General needs

Primary Needs

Primary needs are also known as physiological, biological, basic, or unlearned needs. However, the term primary is more comprehensive as compared to other terms. Primary needs are animal drives which are essential for survival. These needs are common to all human beings, though their intensity may differ. Some of the needs are food, sex, sleep, air to breathe, satisfactory temperature, etc. These needs arise out of the basic physiology of life and are important to survival and preservation of species. These needs are also conditioned by social practices.

According to the concept of 'economic man,' these are the only wants of a human being and he attempts to satisfy them only. But researches in human behaviour show that psychological needs are equally rather more important for human beings.

Secondary Needs

As contrast to the primary needs, secondary needs are not natural but are learned by the individual through his experience and interaction. Therefore, these are also called learned or derived needs. Emergence of these needs depends on learning. This is the reason why we find differences among need pattern of a child and a matured individual. There may be different types of secondary needs like need for power, achievement, status, affiliation, etc.

General Needs

Though a separate classification for general needs is not always given, such a category seems necessary because there are a number of needs which lie in the grey area between the primary and secondary classifications. To be included in this category, a need must not be learned but at the same time, it is not completely physiological. In fact, there are certain such needs like need for competence, curiosity, manipulation, affection, etc. Here, we have just mentioned the classification of various needs into different categories for providing an understanding of the way needs emerge. Their detailed description will be provided in various theories of motivation, particularly based on contents, as these theories try to explain the different needs which people seek to satisfy.

MOTIVATIONAL FACTORS

There are several factors that motivate a person to work. The motivational factors can be broadly divided into two groups:

I. MONETARY FACTORS

Salaries or Wages

Salaries or wages is one of the most important motivational factors. Reasonable salaries must be paid on time. While fixing salaries the organisation must consider such as:

- o Cost of living
- o Company ability to pay
- o Capability of company to pay, etc.

Bonus

It refers to extra payment to employee over and above salary given as an incentive. The employees must be given adequate rate of bonus.

Incentives

The organisation may also provide additional incentives such as medical allowance, educational allowance, HRA allowance, etc.

Special Individual Incentives

The company may provide special individual incentives. Such incentives are to be given to deserving employees for giving valuable suggestions.

II. NON-MONETARY FACTORS

Status or Job Title

By providing a higher status or designations the employee must be motivated. Employees prefer and proud of higher designations.

Appreciation and Recognition

Employees must be appreciated for their services. The praise should not come from immediate superior but also from higher authorities.

Delegation of Authority

Delegation of authority motivates a subordinate to perform the tasks with dedication and commitment. When authority is delegated, the subordinate knows that his superior has placed faith and trust in him.

Working Conditions

Provision for better working conditions such as air-conditioned rooms, proper plant layout, proper sanitation, equipment, machines. etc. motivates the employees.

Job Security

Guarantee of job security or lack of fear dismissal, etc. can also be a good way to motivate the employees. Employees who are kept temporarily for a long time may be frustrated and may leave. the organisation.

Job Enrichment

Job enrichment involves more challenging tasks and responsibilities. For instance, an executive, who is involved in preparing and presenting reports of performance, may also be asked to frame plans.

Workers' Participation

Inviting the employee to be a member of quality circle, or a committee, or some other form of employee participation can also motivate the work-force.

Cordial Relations

Good and healthy relations must exist throughout the organisation. This would definitely motivate the employees.

Good Superiors

Subordinates want their superiors to be intelligent, experienced, matured, and having a good personality. In fact, the superior needs to have superior knowledge and skills than that of his subordinates. The very presence of superiors can motivate the subordinates.

Other Factors

There are several other factors of motivating the employees:

- o Providing training to the employees.
- o Proper job placements.
- o Proper promotions and transfers.
- o Proper performance feedback.
- o Proper welfare facilities.
- o Flexible working hours.

Motivation and Behaviour

Motivation causes goal-directed behaviour as indicated in its nature. Feeling of a need by an individual generates a feeling that he lacks something. This lack of something creates tension in the mind of the individual. Since the tension is not an ideal state of mind, the individual tries to overcome this by engaging himself in a behaviour through which he satisfies his needs.

Goal-directed behaviour leads to goal-fulfilment and the individual succeeds in fulfilling his needs and thereby overcoming his tension in the favourable environment. Behaviour ends the moment tension is released. However, satisfaction of one need leads to feeling of another need, either same need after the lapse of certain time or different need and goal-directed behaviour goes on. Thus, goal-directed behaviour is a continuous process.

Consequences of Non-fulfilment of Need

If the need is not satisfied even after the goal-directed behaviour, the person may feel frustration which can be defined here as the accumulation of tension because of non-fulfilment of needs. At this stage, the person will try to modify his behaviour to eliminate factors responsible for non-fulfilment of his needs, for example, putting more force for need satisfaction. However, there may be numerous such factors and many of them may be beyond his control. As such he is not able to remove the frustration through need satisfaction. Since frustration is not an ideal position for the person, he will try to bring him back by alternative behaviour.

The person would try to modify his behaviour to eliminate factors responsible for non-fulfilment of his need. However, the things blocking the person in achieving his goal are numerous and many of them may be beyond his control. He fails to control these factors and frustration remains there.

Reactions to Non-satisfaction of Needs

1. Flight

One way of handling a frustration is to leave the field or withdraw from the scene. Employees quit jobs that prove to be frustrating.

2. Apathy

Another method of withdrawal is showing indifference. If an employee does not leave frustrating jobs physically, he may remain absent psychologically, that is reading on the job, daydreaming, thinking of almost anything except the work at hand, etc.

3. Aggression

A more common reaction to frustration is aggression, an act against someone or something. An employee being denied a promotion may become aggressive and verbally berate his superior. The aggression may be internalised and in that case frustrated person finds fault with himself while the externalized aggression may be either to the source causing frustration (superior, etc.) or it may be displaced to others also.

The displaced aggression may be either towards a person or towards inanimate object. For example, a frustrated employee, if not able to kick his superior causing frustration, may attack his wife or son. However, if this is not possible, he may kick an inanimate object, e.g., door or so.

Motivation and Performance

Motivation is necessary for work performance because if people do not feel inclined to engage themselves in work behaviour, they will not put in necessary efforts to perform well. However, performance of an individual in the organisation depends on a variety of factors besides motivation. Therefore, it is desirable to identify various factors which affect individual performance and the role that motivation plays in this.

Factors Affecting Individual Performance

Observations show that:

- Various individuals perform differently in the same work situations, and
- The same individual performs differently in different work situations.

These statements suggest that various factors which affect an individual's performance are broadly of two types—individual and situational—and within each type, there may be several factors, that is,

Motivation of individual,
His sense of competence,
His ability,
His role perception, and
Organisational resources.

To conclude, if any of the elements is taken away, performance will be affected adversely. The double-headed arrow between motivation and sense of competence indicates that the two variables mutually influence each other. Reward, as a result of individual's performance affects his level of motivation. If the reward is perceived to be of valence and equitable, it energizes the individual for still better performance and this process goes on.

REFERENCES

I. Books

"Human Needs in Organisational Settings" by Alderfer
"The Practice of Management" by Drucker
"The Motivation to Work" by Herzberg
"Human Resource Management" by Suba Rao
"Personnel Management" by Tripathi
"Personnel Management" by Monappa
"Research Methodology" by C.R. Kothari

II. Magazines

Business Today
Business India
HR Review

III. Newspapers

The Economic Times
Business Standard

CHAPTER

35

Motivation and People Capability Maturity Model

G. Bhuvaneswari, Dr. P.T. Vijaya Rajakumar
and Dr. S. Kaliyamoorthy

INTRODUCTION

People Capability Maturity Model is a galaxy which amalgamates all the human resources development practices. Rudolp and Kleiner (1989) define work motivation as follows: "Motivation is the development of a desire within an employee to perform a task to his or her greatest ability based on that individual's own initiative."

People Capability Maturity Model (PCMM) is the exclusive model which concentrates on the step by step improvement and refinement of individual's capability and makes them matured to move the organisation towards the matured process and product. This people capability maturity model has been developed by Software engineering Institute (SEI) and it has been practiced by software companies. This model is the staged implementation practices with five levels of maturity and each level consists of five to seven key process areas (also called as KPAs). Each key process area has certain goals and practices to achieve the goals.

The step-by-step improvement of individuals won't be possible, if they are not interested in initiating their developmental practices. So, motivational practices are the apposite practices that are needed in the every key process area of PCMM.

PCMM MODEL

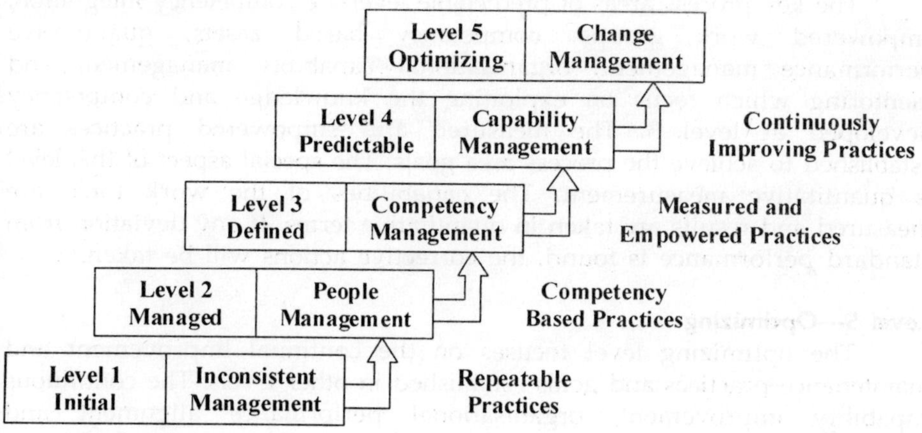

Level 1—Initial

This level is termed as inconsistent management. In this level, there are no standard practices. Project never meets its quality requirement and timely installation. The skilled people suffer in this level because of work overload. The initial level organisations have to put much more effort to achieve the maturity. In order to remove the inconsistencies, PCMM suggests stage wise practices to attain the maturity. PCMM stage-wise improvement practices are started in the managed level—level 2.

Level 2—Managed

The main objective of this level is to eliminate the barriers at unit level which resists the capabilities of the workforce. The people management at unit level is the main concern of this level. The key process areas in this level are work environment, communication, staffing, performance management, training and compensation. Certain goals are determined to achieve the maturity in these key process areas. A number of practices are established to achieve the goals. These practices are repeatable in the unit level so that workforce can feel accustomed to these practices without expecting someone to induce them to do the work.

Level 3—Defined

The level three moves the organisation from unit level issues to organisational issues. The key process areas in this level establish the competency-based practices to enhance the core competencies needed for the business. The key process areas of level 3 such as knowledge and skill analysis, workforce planning, competency development, career development, and competency-based practices, work group development and participatory culture have the goals to improve the work force capabilities which are important to improve the core competencies of the business.

Level 4—Predictable

The key process areas of predictable level are competency integration, empowered work groups, competency based assets, quantitative performance management, organisational capability management and mentoring which focus on exploiting the knowledge and competency developed at level 3. The measured and empowered practices are established to achieve the process area goals. The special aspect of this level is quantitative measurement. The capabilities of the work force are measured and results are taken in quantitative terms. If any deviation from standard performance is found, the corrective actions will be taken.

Level 5—Optimizing

The optimizing level focuses on the continual improvement and maintenance practices and goals established in other levels. The continuous capability improvement, organisational performance alignment and continuous work force innovation are the key process areas. The workforces are trained to continually improve the capabilities so that the performance can be aligned with organisational expectation. This can be achieved through continuous innovative practices.

Motivation as a Part of Strategic Objectives Pursued in the PCMM

PCMM has the following four objectives as its strategic objectives:

- Developing individual capability
- Building work groups and culture
- Motivating and managing performance
- Shaping the work force

These objectives are addressed in each maturity level in different ways. The third objective of PCMM shows that it gives special emphasis for motivation.

Key Process Areas Designed for Motivating and Managing Performance

Level in PCMM	*Key Process Areas for Motivating and Managing Performance*
Level 2—Managed	Work Environment Performance Management Compensation
Level 3—Defined	Competency Based Practices Career Development
Level 4—Predictable	Quantitative Performance Management
Level 5—Optimizing	Organisational Performance Alignment

Continuous Work Force Innovation

In any motivation theory, normally special emphasis is on work environment. The secured and adequate work resources and distraction free environment lead to performance improvement. In PCMM managed level, the practices lead to this kind of environment and the goals are established for improvement and management of performance. Any deviation in performance is corrected and managed; at the same time outstanding performances are recognized and rewarded. The compensation includes performance so that performance-based compensation is also a motivating factor for work forces.

In the defined level, people are motivated to improve their performance by development work force competencies needed for that particular project. The compensation system developed at the managed level is the main motivator for the competency-based practices. Also in the defined level, there is an establishment of career opportunities for work force which helps them in their career development.

In the predictable level, the work force performance is measured on the quantitative terms, and these quantitative values are compared with expected results. When the work force performance is compared with past performance, it would give a great prediction for future performance. This quantitative measurement creates the quantitative expectation of future performance among individuals which enables them to improve the performance by improving work force competencies which was practiced in the defined level.

In the optimizing level, the evaluation of quantitative measurement of performance used to check whether the performance at all levels of the organisation is aligned with the organisational objectives. It also checks that all the workforce practices are motivating aligned performance. The work force practices in the organisational performance alignment key process area are used to check whether the performance is aligned across the individual, work group and units.

PCMM connects all the theories in its key process area practices. Here, the PCMM Connectivity with Mc-Gregor's theory X and theory Y and Herzberg's theory has been discussed.

PCMM Connectivity with Mc-Gregor's Theory X and Theory Y

The practices carried out in PCMM try to convert even theory X people to theory Y. The practices in the PCMM different levels Key process areas coincide with the assumption in Theory Y.

Assumption in Theory Y	*Related Key Process Area in PCMM*
Under proper conditions, the average human being accepts responsibility	Work Environment (Level 2)

People will be committed to the objectives if they are properly rewarded	Performance Management and Compensation (Level 2)
Large number of people are capable of solving the organisational problems in an organisation with high degree of imagination, ingenuity and creativity	Continuous work force innovation (Level 5)

PCMM Connectivity with Herzberg's Two Factor Theories

According to Herzberg, maintenance or hygiene factors are necessary to maintain the reasonable level of satisfaction among employees. These factors do not provide satisfaction to employees but their absence will dissatisfy them. Therefore, these factors are called dissatisfiers. On the other hand, motivational factors create satisfaction to the employees but their absence does not cause dissatisfaction.

In PCMM model, the emphasis is given to hygiene as well as motivation factor. The key process areas which are related to Herzberg motivation theory are listed below:

Hygiene Factors	*Related Key Process Area in PCMM*
Interpersonal relations with subordinates	Communication (Level 2) Participatory Culture (Level 3)
Salary	Compensation (Level 2)
Working Conditions	Work environment (Level 2)
Interpersonal relations with superiors	Participatory Culture (Level 3) Mentoring (Level 4)
Interpersonal relations with peers	Communication (Level 2) Participatory Culture (Level 3) Team building (Level 4)
Achievement	Quantitative Performance Management (Level 4)
Advancement, Opportunity for growth	Career Development (Level 3)
Recognition	Performance Management (Level 2)

Motivational Practices PCMM

Motivational practices in level 2 key process areas are:

Work Environment

- Within prudent limits, adequate resources and funding are provided for implementing improvements to the work environment.
- Individuals receive the training necessary to maintain an effective work environment.
- Laws and regulations governing the work environment are communicated to the workforce.
- The resources needed to accomplish a unit's business processes are made available in a timely manner.
- Individual workspaces provide an adequate personal environment for performing assigned work responsibilities.
- Environmental factors that degrade or endanger the health of the workforce, Physical factors that degrade the effectiveness of the work environment, Sources of frequent interruption or distraction that degrade the effectiveness of the work environment are identified and minimized.

Performance Management

- Adequate resources and funding are provided for the performance management activities.
- All individuals receive orientation in the performance management process
- Adequate resources and funding are provided for recognition and reward activities.

Compensation

- Within each unit, an individual is assigned responsibility for ensuring that compensation activities are performed.
- Adequate resources and funding are provided for the planned compensation activities.
- All individuals responsible for performing compensation activities are trained in those components of the organisation's compensation strategy and practices that they need to understand to perform their responsibilities.

Motivational practices in level 3 key process areas are:

Competency-based practices

- Within each unit, an individual(s) is assigned responsibility for ensuring that workforce practices and activities are adjusted to motivate development in core competencies by all individuals and groups.

- Adequate resources and funding are provided for the planned alignment of workforce practices with the core competencies of the organisation.
- All individuals responsible for performing competency-based workforce activities are trained in the skills needed to perform them.

Career Development

- An individual is assigned responsibility to ensure career development activities are performed within each unit.
- Adequate resources and funding are provided for implementing the planned career development activities.

Motivational practices in level 4 key process areas are:

Quantitative Performance Management

- Adequate resources are provided for performing Quantitative Performance Management activities.
- Individuals who participate in Quantitative Performance Management activities develop the knowledge, skills, and process abilities needed to perform their responsibilities.

Motivational practices in level 5 key process areas are:

Organisational Performance Alignment

- Adequate resources and funding are provided for the planned performance alignment activities.
- All individuals analyzing and reporting performance data have been trained in quantitative data analysis and other relevant topics.
- All individuals involved in performance alignment activities receive appropriate orientation or training

Continuous workforce Innovation

- Within each unit, a responsible individual coordinates actions regarding proposals for improving workforce practices and activities and manages deployment of improvements or innovations.
- Adequate resources are provided for continuously improving workforce practices and activities.
- Individuals receive orientation or preparation in the innovative or improved workforce practices and technologies adopted by the organisation.

CONCLUSION

PCMM Model motivates the workforce by providing adequate resources to perform the activities, providing proper orientation and training, recognizing the workforce knowledge and skills and making avenues to improve them. This model is now applied in software organisations. But it is the universal model for all industries which would give the continuous improvement in people capability.

References

Stephen, P. Robbins and Timothy, A. Judge, "Organisational Behaviour", 13th edition, Prentice Hall India Publishers.

www.sei.cmu.edu

CHAPTER

36

Motivation through Shakespeare's Henry V and Hemingway's The Old Man and the Sea

DR. K. MUTHURAMAN

Nothing great in the world of organisation has ever been achieved without motivation. More things can be wrought by motivation than the world dreams of. Motivation imbues the employees with a passion for achieving the goals of an organisation. If the executives succeed in motivating the employees to cherish such an ideal, they won't find it difficult to achieve the goals of their organisations.

Motivation can be either intrinsic or extrinsic. Money and rewards can not work beyond a level. Self-satisfaction may fade with growing older. When the expectations of the employees are fulfilled, or when the organisation fails to fulfil their expectations, they may lose interest in their job and experience stagnation." In order to avoid this, which is detrimental to the vision of the company, employees must be motivated to have a constant "search" in their career. Though this job is very difficult for the executives, it can be achieved, but only by the motivated executives.

Experience is a great teacher. It is not only our experience, but also others' experiences, which can be learnt through historical, biographical, autobiographical, and, above all, literary works, which are a treasure-house of motivation. All these works provide examples of both "to-be" and "not-to-be" executives. A careful reading of all these works will certainly help the executives to motivate their employees and run their organisations successfully.

As literary works deal with human life, they are immensely useful to executives to acquaint themselves not only with the motivational techniques of various personalities, but also with universal human passions such as anger, jealousy, pride, ambition, lust, and avarice, a knowledge of which is indispensable to executives to deal with employees effectively and efficiently. As it is practically impossible to deal with all the literary works of various genres such as poetry, novel, and drama, I have confined myself to the leadership characteristics of the Sixteenth century British dramatist William Shakespeare's creation Henry V in the play *Henry V* and of the twentieth-century American novelist Ernest Hemingway's Santiago in the novel *The Old Man and the Sea*.

While management may appear to be a part of modern society, the experience of running organisations is actually an old one. During the period of Shakespeare, the "Senior Manager" was well known as the "Leader." His responsibility was to lead a nation, a clan, or a country. Leaders were called kings, queens, dukes, or lords. The organisations of the past, as of now, needed managers. These managers either led or failed. Efficient leaders managed their staff well and inefficient ones managed badly or not at all. Efficient managers understood the essential need for information and inefficient managers ignored it, feeling that communication with the subordinates was not necessary.

During the sixteenth century, management literature was not extensive; it was scarce (Though Machiavelli's *The Prince was the Best Seller*). However people had fascination for good stories about leadership, and Shakespeare wrote successful plays for the audience. In many of his plays, Shakespeare deals with a central character whose rise and fall from a monarchy form the nucleus of the story. In all these plays, the audience was taught lessons about how leaders organized their rise and how their failures precipitated their fall. As many of Shakespeare's plays are about politics, authority, and power, they quite naturally tell stories more of leadership than of romantic love.

For the past five decades or more, management literature has emphasized the importance of leadership in achieving the goals of an organisation. All the books on management argue that without leadership, executives and organisations will fail, and that is the characteristic that is missing in the management of executives.

An exploration of the congruence between Shakespeare's lessons on leadership and motivation with similar views of modern management theorists in the last few years of the twentieth century is worth rewarding. For example, the issue of motivating staff is at the core of much modern management literature. It is of utmost importance to reflect on how a senior manager reaches everyone in an organisation with the message that links an employee's actions to the organisation's vision. All managers, however large their staff group, have to struggle with the importance of communicating motivation. By now everyone recognizes this as an essential but difficult task.

Though we can cite several examples from the plays of Shakespeare to show the difficult job of a leader, it is difficult to think of a better example than the speech of Henry V during the battle of Harfleur. The battle has been going on for some time. Henry with his English troops is besieging the northern French town, but they are facing strong French defensive opposition and Henry's troops are beginning to falter. He rallies them with a speech that represents one of the clearest examples of a leader providing a lasting commitment to a new strategic direction:

> For there is none of you so mean and base;
> That hath not noble luster in your eyes.
> I see you stand like greyhounds in the slips,
> Straining upon the start. The game's afoot:
> Follow your spirit, and upon this charge
> Cry, "God for Henry, England, and Saint George!
>
> *(Henry V, Act III, Scene 1, 29-34)*

All managers would like to make a speech similar to that of Shakespeare's Henry V, because they want to be as certain as Henry so that their people will follow them. At the end of his speech, Henry is sure that his troops will follow him into danger. Such an assurance alone will help the managers to achieve the goals of the organisation. Henry has motivated his troops not with money or promotion or threat, but with effective communication. And all managers would like to create in their staff what Henry has created in his troops. In this connection, Kenneth observes: "The staff that Shakespeare's Henry needs to motivate are soldiers. The speech . . . appeals to their skill, enterprise, and courage" (79).

Shakespeare's Henry has motivated the soldiers through his powerful communication. In order to possess such ability, modern managers must be prepared to spend considerable time learning how to communicate and motivate employees. If the modern managers would like to communicate with the strength of Henry, they must spend their time and effort to understand their staff in the way Henry has done. Before becoming the king, Henry spent his time with young men in the bars of London and found what they were like through communicating with them. Henry presents a clear lesson for the corporate executive of the twenty-first century: "As an executive, how can I excel as a leader by being as wonderful source of motivation and achieving the goals of the organisation?"

As Rudolph and Kleinberg observe, "Motivation is the development of a desire within an employee to perform a task to his greatest ability based on that individual's own initiative." If an employee has such a desire or motivated to have such a desire, he will be determined to fight against odds. This desire to perform a task to one's greatest ability is manifested in the character of Santiago in Hemingway's novel *The Old Man and the Sea*. Hemingway's determined Santiago cherishes "one aim, one business, and one desire (12).

From the very opening of the novel, Santiago is portrayed as someone determined to fight against odds and struggle against defeat. He has gone eighty four days without catching a fish—he will very soon pass his own record of eighty-five days. But the old man refuses defeat at every turn. He is resolved to sail out beyond other fishermen to where the biggest fish promise to be. He lands the marlin, tying his record of eighty-seven days after a three-day brutal battle, and he continues to ward-off sharks from stealing his prey, even though he knows that the battle is useless.

Despite the odds against them, both Santiago and marlin display qualities of pride, honour, and bravery, and both are subject to the law of survival: They must kill or be killed. Santiago is well aware of the fact that no living thing can escape the inevitable struggle that may lead to its own death. But Santiago's undaunted spirit is determined to fight and succeed. To him,"Man is not made for defeat. . . . Man can be destroyed, but not defeated." Such an undaunted spirit is the prerequisite of leaders, and only such leaders can efficiently guide and motivate the other staff of an organisation.

Man may not succeed in all his endeavours, but he should never entertain the feeling he will fail; only then he will be successful in many of his endeavours. Further IL is not only the end, but also the effort that is important. Man can prove himself only through his efforts to battle the inevitable. Though, in the end, Santiago could not return to the shore with the flesh of marlin, but only with its skeleton, he is not defeated, though destroyed. His struggle is heroic, and he emerges as a true hero.

Besides his terrific strength, bravery, and moral certainty, Santiago possesses pride. His pride is not a flaw, but a virtue in his character. Santiago stands as a proof that pride motivates man to greatness. The old man acknowledges that he has killed marlin largely out of pride, and this pride becomes the source of his strength.

Santiago suggests that victory is not a prerequisite for honour. Instead glory depends on having the pride to see a struggle through its end, regardless of the outcome. The glory and the honour Santiago accrues come not from his battle itself, but from his pride and determination to fight. The leaders and the other staff of organisations must emulate Santiago's pride and determination.

When managers and staff of an organisation begin to falter, Shakespeare's Henry and Hemingway's Santiago will serve as a source of inspiration and motivation, and will definitely lift them to greater heights. When leaders and other employees lack confidence, they should remember Henry and Santiago, who will imbue them with courage and confidence. The role of literary works in human life, especially organisational life, is immense. If we unlock the treasure house of literature, we will be surprised to know that the solutions for many of our unsolved problems remain buried in literary works.

REFERENCES

Shakespeare, William. *Henry V*. New York: Dover Publishers, 2003.

Hemingway, Ernest. *The Old Man and the Sea*. New York: Charles Scribner's Sons, 1952.

Young, Philip.'The Old Man and the Sea: Vision/Revision." Ed. Katherine T. Jones. New Jersey: Prentice Hall, 1968.

Gurko, Leo. "The Heroic Impulse in *The Old Man and the Sea*." Ed. Katherine T. Jones. New Jersey: Prentice Hall, 1968.

Right Motivation Formula

MR. S. NASAR AND D.J. LINI MOL

ABSTRACT

This study investigates the relationship between transformational leadership and work motivation in modern organisations. Critical attention is given to transformational leaders' competencies needed to motivate individuals/teams effectively and improve employee performance. Some implications of the study are discussed including the need for supervisors to acquire and use emotional intelligence competencies and empowerment tools in order to enhance their own transformational leadership and develop motivational strategies. Moreover, organisational culture and design can affect skilled employee motivation levels in several ways such as job rotation, participation, employment security, performance appraisal, compensation systems, training and task allocation.

INTRODUCTION

The role of leadership in management is largely determined by the organisational culture of the company. Managers' beliefs, values and assumptions are of critical importance to the overall style of leadership that they adopt. There are several different leadership styles that can be identified within organisational context. Each style has its own set of good and not-so-good characteristics, and each uses leadership in a different way.

Perhaps the most difficult aspect of being a work team leader is motivation of team members. Work teams may be more successful in achieving organisational goals if their members are empowerment to do their jobs. Conversely, if their authority and responsibility are restricted, team members may well reduce their levels of commitment. They might continue to perform satisfactorily but with little enthusiasm for improving quality and productivity.

Informal meetings between individuals on regular basis empower joint decision-making and participative management. Moreover, the existence of accurate job description on individual/team basis is associated positively with effective task allocation and the absence of role conflict. Under these conditions, it is more likely to assign jobs to employees, so as to minimize costs and to ensure that the allocation respects the employees' abilities and fosters job satisfaction.

TRANSFORMATIONAL LEADERSHIP

Transformational leaders provide extraordinary motivation by appealing to follower's ideals and moral values and inspiring them to think about problems in new ways. A leader can motivate followers by making them more aware of the importance and value of their tasks and the need to place them ahead of their own self-interests. Transformational leaders influence rests on their ability to inspire others through their words, visions and actions. In essence, transformational leaders make tomorrow's dreams a reality for their followers.

Following Burns and Bass transformational leadership is associated with distinct dimensions of charisma or idealized influence (extent of pride, trust and respect engendered by and emotional identification with the leader), intellectual stimulation (extent the leader encourages followers to question their own way of doing things and become innovative) and individualized consideration (extent the leader provides personal attention and encouragement for self-development of followers). Charisma is a form of interpersonal attraction that inspires support and acceptance. All else being equal, then, someone with charisma is more likely to be able to influence others than is someone without charisma. Thus, influence is again a fundamental element of this perspective. Charismatic leadership goes beyond transactional leadership styles. The charismatic leader has the capacity to motivate people to do more than normally expected. The impact of charismatic leaders is normally from stating a lofty vision of an imagined future that employee identify with, shaping a corporate value system for which everyone stands, and trusting subordinates and earning followers' complete trust in return.

Charismatic leaders raise subordinates consciousness about new outcomes and motivate them to transcend their own interests for the sake of the department of organisation. They create an atmosphere of change and they may be obsessed by visionary ideas that excite, stimulate and drive other people to work hard. Charismatic leaders have an emotional impact on subordinates. They stand for something, have a vision of the future, are able to communicate that vision to subordinates and motivate them to realize it. The true charismatic leader often does not fit within a traditional organisation and may lead a social movement rather than a formal organisation.

On another but related issue the leaders who possess interpersonal intelligence may be associated with transformational leadership for several reasons. Leaders who possess empathy aspect of emotional intelligence (EQ) are likely to recognize followers' need, take active interest in them, and respond to changes in their emotional states. Empathy is likely to be associated with individualized consideration. Social skills aspect of EQ, which is associated with enabling followers to engage in desirable behaviours, is likely to be associated with intellectual stimulation. Employees are likely to respect and emotionally identify with a leader who is considerate and is willing to help employees to be effective, integrate goals and improve their job performance.

WORK MOTIVATION

The term motivation derives from the Latin word for movement (movere). Building on this concept, Atkinson defines motivation as "the contemporary (immediate) influence on direction, vigor, and persistence of action", while Vroom defines it as "a process governing choice made by persons... among alternative forms of voluntary activity". When studying motivation as it relates to the work place, the goal is to define what is more appropriate in terms of motivation to excel in a particular job requirement. One's overall motivation is too broad of a concept to be dealt with scientifically.

The fields of economics, decision-making, sociology and psychology share a common desire to understand our human nature that is, our essential character. disposition, or temperament. This extensive, multi-disciplinary interest in establishing who we are reflects the enormous ramifications of the endeavor. As Pinker catalogs, theories of human nature have been used to direct relationships, lifestyles and governments with disastrous effects when based on faulty models. On a smaller applied scale, treatments, training, compensation and selection all depend on our theories of human behaviour. Even job design, which is an overtly physical enterprise, requires positing human elements such as "growth need strength".

To ensure the efficacy of our interventions, we need to determine what describes, drives, or decides our actions. Our understanding of behaviour has been hindered by the very extent of our efforts. There is a superabundance of motivational theories. Not only does each field have its particular interpretation, but there are ample sub-divisions within each discipline.

Critical attention is given to the predicted relationship between perceived task scope and employee motivation. The task allocation/ employee reaction situation involves the transformation of objective task characteristics into perceived characteristics. Most of the widely accepted theories of job design support the existence of such a transformation process and pay at least some attention to its inherent importance in job design.

Hackman and Oldham suggest that employees work harder to the extent that their individual needs and organisational goals are congruent. Task allocation is more frequently associated with positive affective, behavioural and motivational responses than are narrowly defined tasks. Affective and motivational responses appear to be more strongly related to task allocation than are behavioural responses. Satisfaction with work is more strongly related to task allocation than are other affective, behavioural, or motivational variables. Motivation is a very complex subject and many theories have been developed with respect to its use in the work environment. There are many theories of motivation, however scholars agree that no single theory provides all the answers. Work motivation needs to be studied from new perspectives. Many topics have yet to be sufficiently studied and certain methods have been underutilized.

TRANSFORMATIONAL LEADERSHIP IN MODERN ORGANISATIONS

Modern organisations can adopt various human resource management practices to enhance employee satisfaction. Efforts can focus on improving the quality of the individuals hired, or on raising the skills and abilities of current employees, or on both. Moreover, organisations can improve the quality of current employees by providing comprehensive training and development activities after selection. The effectiveness of skilled employees will be limited, however, if they are not motivated to perform their jobs. The form and structure of an organisation's human resources system can affect employee motivation levels in several ways. Job rotation, employment security, performance appraisal and compensation systems can motivate skilled employees to engage in effective discretionary decision-making and behaviour in response to a variety of environmental contingencies.

In today's battle for excellent employees, management has to offer more than high pay to win employees' trust and motivate employees. Employee loyalty is at an all-time low. Workers now focus on maintaining a portable skill set so they can move from opportunity to opportunity, rather than making a long-term commitment. Managers are forced to learn motivational strategies to keep the best workers. Part of a manager's job is to motivate everyone, at all times, and using every possible technique or approach available. Because of all the different and varying elements in motivation, this is not a simple or easy task. The main reason for this difficulty is that all people are different hence what might motivate one person does not necessarily work for another person. Individual performance is generally determined by three things, motivation, ability and the work environment. If an employee lacks ability, the manager can provide training or replace the worker. If there is a resource problem, the manager can correct it. But if motivation is the problem, the task for the manager is more challenging.

Individual behaviour is a complex phenomenon and the manager may be hard-pressed to figure out the precise nature of the problem and how to solve it. Thus. motivation is important because of its significance as a determinant of performance and because of its intangible character.

Work teams may be more successful in achieving organisational goals if their members are empowerment to do their jobs. For some managers, learning how to empower team members means realizing that empowerment of self-managed work teams doesn't imply adopting a strictly hands-off style. Especially leader needs to take responsibility for ensuring that the team has clear goals. Some planning and monitoring of the team's work also is necessary.

Leaders newly created self-managing work teams should take responsibility for explaining the organisation's business plan and then help the team define the results to be achieved. The work team leader may also need to handle the budget, monitor team results and provide feed-back to team members, and provide coaching as needed. On another but related issue, scholars and writers in management are beginning to emphasize the importance of EQ on leadership effectiveness. These theoretical contributions suggest that some aspects of EQ may be associated with effective leadership. In general leaders who possess empathy and social skills aspects of EQ are likely to exhibit behaviours associated with transformational leadership.

Emotional intelligence refers to one's ability to be aware of one's own feelings, be aware of others' feelings, to differentiate among them and to use the information to guide one's thinking and behaviour. This definition consists of three categories of abilities: evaluation and expression of emotion, regulation of emotion and using emotions in decision-making. Goleman provides a similar definition: "the capacity for organizing our own feelings and those of others, for motivating ourselves and for managing emotions well in ourselves and in our relationships." These and other definitions by Bar-On Boyatzis are also complimentary. It appears that EQ relates to a number of non-cognitive skills, abilities, or competencies that influence an individual's capacity to deal with environmental demands and pressures. Goleman has found that emotional intelligence is twice as important as technical skills and IQ for jobs at all levels.

CONCLUSION

Leadership is a process of influencing others to achieve the goals of an organisation, creating a vision for others and having the power to translate the vision into reality. The definition of leadership implies that leaders influence followers through the use of power. Different ways of leadership, different types of leaders lead to different output in a group or in an organisation.

In general, supervisors need to acquire and use their empathy and social skills competencies to enhance their own transformational leadership. Therefore, the challenge for a contemporary organisation is to enhance emotional intelligence of their managers. Appropriate interventions may be needed to enhance their social competencies that would involve education and specific job-related training. Managers should also be encouraged to enhance their skills through continuous self-learning. Organisations should provide positive reinforcements for learning and improving managers' essential emotional competencies, motivation and empowerment tools needed for specific jobs. Organisations may have to adapt the policy of recruiting managers with vision and charisma who are likely to be high on EQ. There should also be appropriate changes in the organisation design that would require creating flatter, decentralized and less complex structures. Also there should be appropriate changes in organisational culture that provides rewards for learning new competence and continuous questioning and inquiry.

The prescribed changes in the organisation design, culture and positive reinforcements will encourage managers to acquire emotional competencies needed for motivating their subordinates effectively. As it was stated, perhaps the most difficult aspect of being a work team leader is motivation of team members. The topic of employee motivation plays a central role in the field of management—both practically and theoretically.

Managers see motivation as an integral part of the performance equation at all levels, while organisational researchers see it as a fundamental building block in the development of useful theories of effective management practice. Indeed, the topic of motivation permeates many of the sub-fields that compose the study of management, including leadership, teams, performance management, managerial ethics, decision-making and organisational change.

The issue of time perspective in work motivation is important at both the individual and organisational levels. Individuals and organisations have to survive in the short-term; otherwise, there is no long-term. But focusing only on "today," without regard for long-term consequences can be disastrous. A second issue, related to time perspective, is that of how people and organisational leaders prioritize their goals and values and the consequences of different types of priorities. We know very little about how employees and organisational leaders actually do this, and even less about what makes some people better at it, in terms of positive decision outcomes, than others. Finally, a third issue that needs to be addressed in the field of work motivation is that of definitions. Even the term motivation is not always used clearly. The failure to define terms in a clear and valid way stifles cognitive clarity and progress in the field of work motivation.

New Employer-Employee Relationship: A Tune for Company Success

R. Christina Jeya Nithila, Jeyakodeeswari Pratap and Cyriac Meppuram

"Motivation stands out the people
People deliver Innovations
Innovations deliver success."

The relationship between the employer and employees is an important factor in the company's success. Employers will treat their employees with respect and *vice-versa* if they all want to succeed and achieve goals. Some companies forget to focus on employee retention and appreciation, and then they lose productivity. According to Balanced Score Card Approach, most important pillars are the Healthy Employees of the company, more specifically, the benefits of Employees.

Wellness to the company are:

- Reduction in physical stress and strains because of better health and strength.
- Reduction in absenteeism leading to higher output.
- High energy levels contributing to increased productivity.
- Improved creativity levels.

Improved working relationships from reduced stress and strain.

- Happier employees and their families by experiencing holistic Wellness Lifestyle.
- Goodwill to company for perceptible contribution to employees wellbeing.

Therefore, researchers have undergone a study to find out the relationship between employees and the employer existing in Apollo Tyres, for better productivity and satisfaction of employees with the objectives of: 1. critical analysis of various factors like Safety measures, Work environment, Job satisfaction, Employee benefits, Employee morale, Organisation policies, and 2. The employee attitude towards the management

RESEARCH METHODOLOGY

Out of 136 employees in officers' cadre of Apollo Tyres, Kalamasserry, the researchers have taken 50% of employees from the officers, a sample size of 100.

Sampling Method

The researchers have used random sampling method for the study.

Tools for Data Collection

The researchers have used 5 point rating scale as the main tool for data collection and adopted scoring method for analysis.

The scores are given as follows:

Strongly agree	5
Agree	4
Not sure	3
Disagree	2
Strongly disagree	1

DESCRIPTION ABOUT APOLLO TYRES, KALAMASSERRY

Named after the Greek Sun God, Apollo, the company Apollo Tyres has created a niche for itself in the Indian tyre market after three decades of consistent growth, today it is the premier tyre manufacturing company of India.

Achievements

First Indian Tyre Company to launch exclusive branded outlets—Apollo Tyre World—for truck tyres.

First Indian Tyre Company to segment the market on the basis of load and mileage requirements.

First Indian Tyre Company to introduce packaging for car and two-wheeler tyres and tubes.

First Indian Tyre Company to run a customer loyalty programme.

First Indian Tyre Company to introduce radial tyres for the farm category.

First Tyre Company in India to obtain ISO Certification for all its operations.

First Indian Tyre Company to produce H, V and W-speed rated tubeless tyres.

First Indian Tyre Company to run HIV-AIDS awareness and prevention clinics for the trucking community.

First Indian Tyre Company to support the creation of an Emergency Medical Service in an Indian city.

First Indian Tyre Company to execute an overseas acquisition.

First Indian Tyre Company to reach revenue of over US$ 1 billion.

Vision and Values

"A significant player in the global tyre industry and a brand of choices providing customer delight and continuously enhancing stakeholder value".

Vision

A leader in the Indian tyre industry and a significant global player, providing customer delight and enhancing shareholder value.

Corporate Objectives

- Employee Satisfaction
- Customer Delight
- Revenue Growth
- Operating Margin Improvements
- Care for Customer
- Respect for Associates
- Excellence through Teamwork
- Always Learning
- Trust Mutually
- Ethical Practices

Analysis and Interpretation

The scores are given as follows:

Strongly agree		5
Agree	:	4
Not sure	:	3
Disagree	:	2
Strongly disagree		1

The score assigned by the researchers is multiplied by the response given by the respondents. The ultimate results are shown by the following tabulation.

Sl. No.	Factors	Scores	Relationship level
1.	Relationship between employees and management	848	Strong
2.	Optimistic about the future of the company	314	Medium
3.	More committed to the career with the company than last year	358	Medium
4.	The company cares about the people	340	Medium
5.	The company leadership has clear vision of the future	426	Strong
6.	Leadership making changes positive to the company	402	Strong
7.	Leadership responding to major external issues	400	Strong
8.	Leadership responding to major internal issues	398	Medium
9.	Employees' views and participations are valued	450	Medium
10.	Work gives the feeling of personal accomplishment	460	Strong
11.	Receive appropriate recognition for the work	312	Medium
12.	Empowerment to influence the quality of work	465	Strong
13.	Reasonable work responsibilities	420	Strong
14.	Frequency of informal appreciation receive from superiors	455	Strong
15.	Supervisors care employees as persons at work	426	Strong
16.	There is encouragement for the development	482	Strong
17.	The mission of the company makes me feel my job is important	480	Strong
18.	Getting the opportunities at work to learn and grow	478	Strong

To identify the relationship between employer and assigned by the researchers employee the ranges for scores are:

(1) If the range is between <200, then the relationship between the employee and employer is weak.
(2) If the range is between 200 and 400, then the relationship between the employee and employer is medium.
(3) If the range is between 400 and 600, then the relationship between the employee and employer is strong.
(4) If the range is above 600, then the relationship between the employee and employer is very strong.

FINDINGS

By analyzing the data collected from the respondents with the use of scoring method, it is apparent that maximum of the scores comes at the range between 400 and 550. Therefore, it is concluded that the relationship level of the employer and the employees is strong.

SUGGESTIONS

For every organisation correction is needed for making high growth, and especially in this case, it is need to be very strong.

- Here they should imbibe good informal talk with the employees to make them more effective and dynamic
  - o Recreation
  - o Tea break talk
  - o Friendly talk
  - o Make the employees feel free to speak with superiors.
- Create good and healthy awareness related to the relationship, according to;
  - o Conduct group programmes
  - o Training
  - o Feedback/Follow-up
  - o Seminars
  - o Holyday tours, etc.
- Give more values to the suggestions of employees.
- The employees must be given a feeling that they are very important for the organisation.
- Cultural events and sports events should be conducted to enhance team spirit.
- The management should involve the employees in the decision-making process of the organisation.
- Conduct periodic meetings with employees to communicate good news, challenges etc.

CONCLUSION

Many studies have accounted in connection with motivation, job satisfaction and the climate. These studies are often manifesting the needs for the betterment of improving satisfaction level and climate. Here the study "employee-employer relationship—a tune for company success in Apollo tyres" reveals that the various facts of industrial relation or employee employer relationship that contains job satisfaction, climate, welfare, communication, etc.

The study concludes that the industrial relation or employee employer-relation in the organisation is outstanding and the relationship is favourable for the employees and if the same condition practiced throughout or the implementation of the suggestions given by the researcher will make the workers happy and consequently the production and productivity of organisation will further improve and the organisation will reach the greater heights in the years to come.

REFERENCES

Books

Kothari, C.R., Research Methodology, New Delhi, Whiswa Prakashan, 2004.

C.B. Memoria, Personal Management, Himalayan Publications.

L.M. Prasad, "Organisational Behaviour", Sultan Chand & Sons, Reprint, 1998.

Internet:

Official website of Apollo tyres and other websites; www.apollotyres.com
www.indiantyres.com
www.tyreindustry.corn
www.ehow. com
www.hrm.com

Motivation and Academic Staff in Higher Education

N. Palaniappan

ABSTRACT

Motivation is the key for the development of quality in higher education. This article explores some of the tensions associated with motivation of teaching staff in higher education. It argues that formal reward systems are only one tool which may be used by the effective manager. The effective manager needs to recognize that different motivators are appropriate for different staff and that different staff will demonstrate differing inherent levels of motivation in setting their own targets and striving towards them. Good management consists of recognizing and working with those individual differences. Many teaching staff in higher education are inherently well motivated and work in an environment where the development of professional skills and subject knowledge is the accepted norm. After exploring the relationship between quality, culture and motivation, the article reviews some traditional models of motivation. Despite their longevity these models still offer a useful framework for the consideration of motivation.

The staff of a higher education institution are a key resource. Academic staff, in particular, account for a significant component of the budget of higher education institutions and have a major role to play in achieving the objectives of the institution. The performance of academic staff, both as teachers and researchers and also as managers, determines, to a large extent, the quality of the student experience of higher education and has a significant impact on student learning and thereby on the contributions of such institutions to society.

Most higher education institutions have an implicit or explicit mission to offer a high quality learning experience to all their students. Academic staff manage this learning experience and are the main interface with students. Consequently, their motivation is crucial in determining the quality of this interface. In addition, research is important in revitalizing staff interest in their subject and in keeping their enthusiasm alive, and also in building a research and publishing profile for the institution. Exceptionally well motivated academic staff can, with appropriate support, build a national and international reputation for themselves and the institution in the research, publishing and professional areas. Such a profile may have a significant impact on the ability of the institution to attract high calibre students, research funds and consultancy contracts. However, such achievements depend on an exceptionally high level of commitment.

QUALITY, CULTURE AND MOTIVATION

Quality, and in particular, quality assessment and assurance procedures have received much attention in higher education in India in recent years.

"Quality of education" has been described as the success with which an institution provides educational environments which enable students effectively to achieve worth learning goals including appropriate academic standards (Gordon and Partington, 1993).

Clearly, the student/lecturer interface is important in determining quality and it is appropriate to seek to monitor this quality through appropriate quality assurance processes.

Shoolbred (1993) also seeks to emphasize the relationship between quality and culture: A quality management system ... is after all concerned with how people behave and this behaviour is made manifest in an organisation's climate and culture. They conclude: If higher education institutions are going to make serious moves towards effective quality assurance ... they need to be aware how much the culture may have to change. This may be highly uncomfortable for senior management and for the workforce. In the context of their central theme of culture and cultural change, they start to explore some of the mechanisms for harnessing commitment.

Four well-established models of motivation:

1. rational-economic
2. social
3. self-actualizing
4. complex models

The first three of these can be regarded as content models of motivation. Content theories of motivation try to explain the factors within a person which motivate them. Although these models were first introduced some 40 to 50 years ago, they are still a useful framework . The complex model introduces some aspects of the process theory of motivation. Each of these is described briefly, as a basis for later discussion.

The Rational-Economic Model

This suggests that people are motivated primarily by economic self-interest, and will act to maximize their own financial and material rewards (e.g. Taylor, 1947). People's motivation then can be controlled largely by offering or withholding financial rewards.

The Social Model

This can be summarized in the following terms (e.g. Mayo, 1975):

(1) People at work are motivated primarily by social needs, such as the need for friendship and acceptance, and their sense of identity is formed through relationships with other people.
(2) As a result of increased mechanization and rationalization, work has lost some of its meaning, and people increasingly seek meaning in social relationships at work.
(3) People are more responsive to the pressures of their peer groups at work than to management controls and incentives.
(4) People respond when management meets their needs for belonging, acceptance and sense of identity.

The Self-actualizing Model

Maslow (e.g. Maslow, 1970) first developed the idea of self-actualization needs. According to Maslow, self-actualization is the need a person has to fulfil his or her capabilities and potential, that is, his or her desire for growth.

The Complex Model

Schein (1980) argues that the problem with each of the preceding models of human behaviour is their claim to universality and generality. Schein, instead, sees human nature as complex, with human needs and motivations varying according to the different circumstances people face, their life experience, expectations and age. People are motivated to work when they believe that they can get what they want from their jobs. This might include the satisfaction of safety needs, the excitement of doing challenging work, or the ability to set and achieve goals.

Schein emphasizes that those with responsibility for managing people need to be sensitive to people's differing circumstances and different cultural backgrounds and that strategies for motivating staff need to accommodate this diversity. Schein also introduces the concept of psychological contract. This contract is essentially a set of expectations on both sides and a match is important if efforts to improve motivation are likely to be effective. This model suggests a process of enquiry and negotiation, where each side makes its expectations explicit, and some kind of workable agreement is reached. The manager also needs to recognize that people are not fully aware of their expectations or most find it difficult to express them, so the manager needs to be sensitive and open to signs.

ACADEMIC STAFF—ENVIRONMENT AND CULTURE

This section seeks to draw on some of the concepts introduced in the last section in explaining cultural and environmental factors which impinge on motivation in higher education. Important aspects of the environment which impinge on the management of motivation include the following.

Financial Rewards

Academic staff are appointed to a single salary scale. Their position on that scale is determined by their qualifications and experience, and possibly previous salary, at the time of their appointment. Progression through the scale is by annual increments. In some institutions additional increments may be awarded for special achievements, but in others there is no such scheme. In some subject areas, notably the professional disciplines, it is possible for staff to earn additional income by participation in external, income-generating activities, but arrangements surrounding these opportunities vary between institutions. Promotion is relatively rare, and may reward many years' work. In this environment, financial reward is remote from day-to-day experience, and other sources of motivation are important. On the other hand some new staff are on a very low point on the salary scale and this can act as a dissatisfier, particularly if they have entered a lecturing post after employment in a sector where performance is rewarded by promotion or increased pay.

The Culture of Teaching and Higher Education

Higher education is by culture a developmental environment. All staff has a significant role as teachers, and are subject to the person-to-person pressure to perform that is inherent in this contact. Most staff gain gratification from working with students and witnessing the achievement and development of those students. This is associated with having a professional pride in their work. It is important for them to be accepted by the students, when they work as a leader and facilitator. Frustration may develop from dissatisfiers which prevent staff from doing a good job, including poor timetable organisation, inadequate maintenance of educational equipment, or too many assorted demands on their time.

Diversity of Staff Experience and Roles

It is easy to view the academic staff in higher education as a body, and to seek to introduce motivation and rewards for the body as a whole. It is important to recognize that staff are motivated by different factors, depending on their length of service in higher education, their other work experience, their age, their aspirations with respect to career development and the relative priorities which they attach to achievement and social factors, such as their personal life and being accepted as a team member.

Personal Autonomy

All staff have significant autonomy over their own time management, working hours, priorities, development agendas and the relationships they establish with students and other staff. Indeed, one of the main reasons why staff selects higher education as a career stems from the opportunity for this level of personal autonomy. Conflict can arise later when, having exercised this autonomy which is inherent in the system, staff seek rewards. Job descriptions are typically very broad and there is scope for a mismatch of expectations between the member of staff and their manager which can be corrected only by effective communication.

Strategies for Motivation

In an environment where there is already a strong development a culture, strategies which support self-actualization and growth are strong contenders. These include the following.

Appraisal and Development Schemes

These schemes which offer the opportunity for staff to explore their development needs with their line manager. Interviews held as part of this process can be an important area for developing the psychological contract.

Opportunities for Personal Development

Opportunities for personal development include:

- experience in teaching different groups of students
- visiting students on work placement
- research and publishing activities
- consultancy
- study for higher degrees
- attendance at conferences and workshops
- management/team leadership experience
- training in teaching and/or management skills

Managing Dissatisfiers

The manager has a significant role in eliminating or reducing dissatisfiers. This is often achieved through negotiation and allocation of resources. This must clearly be achieved within organisational constraints, and where it is not possible to modify the dissatisfiers, managers should seek to eliminate their effects and communicate the constraints. For example, currently all funding to higher education institutions (for teaching) is based on total number of students. Most institutions, therefore, allocate staffing resources on this basis. Staff need to appreciate that staffing resources in specific subject areas are determined by such criteria and not by the number of teaching or contact hours, as was to some extent the case in the polytechnic sector in the past. Communication is necessary to ensure that staff expectations change with the changes in the environment.

The Financial Dimension

The usual strategies for financial motivation are performance-related pay and promotion. Such strategies are not usually within the control of the individual head of department or line manager and will be controlled by institutional norms and Funding Council initiatives. As such, when the opportunity arises, these strategies can be used by the individual manager to encourage motivation, but their intermittent and uncontrollable nature presents a lot of problems.

The Social Factor

Many staff work in the same higher education institution for many years. It is particularly important that they are accepted as part of the social group or team. Most staff have an acute need to feel that their contribution is worthwhile, appreciated and acknowledged. My experience is that this need is particularly evident among those staff who realistically recognize they have no further worthwhile career aspirations, yet need reassurance that their existing skills are still valued in the ever changing environment. This need to continue to contribute will be a major factor in these staff accommodating to change.

CONCLUSIONS

This article has sought to identify some of the issues related to the motivation of academic staff in higher education. It argues that such motivation is central to a quality culture. As higher education institutions become more sophisticated in their approach to quality and move on from the current emphasis on quality assurance to a stronger focus on quality enhancement, motivation will become an even more central issue. Further survey-based research, which investigates the relative importance of a variety of factors on staff motivation, will offer additional insights, but will be no substitute for the development of psychological contracts between staff and their managers.

Factors of Organisational Commitment: An Overview

Dr. V. Parthiban

The subject of Work Commitment (WC) is of increasing concern among researchers and practitioners. Although organisational commitment is attracting the most attention. Recently there has been a strong tendency to focus on the broader concept of Work Commitment that includes specific objects of commitment such as organisation, occupation and one's job. Employees' organisational commitment is important because high levels of commitment lead to several favourable organisational outcomes. Occupationally committed employees are more satisfied and more committed to the organisation.

Organisational Commitment refers to the strength of an employee's involvement in the organisation and identification with it. It goes beyond loyalty to include an active contribution to accomplishing organisational goals. It represents a broader work attitude than job satisfaction because it applies to the entire organisation rather than just to the job.

This article focuses on the factors of Organisational Commitment identified by the various researchers and the extent of the influence of these factors on Organisational Commitment.

DEFINITION, MEANING AND ELEMENTS OF ORGANISATIONAL COMMITMENT

Porter and his associates (1982) define Organisational Commitment to be an effective attitude (Psychological Attachment) towards his organisation. Operationally, Organisational Commitment is seen to be characterized by (a) a strong belief in and acceptance of the organisation's goals and values; (b) a willingness to exert considerable effort on behalf of the organisation; and (c) a strong desire to maintain membership in the organisation.

According to Reicher (1985), "Commitment is a process of identification with the goals of an organisation's multiple constituencies." It is the acceptance of goals as the object of commitment. This means that organisation, in Organisational Commitment, is equated with only goals of different constituencies. Obviously, an organisation is much more than goals and consists of several parts, one set of which may be the goals of different constituents.

Jans (1989) define Organisational Commitment as the degree that an individual in an organisation accepts, internalizes, and views his or her role. The process of becoming committed to an organisation involves internalizing the values and goals remain part of the organisation.

O'Reilly (1991) has defined commitment in the following words: "Commitment is typically conceived of as an individuals' psychological bond to the organisation, including a sense of job involvement, loyalty and a belief in the values of the organisation."

Meyer and Allen (1991) has identified three themes in the definition of commitment. Commitment as an affective attachment to the organisation, commitment as a perceived cost associated with leaving the organisation, and commitment as an obligation to remain in the organisation. They referred to these three forms of commitment as *affective, continuance and normative commitment* respectively.

Meyer and Allen have found out that a person becomes committed to an organisation for many reasons and it is the combination of the individual's affective continuance and normative commitments that makes up a complete picture of commitment to the organisation.

According to them, affective commitment refers to the employee's emotional attachment to, identification with, and involvement in the organisation. A person with high affective commitment belongs to an organisation because they want to continuance commitment refers to "an awareness of the costs associated with leaving the organisation" such as loss of prestige, status, or monetary incentives. An individual who has high levels of continuance commitment stays with an organisation because they need to do so. Normative commitment "reflects a feeling of obligation to continue employment". Individuals with high levels of commitment stay with an organisation because they feel it is the "morally right" thing to do for the organisation.

It is important to point out that Meyer and Allen do not see these three components as separate "types" of commitment, but interconnected in a way that reflects the unique nature of each individual's level of commitment to an organisation. The model assumes that each individual will have some level of all three commitments.

David Goss (1995) has rightly observed that commitment is a complex phenomenon that operates in different directions and levels. It is not something which can easily be generated, sustained, neither does it necessarily lead to improved performance.

Salanicik (1977) emphasizes that the commitment of an employee must be reflected in his behaviour rather than attitude. According to him, the elements that determine commitment are:

(i) *Explicitness*—It relates to the "deniability" of an act—It refers to with what level of certainty can we say that a specific act has taken place;
(ii) *Revocability*—It refers to "reversibility" of an act. Many actions are reversible to the extent that if we do not like them we can change our minds and do something else. Others, however, are irrevocable; once committed they cannot be taken back;
(iii) *Volition*—It refers to the complex relationship between freedom and constraint in making of choices; and
(iv) *Publicity*—It is the factor which links action to its social context. Thus publicity refers to the extent to which others know of an action and its importance to the actor.

Meyer and Allen (1997) point out that commitment can have positive and negative aspects for both the employee and the organisation. While the organisation wants committed employees, there is a danger of employees being so committed to the *status quo* that the organisation loses its competitive edge. For the employee, an over commitment to an organisation may lead to reduced time for outside activities and diminished marketability for jobs outside the organisation.

FACTORS RELATED TO ORGANISATIONAL COMMITMENT

The sources of organisational commitment may vary from person to person. Employees' initial commitment to an organisation is determined largely by their individual characteristics (e.g. personality and values) and how well their early job experiences match their expectations. Later, organisational commitment continues to be influenced by job experiences, with many of the same factors that lead to job satisfaction also contributing to organisational commitment or lack of commitment: pay, relationships with supervisors and co-workers, working conditions, opportunities for advancement, and so on.

Over time, organisational commitment tends to become stronger because: (1) Individuals develop deeper ties to the organisation and their co-workers as they spend more time with them; (2) seniority often brings advantages that tend to develop more positive work attitudes; and (3) opportunities in the job market may decrease with age, causing workers to become more strongly attached to their current job.

The various studies brought out the factors that have relationship with organisational commitment. Some of these factors are explained below.

(I) Individual Factors

It is found that the individual factors such as Age, Experience, etc. are related to Organisational Commitment. Some of the individual factors that influence Organisational Commitment are discussed below.

(i) Organisational Commitment and Age

The study conducted by Morrow and McElroy (1987) indicates that younger employees are significantly less affectively committed to their organisations than those in the middle age range, who were, in turn, less committed than the oldest employees.

The study of Chang (1990) and Reyes (1992) reveal that Organisational Commitment is related positively with age. According to Mathieu and Zajac (1990), commitment is positively related to age. One possible explanation for this relationship is that there are few employment options available to older employees (Mowday *et al.*, 1982), and older employees realize that leaving may cost them more than staying (Parasuraman and Nachman, 1987).

(ii) Organisational Commitment and Education

Steers (1977) and Glisson and Durick (1988) have reported in their studies that level of education has negative relationship with Organisational Commitment. The studies by Mowday, *et. at.* (1982) also revealed that Organisational Commitment is inversely related with educational attainment.

(iii) Organisational Commitment and Experience

According to Luthans, McCaud and Dodd (1985), commitment is positively related to length of service in particular organisation. According to Kushman (1992), Mathieu and Zajac (1990) and Meyer and Allen (1997), Organisation tenure is positively related to Organisational Commitment. According to Hrebiniak and Alutto (1992) and Steers (1977), length of organisational tenure is found to be significant positive predictor of Organisational Commitment of employees.

Buchanan's (1974) study of employees at their organisational tenure stages are instructive. He found that for new comers (<1 year), affective commitment was best predicted by job challenge, while for those in the 1-5 year range, feelings of acceptance and a belief that their work was important to the organisation contributed the most. Finally, for those with 5 or more years' tenure, commitment was most strongly related to perceptions that the organisation had a commitment norms and the extent to which employee expectations had been met.

Results of several studies (Meyer and Allen, 1987; Mowday and McDade, 1980) suggest that affective commitment declines in the first year of employment. A reasonable explanation for this is that new employees enter organisations with unrealistically high expectations (Wanous, 1980). As they lean more without their work, however, many experiences "reality shock" and affective reactions alter accordingly. Many employees leave the organisation during this period for those who stay, however, the effective commitment developed during this early period may set the stage for subsequent levels of commitment.

(iv) Organisational Commitment and Job Investment

According to Becker (1960) the more an individual has invested in a company and the lower his or her perceived job mobility, the higher the individual's calculative commitment. Regardless of people's investment in an organisation, if they are responsible for many dependents, have few sources of income, and perceive themselves as having low mobility, dependency on their jobs should be high.

(v) Organisational Commitment and Job Satisfaction

Yoon and Thye (2002) posited that job satisfaction and Perceived Organisations Support (POS) were "dual pathways to commitment" in order to explore the emotional and cognitive aspects of commitment. Their study found that both satisfaction and POS "significantly enhance organisational commitment". The results of the study indicated that satisfaction and POS played equal mediating roles on commitment. Coberly (2004) has found that satisfaction has a mediating effect on commitment as well, and reported a strong casual relationship between satisfaction and commitment.

Several studies provided inconclusive results for casual ordering. Brooke, Russell, and Price (1988) in their study of the relationship between satisfaction, commitment and job involvement, found that the three factors strongly correlated for one another. Furthermore, they found that any model that attempted to force a one factor construct lacked discriminant validity.

Farkas and Tetrick (1989) attempted to discover the casual ordering of satisfaction and commitment on turnover intentions. While their findings did indicate the necessity of some link between satisfaction and commitment, they were unable to find a model that favoured one direction of the relationship over another. The conclusion of the study was that relationship between satisfaction and commitment may be cyclical or possibly reciprocal. Curry, Wakefield, Price and Mueller (1986) also attempted to determine the casual ordering of satisfaction and commitment. Their findings could not support a casual link in either direction.

(vi) Organisational Commitment and Job Involvement

Lodahl and Kejner (1965) have found that Job Involvement is positively linked with Organisational Commitment. Studies by Jans (1989), Stevens, Beyer and Trice (1978) and Loui (1995) reveal a significant positive relationship between Organisational Commitment and Job Involvement.

(vii) Organisational Commitment and Team Spirit

In his work on employee commitment, Steers (1977) found that opportunities for social interaction positively correlated with feelings of commitment.

(viii) Organisational Commitment and Job Performance

Konovsky and Cropanzano (1991) and Meyer and Others (1989) have uncovered a positive relationship between Commitment and Job Performance. Employees who are committed to their respective institutions are more likely not only to remain with the institution but are also likely to exert more effort on belief of the organisation and work towards its success and therefore are also likely to be better performers than the uncommitted employees.

(ix) Organisational Commitment and Behaviour

Mathieu and Zajac (1990) highlight the need for further research as moderators to clarify the relationships between organisational commitment and employee behaviour.

They focused on attitudinal commitment and they defined it as the strength of an employee's emotional attachment to an organisation and acceptance of the organisation's goals and values. According to them relationship between organisational commitment and performance was stronger when financial requirements were low than it was when financial requirements were high.

(x) Organisational Commitment and Organisational Citizenship Behaviour

Findings on commitment outcomes, particularly turnover, absenteeism, tardiness, and work performance are also mixed, weak, or inconsistent (Leung, 1997; Mathieu and Zajac, 1990; Tett and Meyer 1993). The only exception is Organisational Citizenship Behaviour (i.e. discretionary job-related behaviours that promote organisational effectiveness), which has shown a weak but consistent relationship with commitment (Niehoff, Enz and Grover, 1990), although Morrison (1994) has since questioned the construct validity of this concept.

(II) Institutional Factors

(i) Organisational Commitment and Flexible Working Schedule

As the corporate "safety net" of a job guarantee and pension has diminished, employees do not feel as committed to working increased hours. Gonyea and Googins (1996) suggest that organisations and employees adopt a concept of "mutual flexibility". For the organisation, a "flexible" workforce allows for increased hours of operation which helps the organisation maintain a competitive edge for a global economy.

For the employee, flexible schedules may provide assistance in managing work/non-work interaction. This type of arrangement increases the sense of mutual obligation between the benefit from the exchange for both parties.

(ii) Organisational Commitment and Work Assignment

Brehm and Kassin (1990) indicate that individuals given unsatisfactory initial work assignments may be less likely to develop organisational commitment to the organisation than those given satisfactory initial work assignments.

(iii) Organisational Commitment and Support and Politics

According to DeCotiis and Summers (1987), Organisational Commitment is positively related to supportive and considerate leadership. Kinicki *et. al.* (2002) have found that group integration, participative involvement, and organisational climate characteristics are the antecedents of job satisfaction as well. There is evidence that politics, support. and organisational structure could be viewed as antecedents for both satisfaction and commitment.

(iv) Organisational Commitment and Autonomy

According to Dunham, Grube and Castaneda (1994), Organisational Commitment is related to task autonomy.

CONCLUSION

Going by the various findings of the past studies, it is obvious that the concept of organisational commitment is of recent origin and off late the concept and the studies related to it have gained much importance among the academicians and researchers and administrators of organisations.

It is evident that a number of studies regarding organisational commitment are available in plenty at the international level. However, only a few studies are available at the national level. The contribution of Meyer and Allen to the study of organisational commitment is very significant. They postulated three types of commitment viz., affective, continuance and normative commitment. Many studies regarding organisational commitment were based on the study of Meyer and Allen.

Over the years different aspects of organisational commitment were studied and some relationships were established and models were evolved. A few studies brought out the various dimensions of organisational commitment and a few studies found the relationship between organisational commitment and behaviour, nature of job, turnover, organisational support and politics. These findings would be of great help for the future researchers to probe the dimensions of Organisational Commitment in a more precise manner.

REFERENCES

Becker, H.S. (1960), Notes on the Concept of Commitment. *American Journal of Sociology*, 66, 32-42.

Brehm, Sharan S., and Kassin, Saul M. (1990), Social Psychology, Houghton Miffin. Boston.

Brooke, P.P. Jr., Russell, D.W., and Price, J.L. (1988), Discriminant Validation of measures of Job Satisfaction, Job Involvement and Organisational Commitment, *Journal of Applied Psychology*, 73(2), 139-45.

Buchanan, B. (1974), Building organisational commitment: The socialization of managers in work organisations. *Administrative Science Quarterly*. 19, 533-46.

Chang, Y.C. (1990), The relationship of Job attitudes and Organisational Commitment to different aspects of Organisational Environment, Boston, Ma: American Educational Research Association, (ERIC Document Service Reproduction ED 31-8-779)

Coberly, B.M. (2004), Faculty Satisfaction and Organisational Commitment with Industry, University Research Centre, Unpublished Doctoral Dissertation, North Carolina State University, Raleigh.

Curry, J.P. Wakefield, D.S., Price, J.L., and Mueller, C.W. (1986), One the causal ordering of Job Satisfaction and Organisational Commitment. *Academy of Management Journal*. 29(4), 847-58.

David Goss (1995). Principles of Human Resource Management, London, International Thomson Business Press.

DeCotiis, T.A. and Summers, T.P. (1987), A path analysis of a model of the antecedents and consequences of organisational commitment, *Human Relations*, 40(7), 445-70.

Dunham, R.B., Grube, J.A. and Castaneda, M.B. (1994), Organisational Commitment: The utility of an integrative definition, *Journal of Applied Psychology*, 79, 370-80.

Farkas, A.J. and Tetrick, L.E. (1989), A Three-Wave Longitudinal Analysis of the Casual Ordering of Satisfaction and Commitment on Turnover Decisions, *Journal of Applied Psychology*, 74(6), 855-68.

Glisson, C., and Durick. M., (1988) Predictors of Job Satisfaction and Organisational Commitment in Human Service Organisations, *Administrative Science Quarterly*, 33(1), 61-81.

Gonyea, J.G. and Googins, B.K. (1996), The Restructuring of Work and Family in the United States : A New Challenge for American Cooperations. In S. Lewis and I. Lewis (Eds.).

Hrebiniak, L.G. and Alutto, J.A. (1992), Personal and Role-related Factors in the Development of Organisational Commitment, *Administrative Science Quarterly*, 17, 555-72.

Jans, N.A. (1989), Organisational Commitment, Career Factors and Career/Life Stage, *Journal of Organisational Behaviour*, 10(3), 247-66, Retrieved August 27, 2004 from http ://www.jstor.org.

Kinicki A.J., McKee-Ryan, F.M., Schriesheim, C.A. and Carson K.P. (2002), Assessing the construct validity of the Job Descriptive Index: A Review and Meta-Analysis, *Journal of Applied Psychology*, 87(1), 14-32.

Konovsky, M.A. and Cropanzano, R. (1991), Perceived fairness employees drug testing as a predictor of employee attitudes and job performance, *Journal of Applied Psychology*, 76, 698-707.

Kushman, J.W. (1992), The organisational dynamics of Teacher Workplace Commitment A study of urban elementary and middle schools, *Educational Administration Quarterly*, 28(1), 5-42.

Leung, K. (1997), Relationships among satisfaction, commitment and performance : A group level analysis, *Applied Psychology: An International Review*, 46(2), 199-205.

Lodahl, T. and Kejner, M. (1965), The definition and measurement of job involvement, *Journal of Applied Psychology*, 49, 24-33.

Loui, K. (1995), Understanding employee commitment in the public organisation: A study of the juvenile detention center, *International Journal of Public Administration*, 18(8), 1269-95.

Luthans, F. McCaul, H.S., and Dodd, N.G. (1985), Organisational Commitment: A Comparison of American, Japanese and Korian Employees, *The Academy of Management Journal,* 28(1), 213-17.

Mathieu, J.E., and Zajac, D. (1990), A review and meta analysis of the antecedents, correlates, and consequences of organisational commitment, *Psychological Bulletin,* 108, 171-94.

Meyer, J.P. and Allen, N.J. (1987), A Longitudinal Analysis of the Early Development and Consequences of Organisational Commitment, *Canadian Journal of Behavioural Science* 19, 199-215.

Meyer, J.P. and Allen, N.J. (1991), A three component conceptualization of organisational commitment. Human Resource Management Review, 198.

Meyer, J.P. and Allen, N.J. (1997), Commitment in the work place: Theory, Research and Application. Thousand Oats, CA: Sage.

Meyer, J.P., Paunonen, S.V. Gellatly, J.R. Goffin, R.D. and Jackson, D.N. (1989). Organisational commitment and job performance : It's the nature of the commitment that counts, *Journal of Applied Psychology*, 74, 156.

Morrison, W.E., (1994), Role definitions and organisational citizenship behaviour: The importance of the employees' perspective, *Academy of Management Journal*, 37(6), 1543-67.

Morrow, P.C., Mcelroy, J.C. (1987), Work Commitment and Job Satisfaction over three career stages, *Journal of Vocational Behaviour*, 30: 330-46.

Mowday, R.T. and Mc Dade, T.W. (1980), The Development of Job Attitudes. Job perceptions and withdrawal propensities during the early employment period, Detroit MI.

Mowday, R.T. Porter, L.W., and Steers, R.M. (1982), Employee-Organisation Linkages, The Psychology of Commitment Absenteeism and Turnover, Academic Press, New York.

Niehoff, B.P., Enz, C.A. and Grover, R.A. (1990), The impact of top management actions on employee attitudes and perceptions, Group and Organisation's Studies, 15(3), 337-52.

O'Reilly, C. (1991) Corporations, Control and Commitment in Steers and Porter (eds.), Motivation and Work Behaviour, New York, McGraw Hill.

Parasuraman, S. and Nachman, S. (1987), Correlation of Organisational and Professional Commitment, Group and Organisation Studies, Vol. 12, 287-303.

Reichers, A.E. (1985), A review and reconceptualization of organisational commitment, *Academy of Management Review*, 10, 465-76.

Reyes, P. (1992) Preliminary models of Teacher Organisation Commitment : Implication for restructuring the work place, Washington, DC: Office of Educational Research and Improvement (ERIC Document Reproduction Service No. ED 349680),

Salanicik, G. (1977), Commitment: New Directions in Behaviour, Chicago: St. Clair Press.

Steers, R.M. (1977), Antecedents of outcomes of organisational commitment, *Administrative Science Quarterly*, 22, 46-56.

Stevens, J.M., Beyer, J.M. and Trice, H.M. (1978), Assessing personal role and organisational predictors of managerial commitment, *Academy of Management Journal*, 21: 380-96.

Tett, R.P. and Meyer, J.P. (1993), Job Satisfaction, Commitment, turnover intention, turnover: Path analysis based on meta-analytic findings, *Personnel Psychology*. 64. 259-87.

Wanous, J.P. (1980), Organisational Entry, Addision-Wesley, Reading.

Yoon, J. and Thye. S.R. (2002): A dual process model of OC: Job Satisfaction and Organisational Support, *Work and Occupations*, 29(1), 97-124.

Consumer Motivation

DR. S. DHINESH BABU

ABSTRACT

Motivation is the driving force within consumers that impels them to action. This driving force is generated by a state of uncomfortable tension, which exists as the result of an unsatisfied need or want. All human beings have needs, wants, requirements and desires. The individual's subconscious drive to reduce need-induced tensions results in behaviour that he expects will fulfil needs and wants and thus bring about a more comfortable internal state.

The widely accepted belief of consumer situation is that of an individual making a purchase with little influence or no influence from others. However, in some instances a number of people can be jointly involved in a purchase decision. Needs and wants are the basis of all modern marketing. Human need is the key to the survival, profitability and growth of an organisation in a competitive environment, if it succeeds in satisfying the unfulfilled needs of the consumer better and sooner than competitors. Marketer can also make aware the customers of their unfelt needs and may succeed in covering that unfelt needs into real needs through promotional mix. Thus, need is a motivating factor that makes people buy.

IMPORTANCE OF KNOWING CONSUMER MOTIVATION

Success of Salesmanship

A sales person can attain success by knowing about the consumer's motivation. This can also assist the salesman to make available the goods and services to the customer's choice in price, quality and other specifications.

Facilitates Product Planning

Knowledge about the consumer motivation can facilitate product planning, by way of using appropriate colour, size, design, package, price, etc. to the product in accordance with consumer preferences.

Facilitates Product Pricing

Knowledge about the consumers can helpful in pricing the product. Knowledgeable buyer will be prepared to pay a reasonable price, whereas emotion-oriented buyer may be prepared to pay a higher price.

Facilitates to Promotional Materials

Consumer motivation can help the marketing manager to select appropriate promotional tools, in order to induce his customers more effectively.

Facilitates the Selection of Distribution Channels

Most of the customers are influenced by "self-protective" buying motives and they like to purchase products from the wholesalers, because of the facilities extended by the middlemen to their customers.

Creation of Goodwill

Any marketer can satisfy the customers by learning their buying motives and habits, which can create goodwill of the firm and its producers.

Efforts to make Change in Buying Motives

Attempts can be made by learning from the buying motives of a customer, to bring changes in his motives.

CONSUMER MOTIVATION

Motivation is the driving force within consumers that instigates them to act. Motivation is generated by a state of uncomfortable tension, which exists as the result of an unsatisfied need or want. Every individual consumer has needs, wants and desires. The individual's subconscious drive to reduce need-induced tensions results in behaviour that he anticipates will satisfy needs and thus bring about a internal state more comfortably.

Human behaviour is goal-oriented. Goals are the sought-after end-results of motivated behaviour. The direction that behaviour makes—the goal that is chosen—is a end-result of thinking processes and previous experience.

Goals are of two types:

Generic Goals

A generic goal is a general category of goal that may satisfy a certain need.

Product-specific Goals

Product-specific needs are also referred to as wants. A product-specific goal is a specifically labeled or branded product item that individual sees as a way to fulfil his need.

Innate Needs

An individual is born with innate needs. They are Physiological in nature; they include all factors required to sustain physical life (e.g. food, water, shelter, clothing, sex, safety and so on).

Acquired Needs

These are psychological needs. Acquired needs are those which an individual develops after birth are primarily psychological. They include love and affection, recognition, esteem, and self attainment.

For any given need, there are many different and appropriate goals. The specific goal selected relies on the individual consumer's experiences, physical capability, existing cultural norms and value systems, and the goal's accessibility in the physical and social set-up.

Relationship between Needs and Goals

Needs and goals are interdependent and change in response to the individual consumer's physical conditions, circumstances, sociability, and experiences. As lower order needs become satisfied, new, higher order needs emerge that must be fulfilled.

How do People deal with Failure in achieving the Goals?

Failure to attain a goal very often results in frustration feelings. Individuals react to frustration in two different methods: "fight" or "flight". They may cope by finding a way around the obstacle that prohibits goal accomplishment or by adopting a substitute goal (fight); or they may adopt a defense mechanism that enables them to safeguard their self-esteem (flight). Aggression, regression, rationalization, withdrawal, projection, day-dreaming, identification. and repression are the popular defense mechanisms.

Motives and Behaviours

Motives cannot easily be inferred from the behaviour of consumers. Consumers with the same needs may seek fulfilment through different goals. Consumers with different needs may get fulfilment through selection of the similar goals.

Abraham Maslow's hierarchy of needs theory proposes five levels of human needs, physiological needs, safety needs, social needs, egoistic needs and self-realization needs. And other needs widely integrated into consumer advertising include the needs for power, needs for affiliation and needs for achievement.

The common methods for identifying and measuring human motives are, observation and inference, subjective reports and qualitative research—including projective techniques. Since none of these methods is completely reliable by itself, and so, therefore, researchers often use a combination of two or three techniques in tandem to measure the presence or strength of consumer motives.

Motivational Research

It is a qualitative research developed to delve below the consumer's level of conscious awareness. Motivational researches have proved to be of great value to marketers concerned with developing new ideas and new copy appeals.

TYPES OF MOTIVATION

Motivation involves the basic psychological reasons for an individual's actions and behaviour. These are the forces that make the individual to act in a certain way or to behave in the manner that they do.

There are various types of motivations that can influence a person, which are detailed below.

Basic or Primary Motivation

Primary motivation mainly pertains to motives involved with people's need for self-preservation. This includes needs such as thirst and hunger, warmth, sex, avoidance of pain and other primary motives which influence a person's behaviour at a very basic level.

Secondary Motivation

In many ways they involve a person's own sense of values and priorities in life. Secondary motivation is learned motivation.

Most of the behaviours derived from secondary motivation are conscious ones, i.e. a person consciously desires a particular goal or end-result, and behaves in a way that brings them closer to that specific goal. What drives them to do something or to act in a particular way is the longing for something which they currently do not possess.

In general, this type of motivation falls into two basic types: intrinsic and extrinsic motivation.

Intrinsic Motivation

Here, the goal or end-result is not a visible or external thing, but more internal and psychological. The attainment of these goals—by itself also correctly seen as a reward—is in general not visible to others.

Thus, for example, a student is motivated to get good marks (external motivation) or simply, he desires to learn more about a particular subject (intrinsic motivation). Getting good marks is the reward visible to other persons. For the student, the fact that he has become an expert in a particular subject is also a psychological reward for his intrinsic desire.

Extrinsic Motivation

It is likely to involve the concept of rewarded behaviour. Thus, by engaging in a particular type of activity or behaving in a particular manner, one can be "rewarded" by a desired end result.

For instance, an individual is motivated to save money for a vacation.

Hence, he resists the urge to make impulsive purchases and in general become more discriminating in how he spends his money. After a time he founds out that he has a steadily growing amount of savings which he sets aside. When he finds that he has saved enough for that trip, he can make use of his savings for the intended purpose of going for on vacation. The external motivation is the vacation, which is also the reward for his action of saving for it.

Successful Motivated Behaviour

In general, Good and effective behaviour or actions involves the harmonizing of these two types of motivation—intrinsic and extrinsic. When an individual is driven by both intrinsic and extrinsic motivations, then inner conflict is reduced and a person is more likely to devote uninterrupted and harmonious actions towards a specific goal or task.

The inner and external rewards too, are good reinforcing mechanisms. For most of the people, this is really the means to success. By selecting goals that anyone desires—both in its intrinsic and extrinsic rewards—he can harmonize his own actions and devote his energies towards his goals. In such instances, the chances of goal accomplishment increases greatly.

Another study reveals the following six types of motivation, which need to be considered in this context.

Six Types of Motivation

1. *Utilitarian*—motivation for money as well as efficiency.
2. *Knowledge*—motivation to learn, to know the "truth" about something.
3. *Social*—motivation to help others.
4. *Aesthetic*—motivation for nice things, surroundings, clothing, life-fulfilment.
5. *Power*—motivation to control one's own destiny as well as the destiny of others.
6. *Tradition*—motivation to live one's life according to a set standard.

CONCLUSION

Even though there are methods to find out or learn the customers' motivation, it becomes tedious to judge the buying motives due to the following reasons:

- Customers are not literate.
- Non-disclosure of motives by the customers knowingly.
- Multiplicity of buying motives.
- Changes in buying motives with respect to age, income, living standard, etc.

- Difficulties in identifying the specific buying motives.
- Unable to contact each and every customer.
- Individual differences between the people and their buying motives.

References

Leon G. Schiffman, Leslie Lazar Kanuk, "Consumer Behaviour", Prentice-Hall of India, New Delhi, 9th edition, 2007.

Roger D. Blackwell, Paul W. Miniard, James F. Engel, "Consumer Behaviour", Thomson Learning, Inc., 9th edition, 2002.

David L. Loudon and Albert J. Della Bitta, "Consumer Behaviour", Tata McGraw Hill, New Delhi, Fourth edition, 2002.

Philip Kotler, "Marketing Management", Prentice Hall of India Private Limited, New Delhi. Millennium edition (10th edition), 1999.

Prof. M.K. Rampal and Dr. S.L. Gupta, "Cases and Simulations in Marketing Management", 1st edition, New Delhi, Galgotia Publishing Company, 1999.

Motivation, the Key to Empower—A Case Study with Reference to BSNL, Tirunelveli District

DR. B. REVATHY AND SHEEBA, E.

ABSTRACT

The achievement of objectives by an organisation critically depends upon the performance of the employees, which in turn depends upon their abilities and motivation. While ability determines what an employee can do, motivation determines what the employee will do. Work motivation in the average Indian firm is poor. Motivating employees and driving their energy towards organisational goals have been a major question for managers. In the public sector, though the employees are provided with all the possible benefits, their performances are not up to the mark. When we take the field of communication, private companies provide better services and earn better profit than the public sector. Why does this fail in the case of the public sector? This paper is designed to highlight the motivational practices in BSNL and to find out what sort of motivational practices steer the employees of BSNL.

INTRODUCTION

Psychologists in general are of the opinion that the organisational performance is the most important asset for any organisation. This is created through the constant motivation of employees in the organisational set-up. Motivation refers to the internal environment in which the human efficiency is developed to ensure higher productivity and better performance of the employees in the organisation. The concept of motivation is extremely important for the understanding of individual and organisational behaviours and for efficiency. Motivation is common concept covering all factors of production that initiate, direct and organize the behaviour of the individual and determine the intensity, propensity and persistence of that behaviour. It is a very complex and fluid concept influenced by many broader—social, organisational and individual factors.

Many people claim that money is the main motivating factor of production in the world. Research studies also highlight that money is important, however, it is never deemed to be the only factor that is the source of motivation. An alternative approach to motivation requires, examining the cognitive processes that are involved. Distinction should be made between "capacity to work and willingness to work". One can be physically, mentally and technically fit to work but may not be willing to work. Motivation concerns to create a need and desire on the part of the workman to offer a better performance. Thus, it bridges the gap between capacity to work and willingness to work. All the employees in an organisation should aim to improve their skill and knowledge so as to contribute to the progress of the organisation. This helps them to achieve personal satisfaction and fulfil the demand of Basic, Physical, Safety, Social, Self-actualization and other needs.

A firm that provides opportunity for the advancement of its people has a better image in the minds of the public. In an organisation, management tries to co-ordinate various factors of production in such a way that each factor contribute to its maximum to achieve organisational goals. A motive is any particular internal factor or condition that tends to initiate and sustain activity. In fact, without motivation man would be a stagnant creature, never moving, never acting.

STATEMENT OF THE PROBLEM

The most astounding problem for any organisation today is to comfort its employees and ensure their co-operation to the organisation, as these workers can make and mar the future of the organisation. Their co-operation also depends on their attitude towards the organisation and the way in which they develop their attitude. Human Resource Management (HRM) practices influence the satisfaction of employees in meeting their expectations. HRM practices like involvement programmes, performance-linked compensation, career management practices, per-formic management, open job posting and job transfer practices are critical for enhancing motivation levels. However, the response of the average Indian firm to these factors has been inadequate.

After having invested considerable time and money in recruiting and training employees, an organisation must identify means to ensure that those valuable employees are productive and remain loyal to the organisation. Employee retention is of great significance towards maintaining client relationships and, more importantly, in keeping recruitment and training costs under control. Losing talented and experienced employees generally results in additional costs to the firm in the form of replacement of the skilled employees. Several studies have proved that employee motivation, satisfaction and retention are based on strong leadership and sound management practices. If a leader can master the art of motivating and retaining his staff, an organisation can be best assured of the fact that it has indeed achieved the objective of having a happy, loyal employee force resulting in growth and profits. In today's knowledge-based economy, the most challenging task before a HR Manager is to motivate and retain employees. Though various attempts have been made in this direction, there has not been much of success and no one knows as to what exactly is the route to employees' heart.

The major problem is Dc-Motivation, is the devil for an organisation. Even a small piece of bitter or harsh word from the superior affects the employees physically and mentally. It also affects the well-being of the employees. In this situation, it is essential to study the motivational practices followed in organisations. The emotional and economic expectations of the employees are not being met. Economic expectations have moved upwards significantly in the last decade. But organisations, especially those in the manufacturing sector, are finding it increasingly difficult to meet these rising expectations. Emotionally, the identification of employees with their organisations is moderate. The challenge of organisational leadership is to design a business with a compelling vision and to align the organisation to the company's vision through motivation.

IMPORTANCE OF THE STUDY

With the growing competition in the corporate world, the need to continually recruit employees and ensuring that they stay for a considerably long period of time is indeed turning into a challenging feat. It is no longer money alone which makes an employee job hop. Many a time, employees are forced to quit for reasons like improper behaviour of their immediate supervisor or colleagues, lack of recognition for the hard work put in by them and a word of appreciation, which they look forward to on a regular basis. It is a well-known fact, though not acknowledged, that employees do not leave an organisation because it is bad; they leave with a hope to get a better set of people in another organisation. If there is somebody who can make the difference, it is undoubtedly the leaders, with adequate backup from the HR and the management.

Motivating employees and retaining them is altogether a different ball game as compared to those five years ago so much so that employee retention has almost become synonymous with employee motivation. A motivated employee is satisfied with his job, more productive and is more likely to stay with the organisation. Therefore, a key issue to address while handling 'employee retention' is the ways and means of motivating them. Companies are increasingly becoming aware of the fact that only a motivated person can do full justice to his/her work. Having a driven workforce also acts as a key differentiator, giving companies an edge over others.

In turbulent times, every organisation counts on the performance of its employees for growth and success. The progress of development depends upon the personnel in an organisation. The performance of personnel either as individual or member of a group is less as compared to their capabilities in term of skill, abilities and capacities. In this competitive world, performance and capabilities are measured by their efficiency. Keeping an employee working at full potential is the best way to achieve results. It is the ultimate goal of employee motivation programmes.

In the public sector, though the employees are provided with all the possible benefits, their performances are not up to the mark. When we take the field of communication, private companies provide better services and earn better profit than the public sector. Why does this fail in the case of the public sector? The aim of the study is to find the motivational practices that steer the employees of the public sector with specific reference to BSNL.

OBJECTIVES OF THE STUDY

- To ascertain the factors those motivate the employees for the smooth and efficient functioning of BSNL.
- To evaluate the extent and the level of influence of different motivational practices in BSNL.
- To provide suggestions to improve the motivational techniques so as to fulfil the expectations of the employees of BSNL.

SCOPE OF THE STUDY

This study is undertaken to highlight the motivational practices in the field of communication with special reference to the public sector viz., BSNL in Tirunelveli district. In the field of communication, BSNL is the leading enterprise with the caption "Connecting India". This study is designed to collect opinions from the employees of various departments of BSNL in the Tirunelveli district regarding the motivational practices prevailing in their concern. Four main towns namely Vickramasingapuram, Ambasamudram, Veeravanallure and Ceranmahadevi are chosen for the study.

METHODOLOGY OF THE STUDY

- *Sample for the study*—120 employees of BSNL comprising 30 employees from each of these four main towns are chosen for study on convenience sampling method.
- *Sources of data*—The study is based on both primary and secondary data. The theoretical concept is from various secondary sources such as Texts, Journals and Magazines. Questionnaire is used to collect the primary data. Questionnaire consists of 42 questions—8 factor-based questions and 35

component-based questions, to tap the information such as Socio-economic background of the respondents and the motivational practices in the concern and its impact on the performance of the individual employees.

- *Statistical Tools used*—The variables identified in the study are analyzed with the help of Classification table, Percentage analysis, Chi-square test and z-test. The extent of motivational practices is measured by the statistical tools such as Ranking, Karl Pearson's co-efficient of correlation and inter-correlation matrix.

REVIEW OF LITERATURE

Vivek Deolankar (1996) narrated that the most important task of the management is to get work done by the subordinates and to achieve results. Getting the work done depends mainly on whether a person has been motivated to do it or not. Motivating a worker is to create a need, a desire on the part of the worker to better his present performance.

Davar, R.S. (1999) on the basis of experience and information he gathered from a large number of executives at different levels arrived at the conclusion, that at lower level, executives are motivated by status, appreciation from superiors and from their peers and to a limited extent, also motivated by pay security.

Gupta, M.C. (2002) has pointed out three motivating factors in his study "Motivation and Moral in Industry". They are Right men in the Right job, Proper induction, training and information and wages, incentives and bonus.

Deenadayalu, N. (2005) suggested that in motivating employees in order to achieve organisational goals one needs healthy working conditions, high morale of employees, high salary and other provisions, and good leader with requisite leadership qualities.

Douglas (2007) has made some improvement in Maslow's hierarchy of need. The content theories of work motivation attempt to determine what are motivating factors at work. This theory is concerned with identifying the needs of the people and how these needs are satisfied. This study is based on Abraham Maslow's hierarchy of needs. The author said that when there is satisfaction at one level of need the individual skips to the next higher level of need. Hence, he concluded that people who have been sufficient with the basic needs moves to the next level and it varies according to time, place and environment.

Sanjeev Sharma (2008) investigated the reasons why motivation is ignored even though it is of greater significance-motivation is intangible, drives all human actions, can be observed but not measured and is lost in a twilight zone he compared motivation to that of a pop-up fly ball which can fall into cracks, if not handled or played effectively. Further, he explained the need for motivation and profiled 10 areas that powerfully impact motivation which include economic rewards, promotion and transfers, opportunity to grow, challenging and stimulating work, autonomy, leadership, informal psychic rewards, goals and fun. Helping the management team optimize employees' emotions will enable the organisation to make significant impact on the primary sources of competitive advantage in today's market place.

The book attempted to capture those aspects of motivation which play a pivotal role in keeping the employee morale high which, in turn, will help managers keep him bonded with the organisation. An attempt was made to explore various tools for motivating employees, which may be handy for practicing managers in dealing with attrition. Whether organisations adhere to different theories of motivation such as Maslow's hierarchy of needs. McGregor's theory of X and Y or Herzberg's 'hygiene factors' and 'motivators' or Vroom or McClelland etc., the underlying implication is that 'the more motivated an employee is the more he/she is likely to be retained'.

Over the past years, organisations have begun to recognize that the area of motivation has become incredibly successful. Organisations have worked to understand the critical elements of the motivation programs, to capture this experience and replicate it in other areas of business.

DATA ANALYSIS AND INTERPRETATION

Motivation is the process, which creates an atmosphere that is conducive, which facilitates the integration of personal interest and organisational interest. This environment is the pre-requisite for ensuring a comprehensive development of an organisation. Unless the organisation identifies and evolves right kind of motivational techniques, it may remain a mirage for an organisation to achieve higher performance, productivity and co-operation. Keeping this in focus, the study is conducted to ascertain the ways and means through which the employees are motivated in BSNL.

FACTOR-WISE ANALYSIS

TABLE I

Age-wise Distribution of Respondents

Sl. No.	*Age*	*No. of respondents*	*Percentage (%)*
1.	20-30 years	12	10
2.	30-40 years	12	10
3.	40-50 years	52	43
4.	Above 50 years	44	37
	Total	120	100

Source: Primary Data.

The table shows that majority of the respondents, i.e. 43% are in the age group of 40-50 years. There is an opinion among the employees that this high proportion of employees in the age group 50 years is not conducive for the progress of the organisation. It is followed by the age group above 50 years and this is also not a good sign. The employees of productive group together form just 20%. Thus the employees are in the stagnant age group, not with high inspiration or motivation to contribute more for the attainment of the organisational goals.

TABLE 2

Association between Age of the Respondents and Various Dimensions of Motivation of Employees

(Chi-square test (χ^2))

Sl. No.	*Age*	*Various dimensions of motivation*		*Calculation*	*Statistical Inference*
		Low	*High*		
1.	Basic needs	N:44	N:76		
	20-30 years	4	8	χ^2=2.727	
	30-40 years	0	12	Degrees of freedom=3	Not significant
	40-50 years	24	24	P> 0.05	
	Above 50 years	16	32		
2.	Physical needs	N:56	N:64		
	20-30 years	8	4	χ^2=0.871	
	30-40 years	4	8	Degrees of freedom=3	Not significant
	40-50 years	24	24	P> 0.05	
	Above 50 years	20	28		
3.	Safety needs	N:60	N:60		
	20-30 years	8	4	χ^2=3.667	
	30-40 years	0	12	Degrees of freedom=3	Not significant
	40-50 years	24	24	P> 0.05	
	Above 50 years	28	20		
4.	Social needs	N:52	N:68		
	20-30 years	4	8	χ^2=3.529	
	30-40 years	0	12	Degrees of freedom=3	Not significant
	40-50 years	28	20	P> 0.05	
	Above 50 years	20	28		
5.	Self-actualization needs	N:60	N:60		
	20-30 years	4	8	χ^2=1,000	
	30-40 years	4	8	Degrees of freedom=3	Not significant
	40-50 years	28	20	P> 0.05	
	Above 50 years	24	24		
6.	Other needs	N:48	N:72		
	20-30 years	4	8	χ^2=2.569	
	30-40 years	0	12	Degrees of freedom=3	Not significant
	40-50 years	24	24	p>0.05	
	Above 50 years	20	28		

Source: Primary Data.

The table value is 7.815 at 5% level of significance for 3 degrees of freedom. The calculated value of χ^2 is less than the table value. So it is evident that the motivation of the employees is not associated with the age of the employees. Thus age does not influence the motivational practices in BSNL.

TABLE 3

Distribution of Respondents by their Marital Status

Sl. No.	Marital status	No. of respondents	Percentage (%)
1.	Married	104	86.7
2.	Unmarried	16	13.3
	Total	120	100

Source: Primary Data.

Nearly 87% of the employees are married. Majority of the respondents are married and these employees have multiple responsibilities to be fulfilled both in work and in personal life. They are bound by family burdens and sentiments. Only 13% of the respondents are unmarried and are not bound by dual responsibilities.

TABLE 4

Association between Marital Status of the Respondents and Various Dimensions of Motivation of Employees

(Chi-square test (χ^2))

Sl. No.	Age	Various dimensions of motivation		Calculation	Statistical Inference
		Low	High		
1.	Basic needs	N:44	N:76	χ^2=0.271	
	Married	40	64	Degrees of freedom=l	Not
	Unmarried	4	2	P> 0.05	significant
2.	Physical needs	N:56	N:64	χ^2=0.021	
	Married	48	56	Degrees of freedom=l	Not
	Unmarried	8	8	P> 0.05	significant
3.	Safety needs	N:60	N:60	χ^2=0.000	
	Married	52	52	Degrees of freedom=1	Not
	Unmarried	8	8	P> 0.05	significant
4.	Social needs	N:52	N:68	χ^2=0.632	
	Married	48	56	Degrees of freedom=1	Not
	Un married	4	12	P> 0.05	significant
5.	Self-actualization needs	N:60	N:60	χ^2=1.154	
	Married	56	48	Degrees of freedom=l	Not
	Unmarried	4	12	p> 0.05	significant
6.	Other needs	N:48	N:72	χ^2=0.433	
	Married	44	60	Degrees of freedom=l	Not
	Unmarried	4	12	P> 0.05	significant

Source: Primary Data.

The table value is 3.841 at 5% level of significance for 1 degree of freedom. The calculated value of 2 is less than the table value. So it is evident that motivation of the employees is not associated with the marital status of the employees. Therefore, it is proved that marital status does not have any influence on the motivational practices in the organisation.

TABLE 5

Distribution of Respondents by their Educational Qualification

Sl. No.	*Educational Qualification*	*No. of respondents*	*Percentage (%)*
1.	Higher secondary education and below	32	26.7
2.	Graduation and above	88	73.3
	Total	120	100

Source: Primary Data.

This table reveals that majority of the respondents, i.e., 73% of the total respondents are graduates, whereas 27% of them are qualified upto the level of higher secondary. Thus it could be interpreted that almost all the respondents have qualified for their jobs and are suitable to their nature of work. This condition of having more literates and technical employees may help the organisation to better attain its goals.

TABLE 6

Association between Educational Qualifications of the Respondents and Various Dimensions of Motivation of Employees

Sl. No.	*Educational Qualification*	*X*	*S.D.*		*Statistical Inference*
1.	Basic needs				
	Higher secondary education and below	22.63	2.39	Z=11.4622	
	Graduation and above	19.82	3.62	P>0.05	Not significant
2.	Physical needs				
	Higher secondary education and below	23.50	1.51	Z=-6.5437	
	Graduation and above	24.95	3.40	p>0.05	Significant
3.	Safety needs				
	Higher secondary education and below	17.63	2.20	Z=4.9606	
	Graduation and above	16.55	2.54	P>0.05	Not significant
4.	Social needs				
	Higher secondary education and below	22.75	2.96	Z=l.7735	
	Graduation and above	21.45	4.37	p>0.05	Not significant

5.	Self-actualization needs				
	Higher secondary education and below	17.25	1.83	Z=-0.1015	
	Graduation and above	17.27	2.05	p>0.05	Significant
6.	Other needs				
	Higher secondary education and below	1.04	1.04	Z=-4.4149	
	Graduation and above	2.58	2.58	P>0.05	Significant

Source: Primary Data.

From the above analysis, it is found that there is inter-relationship between educational qualification and the physical, self-actualization, and other needs but the other needs such as basic, safety and social needs are independent.

TABLE 7

Distribution of Respondents by their Educational Qualification

Sl. No.	*Designation*	*No. of respondents*	*Percentage (%)*
1.	Grade 1	32	26
2.	Grade 2	40	33
3.	Grade 3	12	10
4.	Grade 4	16	14
5.	Grade 5	12	10
6.	Grade 6	8	07
	Total	120	100

Source: Primary Data.

The table depicts that 33% of the total respondents are of Grade 2 category, 26% Grade 1, 14% Grade 4, 10% Grades 3 and 5 and just 7% of

TABLE 8

Distribution of Respondents by their Educational Qualification

Sl. No.	*Monthly Income (Rs.)*	*No. of respondents*	*Percentage (%)*
1.	Upto 8000	8	06.7
2.	8000-10000	16	13.3
3.	10000-15000	60	50.0
4.	Above 15000	36	30.0
	Total	120	100

Source: Primary Data.

the total respondents are of Grade 6 category. Total respondents are composed of employees of different grades and designations. It can also be predicted that having different grades of employees in their enterprise may help the higher authorities in appropriate allocation of tasks amongst the employees. This in turn assures Right man in the Right job which itself serves as a motivation for the employees for enhanced performance and productivity.

From the above table, it is clear that 70% of the employees are paid remuneration below Rs. 15000 per month and 30% are paid remuneration above Rs. 15000 per month. Majority of the employees are paid less amount of salary. This may demotivate the employees, because salary is one of the major factors that motivate the employees.

TABLE 9

Association between Marital Status of the Respondents and Various Dimensions of Motivation of Employees

(Chi-square test (χ^2))

Sl. No.	*Monthly Income (Rs.)*	*Various dimensions of motivation*		*Calculation*	*Statistical Inference*
		Low	*High*		
1.	Basic needs	N:44	N:76		
	Upto 8000	0	8	χ^2=8.947	
	8000-10000	16	0	Degrees of freedom=3	Not significant
	10000-15000	20	40	P>0.05	
	Above 15000	8	28		
2.	Physical needs	N:56	N:64		
	Upto 8000	8	0	χ^2=2.589	
	8000-10000	8	8	Degrees of freedom=3	Not significant
	10000-15000	24	36	P>0.05	
	Above 15000	16	20		
3.	Safety needs	N:60	N:60		
	Upto 8000	8	8	χ^2=7.444	
	8000-10000	8	4	Degrees of freedom=3	Not significant
	10000-15000	24	40	P>0.05	
	Above 15000	16	8		
4.	Social needs	N:52	N:68		
	Upto 8000	0	8	χ^2=235	
	8000-10000	12	4	Degrees of freedom=3	Not significant
	10000-15000	16	36	P>0.05	
	Above 15000	16	20		
5.	Self-actualization needs	N:60	N:60		
	Upto 8000	0	8	χ^2=7.267	
	8000-10000	4	12	Degrees of freedom=3	Not significant
	10000-15000	44	16	P>0.05	
	Above 15000	12	24		
6.	Other needs	N:48	N:72		
	Upto 8000	0	8	χ^2=6.711	
	8000-10000	12	4	Degrees of freedom=3	Not significant
	10000-15000	16	36	P>0.05	
	Above 15000	12	16		

Source: Primary Data.

The table value is 7.815 at 5% level of significance for 3 degrees of freedom. The calculated value of χ^2 is less than the table value. So it is statistically evident that the motivation of the employees is not associated with the monthly income of the employees. Therefore, it is proved that monthly income does not have any influence on the motivational practices in the organisation. Thus it is a deviation from the normal belief that employees shall be mostly motivated through monetary benefits but contradictorily there is no association between monthly income of the employees and motivational practices in BSNL.

COMPONENT-WISE ANALYSIS

TABLE 10

Karl Pearson's Co-efficient of Correlation between the Respondents' Promotion and Various Dimensions of Motivation of Employees

Sl. No.	*Variable*	*Correlation value*	*Comparison*	*Statistical Inference*
1.	Promotion and basic needs	0.066	p>0.05	Not significant
2.	Promotion and physical needs	-0.255	P<0.01	Significant
3.	Promotion and safety needs	0.157	P>0.05	Not significant
4.	Promotion and social needs	0.138	P>0.05	Not significant
5.	Promotion and self-actualization needs	0.106	P>0.05	Not significant
6.	Promotion and other needs	0.184	P>0.05	Not significant

Source: Primary Data.

From the table it is clear that except the physical needs, all the other five needs are not associated with promotion, one of the techniques of motivation followed in the organisation.

TABLE 10

Karl Pearson's Co-efficient of Correlation between the Respondents' Transfers and Various Dimensions of Motivation of Employees

Sl. No.	*Variable*	*Correlation value*	*Comparison*	*Statistical Inference*
1.	Transfer and basic needs	-0.250	P<0.05	Significant
2.	Transfer and physical needs	-0.254	P<0.0l	Significant
3.	Transfer and safety needs	0.123	P>0.05	Not Significant
4.	Transfer and social needs	0.020	P>0.05	Not Significant
5.	Transfer and self-actualization needs	-0.218	P<0.05	Not Significant
6.	Transfer and other needs	0.153	P>0.05	Not significant

Source: Primary Data.

This table makes it clear that there is significant relationship between transfer, one of the motivational techniques and the basic, physical and self-actualization needs. The other three needs are independent.

TABLE 12

Overall Impact of the Components

Sl. No	Components	Total score	Mean score	Rank
1.	Annual hike in pay	448	4.48	
2.	Opportunities for promotion	445	4.45	2
3.	Favourable transfers	441	4.41	3
4.	More attractive perquisites	430	4.30	4
5.	Conducive working conditions	413	4.13	5
6.	Adequate and comfortable extra facilities	407	4.07	6
7.	Normal hours of work	407	4.07	6
8.	Opportunities for training and development	405	4.05	8
9.	Recognition for excellence in performance	399	3.99	9
10.	High level of involvement among the employees	398	3.98	10
11.	Sufficient safety measures	393	3.93	11
12.	Effective channels of communication	390	3.90	12
13.	Encouragement for participative management	389	3.89	13
14.	High level of job security	384	3.84	14
15.	Cordial public relationship	384	3.84	14
16.	Adequate opportunity for career advancement	382	3.82	16
17.	Unbiased performance appraisal	373	3.73	17
18.	Extraction of services from the personnel is in accordance with their skill and competency	373	3.73	17
19.	High recognition and reward for knowledge and experience	370	3.70	19
20.	Promotions are based purely on performance	368	3.68	20
21.	Encouragement for workers' participation at all levels	366	3.6621	
22.	Cordial supervisor and subordinate relationship	358	3.58	22
23.	Encouragement from superior for further studies	340	3.40	23
24.	Plenty of career opportunities	322	3.22	24
25.	Enterprise shape employees to realize the pride of their job	297	2.97	25
26.	As an employee in the organisation, if high in the recognition in the society	284	2.84	26
27.	Adequate conveyance facilities provided by the enterprise	282	2.82	27
28.	Enterprise make employees to realize self-esteem and self-appreciation	280	2.80	28
29.	Regular counseling to alleviate personal and organisational difficulties	278	2.78	29
30.	Amicable grievances handling mechanism	262	2.62	30
31.	Attractive retirement benefits	260	2.60	31
32.	Absence of unwarranted intervention by the employer	260	2.6031	
33.	Due consideration of the suggestions of employees	256	2.56	33
34.	Encouragement from trade union	239	2.39	34
35.	Job is challenging and stimulating	236	2.36	35

Source: Primary Data.

As to the ranking of the components of motivation, annual hike in pay. opportunities for promotion and favourable transfers score the first three ranks. Least ranking is for the component, "Job is challenging and stimulating".

TABLE 13

Inter-correlation Matrix among Various Dimensions of Motivation

Dimensions	*Basic needs*	*Physical needs*	*Safety needs*	*Social needs*	*Self-actualization needs*	*Other needs*
Basic needs	1.000					
Physical needs	-0.165	1.000				
Safety needs	0.388**	0.173	1.000			
Social needs	0.608**	0.242*	-0.211*	1.000		
Self-actualization needs	0.311**	0.186	-0.266**	-0.523**	1.000	
Other needs	0.303**	0.555**	0.038	0.250*	0.502**	l.000

Source: Primary Data. **0.01 Level of significance *0.05 Level of significance

The table depicts that there is high correlation between basic and social needs, followed by correlation between physical and other needs and between social and self-actualization needs.

FINDINGS

1. Majority of the respondents, i.e., 43% are in the age group of 40-50 years. There is an opinion among the employees that this high proportion of employees in the age group 50 years is not conducive for the progress of the organisation. It is followed by the age group above 50 years and this is also not a good sign. The employees of productive group together form just 20%. Thus the employees are in the stagnant age group not with high inspiration or motivation to contribute more for the attainment of the organisational goals.
2. Majority of the respondents are married and these employees have multiple responsibilities to be fulfilled both in work and in personal life. They are bound by family burdens and sentiments. Only 13% of the respondents are unmarried and are not bound by dual responsibilities. But it is statistically evident that motivation of the employees is not associated with the marital status of the employees. Therefore, it is proved that marital status does not have any influence on the motivational practices in the organisation.
3. 73% of the total respondents are graduates, whereas 27% of them are qualified only upto the level of higher secondary. Thus,

it could be interpreted that almost all the respondents have qualified for their jobs and are suitable to their nature of work. This condition of having more literates and technical employees may help the organisation to better achieve its goals.

4. There is inter-relationship between educational qualification and the physical, self-actualization, and other needs but the other needs such as basic, safety and social needs are independent.
5. 33% of the total respondents are of Grade 2 category, 26% Grade 1, 14% Grade 4, 10% Grades 3 and 5 and just 7% of the total respondents are of Grade 6 category. Total respondents are composed of employees of different grades and designations. It is found that the different grades of employees with distinct qualification help the higher authorities in appropriate allocation of tasks amongst the employees. This in turn assures Right man in the Right job which itself serves as a motivation for the employees for enhanced performance and productivity.
6. 70% of the employees are paid remuneration below Rs. 15000 per month and 30% are paid remuneration above Rs. 15000 per month. Majority of the employees are paid less amount of salary. This may demotivate the employees, because salary is one of the major factors that motivate the employees. But, it is statistically evident that the motivation of the employees of BSNL is not associated with the monthly income of the employees. Therefore, it is proved that monthly income does not have any influence on the motivational practices in the organisation. Thus, it is a deviation from the normal belief that employees shall be mostly motivated through monetary benefits but contradictorily there is no association between monthly income of the employees and motivational practices in BSNL.
7. As to the correlation between promotion and various dimensions of motivation except the physical needs, all the other five needs are not associated with promotion, one of the techniques of motivation followed in the organisation.
8. There is significant relationship between transfer, one of the motivational techniques and the basic, physical and self-actualization needs. The other three needs viz., safety, social and other needs are independent.
9. Annual hike in pay, opportunities for promotion and favourable transfers score the first three ranks in the ranking of the components of motivation. Least ranking is for the component "Job is challenging and stimulating".
10. High correlation is evident between basic and social needs, followed by correlation between physical and other needs and between social and self-actualization needs.

Grievances of the Respondents

- There is no fresh recruitment which in turn results in excessive workload for the existing employees.
- Innovative ideas and creative measures are not encouraged in the study unit.
- Opportunities are not given to acquire more knowledge.
- Seniority is not considered for promotion.
- There is no proper job description. Unless there is clarity and unambiguity among the employees as to what is expected of them. There is total chaos in the enterprise.
- Though the employees are provided with all infrastructural facilities to maintain good standard of living, employees are devoid of initiativeness.
- BSNL is unable to effectively implement practices such as suggestion schemes, which leads to weak synergy between organisational values and individual expectations.
- Reward systems and forms of pay structures have their own implications on motivation. Long-term benefits and retained benefits like provident fund and pension scheme (also including employee stock options) and tenure-linked bonus are useful in eliciting motivation by responding to the employees' economic expectations. However, with the expectations of employees having gone up in recent years, it has led to unmet expectations.
- Performance appraisals that enhance job clarity also induce employees to enhance motivation. Compensation-linked appraisal leads to greater effort by employees to perform. However, such intensely linked appraisal also leads to a sense of relative deprivation and burn-out among employees.

SUGGESTIONS

- The employees must be periodically promoted to higher designations as per the norms of the organisation and on the basis of their work experiences.
- Though the employees are satisfied with the working conditions, it needs to be improved further in order to achieve more positive output.
- The employees need to be more creative in the work place. Monotonous work over the years will kill the efficiency and productivity of employees. Job rotation shall be helpful to overcome monotony of the job.
- Various steps like training programmes, seminars, guest lectures and the like could be arranged in order to avoid the stagnating situation.
- Although most of the respondents are satisfied with

management's overall approach towards employees, it must be improved further to be more cordial.

- The employees must be assured with new reward system. Organisation must take necessary steps to improve the employees' motivation every now and then.
- Through involvement programmes, managers can attempt to foster better employee understanding of organisational values, norms and objectives, leading to employees identifying themselves with the organisation.
- Objectives should be defined in a context that is meaningful to the individual and to the team. Rewards and recognition should be timely and frequent. The more closely a reward is tied to accomplishment, the more meaningful it is to the recipient. In a positive environment, competition is healthy. Recognition and appreciation are fundamental to the success of motivational programmes.
- Employees are to be educated on optimum utilization of various facilitates and available resources so that there is no unnecessary wastage in the organisation.
- The focus would be more on performance linked increments rather than the vanilla percentage increments for all employees at certain level or function as in the past. Hence, within a given salary band or employee level, the percentage range of increment would be wide so as to motivate and incentivize the good performers within the existing salary increment budget. Also, going forward, the salary increase as percentage would be more in the variable performance linked components like incentives and lesser increase in the fixed salary components. The better an employee performs the higher would be his take home salary, linked directly to the performance/productivity. Individual incentives would be implemented and may replace group incentives.
- Enterprise has to come up with innovative ways to encourage employees to garner the maximum performance even when the going gets tough and the returns may not justify the efforts put in. They need to work a way round to camouflage for the lack of monetary privileges that they are usually furnished with. Clear communication, moderate fun activities, and a transparent functioning system will aid in creating a positive and assertive work atmosphere.
- Managers should be specifically directed to proactively communicate with their team members through discussions, meetings, etc., to maintain the employee engagement levels.
- The right employees placed at the right job position will result in effective deployment of employees' skills, where the employees have the feeling of involvement, a sense of

participation and contribution to the final product. Employers providing the employees with the judicious use of freedom of autonomy and empowerment build commitment and improve effectiveness.

- A clear picture of role clarity to the employees will enable them perform well and take right decisions. Providing essential tools, techniques and vital information for timely decision-making and effective role discharge make the employees empowered, motivated and committed to the organisation.
- It is imperative to create an environment in which each stakeholder in the enterprise feels valued and understands how their role impacts the vision of the company. Every function in the organisation should have motivational programmes that respect the individual reward targeted behaviour, and are in harmony with the organisational vision.

CONCLUSION

The invaluable asset of any organisation is its employees who shall take the organisation to a soaring height or bring havoc, depending on the satisfaction they gain from the work and their level of motivation. Smart companies recognize that people are the only true source of competitive advantage in the dynamic business environment today. If organisations recognize that people are the most valuable fundamental asset in any business, then they must also recognize that 'motivation' is the most critical activity for organisational success. A motivated, efficient, and committed workforce steers the organisation towards success. The more an organisation understands and strategize to fulfil employees' requirements, the more will be the employees' commitment and motivation that impact the work performance and business success.

"Motivating people to achieve social and organisational goals and objectives may be the greatest challenge before the management in the new century.

REFERENCES

Davar, R.S. (1999), "Executive Motivation—A Behavioural Approach" Progressive Corporation Pvt. Ltd., Mumbai.

Douglas, G. Mook (2007), Motivation—The Organisation of Action", W.W. Norton and Company, New York.

Manoj Kumar Sarkar (2004), "Personal Management", Crest Publishing House, New Delhi.

Momoria, C.B. (2003), "Personal Management", Himalaya Publishing House, Mumbai.

Prasad, L.M. (2007), "Principles and Practice of Management", Sultan Chand and Sons, New Delhi.

Rudrabasavaraj, M.N. (2005), "Human Factor in Management", Himalaya Publishing House, New Delhi.

Sanjeev Sharma (2008), "A Right Way to Motivate an Employee is to win his Heart", New Age international (P) Ltd, Lucknow.

Scoot, W.G. (1999), "Organisation Theory", Sultan Chand and Sons, New Delhi.

Sharma, A.K. (2007), "Motivational Dynamics", Rawat Publications, Jaipur.

Subba Rao (2003), "Essentials of Human Resources Management and Industrial Relations", Himalaya Publishing House, New Delhi

Influence of Variables on Work Life Balance among Women Professionals

K. Sirajunisa and Prof. N. Panchanatham

ABSTRACT

This was the most important obstacle to the women achieving a high position in occupations and professions. Since both these roles are equally demanding and important. It affects women more. They do more of the work associated with the household activities, apart from taking care of children, older family members, and other dependents. Though multiple roles in work and family can be a source of multiple satisfaction for employed women (Crosby, 1987), a combination of career and family roles is often associated with conflict, over-load and stress (Frone *et al*, 1991). Working mothers that difficulty in combining the roles of working and mothering often affects career growth of the women (Knight, 1994). Hence this study was focused to investigate the influencing effects of demographic variables on the professional's work life balance. Work Life Balance Scale—Gen Fishers (2001), were administered on a sample of 150 professionals in Chidambaram, Tamil Nadu. Professionals were selected on stratified random sample basis by considering their different categories of lecturers, bank officers, doctors, engineers. With the help of SPSS package, One Way ANOVA test was carried out. That the results revealed that there is a significant difference between influences of demographic variables on the professionals work life balance dimensions.

INTRODUCTION

The term work life balance was used for the first time in 1986 to provide an explanation for the unhealthy life choices that many people began to adopt to ensue processional success while neglecting other important aspects of their lives like family, friends and hobbies. In evitable the consequences of such a phenomena have begun to be felt strongly, as globalization, advent of new technologies have posed new challenges to the conventional patterns of paid work. Work Life Balance (WLB) is a term that refers to the desire on the part of both employees and employers to achieve a balance between workplace obligations and personal responsibilities. Work Life Conflict (WLC) occurs when the cumulative demands of work and non-work roles are incompatible in some respect so that participation in one role is made more difficult by participation in the other. Sometimes described as having too much to do and too little time to do it, role overload is a term that is sometimes used as a means of examining the conditions that give rise to WLC. (www. Labour. gu.com). WLC has three components;

- Role overload;
- Work to family interference (i.e., long work hours limits an employee's ability to participate in family roles); and
- Family interferes with work (i.e., family demands prevent attendance at work).

Objective

The objective of the present study is to find out the difference between influences of demographic variables (experience, age, education, and income) on the professionals work life balance dimensions.

Methodology

Study participants were 150 professionals in Chidambaram town, Tamil Nadu. Professionals were selected on stratified random sample basis by considering their different categories of lecturers, bank officers, doctors, engineers. The mean age of respondents was 20-above 50 years. Their average income was Rs. 15,000- above 30,000. The educational attainment of the participants range U.G., P.G., and Profession with experience range of 1- above 15 years. With the help of SPSS package, One Way ANOVA test was carried out.

Hypotheses

"There is no significant difference between experience, age, education and income groups on the professionals' work life balance dimensions."

REVIEWS

We argue that there is a need for organisations in the current business environment to adopt HR strategies and policies that accommodate the work life needs of a diverse workforce (Cox and Blake, 1991), and WLB strategies are a key element of this. Each form of diversity may present particular challenges for management and employees, and create an imperative for flexible and inclusive management strategies (Dass and Parker, 1999). WLB strategies may include flexible policies such as temporal flexibility, telecommuting, part-time and job-sharing employment, leave options (e.g. paid study or parental leave), as part of a strategic approach to managing HR (Nord *et al.*, 2002).

Daga and Hussain (1997) conducted a study to examine the influence of stress and quality of life among working women. The sample consisted of 300 working women (doctors, lecturers and clerks). The quality of life scale (Daga and Husain, 1977) was administered to the respondents. The main findings of the study were quality of life was correlated negatively and significantly with stress among working women. Quality of life was found to be a significant predictor of stress.

TABLE I

One Way ANOVA Results and Group Comparison for the Influence of Work Life Balance Based on Professional's Experience

S. No.	*Work Life Balance*	*Age*	*Mean*	*S.D*	*Sample Size*	*F-value*	*Sig.*	*Scheffe value*
1	Work-Interferes with Personal Life	Between 1-5 Years	21.37	5.08	35	40.515	.000	1Vs2
		Between 6-10 Years	16.38	4.48	68			1Vs3
		Between 11-15 and above Years	11.7	84.96	47			2Vs3
		Total	16.106	5.91	150			
2.	Personal Life–Interferes with Work	Between 1-5 Years	22.48	2.42	35	227.05	.000	1Vs2
		Between 6-10 Years	18.29	2.31	68			1Vs3
		Between 11-15 and above Years	12.29	1.79	47			2Vs3
		Total	17.393	.403	150			
3	Work–Personal Life Enhancement	Between 1-5 Years	7.77	2.07	35	126.85	.000	1Vs2
		Between 6-10 Years	11.16	2.99	68			1Vs3
		Between 11-15 and above Years	17.23	2.89	47			2Vs3
		Total	12.273	4.546	150			

It is observed from the Table 1 that the F-value of interaction effects, (i.e., Impact of experience on Work Life Balance) is significant for the dimensions are Work-Interferes with Personal Life, Personal Life–Interferes with Work, Work-Personal Life Enhancement and over all total are significant and found to be at 0.05 level showing the dominance of professionals experience. Therefore, the stated hypothesis is rejected.

Professional's Work Life Balance differs significantly at different experience levels. It is clear that work-personal life enhancement is getting lesser mean value. It implies that the professionals are not satisfied with their experience levels of work life balance relationship and they are having lot of conflict in their experience. Compare to other dimensions the dimension personal life-interferes with work has received the higher value which implies that neither they have too much of family interferes with work nor do they have too little family interferes with work.

TABLE 2

One Way ANOVA Results and Group Comparison for the Influence of Work Life Balance Based on Professionals' Age

S. No.	Work Life Balance	Age	Mean	S.D.	Sample Size	F-value	Sig.	Scheffe value
1.	Work-Interferes with Personal Life	20-30 Years	1.52	5.01	38			1Vs2
		31-40 Years	16.14	4.22	67	49.008	.000	1Vs3
		41-50 and above Years	11.46	4.80	45			2Vs3
		Total	16.106	5.91	150			
2.	Personal Life-Interferes with Work	20-30 Years	22.44	2.33	38			1Vs3
		31-40 Years	18.05	2.21	67	256.131	.000	2Vs2
		41-50 and above Years	12.13	1.64	45			1Vs3
		Total	17.393	4.403	150			
3.	Work-Personal Life Enhancement	20-30 Years	7.65	2.03	38			1Vs2
		31-40 Years	1.40	2.82	67	151.543	.000	1Vs3
		41-50 and above Years	7.46	2.72	45			2Vs3
		Total	2.273	4.546	150			

It is observed from the Table 2 that the F-value of interaction effects (i.e., Impact of age on Work Life Balance) is significant for the dimensions are Work-Interferes with Personal Life, Personal Life-Interferes with Work, Work-Personal Life Enhancement and over all total are significant and found to be at 0.05 level showing the dominance of professionals' age. Therefore, the stated hypothesis is rejected. Professionals' Work Life Balance differs significantly at different age levels. It is clear that work-personal life enhancement is getting lesser mean value. It implies that the professionals are not satisfied with their age levels of work life balance relationship and they are having lot of conflict in their age. So the professional's has to concentrate more on this dimension. Compare to other dimensions the dimension personal life-interferes with work has received the higher value which implies that neither they have too much of family interferes with work nor do they have too little family interferes with work.

TABLE 3

One Way ANOVA Results and Group Comparison for the Influence of Work Life Balance Based on Professionals' Education

S. No.	Work Life Balance	Education	Mean	S.D.	Sample Size	F-value	Sig.	Scheffe value
1.	Work-Interferes with Personal Life	U.G.	24.9	3.63	20			1Vs2
		P.G.	18.70	3.52	30	105.738	.000	1Vs3
		Professional	12.27	4.01	80			3Vs2
		Total	16.106	5.91	150			
2.	Personal Life-Interferes with Work	U.G.	24.10	1.51	20			1Vs3
		P.G.	20.10	1.50	30	223.044	.000	1Vs2
		Professional	14.02	2.66	80			3Vs3
		Total	17.393	4.403	150			
3.	Work-Personal Life Enhancement	U.G.	6.40	1.69	20			1Vs2
		P.G.	8.96	1.53	30	196.333	.000	1Vs3
		Professional	15.81	2.90	80			2Vs3
		Total	12.273	4.546	150			

It is observed from the Table 3 that the F-value of interaction effects (i.e., Impact of education on Work Life Balance) is significant for the dimensions are Work-Interferes with Personal Life, Personal Life–Interferes with Work, Work-Personal Life Enhancement and over all total are significant and found to be at 0.05 level showing the dominance of professionals' education. Therefore, the stated hypothesis is rejected. Professionals' Work Life Balance differs significantly at different education levels. It is clear that work-personal life enhancement is getting lesser mean value. It implies that the professionals are not satisfied with their education levels of work life balance relationship and they are having lot of conflict in their education. Compare to other dimensions the dimension work-interferes with personal life has received the higher value which implies that neither they have too much of family interferes with work nor do they have too little family interferes with work.

TABLE 4

One Way ANOVA Results and Group Comparison for the Influence of Work Life Balance Based on Professionals' Total Monthly Income

S. No.	*Work Life Balance*	*Total Monthly Income*	*Mean*	*S.D.*	*Sample Size*	*F-value*	*Sig.*	*Scheffe value*
1.	Work-Interferes with Personal Life	Rs. 15,000-20,000	22.20	4.96	30			1Vs2
		Rs. 21,000-25,000	16.37	4.38	72	44.4663	.000	1Vs3
		Rs. 26,000-30,000 and above	11.89	4.96	48			2Vs3
		Total	16.106	5.914	150			
2.	Personal Life-Interferes with Work	Rs. 15,000-20,000	22.56	2.54	30			1Vs2
		Rs. 21,000-25,000	18.58	2.45	72	200.170	.000	1Vs3
		Rs. 26,000-30,000 and above	12.37	1.85	48			2Vs3
		Total	17.393	4.403	150			
3.	Work-Personal Life Enhancement	Rs. 15,000-20,000	7.40	2.01	30			1Vs2
		Rs. 21,000-25,000	11.06	2.91	72	126.274	.000	1Vs3
		Rs. 26,000-30,000 and above	17.12	2.95	48			2Vs3
		Total	12.273	4.546	150			

It is observed from the Table 4 that the F-value of interaction effects (i.e., Impact of total monthly income on Work Life Balance) is significant for the dimensions are Work-Interferes with Personal Life, Personal Life-Interferes with Work, Work-Personal Life Enhancement and over all total are significant and found to be at 0.05 level showing the dominance of professionals' total monthly income. Therefore, the stated hypothesis is rejected. Professionals' Work Life Balance differs significantly at different total monthly income levels. It is clear that work-personal life enhancement is getting lesser mean value. It implies that the professionals are not satisfied with their income levels of work life balance relationship and they are having lot of conflict in their income. Compare to other dimensions the dimension personal life-interferes with work has received the higher value which implies that neither they have too much of family interferes with work nor do they have too little family interferes with work.

CONCLUSIONS

Work life balance defined as the conflict between the demands of work and demands of personal life (Family commitments, leisure time activities, etc.) when wither side becomes unbalanced for extended periods of time, the effects is likely to manifest in unhealthy symptoms (fatigue, stress, depression, etc.). Spending quality time family, meditation, and listening to music were the fruitful coping strategies to reduce stress. Stress management techniques like time management, physical exercises, relaxation, yoga, social support to help effective for professionals. Striking an appropriate balance between one's personal and professional lives is bit of an art and science too. Work Life balance concerns adjusting working patterns so that women can combine work with their responsibilities. Work life imbalance results in job stress, burn out, job dissatisfaction, work-family conflict, poor physical and mental health and poor quality of life, Gunavathy and Suganya (2007). To achieve fulfilment and success at home and work, leisure and personal time must complement one's job passion and work and responsibilities, and reducing work-family conflict and increasing work family enhancement.

References

Abbott, J., De Cieri, H. and Iverson, R.D. (1998), 'Costing turnover: Implications of work-family conflict at management level', *Asia Pacific Journal of Human Resources*, 36(1): pp. 25-43.

Bardoel, E., Tharenou, P. and Moss, S. (1998), 'Organisational Predictors of Work–Family Practices', *Asia Pacific Journal of Human Resources*, 36(3): 31–49.

Best advice on Stress Risk Management in the Workplace (2000), *Health Canada*.

Bond, J.T., Galinsky, E. and Swanberg, J.E. (1997), The National Study of the Changing Workforce. New York: Families and Work Institute.

Dass, P. and Parker, B. (1999), 'Strategies for Managing Human Resource Diversity: From Resistance to Learning', *Academy of Management Executive*, 13(2): 68–80.

Felstead, A., Jewson, N., Phizacklea, A. and Walters, S. (2002), 'Opportunities to Work at Home in the Context of Work Life Balance', *Human Resource Management Journal*, 12(1):54–77.

Flora, F.T. Chianga, Thomas A. Birtchb and Ho Kwong Kwanc, 'The moderating roles of job control and work life balance practices on employee stress in the hotel and catering industry', *International Journal of Hospitality Management*, Volume 29, Issue 1, March 2010, pp. 25-32.

Improving Yours Own Effectiveness, Organisational Effectiveness, Chapter 21, pp. 433-435.

Kapur, Promilla (1970), Marriage and the Working Women in India, New Delhi; Vikas Publishing House.

Nord, W.R., Fox, S., Phoenix, A. and Viano, K. (2002), 'Real-world Reactions to Work Life Balance Programs: Lessons for Effective Implementation', *Organisational Dynamics*, 30(3): 223–38.

Rashmi Joshi, December 2007, Making Work Life Balance for Your Business, *Journal of HRM Review*, pp. 20-24.

HR Practices for Motivating Banking Employees

DR. P. KAMESWARA RAO AND K. SANKAR GANESH

ABSTRACT

Banking sector is found to be one of the major developing sectors in Indian Economy and the world economies are seeing India as one of the most potential market. There are more studies and researches focusing on core areas like retail banking, CRM, Servqual, marketing strategies, etc. Similarly, the HR Issues related to Banking sector has been much focused about and written about in recent years. The factor determinant for the development of the new age of banking sector is the development of human resource. Issues related to HR have become more significant in the consideration of business strategy and hence the management has to come out with a model to answer HR issues and to retain knowledge workers. This paper emphasizes on the developing best practices to address HR issues and to strategies the action plan for sustainable growth.

Key Words: Strategy, knowledge workers, motivators, organizational culture, competency mapping, and balance score card.

INTRODUCTION

The major contributor in service sector for the national development is banking sector. The banks are operating in the era of Liberalization, Privatization and globalization hence it is vital for the banks to perform dynamically. Moreover the economic trend globally is not showing good sign. But still banks and other industrial operations in India is able to withstand recession. On the other side of globalization, new opportunities are emerging in which banks are needed to harness in order to attain competitive advantage. HR being one of the essential drivers for growth for any sector, benchmarking of best practices among banks are the first step towards achieving excellence in HR management. The common challenge that the Indian banking industry is facing today is talent acquisition and retention. Generally the key reasons for attrition in any organisation, can be either he does not like the environment of the work place, the employee may also be not happy with his boss or not sure of the future of the organisation or he is not happy with the compensation package. Hence developing people with better training and working on recruitment and retention of people is the top priority for Indian bank industry.

NEED FOR HR MODEL TO FACILITATE SUSTAINABLE GROWTH

Standardization of employees' performance and to better organisational culture in the organisation is very essential today. The visionary activities of the banking sector are to be attained through the strategic intervention of the employees. It is need of the hour to plan strategically to sustain the competition and to aim for growth. Banks has to design their own HR strategy to maximize the utilization of the human resource. This paper focuses on developing a model to strategies employees.

Strategic Model

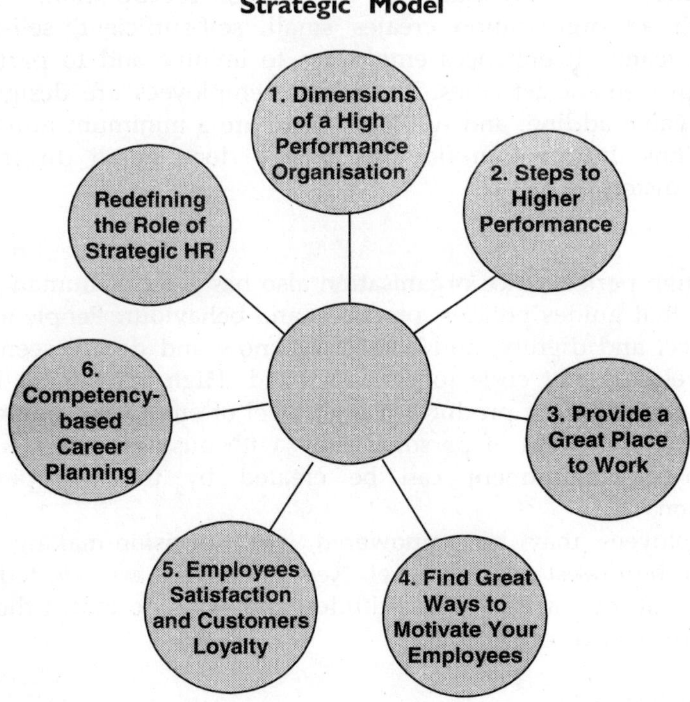

Source: By the Author.

I. Dimensions of a High Performance Organisation

A high-performance organisation is comprised of four interdependent dimensions that must be designed so they complement and support one another. These elements are : work process and technology, culture, structure, and people. One clear finding is that the greater the number of the key elements of a high-performance organisation that were present and congruent, the bigger the pay-off

(a) Work Processes and Technology

High-performance work processes produces products or services of more value to customers and to the society and meets the organisation's goals for quality, cost, timeliness, customer satisfaction, quantity, innovation, efficiency, and safety. These work processes have clear goal measures, and feedback provisions. The technology associated with the work processes efficiently supports and enables effective operation.

(b) Organisation Structure

A high-performance organisation structure aligns the resources appropriately both core work processes and functions. It develops a flexible and responsive work system with the fewest possible organisation levels. It facilitates good understanding of individual's roles and responsibilities, which reduces the effort that must be spent on coordination.

Such an organisation creates small, self-sufficient, self-managing units and teams. It enhances employees to involve and to participate in major improvement activities. The jobs of employees are designed to be essential, value adding, and fulfilling; there are a minimum number of job classifications. Information flows is openly done in all directions with minimum distortion.

(c) People

A high-performance organisation also has a set of human goals and principles that guides policies, practices, and behaviour. People are treated with respect and dignity, and what they know and do are seen as assets to be developed, not costs to be minimized. High investment in human resources development produces a high level of employee competence. By enabling the alignment of personal goals with business goals, high levels of employee commitment can be created by the high-performance organisation.

Employees may be empowered, with decision-making authority pushed to the lowest possible level. New employees are selected carefully to ensure that their aspirations, attitudes, and skills do match the needs of a high-performance organisation.

(d) Organisation Culture

Organisation culture is defined as the prevailing patterns of behaviour of the employees learn; it is the way things are done in the organisation, the rules and in an organisation. Culture is the evident in all aspects of the organisation, for example, in its goals, values, and priorities, its structure and systems, and the distribution of power. It also is seen in the nature of the information that is shared, the process of decision-making, the treatment of people, the rewards given, and the nature of internal and external relationships in the organisation. A strong, shared culture will necessarily to support a high-performance organisation. Such a culture has visible characteristics such as clear and accepted business goals and human goals.

2. Eight Steps to Higher Performance

The following eight steps will help the employees to interact in ways that make they work more efficiently and effectively. These steps will help them to feel more motivated on the job and to build the connection between their own interests and the interests of the organisation.

(a) Help Your Employees Look forward

Take your employees above and beyond the monotonous work of just doing the same job the same way. Make their work challenging, and help them to see the big picture.

Most people want to be better and more capable. But they may resist if they feel that higher expectations will be imposed on them. Make sure the employees know that the company is simply trying to help them stretch and grow. You can do this by helping them set individual performance goals that exceed the existing requirements of their jobs.

(b) Set Clear Standards

The standards of performance for a particular job should be clear. Identify them and be specific about the outcomes that characterize outstanding performance and the outcomes that indicate unacceptable performance. Again, invite discussion on this matter and listen carefully to what the employee has to say. Encourage each employee to establish his or her own parameters for measuring performance based on what he or she considers being realistic. Clear goal conveys the visionary actions too.

(c) Define the Scope of Responsibility for Employees

Making sure everyone understands who is responsible for each job activity. When employees know their roles in relationship to those of others, this will reduces confusion and gives them a better sense of how they might work with their fellow employees to meet their individual objectives

(d) Help Your Employees Buy into Higher Performance Standards

Most employees want to have a role in raising their own performance expectations. The more input an employee can provide about the job he or she is expected to perform, the more likely the employee is to buy into the new standards.

(e) Document on What the Employee and the Employer Agree On

Developing a written statement of performance standards for meeting and for exceeding the expectations which have been agreed upon with the employees. Be specific about what it's going to take to reach the standards, in each area of job activities. Then, document those expectations. Give a copy of this document to each employee and keeping one with the organisation.

(f) Decide on a Course of Action

Once the standard is set, review the specific tasks of each person's job. Identify and discuss the areas in which each employee is skilled and qualified. Plan a course of delegation based on each employee's experience and competence. Creating awareness that their work is challenging in nature is essential.

By doing this, we provide a safe environment so that each employee can be open and honest with you about successes and struggles along the way.

(g) Observe and Follow-up

Time is taken to observe how things are going along the way. Depending on each person's expertise and the complexity of the task being performed, follow-up and observe the job being performed while it's in progress.

(h) Be Clear about Rewards

Employees should know what is expected if they meet or exceed the standards developed. Being clear up front about potential rewards. Sure, it may be less expensive for the organisation if employees fall slightly short of the expectations, because we can save on rewards. But the smart manager knows that success—even if it entails certain expenses at first—but brings success later

Results of High-Performance Organisations

In many different companies in the United States and Canada shows that the work system of high-performance organisations has provided the following results:

- o Substantial improvements in quality, productivity, and in costs; also reductions in turnover, absenteeism, and grievances.
- o Moderate improvement in employee attitudes.
- o Increased involvement by members in union affairs.

One clear finding is that the greater the number of the key elements of a high-performance organisation that were present and congruent, the bigger the turnaround. This means that an organisation that had fulfilling jobs for employees, an open flow of information, self-managing work teams, a supportive role for first-line managers, and so on enjoyed the most positive results.

3. Provide a Great Place to Work

(a) A Friendly Place

It is essential to victim that friendliness appears to be one of the distinguishing characteristics of good workplaces. People seem to enjoy each other's involvement and company. Work for an organisation is; after all, work in a group and in a team. When we work for an organisation, other people don't disappear. We are forced to interact with others, with our co-workers and our boss or our subordinates. The main fact about our workplace has to do largely with the quality of those interactions

(b) With Minimized Politics

In the workplace, people compete over choice assignments, promotions, and recognition, among other things. Competition shall be healthy for both the individuals and the organisation. The field tilts when employers tolerate favouritism or practice outright discrimination against people because of sex, age, sexual preference, nationality, religion and more. At good workplaces, employees should not see about backstabbing.

(c) You Get a Fair Shake

Being fair to employees is essential. Few non-unionized firms, for instance, have even an elementary grievance procedure that offers any protections. And even strong union grievance procedures only seem to moderate the worst abuses. They do not create an atmosphere of fairness. It may be nice to run a company that values fairness. Employees at good workplaces are highly motivated and committed. The employees should feel that "They treat us fairly here," or "The Company is not taking advantage of them," or "The employees should feel that they get a fair shake around here."

4. Great Ways to Motivate the Employees

We have discussed how important it is to motivate the employees and keep their morale high in the work place. The bank manager should play the most important part in motivating the employees. These are five more ways that you can effectively create a positive work environment while increasing employee motivation and morale, infact keeping them smile.

(a) Know Your Employees

It is essential that you knowing and understanding employees. Know about their family; know about what they do after work, what interests them. Different people are motivated by different things. What does the employee want? What do they want from this job, from their life, and for their future? Reaching goals can be difficult. If the bank does not know what is the employee's goal then helping them to reach a goal at work is impossible.

(b) Learn More to Motivate Them

It is the manager's responsibility to create motivation in the workplace. Therefore, it is up to you to continue to learn new and innovative ways to motivate employees. Some banks may offer managers an educational assistance plan. This will give a fabulous opportunity to continue to learn new ways to motivate the employees.

(c) Spending Time with the Employees

Taking few minutes a day to just talk with your employees and giving them an opportunity to voice their opinions and concerns or simply how the day is going may make them to feel at home. This will show the employees are cared about his or her happiness within the bank. The schedule performance reviews can be done either once a month, once a year or however often is comfortable for you. This will allow the manager time to sit down and spend a little more time with the employee and give you a chance to discuss the highs and lows of the period in which the review is being done.

(d) Consider the Employees Feelings about the Job

Most employees start out in a job on the bottom with hopes of advancement. One way to increase employee motivation is to discuss the possibility of advancement or anywhere that they would like their career to go. It might be a different position, or a promotion, even working for a different bank, the employees should know that the manager care about the things that they care about. Let them know that the managers are there to help them achieve their goals and they will work harder for the bank!

(e) Share the News

The manager knows what it feels like when a higher employee seems to be keeping something from you. Even though there may not be a secret, the manager still hasn't informed you on what is going on. The employees may feel this way all the time. It is very important to keep employees informed about issues that arise in the bank even if it does not directly affect them. Employees want to know about the company and they want to be involved. It is a good idea to have regular "catch-up" meetings, just to make sure that everyone is on the same track. Ultimately, it is up to the manager to create a work environment that is good for the bank and good for your employees.

5. Employee Satisfaction and Customer Loyalty

The management perspective is simple: Happy employees help create happy customers. This effect has been popularized in the concept of the "satisfaction mirror" (i.e., employee satisfaction leads to customer satisfaction and business results). Virtually all of the studies that tested the satisfaction mirror concept have identified some linkage between employee satisfaction and customer satisfaction, between employee satisfaction and customer loyalty, or both. The lack of a consistent, positive linkage supporting this myth should not be taken as an invitation to abuse employees or treat them with indifference. Unhappy employees can hurt operations in a myriad of ways: absenteeism, low productivity, uncooperative spirit, filing complaints, supporting strikes, and so forth.

While employee satisfaction isn't the boon promised to businesses, employee dissatisfaction has led to disastrous results for many banks.

(a) Employee Satisfaction Leads to Business Results

The belief that employee satisfaction is important to business outcomes has been around for ages. Similarly, studies specifically testing the association between employee satisfaction and business results typically discover some linkage. Just as was the case with examinations of employee satisfaction and customer satisfaction, they have failed to reveal consistent indications. The consistency of employee feelings was more important than the absolute level in building a cause-effect model!

Employees, like customers, appear to establish thresholds of expected performance. If employee attitudes remain constant or advance slowly, without receding, then customer attitudes and profits are more likely to improve. Hence the employees should be satisfied to yield better results

(b) Loyal Employees Create Loyal Customers

Employee satisfaction has not always been shown to link directly to customer loyalty, so a new myth has evolved with a slightly different target. The amended myth holds that it is not employee satisfaction but employee loyalty that results in customer loyalty. This statement also seems intuitively correct. Because the employee's satisfaction may lead them to be loyal and the employees loyalty will boost the loyalty of the customers.

The strength of the relationship may be contingent upon four elements describing employee performance: capability, satisfaction, loyalty, and productivity. These four elements are thought to directly influence customer satisfaction (and ultimately loyalty) in the following manner:

1. *Capability*: Capable employees can deliver high-value service to customers. This implies that employees have the training, tools, procedures, and rules to deliver good service.
2. *Satisfaction*: Satisfied employees are more likely to treat customers better than are their dissatisfied counterparts.
3. *Loyalty*: Loyal employees are more willing to suppress short-term demands for the long-term benefit of the organisation. As such, they may themselves place a priority on good customer service. Loyal employees also stay with their organisations

longer, reducing the cost of turnover and its negative effect on service quality.

4. *Productivity*: Productive employees have the potential to raise the value of a firm's offerings to its customers. Greater productivity can lower costs of operations, which can mean lower prices for customers.

The combination of these four factors makes intuitive sense. In addition to the traditionally emphasized elements of employee satisfaction and loyalty, this perspective adds the dimensions of capability and productivity. The theory, yet to be proven, emphasizes that employee loyalty is not a singular, direct link to customer loyalty.

6. Competency-based Career Planning

Career pathing involves making a series of job-person matches, based on the demands of the job system in the organisation, that enable the person to grow into greater levels of responsibility, thus providing the organisation with the talent that it requires to meet goals.

Best approaches to career pathing combine an analysis of positions in terms of both the tasks and the organisational behaviours needed for superior performance. The combined approach is essential for each of the jobs in the chain, because there may be marked differences between the characteristics demanded in one job and those needed in another in the same career path.

Steps to Implement the Competency-based Career Path

- Career Management Best Practices.
- Providing Employee Assessment and Career Planning Workshops.
- Conducting Career Coaching Workshops for Managers.
- Establishing Employee Career Centers.
- Giving Open Business Briefings.
- Creating an Internal Network of Information Providers.
- Maintaining Internal Job and Talent Banks.
- Establishing Individual Learning Accounts
- Starting a Mentoring Program

7. Redefining the Role of Strategic HR

Redefining the role of strategic HR can be challenging. Here are some reasons. HR may not have credibility with senior managers. Many executives do not view HR as a business. They are used to thinking of HR as an organisational support department and accustomed to telling them what to do. HR will need to achieve the credibility to be accepted in the new role.

HR Client Relationships with Executives

HR professionals' ability to add value through their partnership with senior executives includes the following:

- *A broad understanding of the business*: This helps HR contribute value about the overall direction of the company.
- *A knowledge of how all the activities need to align*: This knowledge helps the company maximize the success of strategic initiatives and eventually deliver value to the customer.
- *A professionalism in investing in human capital and HR processes*: With this ability, HR can help guide people and organisational decision-making.
- *A unique perspective*: This perspective allows HR to be an "idea merchant" to enable strategic advantage through people and organisational process outcomes.

HR Client Relationship with Managers

HR needs to find the path of least resistance to influence managers to change their role so that they take primary responsibility for attending to employee needs. To achieve this end, HR must be skilled at enabling managers to manage their direct reports. HR creates the environment to help managers become people managers and motivates them (in whatever way that works) to recognize that their people responsibilities are equally as important as their functional, product, and process responsibilities.

HR can take a proactive role in seeing that managers can accomplish the function of trainer/educator by:

- Creating an ongoing learning environment in which managers can develop people management skills, in either formal or informal settings.
- Instilling in managers the excitement and spirit of managing their employees and business with a focus on customer needs.

Perhaps the most difficult challenge for HR is to learn how to enable the managers to be people managers rather than step into the void to take over their responsibility—in other words, help them do it rather than do it for them. As Peter Block suggests in Flawless Consulting, HR should not be "an extra pair of hands" for managers but rather enable them to manage their employees effectively. HR professionals should become performance consultants to help managers manage people effectively.

CONCLUSION

HR Policies of the banks should motivate them to achieve high results and targets. This article concludes that the banks are suggested to frame a good strategically HR policy to motivate the employees. Today the employees are aware about all motivational factor hence the banks should show love towards their employees. They should emphasis on offering good policy to keep the employees motivated continuously.

Referrences

www.domainb.com

http://www.explorehr.org/articles/Home/Four_Dimensions_of_A_High_Performance_Organisation.html

http://www.financialexpress.com/news/best-practices-key-to-excellence-in-hr-management/231334/

http://www.coolavenues.com/know/hr/jeevitha-hr-1.php

Zinkham, G.M. and Hong, J.W. (1991), Self-concept and advertising effectiveness: a conceptual model of congruency, conspicuousness, and response mode, in: R. H. Holman and M.R. Solomon (Eds.) Advancesin Consumer Research, pp. 348-54. (Provo, UT: Association for Consumer Research).

Ahmad, Jamal (July 2004), Retail Banking and Customer Behaviour: A Study of Self-concept, Satisfaction and Technology Usage, Int. Rev. of Retail, Distribution and Consumer Research, Vol. 14, No. 3, pp. 357-79.

Motivational Playback to Retain the BPO Employees from Attrition

G. SRI DEVI AND DR. N. PANCHANATHAM

Business Process Outsourcing (BPO) is likely to be the next big, thing for services in this decade. The industry is very diverse, with several sub-segments, each displaying its own unique characteristics. The BPO players need to be excellent in every facet of operations as the market is highly competitive at every level and re-defining itself every day. Being a People-Centric industry what are the people issues that the HR will have to handle?

In today's economy, more so in knowledge-based industry...IT, ITES/ BPO, the biggest task in front of a HR Manager is to motivate and retain employees. All the attempts made in this direction are big failure and no one knows what a route to employees' heart is. Here in this article, I have made an attempt to list some of the innovative ways to motivate an employee. Applying or implementing the below mentioned ideas is not an assurance that an employee will stick to you but still if done in a proper way...in a long-run...these will surely be of benefit for the organisation.

UNDERSTANDING MOTIVATION

Motivation is an organisation's life-blood; yet "motivation," as a business subject, is largely ignored. Even when not ignored, it certainly is not a focal point for strategic thinking.

Seldom is a clear, coherent, and overall approach taken to the challenge of motivating people. Most organisations don't give it much thought until something starts to go wrong. Pain gets people's attention.

Four reasons explain this fact of life:

- Motivation is intangible.
- Motivation drives all human action. It is the energy source. Those seeking to shape the behaviour ultimately wrestle with motivation.
- With a bit of work, we can intuit our own motivation and monitories shifting nature and intensity. But we can only observe and measure the motivation of others indirectly.
- Motivation is lost in a twilight zone.

Like a pop-up fly ball which drops to the ground between a couple of confused fielders, motivation can fall into cracks. Everyone has an interest in motivation, but few, if any, know who is responsible for mapping the overall game plan.

WHY DO WE NEED MOTIVATED EMPLOYEES?

- Motivated employees are needed in our rapidly changing workplaces.
- Motivated employees help organisations survive.
- Motivated employees are more productive.

To be effective, managers need to understand what motivates employees within the context of the roles they perform. Of all the functions a manager performs, motivating employees is arguably the most complex. This is due, in part, to the fact that what motivates employees changes constantly (Bowen and Radhakrishna, 1991).

Research suggests that as employees' income increases, money becomes less of a motivator (Kovach, 1987). Also, as employees get older, interesting work becomes more of a motivator.

THEORIES ON MOTIVATION

Understanding what motivated employees and how they were motivated was the focus of many researchers following the publication of the Hawthorne Study results (Terpstra, 1979).

Five major approaches that have led to our understanding of motivation are:

- Maslow's need-hierarchy theory,
- Herzberg's two-factor theory,
- Vroom's expectancy theory,
- Adams' equity theory, and
- Skinner's reinforcement theory.

Maslow's theory states that employees have five levels of needs (Maslow, 1943): physiological, safety, social, ego, and self-actualizing. Maslow argued that lower level needs had to be satisfied before the next higher level need would motivate employees.

Herzberg's theory categorized motivation into two factors: motivators and hygienes (Herzberg, Mausner, and Snyderman, 1959). Motivator or intrinsic factors, such as achievement and recognition, produce job satisfaction. Hygiene or extrinsic factors, such as pay and job security, produce job dissatisfaction.

Vroom's theory is based on the belief that employee effort will lead to performance and performance will lead to rewards (Vroom, 1964). Rewards may be either positive or negative. The more positive the reward the more likely the employee will be highly motivated. Conversely, the more negative the reward the less likely the employee will be motivated.

Adams' theory states that employees strive for equity between themselves and other workers. Equity is achieved when the ratio of employee outcomes over inputs is equal to other employee outcomes over inputs (Adams, 1965).

Skinner's theory simply states those employees' behaviours that lead to positive outcomes will be repeated and behaviours that lead to negative outcomes will not be repeated (Skinner, 1953). Managers should positively reinforce employee behaviours that lead to positive outcomes. Managers should negatively reinforce employee behaviour that leads to negative outcomes.

MOTIVATIONAL BENEFITS PROVIDED BY THE BPO COMPANIES TO RETAIN THE TALENT POOL

1. Group Medi-claim Insurance Scheme

This insurance scheme is to provide adequate insurance coverage of employees for expenses related to hospitalization due to illness, disease or injury or pregnancy in case of female employees or spouse of male employees. All employees and their dependent family members are eligible. Dependent family members include spouse, non-earning parents and children above three months

2. Personal Accident Insurance Scheme

This scheme is to provide adequate insurance coverage for Hospitalization expenses arising out of injuries sustained in an accident. This covers total/partial disablement/death due to accident and due to accidents.

3. Subsidized Food and Transportation

The organisations provide transportation facility to all the employees from home till office at subsidized rates. The lunch provided is also subsidized.

4. Company Leased Accommodation

Some of the companies provides shared accommodation for all the outstation employees, in fact some of the BPO companies also undertakes to pay electricity/water bills as well as the Society charges for the shared accommodation. The purpose is to provide to the employees to lead a more comfortable work life balance.

5. Recreation, Cafeteria, ATM and Concierge Facilities

The recreation facilities include pool tables, chess tables and coffee bars. Companies also have well equipped gyms, personal trainers and showers at facilities.

6. Corporate Credit Card

The main purpose of the corporate credit card is enable the timely and efficient payment of official expenses which the employees undertake for purposes such as travel related expenses like Hotel bills, Air tickets, etc.

7. Cellular Phone/Laptop

Cellular phone and/or Laptop are provided to the employees on the basis of business need. The employee is responsible for the maintenance and safeguarding of the asset.

8. Personal Health Care (Regular medical check-ups)

Some of the BPO's provides the facility for extensive health check-up. For employees with above 40 years of age, the medical check-up can be done once a year.

9. Loans

Many BPO companies provide loan facility on three different occasions: Employees are provided with financial assistance in case of a medical emergency. Employees are also provided with financial assistance at the time of their wedding. And, the new recruits are provided with interest-free loans to assist them in their initial settlement at the work location.

10. Educational Benefits

Many BPO companies have this policy to develop the personality and knowledge level of their employees and hence reimburses the expenses incurred towards tuition fees, examination fees, and purchase of books subject, for pursuing MBA, and/or other management qualification at India's top most Business Schools.

11. Performance-based Incentives

In many BPO companies they have plans for, performance-based incentive scheme. The parameters for calculation are process performance, i.e. speed, accuracy and productivity of each process. The Pay for Performance can be as much as 22% of the salary.

12. Flexi-time

The main objective of the flexi-time policy is to provide opportunity to employees to work with flexible work schedules and set out conditions for availing this provision. Flexible work schedules are initiated by employees and approved by management to meet business commitments while supporting employee personal life needs. The factors on which Flexi-time is allowed to an employee include: Child or Parent care, Health situation, Maternity, Formal education program.

13. Flexible Salary Benefits

Its main objective is to provide flexibility to the employees to plan a tax-effective compensation structure by balancing the monthly net income, yearly benefits and income tax payable. It is applicable of all the employees of the organisation. The Salary consists of Basic, DA and Conveyance Allowance. The Flexible Benefit Plan consists of: House Rent Allowance, Leave Travel Assistance, Medical Reimbursement, Special Allowance

14. Regular Get Together and Other Cultural Programs

The companies organizes cultural program as and when possible but most of the times, once in a quarter, in which all the employees are given an opportunity to display their talents in dramatics, singing, acting, dancing, etc. Apart from that the organisations also conduct various sports programs such as Cricket, football, etc. and regularly play matches with the teams of other organisations and colleges.

15. Wedding Day Gift

Employee is given a gift voucher of Rs. 2000/- to Rs. 7000/- based on their level in the organisation.

16. Employee Referral Scheme

In several companies employee referral scheme is implemented to encourage employees to refer friends and relatives for employment in the organisation.

17. Economic Rewards

Money is a primary motivator. While base salary remains the largest share of the total cash pie, cash incentive plans continue to grow in popularity. Special achievement incentive rewards, spot bonuses, and cash-equivalent rewards all play a role in the economic reward package. In many companies, stock-based incentive plans, once limited to top executives, are offered to all employees. We are seeing an explosion of creative ideas in the realm of economic rewards, although not all approaches motivate people.

18. Promotions and Transfers

While having economic value, promotions also carry crucial social and psychological meaning (recognition and sense of accomplishment) that, for many, far outweigh additional money or perquisites.

19. Opportunity to Grow

The chance to improve one's self is an enormously important source of motivation. Organisations that offer this advantage are in a win-win partnership with their employees. The company creates and maintains a talented workforce to use as a competitive weapon, and the employees sharpen their own competitive edge as they self-actualize. Talk about synergy.

The following are some of the motivational strategies followed by the IT Giants to retain their young talent pool.

Examples of Motivation Strategies for Young Professionals in India's BPO

Name of the Company	*Motivation Strategy*	*Impact*
Tata Consulting Services (TCS)	• A choice of working in over 170 offices across 40 countries in a variety of areas. • Paternity leave for adoption of a girl child • Discounts on group parties	" Significant impact on job hopping achieved
WIPRO	• 'Wings Within' programme where existing employees get a chance to quit their current job role and join a different firm within WIPRO	" Has led to a higher retention rate
INFOSYS	• Fostering a sense of belongingness, creative artistic and social activities for the employees and their families. • Initiating one of the best 'corporate universities' in the world	" Moderate Retentions rate increase achieved
Microsoft-India	• Excellent sporting and wellness facilities • Employees allowed to choose flexible working schedule • Moving people across functions and sections in assisting employees find their area of interest	" Struggling to minimize job hopping

CONCLUSION

The World Competitiveness Report rated India's human resource capabilities as being comparatively weaker than most Asian nations. The recognition of world class human resource capability as being pivotal to global success has changed Indian HRM cultures in recent years. While the historical and traditional roots remain deeply embedded in the subjective world of managers, emphasis on objective global concepts and practices are becoming more common. Two very different perspectives in HRM especially in BPO are evident. Firstly, Indian firms with a global outlook; secondly, global firms seeking to adapt to the Indian context; these two perspectives will move increasingly towards a cross verging and strengthening the BPO jobs. Interestingly, within the national context, India itself is not a homogenous entity. Regional variations in terms of industry size, provincial business culture, and political issues play very relevant roles. The nature of hierarchy, status, authority, responsibility and similar other concepts vary widely across the nations in this ITES maintenance. Indeed, organisational performance and personal success are critical in the new era.

References

Business Week (2007). A Red-HA Big Blue in India, Sept. 3. Available: http://businessweek.com/magazine/content/07_36/b4048052.htm

Chatterjee, S.R. (2006). Human resource management in India. In: A. Nankervis, Chatterjee, S.R. and J. Coffey (Eds.), *Perspectives of human resource management in the Asia Pacific* (41-62). Pearson Prentice Hall: Malaysia.

Chatterjee, S.R., and Pearson, C.A.L. (2000). Indian managers in transition: Orientations, work goals, values and ethics. *Management International Review*, 40(1), 81-95.

Factors of Employee Motivation in Leading Firm

R. BANILA AND RAJKUMAR

I. INTRODUCTION

"Motivation will almost always beat mere talent."

"The greater the loyalty of a group toward the group, the greater is the motivation among the members to achieve the goals of the group, and the greater the probability that the group will achieve its goals."

Motivation is a set of processes that moves a person towards a goal. It signifies the level, direction and persistence of effort expended in work. Level signifies the quantum of effort put forth, direction refers to the choice made among available alternatives to expend the effort and persistence denotes the tenacity with which the individual perseveres in the job. Thus motivation is linked with the actual behaviour of the individuals.

Since motivation influences productivity, supervisors need to understand what motivates employees to perform effectively and efficiently. Each employee's behaviour is different. So the process of motivating an employee need so many hard steps to take. Motivated behaviours are voluntary choices controlled by the individual employee. In an organisation, if the management or the supervisor (motivator) wants to motivate the employees he should know the factors which influence the motivation of employees.

Factors that affect work motivation are individual differences, job characteristics and organisational practices. Individual differences are the personal needs, values and attitudes, interests and abilities that people bring to their jobs. Job characteristics are the aspects of the position that determine its limitations and challenges. Organisational practices are the rules, human resource policies, managerial practices and rewards systems of an organisation. Supervisors must consider how these factors interact to affect employees' job performance. The present study aims to study the factors influencing the employee motivation.

2. RESEARCH METHODOLOGY

The "Study on factors of Employee Motivation" has been conducted among the employees in a leading pharmaceutical company. The researcher has used "Interview-Schedule" to collect the primary data. The schedule contains the questions on the factors influencing motivation such as interest in job, wages, appreciation of boss, working condition, job security, opportunity for promotion, loyalty towards the company, code of conduct, sympathetic help, rewards, job enrichment and need for prestige, etc. Out of 252 employees 150 employees are selected by using lottery method of simple random sampling technique.

3. CONCEPTUAL FRAMEWORK OF EMPLOYEE MOTIVATION

Environmental cues and fulfilment of the need pattern of individuals help to develop motivation. Unless a person has the necessary abilities and skills to do the work, and perceives the role accurately, mere engagement in work behaviour will not ensure effective or high performance.

In addition to acquainting the employees with the organisation's expectations of their performance and achievement of goals, the manager should also provide the necessary form of encouragement, placement of resources, offering guidance whenever and wherever necessary, and in general fostering the employee's sense of competence. The more motivated the individual, the more likely the person is to interact with the work environment and enhance the sense of competence through success experiences. These success episodes will in turn drive the individual to engage further in work behaviour.

3.1. Factors of Employee Motivation

Traditionally it is believed that employees are motivated by the opportunity to make as much money as possible and will act trationally to maximize their earnings. The assumption is that money, because what it can buy, is the most important motivator of all people. If this is so, why do some employees oppose the introduction of piece rate plans and others refuse to take over time. Obviously, men does not work only for money but to fulfil a variety of needs. Three types of forces generally influences human behaviour:

- Forces operating within the individual
- Forces operating within the organisation
- Forces operating in the environment

The factors which motivate employees are: (a) job security, (b) sympathetic help with personal problems, (c) personal loyalty to employees, (d) interest in work, (e) good working conditions, (f) discipline, (g) good wages, (h) promotions and growth in the organisation, (i) feeling of being on in things, and (j) full appreciation of work done, etc.

3.1.1. The Individuals

Human needs are both numerous and complex. Each person is different and a variety of items may prove to be motivating, depending upon the needs of the individual. It is the duty of the manager to match individual needs and expectations to the type of rewards available in the job setting.

3.1.2. The Organisation

The organisational climate plays an important part in determining worker's motivation. The climate in organisation is determined by a number of variables such as its leadership style, autonomy enjoyed by members, growth prospects, emotional support from members, reward structure, etc.

3.1.3. The Environment

Factors such as social status and social acceptance play an important role in shaping the motivations of people. Culture, norms, customs, images and attributes accorded by society to particular jobs.

3.1.4. Employee Involvement Programmes

Employee involvement is the participative process that uses the inputs of employees to increase their commitment to the organisation's success. The managers of the companies can empower their employees through employee involvement programme. The three major forms of employee involvement programmes are participative management, representative participation and quality circles.

3.1.5. Participative Management

The distinct characteristic common to all participative management programmes is the use of joint decision-making. That is subordinates actually share a significant degree of decision-making power with their immediate superiors.

Representative participation

Rather than participating directly in decisions, workers are represented by a small group of employees who actually participate. The goal of representative participation is to redistribute power within the organisation.

3.1.6. Quality Circles

Quality circles are defined as a work group of 8 to 10 employees and supervisors who have a shared area of responsibility and who meet regularly to discuss their quality problems, investigate causes of the problems, recommend solutions and take corrective action.

3.1.7. Job characteristics

Any job can be described in terms of five core job dimensions. They are skill variety, Task identity, Task significance, Autonomy and feedback. These elements of Job has greater influence in the motivation of employees. In the motivational stand point we can determine that the internal rewards are obtained by individuals when they learn that they personally have performed well on a task that they care about.

3.1.8. Rewarding employees

The rewards to the employees' performance has direct link with the employees' motivation. There are many ways to reward employees. They are piece-rate pay, Merit-based pay, bonuses, profit sharing plans and gain sharing, and employee recognition programmes.

4. ANALYSIS OF THE STUDY

The schedule contains the questions on the factors influencing motivation such as interest in job, wages, appreciation of boss, working condition, job security, opportunity for promotion, loyalty towards the company, code of conduct, sympathetic help, rewards, job enrichment and need for prestige, etc. The employees are asked to respond for the questions which has the options such as Strongly Agree, Agree, Neither agree nor disagree, Disagree and Strongly Disagree. The scores given to the options are 2, 1, 0, -1, -2 respectively.

The scores of the factors are given below:

S. No.	*Factors*	*Score (X)*	*X-A*	*(X-A)²*	*Level*
1.	Self-interest in work	120	-22	484	Medium
2.	Need for achievement	150	8	64	Medium
3.	Wages	210	68	4624	High
4.	Appreciation given by boss	190	48	2304	Medium
5.	Working condition	200	58	3364	Medium
6.	Job security	140	-2	4	Medium
7.	Opportunity for promotion	95	-47	2209	Medium
8.	Loyalty towards company	210	68	4624	High
9.	Code of conduct	70	-72	5184	Low
10.	Sympathetic help during personal problems	220	78	6084	High
11.	Rewards	220	78	6084	High
12.	Freedom of operation	180	38	1444	Medium
13.	Job enrichment	30	-112	12544	Low
14.	Work gives Prestige	195	53	2809	Medium
15.	Popularity of the company	215	63	3969	High

Average (A) = 163
Standard deviation = 60.98
High range = 142+60.98 = 202.98
Low range = 142–60.98 = 81.08
Medium level = in between 81 and 203.

5. FINDINGS

From the analysis it is found that the factors such as employees' loyalty, popularity of the company and sympathetic help provided by the company, wages and rewards highly influence the employees' motivation.

The factors such as Self-interest in work, Need for achievement, Appreciation given by boss, Working condition, Job security, Opportunity for promotion, Freedom of operation, and Prestige in work have medium level influence in the employees' motivation.

The factors such as code of conduct and Job enrichment motivate the employees at a low level.

6. DISCUSSION

From the results, it is quite evident that employees' loyalty, popularity of the company and sympathetic help by the company, wages and rewards are the factors which are highly motivating the employees to work effectively in the organisation. According to Fisher (1990), there are essentially three levels of motivation: intrinsic motivation (the employee's natural interest), extrinsic motivation (the future reward such as enhanced employment prospectus) and the combination of satisfaction and reward (success in the task). True motivation is born when there is combination of satisfaction and reward. Without task-based satisfaction, there would be no foundation to build intrinsic and extrinsic motivation. So it is to be noted that if employees do a work well, they have to be appreciated and rewarded for the best attainment of employee motivation.

7. CONCLUSION

Various points related to employee motivation are discussed in this study. The study reveals the various factors which influence the employee motivation and it depicts the influence level of the motivational factors in the motivation of employees.

Index